THE **COMPLETE WORKS** OF **SWAMI VIVEKANANDA**

VOLUME II

Discovery Publisher

2017, Discovery Publisher

No part of this book may be reproduced in any form or by any electronic or mechanical means including information storage and retrieval systems, without permission in writing from the publisher.

Author: Swami Vivekananda

616 Corporate Way
Valley Cottage, New York, 10989
www.discoverypublisher.com
edition@discoverypublisher.com
facebook.com/discoverypublisher
twitter.com/discoverypb

New York • Paris • Dublin • Tokyo • Hong Kong

TABLE OF CONTENTS

The Complete Works of Swami Vivekananda — 1

WORK AND ITS SECRET — 4
Delivered at Los Angeles, California, January 4, 1900

THE POWERS OF THE MIND — 7
Delivered at Los Angeles, California, January 8, 1900

HINTS ON PRACTICAL SPIRITUALITY — 13
Delivered at the Home of Truth, Los Angeles, California

Bhakti or Devotion — 22

BHAKTI OR DEVOTION — 24

Jnana-Yoga — 32

CHAPTER I: THE NECESSITY OF RELIGION — 33
Delivered in London

CHAPTER II: THE REAL NATURE OF MAN — 38
Delivered in London

CHAPTER III: MAYA AND ILLUSION — 46
Delivered in London

CHAPTER IV: MAYA AND THE EVOLUTION OF THE CONCEPTION OF GOD — 54
Delivered in London, 20th October 1896

CHAPTER V: MAYA AND FREEDOM — 59
Delivered in London, 22nd October 1896

CHAPTER VI: THE ABSOLUTE AND MANIFESTATION — 64
Delivered in London, 1896

CHAPTER VII: GOD IN EVERYTHING — 71
Delivered in London, 27th October 1896

CHAPTER VIII: REALISATION — 75
Delivered in London, 29th October 1896

CHAPTER IX: UNITY IN DIVERSITY — 84
Delivered in London, 3rd November 1896

CHAPTER X: THE FREEDOM OF THE SOUL — 90
Delivered in London, 5th November 1896

CHAPTER XI: THE COSMOS — 96
The Macrocosm — 96
Delivered in New York, 19th January 1896

CHAPTER XII: THE COSMOS — 100
The Microcosm — 100
Delivered in New York, 26th January 1896

CHAPTER XIII: IMMORTALITY — 106
Delivered in America

CHAPTER XIV: THE ATMAN — 111
Delivered in America

CHAPTER XV: THE ATMAN, ITS BONDAGE AND FREEDOM — 118
Delivered in America

CHAPTER XVI: THE REAL AND THE APPARENT MAN — 122
Delivered in New York

Practical Vedanta and other lectures — 136

PRACTICAL VEDANTA: PART I — 138
Delivered in London, 10th November 1896

PRACTICAL VEDANTA: PART II — 145
Delivered in London, 12th November 1896

PRACTICAL VEDANTA: PART III — 153
Delivered in London, 17th November 1896

PRACTICAL VEDANTA: PART IV — 159
Delivered in London, 18th November 1896

THE WAY TO THE REALISATION OF A UNIVERSAL RELIGION — 167
Delivered in the Universalist Church, Pasadena, California, 28th January 1900

THE IDEAL OF A UNIVERSAL RELIGION, HOW IT MUST EMBRACE DIFFERENT TYPES OF MINDS AND METHODS — 174

THE OPEN SECRET — 183
Delivered at Los Angeles, Calif., 5th January 1900

THE WAY TO BLESSEDNESS — 187

YAJNAVALKYA AND MAITREYI — 191

SOUL, NATURE, AND GOD — 194

COSMOLOGY — 198

A STUDY OF THE SANKHYA PHILOSOPHY — 202

SANKHYA AND VEDANTA — 207

THE GOAL — 211
Delivered in San Francisco, March 27, 1900

Reports in American Newspapers — 218

DIVINITY OF MAN — 219
Ada Record, February 28, 1894

SWAMI VIVEKANANDA ON INDIA — 220
Bay City Daily Tribune, March 21, 1894

RELIGIOUS HARMONY — 221
Saginaw Evening News, March 22, 1894

FROM FAR OFF INDIA — 222
Saginaw Courier-Herald, March 22, 1894

AN EVENING WITH OUR HINDU COUSINS — 223
Northampton Daily Herald, April 16, 1894

THE MANNERS AND CUSTOMS OF INDIA — 224
Boston Herald, May 15, 1894

THE RELIGIONS OF INDIA — 225
Boston Herald, May 17, 1894

SECTS AND DOCTRINES IN INDIA — 225
Harvard Crimson, May 17, 1894

LESS DOCTRINE AND MORE BREAD — 226
Baltimore American, October 15, 1894

THE RELIGION OF BUDDHA — 226
Morning Herald, October 22, 1894

The High Priest Speaks — 227
Baltimore American, October 22, 1894

ALL RELIGIONS ARE GOOD — 228
Washington Post, October 29, 1894

He Believes It Blindly — 228

The Yogis Are Jugglers — 228

THE HINDU VIEW OF LIFE — 229
Brooklyn Times, December 31, 1894
Brooklyn Daily Eagle, December 31, 1894

IDEALS OF WOMANHOOD — 231
Brooklyn Standard Union, January 21, 1895

TRUE BUDDHISM — 232
Brooklyn Standard Union, February 4, 1895

INDIA'S GIFT TO THE WORLD — 234
Brooklyn Standard Union, February 27, 1895

CHILD WIDOWS OF INDIA — 235
Daily Eagle, February 27, 1895

SOME CUSTOMS OF THE HINDUS — 236
Brooklyn Standard Union, April 8, 1895

THE **COMPLETE WORKS** OF
SWAMI VIVEKANANDA

VOLUME II

WORK AND ITS SECRET

Delivered at Los Angeles, California, January 4, 1900

One of the greatest lessons I have learnt in my life is to pay as much attention to the means of work as to its end. He was a great man from whom I learnt it, and his own life was a practical demonstration of this great principle I have been always learning great lessons from that one principle, and it appears to me that all the secret of success is there; to pay as much attention to the means as to the end.

Our great defect in life is that we are so much drawn to the ideal, the goal is so much more enchanting, so much more alluring, so much bigger in our mental horizon, that we lose sight of the details altogether.

But whenever failure comes, if we analyse it critically, in ninety-nine per cent of cases we shall find that it was because we did not pay attention to the means. Proper attention to the finishing, strengthening, of the means is what we need. With the means all right, the end must come. We forget that it is the cause that produces the effect; the effect cannot come by itself; and unless the causes are exact, proper, and powerful, the effect will not be produced. Once the ideal is chosen and the means determined, we may almost let go the ideal, because we are sure it will be there, when the means are perfected. When the cause is there, there is no more difficulty about the effect, the effect is bound to come. If we take care of the cause, the effect will take care of itself. The realization of the ideal is the effect. The means are the cause: attention to the means, therefore, is the great secret of life. We also read this in the Gita and learn that we have to work, constantly work with all our power; to put our whole mind in the work, whatever it be, that we are doing. At the same time, we must not be attached. That is to say, we must not be drawn away from the work by anything else; still, we must be able to quit the work whenever we like.

If we examine our own lives, we find that the greatest cause of sorrow is this: we take up something, and put our whole energy on it — perhaps it is a failure and yet we cannot give it up. We know that it is hurting us, that any further clinging to it is simply bringing misery on us; still, we cannot tear ourselves away from it. The bee came to sip the honey, but its feet stuck to the honey-pot and it could not get away. Again and again, we are finding ourselves in that state. That is the whole secret of existence. Why are we here? We came here to sip the honey, and we find our hands and feet sticking to it. We are caught, though we came to catch. We came to enjoy; we are being enjoyed. We came to rule; we are being ruled. We came to work; we are being worked. All the time, we find that. And this comes into every detail of our life. We are being worked upon by other minds, and we are always struggling to work on other minds. We want to enjoy the pleasures of life; and they eat into our vitals. We want to get everything from nature, but we find in the long run that nature takes everything from us — depletes us, and casts us aside.

Had it not been for this, life would have been all sunshine. Never mind! With all its failures and successes, with all its joys and sorrows, it can be one succession of sunshine, if only we are not caught.

That is the one cause of misery: we are attached, we are being caught. Therefore says the Gita: Work constantly; work, but be not attached; be not caught. Reserve unto yourself the power of detaching yourself from everything, however beloved, however much the soul might yearn for it, however great the pangs of misery you feel if you were going to leave it; still, reserve the power of leaving it whenever you want. The weak have no place here, in this life or in any other life. Weakness leads to slavery. Weakness leads to all kinds of misery, physical and mental. Weakness is death. There are hundreds of thousands of microbes surrounding us, but they cannot harm us unless we become weak, until the body is ready and predisposed to receive them. There may be a million microbes of misery, floating about us. Never mind! They dare not approach us, they have no power to get a hold on us, until the mind is weakened. This is the great fact: strength is life, weakness is death. Strength is felicity, life eternal, immortal; weakness is constant strain and misery: weakness is death.

Attachment is the source of all our pleasures now. We are attached to our friends, to our relatives; we are attached to our intellectual and spiritual works; we are attached to external objects, so that we get pleasure from them. What, again, brings misery but this very attachment? We have to detach ourselves to earn joy. If only we had power to detach ourselves at will, there would not be any misery. That man alone will be able to get the best of nature, who, having the power of attaching himself to a thing with all his energy, has also the power to detach himself when he should do so. The difficulty is that there must be as much power of attachment as that of detachment. There are men who are never attracted by anything. They can never love, they are hard-hearted and apathetic; they escape most of the miseries of life. But the wall never feels misery, the wall never loves, is never hurt; but it is the wall, after all. Surely it is better to be attached and caught, than to be a wall. Therefore the man who never loves, who is hard and stony, escaping most of the miseries of life, escapes also its joys. We do not want that. That is weakness, that is death. That soul has not been awakened that never feels weakness, never feels misery. That is a callous state. We do not want that.

At the same time, we not only want this mighty power of love, this mighty power of attachment, the power of throwing our whole soul upon a single object, losing ourselves and letting ourselves be annihilated, as it were, for other souls — which is the power of the gods — but we want to be higher even than the gods. The perfect man can put his whole soul upon that one point of love, yet he is unattached. How comes this? There is another secret to learn.

The beggar is never happy. The beggar only gets a dole with pity and scorn behind it, at least with the thought behind that the beggar is a low object. He never really enjoys what he gets.

We are all beggars. Whatever we do, we want a return. We are all traders. We are traders in life, we are traders in virtue, we are traders in religion. And alas! we are also traders in love.

If you come to trade, if it is a question of give-and-take, if it is a question of buy-and-sell, abide by the laws of buying and selling. There is a bad time and there is a good time; there is a rise and a fall in prices: always you expect the blow to come. It is like looking at the mirrors Your face is reflected: you make a grimace — there is one in the mirror; if you laugh, the mirror laughs. This is buying and selling, giving and taking.

We get caught. How? Not by what we give, but by what we expect. We get misery in return for our love; not from the fact that we love, but from the fact that we want love in return. There is no misery where there is no want. Desire, want, is the father of all misery. Desires are bound by the laws of success and failure. Desires must bring misery.

The great secret of true success, of true happiness, then, is this: the man who asks for no return, the perfectly unselfish man, is the most successful. It seems to be a paradox. Do we not know that every man who is unselfish in life gets cheated, gets hurt? Apparently, yes. "Christ was unselfish, and yet he was crucified." True, but we know that his unselfishness is the reason, the cause of a great victory — the crowning of millions upon millions of lives with the blessings of true success.

Ask nothing; want nothing in return. Give what you have to give; it will come back to you — but do not think of that now, it will come back multiplied a thousandfold — but the attention must not be on that. Yet have the power to give: give, and there it ends. Learn that the whole of life is giving, that nature will force you to give. So, give willingly. Sooner or later you will have to give up. You come into life to accumulate. With clenched hands, you want to take. But nature puts a hand on your throat and makes your hands open. Whether you will it or not, you have to give. The moment you say, "I will not", the blow comes; you are hurt. None is there but will be compelled, in the long run, to give up everything. And the more one struggles against this law, the more miserable one feels. It is because we dare not give, because we are not resigned enough to accede to this grand demand of nature, that we are miserable. The forest is gone, but we get heat in return. The sun is taking up water from the ocean, to return it in showers. You are a machine for taking and giving: you take, in order to give. Ask, therefore, nothing in return; but the more you give, the more will come to you. The quicker you can empty the air out of this room, the quicker it will be filled up by the external air; and if you close all the doors and every aperture, that which is within will remain, but that which is outside will never come in, and that which is within will stagnate, degenerate, and become poisoned. A river is continually emptying itself into the ocean and is continually filling up again. Bar not the exit into the ocean. The moment you do that, death seizes you.

Be, therefore, not a beggar; be unattached This is the most terrible task of life! You do not calculate the dangers on the path. Even by intellectually recognising the difficulties, we really do not know them until we feel them. From a distance we may get a general view of a park: well, what of that? We feel and really know it when we are in it. Even if our every attempt is a failure, and we bleed and are torn asunder, yet, through all this, we have to preserve our heart — we must assert our Godhead in the midst of all these difficulties. Nature wants us to react, to return blow for blow, cheating for cheating, lie for lie, to hit back with all our might. Then it requires a superdivine power not to hit back, to keep control, to be unattached.

Every day we renew our determination to be unattached. We cast our eyes back and look at the past objects of our love and attachment, and feel how every one of them made us miserable. We went down into the depths of despondency because of our "love"! We found ourselves mere slaves in the hands of others, we were dragged down and down! And we make a fresh determination: "Henceforth, I will be master of myself; henceforth, I will have control over myself." But the time comes, and the same story once more! Again the soul is caught and cannot get out. The bird is in a net, struggling and fluttering. This is our life.

I know the difficulties. Tremendous they are, and ninety per cent of us become discouraged and lose heart, and in our turn, often become pessimists and cease to believe in sincerity, love, and all that is grand and noble. So, we find men who in the freshness of their lives have been forgiving, kind, simple, and guileless, become in old age lying masks of men. Their minds are a mass of intricacy. There may be a good deal of external policy, possibly. They are not hot-headed, they do not speak, but it would be better for them to do so; their hearts are dead and, therefore, they do not speak. They do not curse, not become angry; but it would be better for them to be able to be angry, a thousand times better, to be able to curse. They cannot. There is death in the heart, for cold hands have seized upon it, and it can no more act, even to utter a curse, even to use a harsh word.

All this we have to avoid: therefore I say, we require superdivine power. Superhuman power is not strong enough. Superdivine strength is the only way, the one way out. By it alone we can pass through all these intricacies, through these showers of miseries, unscathed. We may be cut to pieces, torn asunder, yet our hearts must grow nobler and nobler all the time.

It is very difficult, but we can overcome the difficulty by constant practice. We must learn that nothing can happen to us, unless we make ourselves susceptible to it. I have just said, no disease can come to me until the body is ready; it does not depend alone on the germs, but upon a certain predisposition which is already in the body. We get only that for which we are fitted. Let us give up our pride and understand this, that never is misery undeserved. There never has been a blow undeserved: there never has been an evil for which I did not pave the way with my own hands. We ought to know that. Analyse yourselves and you will find that every blow you have received, came to you because you prepared yourselves for it. You did half, and the external world did the other half: that is how the blow came. That will sober us down. At the same time, from this very analysis will come a note of hope, and the note of hope is: "I have no control of the external world, but that which is in me and nearer unto me, my own world, is in my control. If the two together are required to make a failure, if the two together are necessary to give me a blow, I will not contribute the one which is in my keeping; and how then can the blow come? If I get real control of myself, the blow will never come."

We are all the time, from our childhood, trying to lay the blame upon something outside ourselves. We are always standing up to set right other people, and not ourselves. If we are miserable, we say, "Oh, the world is a devil's world." We curse others and say, "What infatuated fools!" But why should we be in such a world, if we really are so good? If this is a devil's world, we must be devils also; why else should we be here? "Oh, the people of the world are so selfish!" True enough; but why should we be found in that company, if we be better? Just think of that.

We only get what we deserve. It is a lie when we say, the world is bad and we are good. It can never be so. It is a terrible lie we tell ourselves.

This is the first lesson to learn: be determined not to curse anything outside, not to lay the blame upon any one outside, but be a man, stand up, lay the blame on yourself. You will find, that is always true. Get hold of yourself.

Is it not a shame that at one moment we talk so much of our manhood, of our being gods — that we know everything, we can do everything, we are blameless, spotless, the most unselfish people in the world; and at the next moment a little stone hurts us, a little anger from a little Jack wounds us — any fool in the street makes "these gods" miserable! Should this be so if we are such gods? Is it true that the world is to blame? Could God, who is the purest and the noblest of souls, be made miserable by any of our tricks? If you are so unselfish, you are like God. What world can hurt you? You would go through the seventh hell unscathed, untouched. But the very fact that you complain and want to lay the blame upon the external world shows that you feel the external world — the very fact that you feel shows that you are not what you claim to be. You only make your offence greater by heaping misery upon misery, by imagining that the external world is hurting you, and crying out, "Oh, this devil's world! This man hurts me; that man hurts me! " and so forth. It is adding lies to misery.

We are to take care of ourselves — that much we can do — and give up attending to others for a time. Let us perfect the means; the end will take care of itself. For the world can be good and pure, only if our lives are good and pure. It is an effect, and we are the means. Therefore, let us purify ourselves. Let us make ourselves perfect.

THE POWERS OF THE MIND

Delivered at Los Angeles, California, January 8, 1900

All over the world there has been the belief in the supernatural throughout the ages. All of us have heard of extraordinary happenings, and many of us have had some personal experience of them. I would rather introduce the subject by telling you certain facts which have come within my own experience. I once heard of a man who, if any one went to him with questions in his mind, would answer them immediately; and I was also informed that he foretold events. I was curious and went to see him with a few friends. We each had something in our minds to ask, and, to avoid mistakes, we wrote down our questions and put them in our pockets. As soon as the man saw one of us, he repeated our questions and gave the answers to them. Then he wrote something on paper, which he folded up, asked me to sign on the back, and said, "Don't look at it; put it in your pocket and keep it there till I ask for it again." And so on to each one of us. He next told us about some events that would happen to us in the future. Then he said, "Now, think of a word or a sentence, from any language you like." I thought of a long sentence from Sanskrit, a language of which he was entirely ignorant. "Now, take out the paper from your pocket," he said. The Sanskrit sentence was written there! He had written it an hour before with the remark, "In confirmation of what I have written, this man will think of this sentence." It was correct. Another of us who had been given a similar paper which he had signed and placed in his pocket, was also asked to think of a sentence. He thought of a sentence in Arabic, which it was still less possible for the man to know; it was some passage from the Koran. And my friend found this written down on the paper.

Another of us was a physician. He thought of a sentence from a German medical book. It was written on his paper.

Several days later I went to this man again, thinking possibly I had been deluded somehow before. I took other friends, and on this occasion also he came out wonderfully triumphant.

Another time I was in the city of Hyderabad in India, and I was told of a Brâhmin there who could produce numbers of things from where, nobody knew. This man was in business there; he was a respectable gentleman. And I asked him to show me his tricks. It so happened that this man had a fever, and in India there is a general belief that if a holy man puts his hand on a sick man he would be well. This Brahmin came to me and said, "Sir, put your hand on my head, so that my fever may be cured." I said, "Very good; but you show me your tricks." He promised. I put my hand on his head as desired, and later he came to fulfil his promise. He had only a strip of cloth about his loins, we took off everything else from him. I had a blanket which I gave him to wrap round himself, because it was cold, and made him sit in a corner. Twenty-five pairs of eyes were looking at him. And he said, "Now, look, write down anything you want." We all wrote down names of fruits that never grew in that country, bunches of grapes, oranges, and so on. And we gave him those bits of paper. And there came from under his blanket, bushels of grapes, oranges, and so forth, so much that if all that fruit was weighed, it would have been twice as heavy as the man. He asked us to eat the fruit. Some of us objected, thinking it was hypnotism; but the man began eating himself — so we all ate. It was all right.

He ended by producing a mass of roses. Each flower was perfect, with dew-drops on the petals, not one crushed, not one injured. And masses of them! When I asked the man for an explanation, he said, "It is all sleight of hand."

Whatever it was, it seemed to be impossible that it could be sleight of hand merely. From whence could he have got such large quantities of things?

Well, I saw many things like that. Going about India you find hundreds of similar things in different places. These are in every country. Even in this country you will find some such wonderful things. Of course there is a great deal of fraud, no doubt; but then, whenever you see fraud, you have also to say that fraud is an imitation. There must be some truth somewhere, that is being imitated; you cannot imitate nothing. Imitation must be of something substantially true.

In very remote times in India, thousands of years ago, these facts used to happen even more than they do today. It seems to me that when a country becomes very thickly populated, psychical power deteriorates. Given a vast country thinly inhabited, there will, perhaps, be more of psychical power there. These facts, the Hindus, being analytically minded. Took up and investigated. And they came to certain remarkable conclusions; that is, they made a science of it. They found out that all these, though extraordinary, are also natural; there is nothing supernatural. They are under laws just the same as any other physical phenomenon. It is not a freak of nature that a man is born with such powers. They can be systematically studied, practiced, and acquired. This science they call the science of Râja-Yoga. There are thousands of people who cultivate the study of this science, and for the whole nation it has become a part of daily worship.

The conclusion they have reached is that all these extraordinary powers are in the mind of man. This mind is a part of the universal mind. Each mind is connected with every other mind. And each mind, wherever it is located, is in actual communication with the whole world.

Have you ever noticed the phenomenon that is called thought-transference? A man here is thinking something, and that thought is manifested in somebody else, in some other place. With preparations — not by chance — a man wants to send a thought to another mind at a distance, and this other mind knows that a thought is coming, and he receives it exactly as it is sent out. Distance makes no difference. The thought goes and reaches the other man, and he understands it. If your mind were an isolated something here, and my mind were an isolated something there, and there were no connection between the two, how would it be possible for my thought to reach you? In the ordinary cases, it is not my thought that is reaching you direct; but my thought has got to be dissolved into ethereal vibrations and those ethereal vibrations go into your brain, and they have to be resolved again into your own thoughts. Here is a dissolution of thought, and there is a resolution of thought. It is a roundabout process. But in telepathy, there is no such thing; it is direct.

This shows that there is a continuity of mind, as the Yogis call it. The mind is universal. Your mind, my mind, all these little minds, are fragments of that universal mind, little waves in the ocean; and on account of this continuity, we can convey our thoughts directly to one another.

You see what is happening all around us. The world is one of influence. Part of our energy is used up in the preservation of our own bodies. Beyond that, every particle of our energy is day and night being used in influencing others. Our bodies, our virtues, our intellect, and our spirituality, all these are continuously influencing others; and so, conversely, we are being influenced by them. This is going on all around us. Now, to take a concrete example. A man comes; you know he is very learned, his language is beautiful, and he speaks to you by the hour; but he does not make any impression. Another man comes, and he speaks a few words, not well arranged, ungrammatical perhaps; all the same, he makes an immense impression. Many of you have seen that. So it is evident that words alone cannot always produce an impression. Words, even thoughts contribute only one-third of the influence in making an impression, the man, two-thirds. What you call the personal magnetism of the man — that is what goes out and impresses you.

In our families there are the heads; some of them are successful, others are not. Why? We complain of others in our failures. The moment I am unsuccessful, I say, so-and-so is the cause of the failure. In failure, one does not like to confess one's own faults and weaknesses. Each person tries to hold himself faultless and lay the blame upon somebody or something else, or even on bad luck. When heads of families fail, they should ask themselves, why it is that some persons manage a family so well and others do not. Then you will find that the difference is owing to the man — his presence, his personality.

Coming to great leaders of mankind, we always find that it was the personality of the man that counted. Now, take all the great authors of the past, the great thinkers. Really speaking, how many thoughts have they thought? Take all the writings that have been left to us by the past leaders of mankind; take each one of their books and appraise them. The real thoughts, new and genuine, that have been thought in this world up to this time, amount to only a handful. Read in their books the thoughts they have left to us. The authors do not appear to be giants to us, and yet we know that they were great giants in their days. What made them so? Not simply the thoughts they thought, neither the books they wrote, nor the speeches they made, it was something else that is now gone, that is their personality. As I have already remarked, the personality of the man is two-thirds, and his intellect, his words, are but one-third. It is the real man, the personality of the man, that runs through us. Our actions are but effects. Actions must come when the man is there; the effect is bound to follow the cause.

The ideal of all education, all training, should be this man-making. But, instead of that, we are always trying to polish up the outside. What use in polishing up the outside when there is no inside? The end and aim of all training is to make the man grow. The man who influences, who throws his magic, as it were, upon his fellow-beings, is a dynamo of power, and when that man is ready, he can do anything and everything he likes; that personality put upon anything will make it work.

Now, we see that though this is a fact, no physical laws that we know of will explain this. How can we explain it by chemical and physical knowledge? How much of oxygen, hydrogen, carbon, how many molecules in different positions, and how many cells, etc., etc. can explain this mysterious personality? And we still see, it is a fact, and not only that, it is the real man; and it is that man that lives and moves and works, it is that man that influences, moves his fellow-beings, and passes out, and his intellect and books and works are but traces left behind. Think of this. Compare the great teachers of religion with the great philosophers. The philosophers scarcely influenced anybody's inner man, and yet they wrote most marvellous books. The religious teachers, on the other hand, moved countries in their lifetime. The difference was made by personality. In the philosopher it is a faint personality that influences; in the great prophets it is tremendous. In the former we touch the intellect, in the latter we touch life. In the one case, it is simply a chemical process, putting certain chemical ingredients together which may gradually combine and under proper circumstances bring out a flash of light or may fail. In the other, it is like a torch that goes round quickly, lighting others.

The science of Yoga claims that it has discovered the laws which develop this personality, and by proper attention to those laws and methods, each one can grow and strengthen his personality. This is one of the great practical things, and this is the secret of all education. This has a universal application. In the life of the householder, in the life of the poor, the rich, the man of business, the spiritual man, in every one's life, it is a great thing, the strengthening of this personality. There are laws, very fine, which are behind the physical laws, as we know. That is to say, there are no such realities as a physical world, a mental world, a spiritual world. Whatever is, is one. Let us say, it is a sort of tapering existence; the thickest part is here, it tapers and becomes finer and finer. The finest is what we call spirit, the grossest, the body. And just as it is here in microcosm, it is exactly the same in the macrocosm. The universe of ours is exactly like that; it is the gross external thickness, and it tapers into something finer and finer until it becomes God.

We also know that the greatest power is lodged in the fine, not in the coarse. We see a man take up a huge weight, we see his muscles swell, and all over his body we see signs of exertion, and we think the muscles are powerful things. But it is the thin thread-like things, the nerves, which bring power to the muscles; the moment one of these threads is cut off from reaching the muscles, they are not able to work at all. These tiny nerves bring the power from something still finer, and that again in its turn brings it from something finer still — thought, and so on. So, it is the fine that is really the seat of power. Of course we can see the movements in the gross; but when fine movements take place, we cannot see them. When a gross thing moves, we catch it, and thus we naturally identify movement with things which are gross. But all the power is really in the fine. We do not see any movement in the fine, perhaps, because the movement is so intense that we cannot perceive it. But if by any science, any investigation, we are helped to get hold of these finer forces which are the cause of the expression, the expression itself will be under control. There is a little bubble coming from the bottom of a lake; we do not see it coming all the time, we see it only when it bursts on the surface; so, we can perceive thoughts only after they develop a great deal, or after they become actions. We constantly complain that we have no control over our actions, over our thoughts. But how can we have it? If we can get control over the fine movements, if we can get hold of thought at the root, before it has become thought, before it has become action, then it would be possible for us to control the whole. Now, if there is a method by which we can analyse, investigate, understand, and finally grapple with those finer powers, the finer causes, then alone is it possible to have control over ourselves, and the man who has control over his own mind assuredly will have control over every other mind. That is why purity and morality have been always the object of religion; a pure, moral man has control of himself. And all minds are the same, different parts of one Mind. He who knows one lump of clay has known all the clay in the universe. He who knows and controls his own mind knows the secret of every mind and has power over every mind

Now, a good deal of our physical evil we can get rid of, if we have control over the fine parts; a good many worries we can throw off, if we have control over the fine movements; a good many failures can be averted, if we have control over these fine powers. So far, is utility. Yet beyond, there is something higher.

Now, I shall tell you a theory, which I will not argue now, but simply place before you the conclusion. Each man in his childhood runs through the stages through which his race has come up; only the race took thousands of years to do it, while the child takes a few years. The child is first the old savage man — and he crushes a butterfly under his feet. The child is at first like the primitive ancestors of his race. As he grows, he passes through different stages until he reaches the development of his race. Only he does it swiftly and quickly. Now, take the whole of humanity as a race, or take the whole of the animal creation, man and the lower animals, as one whole. There is an end towards which the whole is moving. Let us call it perfection. Some men and women are born who anticipate the whole progress of mankind. Instead of waiting and being reborn over and over again for ages until the whole human race has attained to that perfection, they, as it were, rush through them in a few short years of their life. And we know that we can hasten these processes, if we be true to ourselves. If a number of men, without any culture, be left to live upon an island, and are given barely enough food, clothing, and shelter, they will gradually go on and on, evolving higher and higher stages of civilization. We know also, that this growth can be hastened by additional means. We help the growth of trees, do we not? Left to nature they would have grown, only they would have taken a longer time; we help them to grow in a shorter time than they would otherwise have taken. We are doing all the time the same thing, hastening the growth of things by artificial means. Why cannot we hasten the growth of man? We can do that as a race Why are teachers sent to other countries? Because by these means we can hasten the growth of races. Now, can we not hasten the growth of individuals? We can. Can we put a limit to the hastening? We cannot say how much a man can grow in one life. You have no reason to say that this much a man can do and no more. Circumstances can hasten him wonderfully. Can there be any limit then, till you come to perfection? So, what comes of it? — That a perfect man, that is to say, the type that is to come of this race, perhaps millions of years hence, that man can come today. And this is what the Yogis say, that all great incarnations and prophets are such men; that they reached perfection in this one life. We have had such men at all periods of the world's history and at all times. Quite recently, there was such a man who lived the life of the whole human race and reached the end — even in this life. Even this hastening of the growth must be under laws. Suppose we can investigate these laws and understand their secrets and apply them to our own needs; it follows that we grow. We hasten our growth, we hasten our development, and we become perfect, even in this life. This is the higher part of our life, and the science of the study of mind and its powers has this perfection as its real end. Helping others with money and other material things and teaching them how to go on smoothly in their daily life are mere details.

The utility of this science is to bring out the perfect man, and not let him wait and wait for ages, just a plaything in the hands of the physical world, like a log of drift-wood carried from wave to wave and tossing about in the ocean. This science wants you to be strong, to take the work in your own hand, instead of leaving it in the hands of nature, and get beyond this little life. That is the great idea.

Man is growing in knowledge, in power, in happiness. Continuously, we are growing as a race. We see that is true, perfectly true. Is it true of individuals? To a certain extent, yes. But yet, again comes the question: Where do you fix the limit? I can see only at a distance of so many feet. But I have seen a man close his eyes and see what is happening in another room. If you say you do not believe it, perhaps in three weeks that man can make you do the same. It can be taught to anybody. Some persons, in five minutes even, can be made to read what is happening in another man's mind. These facts can be demonstrated.

Now, if these things are true, where can we put a limit? If a man can read what is happening in another's mind in the corner of this room, why not in the next room? Why not anywhere? We cannot say, why not. We dare not say that it is not possible. We can only say, we do not know how it happens. Material scientists have no right to say that things like this are not possible; they can only say, "We do not know." Science has to collect facts, generalise upon them, deduce principles, and state the truth — that is all. But if we begin by denying the facts, how can a science be?

There is no end to the power a man can obtain. This is the peculiarity of the Indian mind, that when anything interests it, it gets absorbed in it and other things are neglected. You know how many sciences had their origin in India. Mathematics began there. You are even today counting 1, 2, 3, etc. to zero, after Sanskrit figures, and you all know that algebra also originated in India, and that gravitation was known to the Indians thousands of years before Newton was born.

You see the peculiarity. At a certain period of Indian history, this one subject of man and his mind absorbed all their interest. And it was so enticing, because it seemed the easiest way to achieve their ends. Now, the Indian mind became so thoroughly persuaded that the mind could do anything and everything according to law, that its powers became the great object of study. Charms, magic, and other powers, and all that were nothing extraordinary, but a regularly taught science, just as the physical sciences they had taught before that. Such a conviction in these things came upon the race that physical sciences nearly died out. It was the one thing that came before them. Different sects of Yogis began to make all sorts of experiments. Some made experiments with light, trying to find out how lights of different colours produced changes in the body. They wore a certain coloured cloth, lived under a certain colour, and ate certain coloured foods. All sorts of experiments were made in this way. Others made experiments in sound by stopping and unstopping their ears. And still others experimented in the sense of smell, and so on.

The whole idea was to get at the basis, to reach the fine parts of the thing. And some of them really showed most marvellous powers. Many of them were trying to float in the air or pass through it. I shall tell you a story which I heard from a great scholar in the West. It was told him by a Governor of Ceylon who saw the performance. A girl was brought forward and seated cross-legged upon a stool made of sticks crossed. After she had been seated for a time, the show-man began to take out, one after another, these cross-bars; and when all were taken out, the girl was left floating in the air. The Governor thought there was some trick, so he drew his sword and violently passed it under the girl; nothing was there. Now, what was this? It was not magic or something extraordinary. That is the peculiarity. No one in India would tell you that things like this do not exist. To the Hindu it is a matter of course. You know what the Hindus would often say when they have to fight their enemies — "Oh, one of our Yogis will come and drive the whole lot out!" It is the extreme belief of the race. What power is there in the hand or the sword? The power is all in the spirit.

If this is true, it is temptation enough for the mind to exert its highest. But as with every other science it is very difficult to make any great achievement, so also with this, nay much more. Yet most people think that these powers can be easily gained. How many are the years you take to make a fortune? Think of that! First, how many years do you take to learn electrical science or engineering? And then you have to work all the rest of your life.

Again, most of the other sciences deal with things that do not move, that are fixed. You can analyse the chair, the chair does not fly from you. But this science deals with the mind, which moves all the time; the moment you want to study it, it slips. Now the mind is in one mood, the next moment, perhaps, it is different, changing, changing all the time. In the midst of all this change it has to be studied, understood, grasped, and controlled. How much more difficult, then, is this science! It requires rigorous training. People ask me why I do not give them practical lessons. Why, it is no joke. I stand upon this platform talking to you and you go home and find no benefit; nor do I. Then you say, "It is all bosh." It is because you wanted to make a bosh of it. I know very little of this science, but the little that I gained I worked for thirty years of my life, and for six years I have been telling people the little that I know. It took me thirty years to learn it; thirty years of hard struggle. Sometimes I worked at it twenty hours during the twenty-four; sometimes I slept only one hour in the night; sometimes I worked whole nights; sometimes I lived in places where there was hardly a sound, hardly a breath; sometimes I had to live in caves. Think of that. And yet I know little or nothing; I have barely touched the hem of the garment of this science. But I can understand that it is true and vast and wonderful.

Now, if there is any one amongst you who really wants to study this science, he will have to start with that sort of determination, the same as, nay even more than, that which he puts into any business of life.

And what an amount of attention does business require, and what a rigorous taskmaster it is! Even if the father, the mother, the wife, or the child dies, business cannot stop! Even if the heart is breaking, we still have to go to our place of business, when every hour of work is a pang. That is business, and we think that it is just, that it is right.

This science calls for more application than any business can ever require. Many men can succeed in business; very few in this. Because so much depends upon the particular constitution of the person studying it. As in business all may not make a fortune, but everyone can make something, so in the study of this science each one can get a glimpse which will convince him of its truth and of the fact that there have been men who realised it fully.

This is the outline of the science. It stands upon its own feet and in its own light, and challenges comparison with any other science. There have been charlatans, there have been magicians, there have been cheats, and more here than in any other field. Why? For the same reason, that the more profitable the business, the greater the number of charlatans and cheats. But that is no reason why the business should not be good. And one thing more; it may be good intellectual gymnastics to listen to all the arguments and an intellectual satisfaction to hear of wonderful things. But, if any one of you really wants to learn something beyond that, merely attending lectures will not do. That cannot be taught in lectures, for it is life; and life can only convey life. If there are any amongst you who are really determined to learn it, I shall be very glad to help them.

HINTS ON PRACTICAL SPIRITUALITY

Delivered at the Home of Truth, Los Angeles, California

This morning I shall try to present to you some ideas about breathing and other exercises. We have been discussing theories so long that now it will be well to have a little of the practical. A great many books have been written in India upon this subject. Just as your people are practical in many things, so it seems our people are practical in this line. Five persons in this country will join their heads together and say, "We will have a joint-stock company", and in five hours it is done; in India they could not do it in fifty years; they are so unpractical in matters like this. But, mark you, if a man starts a system of philosophy, however wild its theory may be, it will have followers. For instance, a sect is started to teach that if a man stands on one leg for twelve years, day and night, he will get salvation — there will be hundreds ready to stand on one leg. All the suffering will be quietly borne. There are people who keep their arms upraised for years to gain religious merit. I have seen hundreds of them. And, mind you, they are not always ignorant fools, but are men who will astonish you with the depth and breadth of their intellect. So, you see, the word practical is also relative.

We are always making this mistake in judging others; we are always inclined to think that our little mental universe is all that is; our ethics, our morality, our sense of duty, our sense of utility, are the only things that are worth having. The other day when I was going to Europe, I was passing through Marseilles, where a bull-fight was being held. All the Englishmen in the steamer were mad with excitement, abusing and criticising the whole thing as cruel. When I reached England, I heard of a party of prize-fighters who had been to Paris, and were kicked out unceremoniously by the French, who thought prize-fighting very brutal. When I hear these things in various countries, I begin to understand the marvellous saying of Christ: "Judge not that ye be not judged." The more we learn, the more he find out how ignorant we are, how multiform and multi-sided is this mind of man. When I was a boy, I used to criticise the ascetic practices of my countrymen; great preachers in our own land have criticised them; the greatest man that was ever born, Buddha himself, criticised them. But all the same, as I am growing older, I feel that I have no right to judge. Sometimes I wish that, in spite of all their incongruities, I had one fragment of their power to do and suffer. Often I think that my judgment and my criticism do not proceed from any dislike of torture, but from sheer cowardice — because I cannot do it — I dare not do it.

Then, you see that strength, power, and courage are things which are very peculiar. We generally say, "A courageous man, a brave man, a daring man", but we must bear in mind that that courage or bravery or any other trait does not always characterise the man. The same man who would rush to the mouth of a cannon shrinks from the knife of the surgeon; and another man who never dares to face a gun will calmly bear a severe surgical operation, if need be.

Now, in judging others you must always define your terms of courage or greatness. The man whom I am criticising as not good may be wonderfully so in some points in which I am not.

Take another example. You often note, when people are discussing as to what man and woman can do, always the same mistake is made. They think they show man at his best because he can fight, for instance, and undergo tremendous physical exertion; and this is pitted against the physical weakness and the non-combating quality of woman. This is unjust. Woman is as courageous as man. Each is equally good in his or her way. What man can bring up a child with such patience, endurance, and love as the woman can? The one has developed the power of doing; the other, the power of suffering. If woman cannot act, neither can man suffer. The whole universe is one of perfect balance. I do not know, but some day we may wake up and find that the mere worm has something which balances our manhood. The most wicked person may have some good qualities that I entirely lack. I see that every day of my life. Look at the savage! I wish I had such a splendid physique. He eats, he drinks, to his heart's content, without knowing perhaps what sickness is, while I am suffering every minute. How many times would I have been glad to have changed my brain for his body! The whole universe is only a wave and a hollow; there can be no wave without a hollow. Balance everywhere. You have one thing great, your neighbour has another thing great. When you are judging man and woman, judge them by the standard of their respective greatness. One cannot be in other's shoes. The one has no right to say that the other is wicked. It is the same old superstition that says, "If this is done, the world will go to ruin." But in spite of this the world has not yet come to ruin. It was said in this country that if the Negroes were freed, the country would go to ruin — but did it? It was also said that if the masses were educated, the world would come to ruin — but it was only made better. Several years ago a book came out depicting the worst thing that could happen to England. The writer showed that as workmen's wages were rising, English commerce was declining. A cry was raised that the workmen in England were exorbitant in their demands, and that the Germans worked for less wages. A commission was sent over to Germany to investigate this and it reported that the German labourers received higher wages. Why was it so? Because of the education of the masses. Then how about the world going to ruin if the masses are educated? In India, especially, we meet with old fogies all over the land. They want to keep everything secret from the masses. These people come to the very satisfying conclusion that they are the crême de la crême of this universe. They believed they cannot be hurt by these dangerous experiments. It is only the masses that can be hurt by them!

Now, coming back to the practical. The subject of the practical application of psychology has been taken up in India from very early times. About fourteen hundred years before Christ, there flourished in India a great philosopher, Patanjali by name. He collected all the facts, evidences, and researches in psychology and took advantage of all the experiences accumulated in the past. Remember, this world is very old; it was not created only two or three thousand years ago. It is taught here in the West that society began eighteen hundred years ago, with the New Testament. Before that there was no society. That may be true with regard to the West, but it is not true as regards the whole world. Often, while I was lecturing in London, a very intellectual and intelligent friend of mine would argue with me, and one day after using all his weapons against me, he suddenly exclaimed, "But why did not your Rishis come to England to teach us?" I replied, "Because there was no England to come to. Would they preach to the forests?"

"Fifty years ago," said Ingersoll to me, "you would have been hanged in this country if you had come to preach. You would have been burnt alive or you would have been stoned out of the villages."

So there is nothing unreasonable in the supposition that civilisation existed fourteen hundred years before Christ. It is not yet settled whether civilisation has always come from the lower to the higher. The same arguments and proofs that have been brought forward to prove this proposition can also be used to demonstrate that the savage is only a degraded civilised man. The people of China, for instance, can never believe that civilisation sprang from a savage state, because the contrary is within their experience. But when you talk of the civilisation of America, what you mean is the perpetuity and the growth of your own race.

It is very easy to believe that the Hindus, who have been declining for seven hundred years, were highly civilised in the past. We cannot prove that it is not so.

There is not one single instance of any civilisation being spontaneous. There was not a race in the world which became civilised unless another civilised race came and mingled with that race. The origin of civilisation must have belonged, so to say, to one or two races who went abroad, spread their ideas, and intermingled with other races and thus civilisation spread.

For practical purposes, let us talk in the language of modern science. But I must ask you to bear in mind that, as there is religious superstition, so also there is a superstition in the matter of science. There are priests who take up religious work as their speciality; so also there are priests of physical law, scientists. As soon as a great scientist's name, like Darwin or Huxley, is cited, we follow blindly. It is the fashion of the day. Ninety-nine per cent of what we call scientific knowledge is mere theories. And many of them are no better than the old superstitions of ghosts with many heads and hands, but with this difference that the latter differentiated man a little from stocks and stones. True science asks us to be cautious. Just as we should be careful with the priests, so we should be with the scientists. Begin with disbelief. Analyse, test, prove everything, and then take it. Some of the most current beliefs of modern science have not been proved. Even in such a science as mathematics, the vast majority of its theories are only working hypotheses. With the advent of greater knowledge they will be thrown away.

In 1400 B.C. a great sage made an attempt to arrange, analyse, and generalise upon certain psychological facts. He was followed by many others who took up parts of what he had discovered and made a special study of them The Hindus alone of all ancient races took up the study of this branch of knowledge in right earnest. I am teaching you now about it, but how many of you will practice it? How many days, how many months will it be before you give it up? You are impractical on this subject. In India, they will persevere for ages and ages. You will be astonished to hear that they have no churches, no Common Prayers, or anything of the kind; but they, every day, still practice the breathings and try to concentrate the mind; and that is the chief part of their devotion. These are the main points. Every Hindu must do these. It is the religion of the country. Only, each one may have a special method — a special form of breathing, a special form of concentration, and what is one's special method, even one's wife need not know; the father need not know the son's. But they all have to do these. And there is nothing occult about these things. The word "occult" has no bearing on them. Near the Gangâ thousands and thousands of people may be seen daily sitting on its banks breathing and concentrating with closed eyes. There may be two reasons that make certain practices impracticable for the generality of mankind. One is, the teachers hold that the ordinary people are not fit for them. There may be some truth in this, but it is due more to pride. The second is the fear of persecution. A man, for instance, would not like to practice breathing publicly in this country, because he would be thought so queer; it is not the fashion here. On the other hand, in India. If a man prayed, "Give us this day our daily bread", people would laugh at him. Nothing could be more foolish to the Hindu mind than to say, "Our Father which art in Heaven." The Hindu, when he worships, thinks that God is within himself.

According to the Yogis, there are three principal nerve currents: one they call the Idâ, the other the Pingalâ, and the middle one the Sushumnâ, and all these are inside the spinal column. The Ida and the Pingala, the left and the right, are clusters of nerves, while the middle one, the Sushumna, is hollow and is not a cluster of nerves. This Sushumna is closed, and for the ordinary man is of no use, for he works through the Ida and the Pingala only. Currents are continually going down and coming up through these nerves, carrying orders all over the body through other nerves running to the different organs of the body.

It is the regulation and the bringing into rhythm of the Ida and Pingala that is the great object of breathing. But that itself is nothing — it is only so much air taken into the lungs; except for purifying the blood, it is of no more use. There is nothing occult in the air that we take in with our breath and assimilate to purify the blood; the action is merely a motion. This motion can be reduced to the unit movement we call Prâna; and everywhere, all movements are the various manifestations of this Prana. This Prana is electricity, it is magnetism; it is thrown out by the brain as thought. Everything is Prana; it is moving the sun, the moon, and the stars.

We say, whatever is in this universe has been projected by the vibration of the Prana. The highest result of vibration is thought. If there be any higher, we cannot conceive of it. The nerves, Ida and Pingala, work through the Prana. It is the Prana that is moving every part of the body, becoming the different forces. Give up that old idea that God is something that produces the effect and sits on a throne dispensing justice. In working we become exhausted because we use up so much Prana.

The breathing exercises, called Prânâyâma, bring about regulation of the breathing, rhythmic action of the Prana. When the Prana is working rhythmically, everything works properly. When the Yogis get control over their own bodies, if there is any disease in any part, they know that the Prana is not rhythmic there and they direct the Prana to the affected part until the rhythm is re-established.

Just as you can control the Prana in your own body, so, if you are powerful enough, you can control, even from here another man's Prana in India. It is all one. There is no break; unity is the law. Physically, psychically, mentally, morally, metaphysically, it is all one. Life is only a vibration. That which vibrates this ocean of ether, vibrates you. Just as in a lake, various strata of ice of various degrees of solidity are formed, or as in an ocean of vapour there are various degrees of density, so is this universe an ocean of matter. This is an ocean of ether in which we find the sun, moon, stars, and ourselves — in different states of solidity; but the continuity is not broken; it is the same throughout.

Now, when we study metaphysics, we come to know the world is one, not that the spiritual, the material, the mental, and the world of energies are separate. It is all one, but seen from different planes of vision. When you think of yourself as a body, you forget that you are a mind, and when you think of yourself as a mind, you will forget the body. There is only one thing, that you are; you can see it either as matter or body — or you can see it as mind or spirit. Birth, life, and death are but old superstitions. None was ever born, none will ever die; one changes one's position — that is all. I am sorry to see in the West how much they make of death; always trying to catch a little life. "Give us life after death! Give us life!" They are so happy if anybody tells them that they are going to live afterwards! How can I ever doubt such a thing! How can I imagine that I am dead! Try to think of yourself as dead, and you will see that you are present to see your own dead body. Life is such a wonderful reality that you cannot for a moment forget it. You may as well doubt that you exist. This is the first fact of consciousness — I am. Who can imagine a state of things which never existed? It is the most self-evident of all truths. So, the idea of immortality is inherent in man. How can one discuss a subject that is unimaginable? Why should we want to discuss the pros and cons of a subject that is self-evident?

The whole universe, therefore, is a unit, from whatever standpoint you view it. Just now, to us, this universe is a unit of Prana and Âkâsha, force and matter. And mind you, like all other basic principles, this is also self-contradictory. For what is force? — that which moves matter. And what is matter? — that which is moved by force. It is a seesaw! Some of the fundamentals of our reasoning are most curious, in spite of our boast of science and knowledge. "It is a headache without a head", as the Sanskrit proverb says. This state of things has been called Maya. It has neither existence nor non-existence. You cannot call it existence, because that only exists which is beyond time and space, which is self-existence. Yet this world satisfies to a certain degree our idea of existence. Therefore it has an apparent existence.

But there is the real existence in and through everything; and that reality, as it were, is caught in the meshes of time, space, and causation. There is the real man, the infinite, the beginningless, the endless, the ever-blessed, the ever-free. He has been caught in the meshes of time, space, and causation. So has everything in this world. The reality of everything is the same infinite. This is not idealism; it is not that the world does not exist. It has a relative existence, and fulfils all its requirements But it has no independent existence. It exists because of the Absolute Reality beyond time, space, and causation.

I have made long digressions. Now, let us return to our main subject.

All the automatic movements and all the conscious movements are the working of Prana through the nerves. Now, you see, it will be a very good thing to have control over the unconscious actions.

On some other occasions, I told you the definition of God and man. Man is an infinite circle whose circumference is nowhere, but the centre is located in one spot; and God is an infinite circle whose circumference is nowhere, but whose centre is everywhere. He works through all hands, sees through all eyes, walks on all feet, breathes through all bodies, lives in all life, speaks through every mouth, and thinks through every brain. Man can become like God and acquire control over the whole universe if he multiplies infinitely his centre of self-consciousness. Consciousness, therefore, is the chief thing to understand. Let us say that here is an infinite line amid darkness. We do not see the line, but on it there is one luminous point which moves on. As it moves along the line, it lights up its different parts in succession, and all that is left behind becomes dark again. Our consciousness; may well be likened to this luminous point. Its past experiences have been replaced by the present, or have become subconscious. We are not aware of their presence in us;

but there they are, unconsciously influencing our body and mind. Every movement that is now being made without the help of consciousness was previously conscious. Sufficient impetus has been given to it to work of itself.

The great error in all ethical systems, without exception, has been the failure of teaching the means by which man could refrain from doing evil. All the systems of ethics teach, "Do not steal!" Very good; but why does a man steal? Because all stealing, robbing, and other evil actions, as a rule, have become automatic. The systematic robber, thief, liar, unjust man and woman, are all these in spite of themselves! It is really a tremendous psychological problem. We should look upon man in the most charitable light. It is not so easy to be good. What are you but mere machines until you are free? Should you be proud because you are good? Certainly not. You are good because you cannot help it. Another is bad because he cannot help it. If you were in his position, who knows what you would have been? The woman in the street, or the thief in the jail, is the Christ that is being sacrificed that you may be a good man. Such is the law of balance. All the thieves and the murderers, all the unjust, the weakest, the wickedest, the devils, they all are my Christ! I owe a worship to the God Christ and to the demon Christ! That is my doctrine, I cannot help it. My salutation goes to the feet of the good, the saintly, and to the feet of the wicked and the devilish! They are all my teachers, all are my spiritual fathers, all are my Saviours. I may curse one and yet benefit by his failings; I may bless another and benefit by his good deeds. This is as true as that I stand here. I have to sneer at the woman walking in the street, because society wants it! She, my Saviour, she, whose street-walking is the cause of the chastity of other women! Think of that. Think, men and women, of this question in your mind. It is a truth — a bare, bold truth! As I see more of the world, see more of men and women, this conviction grows stronger. Whom shall I blame? Whom shall I praise? Both sides of the shield must be seen.

The task before us is vast; and first and foremost, we must seek to control the vast mass of sunken thoughts which have become automatic with us. The evil deed is, no doubt, on the conscious plane; but the cause which produced the evil deed was far beyond in the realms of the unconscious, unseen, and therefore more potent.

Practical psychology directs first of all its energies in controlling the unconscious, and we know that we can do it. Why? Because we know the cause of the unconscious is the conscious; the unconscious thoughts are the submerged millions of our old conscious thoughts, old conscious actions become petrified — we do not look at them, do not know them, have forgotten them. But mind you, if the power of evil is in the unconscious, so also is the power of good. We have many things stored in us as in a pocket. We have forgotten them, do not even think of them, and there are many of them, rotting, becoming positively dangerous; they come forth, the unconscious causes which kill humanity. True psychology would, therefore, try to bring them under the control of the conscious. The great task is to revive the whole man, as it were, in order to make him the complete master of himself. Even what we call the automatic action of the organs within our bodies, such as the liver etc., can be made to obey our commands.

This is the first part of the study, the control of the unconscious. The next is to go beyond the conscious. Just as unconscious work is beneath consciousness, so there is another work which is above consciousness. When this superconscious state is reached, man becomes free and divine; death becomes immortality, weakness becomes infinite power, and iron bondage becomes liberty. That is the goal, the infinite realm of the superconscious.

So, therefore, we see now that there must be a twofold work. First, by the proper working of the Ida and the Pingala, which are the two existing ordinary currents, to control the subconscious action; and secondly, to go beyond even consciousness.

The books say that he alone is the Yogi who, after long practice in self-concentration, has attained to this truth. The Sushumna now opens and a current which never before entered into this new passage will find its way into it, and gradually ascend to (what we call in figurative language) the different lotus centres, till at last it reaches the brain. Then the Yogi becomes conscious of what he really is, God Himself.

Everyone without exception, everyone of us, can attain to this culmination of Yoga. But it is a terrible task. If a person wants to attain to this truth, he will have to do something more than to listen to lectures and take a few breathing exercises. Everything lies in the preparation. How long does it take to strike a light? Only a second; but how long it takes to make the candle! How long does it take to eat a dinner? Perhaps half an hour. But hours to prepare the food! We want to strike the light in a second, but we forget that the making of the candle is the chief thing.

But though it is so hard to reach the goal, yet even our smallest attempts are not in vain. We know that nothing is lost. In the Gita, Arjuna asks Krishna, "Those who fail in attaining perfection in Yoga in this life, are they destroyed like the clouds of summer?" Krishna replies, "Nothing, my friend, is lost in this world. Whatever one does, that remains as one's own, and if the fruition of Yoga does not come in this life, one takes it up again in the next birth." Otherwise, how do you explain the marvellous childhood of Jesus, Buddha, Shankara?

Breathing, posturing, etc. are no doubt helps in Yoga; but they are merely physical. The great preparations are mental. The first thing necessary is a quiet and peaceable life.

If you want to be a Yogi, you must be free, and place yourself in circumstances where you are alone and free from all anxiety. He who desires a comfortable and nice life and at the same time wants to realise the Self is like the fool who, wanting to cross the river, caught hold of a crocodile, mistaking it for a log of wood (Vivekachudâmani, 84.). "Seek ye first the kingdom of God, and everything shall be added unto you." This is the one great duty, this is renunciation. Live for an ideal, and leave no place in the mind for anything else. Let us put forth all our energies to acquire that, which never fails — our spiritual perfection. If we have true yearning for realisation, we must struggle, and through struggle growth will come. We shall make mistakes, but they may be angels unawares.

The greatest help to spiritual life is meditation (Dhyâna). In meditation we divest ourselves of all material conditions and feel our divine nature. We do not depend upon any external help in meditation. The touch of the soul can paint the brightest colour even in the dingiest places; it can cast a fragrance over the vilest thing; it can make the wicked divine — and all enmity, all selfishness is effaced. The less the thought of the body, the better. For it is the body that drags us down. It is attachment, identification, which makes us miserable. That is the secret: To think that I am the spirit and not the body, and that the whole of this universe with all its relations, with all its good and all its evil, is but as a series of paintings — scenes on a canvas — of which I am the witness.

BHAKTI OR DEVOTION

BHAKTI OR DEVOTION

The idea of a Personal God has obtained in almost every religion, except a very few. With the exception of the Buddhist and the Jain, perhaps all the religions of the world have the idea of a Personal God, and with it comes the idea of devotion and worship. The Buddhists and the Jains, although they have no Personal God, worship the founders of their religions in precisely the same way as others worship a Personal God. This idea of devotion and worship to some higher being who can reflect back the love to man is universal. In various religions this love and devotion is manifested in various degrees, at different stages. The lowest stage is that of ritualism, when abstract ideas are almost impossible, and are dragged down to the lowest plane, and made concrete. Forms come into play, and, along with them, various symbols. Throughout the history of the world, we find that man is trying to grasp the abstract through thought-forms, or symbols. All the external manifestations of religion — bells, music, rituals, books, and images — come under that head. Anything that appeals to the senses, anything that helps man to form a concrete image of the abstract, is taken hold of, and worshipped.

From time to time, there have been reformers in every religion who have stood against all symbols and rituals. But vain has been their opposition, for so long as man will remain as he is, the vast majority will always want something concrete to hold on to, something around which, as it were, to place their ideas, something which will be the centre of all the thought-forms in their minds. The great attempts of the Mohammedans and of the Protestants have been directed to this one end, of doing away with all rituals, and yet we find that even with them, rituals have crept in. They cannot be kept out; after long struggle, the masses simply change one symbol for another. The Mohammedan, who thinks that every ritual, every form, image, or ceremony, used by a non-Mohammedan is sinful, does not think so when he comes to his own shrine, the Caaba. Every religious Mohammedan wherever he prays, must imagine that he is standing before the Caaba. When he makes a pilgrimage there, he must kiss the black stone in the wall of the shrine. All the kisses that have been imprinted on that stone, by millions and millions of pilgrims, will stand up as witnesses for the benefit of the faithful on the last day of judgment. Then, there is the well of Zimzim. Mohammedans believe that whoever draws a little water out of that well will have his sins pardoned, and he will, after the day of resurrection, have a fresh body, and live for ever. In others, we find that the symbology comes in the form of buildings. Protestants hold that churches are more sacred than other places. The church, as it is, stands for a symbol. Or there is the Book. The idea of the Book to them, is much holier than any other symbol.

It is vain to preach against the use of symbols, and why should we preach against them? There is no reason why man should not use symbols. They have them in order to represent the ideas signified behind them. This universe is a symbol, in and through which we are trying to grasp the thing signified, which is beyond and behind. The spirit is the goal, and not matter. Forms, images, bells, candles, books, churches, temples, and all holy symbols are very good, very helpful to the growing plant of spirituality, but thus far and no farther. In the test majority of cases, we find that the plant does not grow. It is very good to be born in a church, but it is very bad to die in a church. It is very good to be born within the limits of certain forms that help the little plant of spirituality, but if a man dies within the bounds of these forms, it shows that he has not grown, that there has been no development of the soul.

If, therefore, any one says that symbols, rituals, and forms are to be kept for ever, he is wrong; but if he says, that these symbols and rituals are a help to the growth of the soul, in its low and undeveloped state, he is right. But, you must not mistake this development of the soul as meaning anything intellectual. A man can be of gigantic intellect, yet spiritually he may be a baby. You can verify it this moment. All of you have been taught to believe in an Omnipresent God. Try to think of it. How few of you can have any idea of what omnipresence means! If you struggle hard, you will get something like the idea of the ocean, or of the sky, or of a vast stretch of green earth, or of a desert. All these are material images, and so long as you cannot conceive of the abstract as abstract, of the ideal as the ideal, you will have to resort to these forms, these material images. It does not make much difference whether these images are inside or outside the mind. We are all born idolaters, and idolatry is good, because it is in the nature of man. Who can get beyond it? Only the perfect man, the God-man. The rest are all idolaters. So long as we see this universe before us, with its forms and shapes, we are all idolaters. This is a gigantic symbol we are worshipping. He who says he is the body is a born idolater. We are spirit, spirit that has no form or shape, spirit that is infinite, and not matter. Therefore, anyone who cannot grasp the abstract, who cannot think of himself as he is, except in and through matter, as the body, is an idolater. And yet how people fight among themselves, calling one another idolaters! In other words, each says, his idol is right, and the others' are wrong.

Therefore, we should get rid of these childish notions. We should get beyond the prattle of men who think that religion is merely a mass of frothy words, that it is only a system of doctrines; to whom religion is only a little intellectual assent or dissent; to whom religion is believing in certain words which their own priests tell them; to whom religion is something which their forefathers believed; to whom religion is a certain form of ideas and superstitions to which they cling because they are their national superstitions. We should get beyond all these and look at humanity as one vast organism, slowly coming towards light — a wonderful plant, slowly unfolding itself to that wonderful truth which is called God — and the first gyrations, the first motions, towards this are always through matter and through ritual.

In the heart of all these ritualisms, there stands one idea prominent above all the rest — the worship of a name. Those of you who have studied the older forms of Christianity, those of you who have studied the other religions of the world, perhaps have marked that there is this idea with them all, the worship of a name. A name is said to be very sacred. In the Bible we read that the holy name of God was considered sacred beyond compare, holy beyond everything. It was the holiest of all names, and it was thought that this very Word was God. This is quite true. What is this universe but name and form? Can you think without words? Word and thought are inseparable. Try if any one of you can separate them. Whenever you think, you are doing so through word forms. The one brings the other; thought brings the word, and the word brings the thought. Thus the whole universe is, as it were, the external symbol of God, and behind that stands His grand name. Each particular body is a form, and behind that particular body is its name. As soon as you think of our friend So-and-so, there comes the idea of his body, and as soon as you think of your friend's body, you get the idea of his name. This is in the constitution of man. That is to say, psychologically, in the mind-stuff of man, there cannot come the idea of name without the idea of form, and there cannot come the idea of form without the idea of name. They are inseparable; they are the external and the internal sides of the same wave. As such, names have been exalted and worshipped all over the world — consciously or unconsciously, man found the glory of names.

Again, we find that in many different religions, holy personages have been worshipped. They worship Krishna, they worship Buddha, they worship Jesus, and so forth. Then, there is the worship of saints; hundreds of them have been worshipped all over the world, and why not? The vibration of light is everywhere. The owl sees it in the dark. That shows it is there, though man cannot see it. To man, that vibration is only visible in the lamp, in the sun, in the moon, etc. God is omnipresent, He is manifesting Himself in every being; but for men, He is only visible, recognisable, in man. When His light, His presence, His spirit, shines through the human face, then and then alone, can man understand Him. Thus, man has been worshipping God through men all the time, and must do so as long as he is a man. He may cry against it, struggle against it, but as soon as he attempts to realise God, he will find the constitutional necessity of thinking of God as a man.

So we find that in almost every religion these are the three primary things which we have in the worship of God — forms or symbols, names, God-men. All religions have these, but you find that they want to fight with each other. One says, "My name is the only name; my form is the only form; and my God-men are the only God-men in the world; yours are simply myths." In modern times, Christian clergymen have become a little kinder, and they allow that in the older religions, the different forms of worship were foreshadowings of Christianity, which of course, they consider, is the only true form. God tested Himself in older times, tested His powers by getting these things into shape which culminated in Christianity. This, at least, is a great advance. Fifty years ago they would not have said even that; nothing was true except their own religion. This idea is not limited to any religion, nation, or class of persons; people are always thinking that the only right thing to be done by others is what they themselves are doing. And it is here that the study of different religions helps us. It shows us that the same thoughts that we have been calling ours, and ours alone, were present hundreds of years ago in others, and sometimes even in a better form of expression than our own.

These are the external forms of devotion, through which man has to pass; but if he is sincere, if he really wants to reach the truth, he goes higher than these, to a plane where forms are as nothing. Temples or churches, books or forms, are simply the kindergarten of religion, to make the spiritual child strong enough to take higher steps; and these first steps are necessary if he wants religion. With the thirst, the longing for God, comes real devotion, real Bhakti. Who has the longing? That is the question. Religion is not in doctrines, in dogmas, nor in intellectual argumentation; it is being and becoming, it is realisation. We hear so many talking about God and the soul, and all the mysteries of the universe, but if you take them one by one, and ask them, "Have you realised God? Have you seen your Soul?" — how many can say they have? And yet they are all fighting with one another! At one time, in India, representatives of different sects met together and began to dispute. One said that the only God was Shiva; another said, the only God was Vishnu, and so on; and there was no end to their discussion. A sage was passing that way, and was invited by the disputants to decide the matter. He first asked the man who was claiming Shiva as the greatest God, "Have you seen Shiva? Are you acquainted with Him? If not, how do you know He is the greatest God?" Then turning to the worshipper of Vishnu, he asked, "Have you seen Vishnu?" And after asking this question to all of them, he found out that not one of them knew anything of God. That was why they were disputing so much, for had they really known, they would not have argued. When a jar is being filled with water, it makes a noise, but when it is full, there is no noise. So, the very fact of these disputations and fighting among sects shows that they do not know anything about religion. Religion to them is a mere mass of frothy words, to be written in books. Each one hurries to write a big book, to make it as massive as possible, stealing his materials from every book he can lay his hands upon, and never acknowledging his indebtedness. Then he launches this book upon the world, adding to the disturbance that is already existing there.

The vast majority of men are atheists. I am glad that, in modern times, another class of atheists has come into existence in the Western world — I mean the materialists. They are sincere atheists. They are better than the religious atheists, who are insincere, who fight and talk about religion, and yet do not want it, never try to realise it, never try to understand it. Remember the words of Christ: "Ask, and it shall be given you; seek, and ye shall find; knock, and it shall be opened unto you." These words are literally true, not figures or fiction. They were the outflow of the heart's blood of one of the greatest sons of God who have ever come to this world of ours; words which came as the fruit of realisation, from a man who had felt and realised God himself; who had spoken with God, lived with

God, a hundred times more intensely than you or I see this building. Who wants God? That is the question. Do you think that all this mass of people in the world want God, and cannot get Him? That cannot be. What want is there without its object outside? Man wants to breathe, and there is air for him to breathe. Man wants to eat, and there is food to eat. What creates these desires? The existence of external things. It was the light that made the eyes; it was the sound that made the ears. So every desire in human beings has been created by something which already existed outside. This desire for perfection, for reaching the goal and getting beyond nature, how can it be there, until something has created it and drilled it into the soul of man, and makes it live there? He, therefore, in whom this desire is awakened, will reach the goal. We want everything but God. This is not religion that you see all around you. My lady has furniture in her parlour, from all over the world, and now it is the fashion to have something Japanese; so she buys a vase and puts it in her room. Such is religion with the vast majority; they have all sorts of things for enjoyment, and unless they add a little flavour of religion, life is not all right, because society would criticise them. Society expects it; so they must have some religion. This is the present state of religion in the world.

A disciple went to his master and said to him, "Sir, I want religion." The master looked at the young man, and did not speak, but only smiled. The young man came every day, and insisted that he wanted religion. But the old man knew better than the young man. One day, when it was very hot, he asked the young man to go to the river with him and take a plunge. The young man plunged in, and the old man followed him and held the young man down under the water by force. After the young man had struggled for a while, he let him go and asked him what he wanted most while he was under the water. "A breath of air", the disciple answered. "Do you want God in that way? If you do, you will get Him in a moment," said the master. Until you have that thirst, that desire, you cannot get religion, however you may struggle with your intellect, or your books, or your forms. Until that thirst is awakened in you, you are no better than any atheist; only the atheist is sincere, and you are not.

A great sage used to say, "Suppose there is a thief in a room, and somehow he comes to know that there is a vast mass of gold in the next room, and that there is only a thin partition between the two rooms What would be the condition of that thief? He would be sleepless, he would not be able to eat or do anything. His whole mind would be on getting that gold. Do you mean to say that, if all these people really believed that the Mine of Happiness, of Blessedness, of Glory were here, they would act as they do in the world, without trying to get God?" As soon as a man begins to believe there is a God, he becomes mad with longing to get to Him. Others may go their way, but as soon as a man is sure that there is a much higher life than that which he is leading here, as soon as he feels sure that the senses are not all, that this limited, material body is as nothing compared with the immortal, eternal, undying bliss of the Self, he becomes mad until he finds out this bliss for himself. And this madness, this thirst, this mania, is what is called the "awakening" to religion, and when that has come, a man is beginning to be religious. But it takes a long time. All these forms and ceremonies, these prayers and pilgrimages, these books, bells, candles, and priests, are the preparations; they take off the impurities from the soul. And when the soul has become pure, it naturally wants to get to the mine of all purity, God Himself. Just as a piece of iron, which had been covered with the dust of centuries, might be lying near a magnet all the time, and yet not be attracted by it, but as soon as the dust is cleared away, the iron is drawn by the magnet; so, when the human soul, covered with the dust of ages, impurities, wickednesses, and sins, after many births, becomes purified enough by these forms and ceremonies, by doing good to others, loving other beings, its natural spiritual attraction comes, it wakes up and struggles towards God.

Yet, all these forms and symbols are simply the beginning, not true love of God. Love we hear spoken of everywhere Everyone says, "Love God." Men do not know what it into love; if they did, they would not talk so glibly about it. Every man says he can love, and then, in no time, finds out that there is no love in his nature. Every woman says she can love and soon finds out that she cannot. The world is full of the talk of love, but it is hard to love. Where is love? How do you know that there is love? The first test of love is that it knows no bargaining. So long as you see a man love another only to get something from him, you know that that is not love; it is shopkeeping. Wherever there is any question of buying and selling, it is not love. So, when a man prays to God, "Give me this, and give me that", it is not love. How can it be? I offer you a prayer, and you give me something in return; that is what it is, mere shopkeeping.

A certain great king went to hunt in a forest, and there he happened to meet a sage. He had a little conversation with him and became so pleased with him that he asked him to accept a present from him. "No," said the sage, "I am perfectly satisfied with my condition; these trees give me enough fruit to eat; these beautiful pure streams supply me with all the water I want; I sleep in these caves. What do I care for your presents, though you be an emperor?" The emperor said, "Just to purify me, to gratify me, come with me into the city and take some present." At last the sage consented to go with the emperor, and he was taken into the emperor's palace, where there were gold, jewellery, marble, and most wonderful things. Wealth and power were manifest everywhere. The emperor asked the sage to wait a minute, while he repeated his prayer, and he went into a corner and began to pray, "Lord, give me more wealth, more children, more territory." In the meanwhile, the sage got up and began to walk away. The emperor saw him going and went after him. "Stay, Sir, you did not take my present and are going away." The sage turned to him and said, "Beggar, I do not beg of beggars. What can you give? You have been begging yourself all the time." That is not the language of love. What is the difference between love and shopkeeping, if you ask God to give you this, and give you that? The first test of love is that it knows no bargaining. Love is always the giver, and never the taker. Says the child of God, "If God wants, I give Him my everything, but I do not want anything of Him. I want nothing in this universe. I love Him, because I want to love Him, and I ask no favour in return. Who cares whether God is almighty or not? I do not want any power from Him nor any manifestation of His power. Sufficient for me that He is the God of love. I ask no more question."

The second test is that love knows no fear. So long as man thinks of God as a Being sitting above the clouds, with rewards in one hand and punishments in the other, there can be no love. Can you frighten one into love? Does the lamb love the lion? The mouse, the cat? The slave, the master? Slaves sometimes simulate love, but is it love? Where do you ever see love in fear? It is always a sham. With love never comes the idea of fear. Think of a young mother in the street: if a dog barks at her, she flees into the nearest house. The next day she is in the street with her child, and suppose a lion rushes upon the child, where will be her position? Just at the mouth of the lion, protecting her child. Love conquered all her fear. So also in the love of God. Who cares whether God is a rewarder or a punisher? That is not the thought of a lover. Think of a judge when he comes home, what does his wife see in him? Not a judge, or a rewarder or punisher, but her husband, her love. What do his children see in him? Their loving father, not the punisher or rewarder. So the children of God never see in Him a punisher or a rewarder. It is only people who have never tasted of love that fear and quake. Cast off all fear — though these horrible ideas of God as a punisher or rewarder may have their use in savage minds. Some men, even the most intellectual, are spiritual savages, and these ideas may help them. But to men who are spiritual, men who are approaching religion, in whom spiritual insight is awakened, such ideas are simply childish, simply foolish. Such men reject all ideas of fear.

The third is a still higher test. Love is always the highest ideal. When one has passed through the first two stages, when one has thrown off all shopkeeping, and cast off all fear, one then begins to realise that love is always the highest ideal. How many times in this world we see a beautiful woman loving an ugly man? How many times we see a handsome man loving an ugly woman! What is the attraction? Lookers-on only see the ugly man or the ugly woman, but not so the lover; to the lover the beloved is the most beautiful being that ever existed. How is it? The woman who loves the ugly man takes, as it were, the ideal of beauty which is in her own mind, and projects it on this ugly man; and what she worships and loves is not the ugly man, but her own ideal. That man is, as it were, only the suggestion, and upon that suggestion she throws her own ideal, and covers it; and it becomes her object of worship. Now, this applies in every case where we love. Many of us have very ordinary looking brothers or sisters; yet the very idea of their being brothers or sisters makes them beautiful to us.

The philosophy in the background is that each one projects his own ideal and worships that. This external world is only the world of suggestion. All that we see, we project out of our own minds. A grain of sand gets washed into the shell of an oyster and irritates it. The irritation produces a secretion in the oyster, which covers the grain of sand and the beautiful pearl is the result. Similarly, external things furnish us with suggestions, over which we project our own ideals and make our objects. The wicked see this world as a perfect hell, and the good as a perfect heaven. Lovers see this world as full of love, and haters as full of hatred; fighters see nothing but strife, and the peaceful nothing but peace. The perfect man sees nothing but God. So we always worship our highest ideal, and when we have reached the point, when we love the ideal as the ideal, all arguments and doubts vanish for ever. Who cares whether God can be demonstrated or not? The ideal can never go, because it is a part of my own nature. I shall only question the ideal when I question my own existence, and as I cannot question the one, I cannot question the other. Who cares whether God can be almighty and all-merciful at the same time or not? Who cares whether He is the rewarder of mankind, whether He looks at us with the eyes of a tyrant or with the eyes of a beneficent monarch?

The lover has passed beyond all these things, beyond rewards and punishments, beyond fears and doubts, beyond scientific or any other demonstration. Sufficient unto him is the ideal of love, and is it not self-evident that this universe is but a manifestation of this love? What is it that makes atoms unite with atoms, molecules with molecules, and causes planets to fly towards each other? What is it that attracts man to man, man to woman, woman to man, and animals to animals, drawing the whole universe, as it were, towards one centre? It is what is called love. Its manifestation is from the lowest atom to the highest being: omnipotent, all-pervading, is this love. What manifests itself as attraction in the sentient and the insentient, in the particular and in the universal, is the love of God. It is the one motive power that is in the universe. Under the impetus of that love, Christ gives his life for humanity, Buddha even for an animal, the mother for the child, the husband for the wife. It is under the impetus of the same love that men are ready to give up their lives for their country, and strange to say, under the impetus of the same love, the thief steals, the murderer murders. Even in these cases, the spirit is the same, but the manifestation is different. This is the one motive power in the universe. The thief has love for gold; the love is there, but it is misdirected. So, in all crimes, as well as in all virtuous actions, behind stands that eternal love. Suppose a man writes a cheque for a thousand dollars for the poor of New York, and at the same time, in the same room, another man forges the name of a friend. The light by which both of them write is the same, but each one will be responsible for the use he makes of it. It is not the light that is to be praised or blamed. Unattached, yet shining in everything, is love, the motive power of the universe, without which the universe would fall to pieces in a moment, and this love is God.

"None, O beloved, loves the husband for the husband's sake, but for the Self that is in the husband; none, O beloved, ever loves the wife for the wife's sake, but for the Self that is in the wife. None ever loves anything else, except for the Self." Even this selfishness, which is so much condemned, is but a manifestation of the same love. Stand aside from this play, do not mix in it, but see this wonderful panorama, this grand drama, played scene after scene, and hear this wonderful harmony; all are the manifestation of the same love. Even in selfishness, that self will multiply, grow and grow. That one self, the one man, will become two selves when he gets married; several, when he gets children; and thus he grows until he feels the whole world as his Self, the whole universe as his Self. He expands into one mass of universal love, infinite love — the love that is God.

Thus we come to what is called supreme Bhakti, supreme devotion, in which forms and symbols fall off. One who has reached that cannot belong to any sect, for all sects are in him. To what shall he belong? For all churches and temples are in him. Where is the church big enough for him? Such a man cannot bind himself down to certain limited forms. Where is the limit for unlimited love, with which he has become one? In all religions which take up this ideal of love, we find the struggle to express it. Although we understand what this love means and see that everything in this world of affections and attractions is a manifestation of that Infinite Love, the expression of which has been attempted by sages and saints of different nations, yet we find them using all the powers of language, transfiguring even the most carnal expression into the divine.

Thus sang the royal Hebrew sage, thus sang they of India. "O beloved, one kiss of Thy lips! Kissed by Thee, one's thirst for Thee increaseth for ever! All sorrows cease, one forgets the past, present, and future, and only thinks of Thee alone." That is the madness of the lover, when all desires have vanished. "Who cares for salvation? Who cares to be saved? Who cares to be perfect even? Who cares for freedom?" — says the lover. "I do not want wealth, nor even health; I do not want beauty, I do not want intellect: let me be born again and again, amid all the evils that are in the world; I will not complain, but let me love Thee, and that for love's sake."

That is the madness of love which finds expression in these songs. The highest, most expressive, strongest, and most attractive human love is that between man and woman, and, therefore, that language was used in expressing the deepest devotion. The madness of this human love was the faintest echo of the mad love of the saints. The true lovers of God want to become mad, inebriated with the love of God, to become "God-intoxicated men". They want to drink of the cup of love which has been prepared by the saints and sages of every religion, who have poured their heart's blood into it, and in which have been concentrated all the hopes of those who have loved God without seeking reward, who wanted love for itself only. The reward of love is love, and what a reward it is! It is the only thing that takes off all sorrows, the only cup, by the drinking of which this disease of the world vanishes Man becomes divinely mad and forgets that be is man.

Lastly, we find that all these various systems, in the end, converge to that one point, that perfect union. We always begin as dualists. God is a separate Being, and I am a separate being. Love comes between, and man begins to approach God, and God, as it were, begins to approach man. Man takes up all the various relationships of life, as father, mother, friend, or lover; and the last point is reached when he becomes one with the object of worship. "I am you, and you are I; and worshipping you, I worship myself; and in worshipping myself, I worship you." There we find the highest culmination of that with which man begins. At the beginning it was love for the self, but the claims of the little self made love selfish; at the end came the full blaze of light, when that self had become the Infinite. That God who at first was a Being somewhere, became resolved, as it were, into Infinite Love. Man himself was also transformed. He was approaching God, he was throwing off all vain desires, of which he was full before. With desires vanished selfishness, and, at the apex, he found that Love, Lover, and Beloved were One.

JNANA-YOGA

CHAPTER I
THE NECESSITY OF RELIGION

Delivered in London

Of all the forces that have worked and are still working to mould the destinies of the human race, none, certainly, is more potent than that, the manifestation of which we call religion. All social organisations have as a background, somewhere, the workings of that peculiar force, and the greatest cohesive impulse ever brought into play amongst human units has been derived from this power. It is obvious to all of us that in very many cases the bonds of religion have proved stronger than the bonds of race, or climate, or even of descent. It is a well-known fact that persons worshipping the same God, believing in the same religion, have stood by each other, with much greater strength and constancy, than people of merely the same descent, or even brothers. Various attempts have been made to trace the beginnings of religion. In all the ancient religions which have come down to us at the present day, we find one claim made — that they are all supernatural, that their genesis is not, as it were, in the human brain, but that they have originated somewhere outside of it.

Two theories have gained some acceptance amongst modern scholars. One is the spirit theory of religion, the other the evolution of the idea of the Infinite. One party maintains that ancestor worship is the beginning of religious ideas; the other, that religion originates in the personification of the powers of nature. Man wants to keep up the memory of his dead relatives and thinks they are living even when the body is dissolved, and he wants to place food for them and, in a certain sense, to worship them. Out of that came the growth we call religion.

Studying the ancient religions of the Egyptians, Babylonians, Chinese, and many other races in America and elsewhere, we find very clear traces of this ancestor worship being the beginning of religion. With the ancient Egyptians, the first idea of the soul was that of a double. Every human body contained in it another being very similar to it; and when a man died, this double went out of the body and yet lived on. But the life of the double lasted only so long as the dead body remained intact, and that is why we find among the Egyptians so much solicitude to keep the body uninjured. And that is why they built those huge pyramids in which they preserved the bodies. For, if any portion of the external body was hurt, the double would be correspondingly injured. This is clearly ancestor worship. With the ancient Babylonians we find the same idea of the double, but with a variation. The double lost all sense of love; it frightened the living to give it food and drink, and to help it in various ways. It even lost all affection for its own children and its own wife. Among the ancient Hindus also, we find traces of this ancestor worship. Among the Chinese, the basis of their religion may also be said to be ancestor worship, and it still permeates the length and breadth of that vast country. In fact, the only religion that can really be said to flourish in China is that of ancestor worship. Thus it seems, on the one hand, a very good position is made out for those who hold the theory of ancestor worship as the beginning of religion.

On the other hand, there are scholars who from the ancient Aryan literature show that religion originated in nature worship. Although in India we find proofs of ancestor worship everywhere, yet in the oldest records there is no trace of it whatsoever. In the Rig-Veda Samhitâ, the most ancient record of the Aryan race, we do not find any trace of it. Modern scholars think, it is the worship of nature that they find there. The human mind seems to struggle to get a peep behind the scenes. The dawn, the evening, the hurricane, the stupendous and gigantic forces of nature, its beauties, these have exercised the human mind, and it aspires to go beyond, to understand something about them. In the struggle they endow these phenomena with personal attributes, giving them souls and bodies, sometimes beautiful, sometimes transcendent. Every attempt ends by these phenomena becoming abstractions whether personalised or not. So also it is found with the ancient Greeks; their whole mythology is simply this abstracted nature worship. So also with the ancient Germans, the Scandinavians, and all the other Aryan races. Thus, on this side, too, a very strong case has been made out, that religion has its origin in the personification of the powers of nature.

These two views, though they seem to be contradictory, can be reconciled on a third basis, which, to my mind, is the real germ of religion, and that I propose to call the struggle to transcend the limitations of the senses. Either, man goes to seek for the spirits of his ancestors, the spirits of the dead, that is, he wants to get a glimpse of what there is after the body is dissolved, or, he desires to understand the power working behind the stupendous phenomena of nature. Whichever of these is the case, one thing is certain, that he tries to transcend the limitations of the senses. He cannot remain satisfied with his senses; he wants to go beyond them. The explanation need not be mysterious. To me it seems very natural that the first glimpse of religion should come through dreams. The first idea of immortality man may well get through dreams. Is that not a most wonderful state? And we know that children and untutored minds find very little difference between dreaming and their awakened state. What can be more natural than that they find, as natural logic, that even during the sleep state when the body is apparently dead, the mind goes on with all its intricate workings? What wonder that men will at once come to the conclusion that when this body is dissolved for ever, the same working will go on? This, to my mind, would be a more natural explanation of the supernatural, and through this dream idea the human mind rises to higher and higher conceptions. Of course, in time, the vast majority of mankind found out that these dreams are not verified by their waking states, and that during the dream state it is not that man has a fresh existence, but simply that he recapitulates the experiences of the awakened state.

But by this time the search had begun, and the search was inward, and man continued inquiring more deeply into the different stages of the mind and discovered higher states than either the waking or the dreaming. This state of things we find in all the organised religions of the world, called either ecstasy or inspiration. In all organised religions, their founders, prophets, and messengers are declared to have gone into states of mind that were neither waking nor sleeping, in which they came face to face with a new series of facts relating to what is called the spiritual kingdom. They realised things there much more intensely than we realise facts around us in our waking state. Take, for instance, the religions of the Brahmins. The Vedas are said to be written by Rishis. These Rishis were sages who realised certain facts. The exact definition of the Sanskrit word Rishi is a Seer of Mantras — of the thoughts conveyed in the Vedic hymns. These men declared that they had realised — sensed, if that word can be used with regard to the supersensuous — certain facts, and these facts they proceeded to put on record. We find the same truth declared amongst both the Jews and the Christians.

Some exceptions may be taken in the case of the Buddhists as represented by the Southern sect. It may be asked — if the Buddhists do not believe in any God or soul, how can their religion be derived from the supersensuous state of existence? The answer to this is that even the Buddhists find an eternal moral law, and that moral law was not reasoned out in our sense of the word But Buddha found it, discovered it, in a supersensuous state. Those of you who have studied the life of Buddha even as briefly given in that beautiful poem, The Light of Asia, may remember that Buddha is represented as sitting under the Bo-tree until he reached that supersensuous state of mind. All his teachings came through this, and not through intellectual cogitations.

Thus, a tremendous statement is made by all religions; that the human mind, at certain moments, transcends not only the limitations of the senses, but also the power of reasoning. It then comes face to face with facts which it could never have sensed, could never have reasoned out. These facts are the basis of all the religions of the world. Of course we have the right to challenge these facts, to put them to the test of reason. Nevertheless, all the existing religions of the world claim for the human mind this peculiar power of transcending the limits of the senses and the limits of reason; and this power they put forward as a statement of fact.

Apart from the consideration of tie question how far these facts claimed by religions are true, we find one characteristic common to them all. They are all abstractions as contrasted with the concrete discoveries of physics, for instance; and in all the highly organised religions they take the purest form of Unit Abstraction, either in the form of an Abstracted Presence, as an Omnipresent Being, as an Abstract Personality called God, as a Moral Law, or in the form of an Abstract Essence underlying every existence. In modern times, too, the attempts made to preach religions without appealing to the supersensuous state if the mind have had to take up the old abstractions of the Ancients and give different names to them as "Moral Law", the "Ideal Unity", and so forth, thus showing that these abstractions are not in the senses. None of us have yet seen an "Ideal Human Being", and yet we are told to believe in it. None of us have yet seen an ideally perfect man, and yet without that ideal we cannot progress. Thus, this one fact stands out from all these different religions, that there is an Ideal Unit Abstraction, which is put before us, either in the form of a Person or an Impersonal Being, or a Law, or a Presence, or an Essence. We are always struggling to raise ourselves up to that ideal. Every human being, whosoever and wheresoever he may be, has an ideal of infinite power. Every human being has an ideal of infinite pleasure. Most of the works that we find around us, the activities displayed everywhere, are due to the struggle for this infinite power or this infinite pleasure. But a few quickly discover that although they are struggling for infinite power, it is not through the senses that it can be reached. They find out very soon that that infinite pleasure is not to be got through the senses, or, in other words, the senses are too limited, and the body is too limited, to express the Infinite. To manifest the Infinite through the finite is impossible, and sooner or later, man learns to give up the attempt to express the Infinite through the finite.

This giving up, this renunciation of the attempt, is the background of ethics. Renunciation is the very basis upon which ethics stands. There never was an ethical code preached which had not renunciation for its basis.

Ethics always says, "Not I, but thou." Its motto is, "Not self, but non-self." The vain ideas of individualism, to which man clings when he is trying to find that Infinite Power or that Infinite Pleasure through the senses, have to be given up — say the laws of ethics. You have to put yourself last, and others before you. The senses say, "Myself first." Ethics says, "I must hold myself last." Thus, all codes of ethics are based upon this renunciation; destruction, not construction, of the individual on the material plane. That Infinite will never find expression upon the material plane, nor is it possible or thinkable.

So, man has to give up the plane of matter and rise to other spheres to seek a deeper expression of that Infinite. In this way the various ethical laws are being moulded, but all have that one central idea, eternal self-abnegation. Perfect self-annihilation is the ideal of ethics. People are startled if they are asked not to think of their individualities. They seem so very much afraid of losing what they call their individuality. At the same time, the same men would declare the highest ideals of ethics to be right, never for a moment thinking that the scope, the goal, the idea of all ethics is the destruction, and not the building up, of the individual.

Utilitarian standards cannot explain the ethical relations of men, for, in the first place, we cannot derive any ethical laws from considerations of utility. Without the supernatural sanction as it is called, or the perception of the superconscious as I prefer to term it, there can be no ethics. Without the struggle towards the Infinite there can be no ideal. Any system that wants to bind men down to the limits of their own societies is not able to find an explanation for the ethical laws of mankind. The Utilitarian wants us to give up the struggle after the Infinite, the reaching-out for the Supersensuous, as impracticable and absurd, and, in the same breath, asks us to take up ethics and do good to society. Why should we do good? Doing good is a secondary consideration. We must have an ideal. Ethics itself is not the end, but the means to the end. If the end is not there, why should we be ethical? Why should I do good to other men, and not injure them? If happiness is the goal of mankind, why should I not make myself happy and others unhappy? What prevents me? In the second place, the basis of utility is too narrow. All the current social forms and methods are derived from society as it exists, but what right has the Utilitarian to assume that society is eternal? Society did not exist ages ago, possibly will not exist ages hence. Most probably it is one of the passing stages through which we are going towards a higher evolution, and any law that is derived from society alone cannot be eternal, cannot cover the whole ground of man's nature. At best, therefore, Utilitarian theories can only work under present social conditions. Beyond that they have no value. But a morality an ethical code, derived from religion and spirituality, has the whole of infinite man for its scope. It takes up the individual, but its relations are to the Infinite, and it takes up society also — because society is nothing but numbers of these individuals grouped together; and as it applies to the individual and his eternal relations, it must necessarily apply to the whole of society, in whatever condition it may be at any given time. Thus we see that there is always the necessity of spiritual religion for mankind. Man cannot always think of matter, however pleasurable it may be.

It has been said that too much attention to things spiritual disturbs our practical relations in this world. As far back as in the days of the Chinese sage Confucius, it was said, "Let us take care of this world: and then, when we have finished with this world, we will take care of other world." It is very well that we should take care of this world. But if too much attention to the spiritual may affect a little our practical relations, too much attention to the so-called practical hurts us here and hereafter. It makes us materialistic. For man is not to regard nature as his goal, but something higher.

Man is man so long as he is struggling to rise above nature, and this nature is both internal and external. Not only does it comprise the laws that govern the particles of matter outside us and in our bodies, but also the more subtle nature within, which is, in fact, the motive power governing the external. It is good and very grand to conquer external nature, but grander still to conquer our internal nature. It is grand and good to know the laws that govern the stars and planets; it is infinitely grander and better to know the laws that govern the passions, the feelings, the will, of mankind. This conquering of the inner man, understanding the secrets of the subtle workings that are within the human mind, and knowing its wonderful secrets, belong entirely to religion. Human nature — the ordinary human nature, I mean — wants to see big material facts. The ordinary man cannot understand anything that is subtle. Well has it been said that the masses admire the lion that kills a thousand lambs, never for a moment thinking that it is death to the lambs. Although a momentary triumph for the lion; because they find pleasure only in manifestations of physical strength. Thus it is with the ordinary run of mankind. They understand and find pleasure in everything that is external. But in every society there is a section whose pleasures are not in the senses, but beyond, and who now and then catch glimpses of something higher than matter and struggle to reach it. And if we read the history of nations between the lines, we shall always find that the rise of a nation comes with an increase in the number of such men; and the fall begins when this pursuit after the Infinite, however vain Utilitarians may call it, has ceased. That is to say, the mainspring of the strength Of every race lies in its spirituality, and the death of that race begins the day that spirituality wanes and materialism gains ground.

Thus, apart from the solid facts and truths that we may learn from religion, apart from the comforts that we may gain from it, religion, as a science, as a study, is the greatest and healthiest exercise that the human mind can have. This pursuit of the Infinite, this struggle to grasp the Infinite, this effort to get beyond the limitations of the senses — out of matter, as it were — and to evolve the spiritual man — this striving day and night to make the Infinite one with our being — this struggle itself is the grandest and most glorious that man can make. Some persons find the greatest pleasure in eating. We have no right to say that they should not. Others find the greatest pleasure in possessing certain things. We have no right to say that they should not. But they also have no right to say "no" to the man who finds his highest pleasure in spiritual thought. The lower the organisation, the greater the pleasure in the senses. Very few men can eat a meal with the same gusto as a dog or a wolf. But all the pleasures of the dog or the wolf have gone, as it were into the senses. The lower types of humanity in all nations find pleasure in the senses, while the cultured and the educated find it in thought, in philosophy, in arts and sciences. Spirituality is a still higher plane. The subject being infinite, that plane is the highest, and the pleasure there is the highest for those who can appreciate it. So, even on the utilitarian ground that man is to seek for pleasure, he should cultivate religious thought, for it is the highest pleasure that exists. Thus religion, as a study, seems to me to be absolutely necessary.

We can see it in its effects. It is the greatest motive power that moves the human mind No other ideal can put into us the same mass of energy as the spiritual. So far as human history goes, it is obvious to all of us that this has been the case and that its powers are not dead. I do not deny that men, on simply utilitarian grounds, can be very good and moral. There have been many great men in this world perfectly sound, moral, and good, simply on utilitarian grounds. But the world-movers, men who bring, as It were, a mass of magnetism into the world whose spirit works in hundreds and in thousands, whose life ignites others with a spiritual fire — such men, we always find, have that spiritual background. Their motive power came from religion. Religion is the greatest motive power for realising that infinite energy which is the birthright and nature of every man. In building up character in making for everything that is good and great, in bringing peace to others and peace to one's own self, religion is the highest motive power and, therefore, ought to be studied from that standpoint. Religion must be studied on a broader basis than formerly. All narrow limited, fighting ideas of religion have to go. All sect ideas and tribal or national ideas of religion must be given up. That each tribe or nation should have its own particular God and think that every other is wrong is a superstition that should belong to the past. All such ideas must be abandoned.

As the human mind broadens, its spiritual steps broaden too. The time has already come when a man cannot record a thought without its reaching to all corners of the earth; by merely physical means, we have come into touch with the whole world; so the future religions of the world have to become as universal, as wide.

The religious ideals of the future must embrace all that exists in the world and is good and great, and, at the same time, have infinite scope for future development. All that was good in the past must be preserved; and the doors must be kept open for future additions to the already existing store. Religions must also be inclusive and not look down with contempt upon one another because their particular ideals of God are different. In my life I have seen a great many spiritual men, a great many sensible persons, who did not believe in God at all that is to say, not in our sense of the word. Perhaps they understood God better than we can ever do. The Personal idea of God or the Impersonal, the Infinite, Moral Law, or the Ideal Man — these all have to come under the definition of religion. And when religions have become thus broadened, their power for good will have increased a hundredfold. Religions, having tremendous power in them, have often done more injury to the world than good, simply on account of their narrowness and limitations.

Even at the present time we find many sects and societies, with almost the same ideas, fighting each other, because one does not want to set forth those ideas in precisely the same way as another. Therefore, religions will have to broaden. Religious ideas will have to become universal, vast, and infinite; and then alone we shall have the fullest play of religion, for the power of religion has only just begun to manifest in the world. It is sometimes said that religions are dying out, that spiritual ideas are dying out of the world. To me it seems that they have just begun to grow. The power of religion, broadened and purified, is going to penetrate every part of human life. So long as religion was in the hands of a chosen few or of a body of priests, it was in temples, churches, books, dogmas, ceremonials, forms, and rituals. But when we come to the real, spiritual, universal concept, then, and then alone religion will become real and living; it will come into our very nature, live in our every movement, penetrate every pore of our society, and be infinitely more a power for good than it has ever been before.

What is needed is a fellow-feeling between the different types of religion, seeing that they all stand or fall together, a fellow-feeling which springs from mutual esteem and mutual respect, and not the condescending, patronising, niggardly expression of goodwill, unfortunately in vogue at the present time with many. And above all, this is needed between types of religious expression coming from the study of mental phenomena — unfortunately, even now laying exclusive claim to the name of religion — and those expressions of religion whose heads, as it were, are penetrating more into the secrets of heaven though their feet are clinging to earth, I mean the so-called materialistic sciences.

To bring about this harmony, both will have to make concessions, sometimes very large, nay more, sometimes painful, but each will find itself the better for the sacrifice and more advanced in truth. And in the end, the knowledge which is confined within the domain of time and space will meet and become one with that which is beyond them both, where the mind and senses cannot reach — the Absolute, the Infinite, the One without a second.

CHAPTER II
THE REAL NATURE OF MAN

Delivered in London

Great is the tenacity with which man clings to the senses. Yet, however substantial he may think the external world in which he lives and moves, there comes a time in the lives of individuals and of races when, involuntarily, they ask, "Is this real?" To the person who never finds a moment to question the credentials of his senses, whose every moment is occupied with some sort of sense-enjoyment — even to him death comes, and he also is compelled to ask, "Is this real?" Religion begins with this question and ends with its answer. Even in the remote past, where recorded history cannot help us, in the mysterious light of mythology, back in the dim twilight of civilisation, we find the same question was asked, "What becomes of this? What is real?"

One of the most poetical of the Upanishads, the Katha Upanishad, begins with the inquiry: "When a man dies, there is a dispute. One party declares that he has gone for ever, the other insists that he is still living. Which is true?" Various answers have been given. The whole sphere of metaphysics, philosophy, and religion is really filled with various answers to this question. At the same time, attempts have been made to suppress it, to put a stop to the unrest of mind which asks, "What is beyond? What is real?" But so long as death remains, all these attempts at suppression will always prove to be unsuccessful. We may talk about seeing nothing beyond and keeping all our hopes and aspirations confined to the present moment, and struggle hard not to think of anything beyond the world of senses; and, perhaps, everything outside helps to keep us limited within its narrow bounds. The whole world may combine to prevent us from broadening out beyond the present. Yet, so long as there is death, the question must come again and again, "Is death the end of all these things to which we are clinging, as if they were the most real of all realities, the most substantial of all substances?" The world vanishes in a moment and is gone. Standing on the brink of a precipice beyond which is the infinite yawning chasm, every mind, however hardened, is bound to recoil and ask, "Is this real?" The hopes of a lifetime, built up little by little with all the energies of a great mind, vanish in a second. Are they real? This question must be answered. Time never lessens its power; on the other hand, it adds strength to it.

Then there is the desire to be happy. We run after everything to make ourselves happy; we pursue our mad career in the external world of senses. If you ask the young man with whom life is successful, he will declare that it is real; and he really thinks so. Perhaps, when the same man grows old and finds fortune ever eluding him, he will then declare that it is fate. He finds at last that his desires cannot be fulfilled. Wherever he goes, there is an adamantine wall beyond which he cannot pass. Every sense-activity results in a reaction. Everything is evanescent. Enjoyment, misery, luxury, wealth, power, and poverty, even life itself, are all evanescent.

Two positions remain to mankind. One is to believe with the nihilists that all is nothing, that we know nothing, that we can never know anything either about the future, the past, or even the present. For we must remember that he who denies the past and the future and wants to stick to the present is simply a madman. One may as well deny the father and mother and assert the child. It would be equally logical. To deny the past and future, the present must inevitably be denied also. This is one position, that of the nihilists. I have never seen a man who could really become a nihilist for one minute. It is very easy to talk.

Then there is the other position — to seek for an explanation, to seek for the real, to discover in the midst of this eternally changing and evanescent world whatever is real. In this body which is an aggregate of molecules of matter, is there anything which is real? This has been the search throughout the history of the, human mind. In the very oldest times, we often find glimpses of light coming into men's minds. We find man, even then, going a step beyond this body, finding something which is not this external body, although very much like it, much more complete, much more perfect, and which remains even when this body is dissolved. We read in the hymns of the Rig-Veda, addressed to the God of Fire who is burning a dead body, "Carry him, O Fire, in your arms gently, give him a perfect body, a bright body, carry him where the fathers live, where there is no more sorrow, where there is no more death." The same idea you will find present in every religion. And we get another idea with it. It is a significant fact that all religions, without one exception, hold that man is a degeneration of what he was, whether they clothe this in mythological words, or in the clear language of philosophy, or in the beautiful expressions of poetry. This is the one fact that comes out of every scripture and of every mythology that the man that is, is a degeneration of what he was. This is the kernel of truth within the story of Adam's fall in the Jewish scripture. This is again and again repeated in the scriptures of the Hindus; the dream of a period which they call the Age of Truth, when no man died unless he wished to die, when he could keep his body as long as he liked, and his mind was pure and strong. There was no evil and no misery; and the present age is a corruption of that state of perfection. Side by side with this, we find the story of the deluge everywhere. That story itself is a proof that this present age is held to be a corruption of a former age by every religion. It went on becoming more and more corrupt until the deluge swept away a large portion of mankind, and again the ascending series began. It is going up slowly again to reach once more that early state of purity. You are all aware of the story of the deluge in the Old Testament. The same story was current among the ancient Babylonians, the Egyptians, the Chinese, and the Hindus. Manu, a great ancient sage, was praying on the bank of the Gangâ, when a little minnow came to him for protection, and he put it into a pot of water he had before him. "What do you want?" asked Manu. The little minnow declared he was pursued by a bigger fish and wanted protection. Manu carried the little fish to his home, and in the morning he had become as big as the pot and said, "I cannot live in this pot any longer". Manu put him in a tank, and the next day he was as big as the tank and declared he could not live there any more. So Manu had to take him to a river, and in the morning the fish filled the river. Then Manu put him in the ocean, and he declared, "Manu, I am the Creator of the universe. I have taken this form to come and warn you that I will deluge the world. You build an ark and in it put a pair of every kind of animal, and let your family enter the ark, and there will project out of the water my horn. Fasten the ark to it; and when the deluge subsides, come out and people the earth." So the world was deluged, and Manu saved his own family and two of every kind of animal and seeds of every plant. When the deluge subsided, he came and peopled the world; and we are all called "man", because we are the progeny of Manu.

Now, human language is the attempt to express the truth that is within. I am fully persuaded that a baby whose language consists of unintelligible sounds is attempting to express the highest philosophy, only the baby has not the organs to express it nor the means. The difference between the language of the highest philosophers and the utterances of babies is one of degree and not of kind. What you call the most correct, systematic, mathematical language of the present time, and the hazy, mystical, mythological languages of the ancients, differ only in degree. All of them have a grand idea behind, which is, as it were, struggling to express itself; and often behind these ancient mythologies are nuggets of truth; and often, I am sorry to say, behind the fine, polished phrases of the moderns is arrant trash. So, we need not throw a thing overboard because it is clothed in mythology, because it does not fit in with the notions of Mr. So-and-so or Mrs. So-and-so of modern times. If people should laugh at religion because most religions declare that men must believe in mythologies taught by such and such a prophet, they ought to laugh more at these moderns. In modern times, if a man quotes a Moses or a Buddha or a Christ, he is laughed at; but let him give the name of a Huxley, a Tyndall, or a Darwin, and it is swallowed without salt. "Huxley has said it", that is enough for many. We are free from superstitions indeed! That was a religious superstition, and this a scientific superstition; only, in and through that superstition came life-giving ideas of spirituality; in and through this modern superstition come lust and greed. That superstition was worship of God, and this superstition is worship of filthy lucre, of fame or power. That is the difference.

To return to mythology. Behind all these stories we find one idea standing supreme — that man is a degeneration of what he was. Coming to the present times, modern research seems to repudiate this position absolutely. Evolutionists seem to contradict entirely this assertion. According to them, man is the evolution of the mollusc; and, therefore, what mythology states cannot be true. There is in India, however, a mythology which is able to reconcile both these positions. The Indian mythology has a theory of cycles, that all progression is in the form of waves. Every wave is attended by a fall, and that by a rise the next moment, that by a fall in the next, and again another rise The motion is in cycles. Certainly it is true, even on the grounds of modern research, that man cannot be simply an evolution. Every evolution presupposes an involution. The modern scientific man will tell you that you can only get the amount of energy out of a machine which you have previously put into it. Something cannot be produced out of nothing. If a man is an evolution of the mollusc, then the perfect man — the Buddha-man, the Christ-man — was involved in the mollusc. If it is not so, whence come these gigantic personalities? Something cannot come out of nothing. Thus we are in the position of reconciling the scriptures with modern light. That energy which manifests itself slowly through various stages until it becomes the perfect man, cannot come out of nothing. It existed somewhere; and if the mollusc or the protoplasm is the first point to which you can trace it, that protoplasm, somehow or other, must have contained the energy.

There is a great discussion going on as to whether the aggregate of materials we call the body is the cause of manifestation of the force we call the soul, thought, etc., or whether it is the thought that manifests this body. The religions of the world of course hold that the force called thought manifests the body, and not the reverse. There are schools of modern thought which hold that what we call thought is simply the outcome of the adjustment of the parts of the machine which we call body. Taking the second position that the soul or the mass of thought, or however you may call it, is the outcome of this machine, the outcome of the chemical and physical combinations of matter making up the body and brain, leaves the question unanswered. What makes the body? What force combines the molecules into the body form? What force is there which takes up material from the mass of matter around and forms my body one way, another body another way, and so on? What makes these infinite distinctions? To say that the force called soul is the outcome of the combinations of the molecules of the body is putting the cart before the horse. How did the combinations come; where was the force to make them? If you say that some other force was the cause of these combinations, and soul was the outcome of that matter, and that soul — which combined a certain mass of matter — was itself the result of the combinations, it is no answer. That theory ought to be taken which explains most of the facts, if not all, and that without contradicting other existing theories. It is more logical to say that the force which takes up the matter and forms the body is the same which manifests through that body. To say, therefore, that the thought forces manifested by the body are the outcome of the arrangement of molecules and have no independent existence has no meaning; neither can force evolve out of matter. Rather it is possible to demonstrate that what we call matter does not exist at all. It is only a certain state of force. Solidity, hardness, or any other state of matter can be proved to be the result of motion. Increase of vortex motion imparted to fluids gives them the force of solids. A mass of air in vortex motion, as in a tornado, becomes solid-like and by its impact breaks or cuts through solids. A thread of a spider's web, if it could be moved at almost infinite velocity, would be as strong as an iron chain and would cut through an oak tree. Looking at it in this way, it would be easier to prove that what we call matter does not exist. But the other way cannot be proved.

What is the force which manifests itself through the body? It is obvious to all of us, whatever that force be, that it is taking particles up, as it were, and manipulating forms out of them — the human body. None else comes here to manipulate bodies for you and me. I never saw anybody eat food for me. I have to assimilate it, manufacture blood and bones and everything out of that food. What is this mysterious force? Ideas about the future and about the past seem to be terrifying to many. To many they seem to be mere speculation.

We will take the present theme. What is this force which is now working through us? We know how in old times, in all the ancient scriptures, this power, this manifestation of power, was thought to be a bright substance having the form of this body, and which remained even after this body fell. Later on, however, we find a higher idea coming — that this bright body did not represent the force. Whatsoever has form must be the result of combinations of particles and requires something else behind it to move it. If this body requires something which is not the body to manipulate it, the bright body, by the same necessity, will also require something other than itself to manipulate it. So, that something was called the soul, the Atman in Sanskrit. It was the Atman which through the bright body, as it were, worked on the gross body outside. The bright body is considered as the receptacle of the mind, and the Atman is beyond that It is not the mind even; it works the mind, and through the mind the body. You have an Atman, I have another each one of us has a separate Atman and a separate fine body, and through that we work on the gross external body. Questions were then asked about this Atman about its nature. What is this Atman, this soul of man which is neither the body nor the mind? Great discussions followed. Speculations were made, various shades of philosophic inquiry came into existence; and I shall try to place before you some of the conclusions that have been reached about this Atman.

The different philosophies seem to agree that this Atman, whatever it be, has neither form nor shape, and that which has neither form nor shape must be omnipresent. Time begins with mind, space also is in the mind. Causation cannot stand without time. Without the idea of succession there cannot be any idea of causation. Time, space and causation, therefore, are in the mind, and as this Atman is beyond the mind and formless, it must be beyond time, beyond space, and beyond causation. Now, if it is beyond time, space, and causation, it must be infinite. Then comes the highest speculation in our philosophy. The infinite cannot be two. If the soul be infinite, there can be only one Soul, and all ideas of various souls — you having one soul, and I having another, and so forth — are not real. The Real Man, therefore, is one and infinite, the omnipresent Spirit. And the apparent man is only a limitation of that Real Man. In that sense the mythologies are true that the apparent man, however great he may be, is only a dim reflection of the Real Man who is beyond. The Real Man, the Spirit, being beyond cause and effect, not bound by time and space, must, therefore, be free. He was never bound, and could not be bound. The apparent man, the reflection, is limited by time, space, and causation, and is, therefore, bound. Or in the language of some of our philosophers, he appears to be bound, but really is not. This is the reality in our souls, this omnipresence, this spiritual nature, this infinity. Every soul is infinite, therefore there is no question of birth and death. Some children were being examined. The examiner put them rather hard questions, and among them was this one: "Why does not the earth fall?" He wanted to evoke answers about gravitation. Most of the children could not answer at all; a few answered that it was gravitation or something. One bright little girl answered it by putting another question: "Where should it fall?" The question is nonsense. Where should the earth fall? There is no falling or rising for the earth. In infinite space there is no up or down; that is only in the relative. Where is the going or coming for the infinite? Whence should it come and whither should it go?

Thus, when people cease to think of the past or future, when they give up the idea of body, because the body comes and goes and is limited, then they have risen to a higher ideal. The body is not the Real Man, neither is the mind, for the mind waxes and wanes. It is the Spirit beyond, which alone can live for ever. The body and mind are continually changing, and are, in fact, only names of series of changeful phenomena, like rivers whose waters are in a constant state of flux, yet presenting the appearance of unbroken streams. Every particle in this body is continually changing; no one has the same body for many minutes together, and yet we think of it as the same body. So with the mind; one moment it is happy, another moment unhappy; one moment strong, another weak; an ever-changing whirlpool. That cannot be the Spirit which is infinite. Change can only be in the limited. To say that the infinite changes in any way is absurd; it cannot be. You can move and I can move, as limited bodies; every particle in this universe is in a constant state of flux, but taking the universe as a unit, as one whole, it cannot move, it cannot change. Motion is always a relative thing. I move in relation to something else. Any particle in this universe can change in relation to any other particle; but take the whole universe as one, and in relation to what can it move? There is nothing besides it. So this infinite Unit is unchangeable, immovable, absolute, and this is the Real Man. Our reality, therefore, consists in the Universal and not in the limited. These are old delusions, however comfortable they are, to think that we are little limited beings, constantly changing. People are frightened when they are told that they are Universal Being, everywhere present. Through everything you work, through every foot you move, through every lip you talk, through every heart you feel.

People are frightened when they are told this. They will again and again ask you if they are not going to keep their individuality. What is individuality? I should like to see it. A baby has no moustache; when he grows to be a man, perhaps he has a moustache and beard. His individuality would be lost, if it were in the body. If I lose one eye, or if I lose one of my hands, my individuality would be lost if it were in the body. Then, a drunkard should not give up drinking because he would lose his individuality. A thief should not be a good man because he would thereby lose his individuality. No man ought to change his habits for fear of this. There is no individuality except in the Infinite. That is the only condition which does not change. Everything else is in a constant state of flux. Neither can individuality be in memory. Suppose, on account of a blow on the head I forget all about my past; then, I have lost all individuality; I am gone. I do not remember two or three years of my childhood, and if memory and existence are one, then whatever I forget is gone. That part of my life which I do not remember, I did not live. That is a very narrow idea of individuality.

We are not individuals yet. We are struggling towards individuality, and that is the Infinite, that is the real nature of man. He alone lives whose life is in the whole universe, and the more we concentrate our lives on limited things, the faster we go towards death. Those moments alone we live when our lives are in the universe, in others; and living this little life is death, simply death, and that is why the fear of death comes. The fear of death can only be conquered when man realises that so long as there is one life in this universe, he is living. When he can say, "I am in everything, in everybody, I am in all lives, I am the universe," then alone comes the state of fearlessness. To talk of immortality in constantly changing things is absurd. Says an old Sanskrit philosopher: It is only the Spirit that is the individual, because it is infinite. No infinity can be divided; infinity cannot be broken into pieces. It is the same one, undivided unit for ever, and this is the individual man, the Real Man. The apparent man is merely a struggle to express, to manifest this individuality which is beyond; and evolution is not in the Spirit. These changes which are going on — the wicked becoming good, the animal becoming man, take them in whatever way you like — are not in the Spirit. They are evolution of nature and manifestation of Spirit. Suppose there is a screen hiding you from me, in which there is a small hole through which I can see some of the faces before me, just a few faces. Now suppose the hole begins to grow larger and larger, and as it does so, more and more of the scene before me reveals itself and when at last the whole screen has disappeared, I stand face to face with you all. You did not change at all in this case; it was the hole that was evolving, and you were gradually manifesting yourselves. So it is with the Spirit. No perfection is going to be attained. You are already free and perfect. What are these ideas of religion and God and searching for the hereafter? Why does man look for a God? Why does man, in every nation, in every state of society, want a perfect ideal somewhere, either in man, in God, or elsewhere? Because that idea is within you. It was your own heart beating and you did not know; you were mistaking it for something external. It is the God within your own self that is propelling you to seek for Him, to realise Him. After long searches here and there, in temples and in churches, in earths and in heavens, at last you come back, completing the circle from where you started, to your own soul and find that He for whom you have been seeking all over the world, for whom you have been weeping and praying in churches and temples, on whom you were looking as the mystery of all mysteries shrouded in the clouds, is nearest of the near, is your own Self, the reality of your life, body, and soul. That is your own nature. Assert it, manifest it. Not to become pure, you are pure already. You are not to be perfect, you are that already. Nature is like that screen which is hiding the reality beyond. Every good thought that you think or act upon is simply tearing the veil, as it were; and the purity, the Infinity, the God behind, manifests Itself more and more.

This is the whole history of man. Finer and finer becomes the veil, more and more of the light behind shines forth, for it is its nature to shine. It cannot be known; in vain we try to know it. Were it knowable, it would not be what it is, for it is the eternal subject. Knowledge is a limitation, knowledge is objectifying. He is the eternal subject of everything, the eternal witness in this universe, your own Self. Knowledge is, as it were, a lower step, a degeneration. We are that eternal subject already; how can we know it? It is the real nature of every man, and he is struggling to express it in various ways; otherwise, why are there so many ethical codes? Where is the explanation of all ethics? One idea stands out as the centre of all ethical systems, expressed in various forms, namely, doing good to others. The guiding motive of mankind should be charity towards men, charity towards all animals. But these are all various expressions of that eternal truth that, "I am the universe; this universe is one." Or else, where is the reason? Why should I do good to my fellowmen? Why should I do good to others? What compels me? It is sympathy, the feeling of sameness everywhere. The hardest hearts feel sympathy for other beings sometimes. Even the man who gets frightened if he is told that this assumed individuality is really a delusion, that it is ignoble to try to cling to this apparent individuality, that very man will tell you that extreme self-abnegation is the centre of all morality. And what is perfect self-abnegation? It means the abnegation of this apparent self, the abnegation of all selfishness. This idea of "me and mine" — Ahamkâra and Mamatâ — is the result of past Superstition, and the more this present self passes away, the more the real Self becomes manifest. This is true self-abnegation, the centre, the basis, the gist of all moral teaching; and whether man knows it or not the whole world is slowly going towards it, practicing it more or less. Only, the vast majority of mankind are doing it unconsciously. Let them do it consciously. Let then make the sacrifice, knowing that this "me and mine" is not the real Self, but only a limitation. But one glimpse Of that infinite reality which is behind — but one spark of that infinite fire that is the All — represents the present man; the Infinite is his true nature.

What is the utility, the effect, the result, of this knowledge? In these days, we have to measure everything by utility — by how many pounds shillings, and pence it represents. What right has a person to ask that truth should be judged by the standard of utility or money? Suppose there is no utility, will it be less true? Utility is not the test of truth. Nevertheless, there is the highest utility in this. Happiness, we see is what everyone is seeking for, but the majority seek it in things which are evanescent and not real. No happiness was ever found in the senses. There never was a person who found happiness in the senses or in enjoyment of the senses. Happiness is only found in the Spirit. Therefore the highest utility for mankind is to find this happiness in the Spirit. The next point is that ignorance is the great mother of all misery, and the fundamental ignorance is to think that the Infinite weeps and cries, that He is finite. This is the basis of all ignorance that we, the immortal, the ever pure, the perfect Spirit, think that we are little minds, that we are little bodies; it is the mother of all selfishness. As soon as I think that I am a little body, I want to preserve it, to protect it, to keep it nice, at the expense of other bodies; then you and I become separate. As soon as this idea of separation comes, it opens the door to all mischief and leads to all misery. This is the utility that if a very small fractional part of human beings living today can put aside the idea of selfishness, narrowness, and littleness, this earth will become a paradise tomorrow; but with machines and improvements of material knowledge only, it will never be. These only increase misery, as oil poured on fire increases the flame all the more. Without the knowledge of the Spirit, all material knowledge is only adding fuel to fire, only giving into the hands of selfish man one more instrument to take what belongs to others, to live upon the life of others, instead of giving up his life for them.

Is it practical ? — is another question. Can it be practised in modern society? Truth does not pay homage to any society, ancient or modern. Society has to pay homage to Truth or die. Societies should be moulded upon truth, and truth has not to adjust itself to society. If such a noble truth as unselfishness cannot be practiced in society, it is better for man to give up society and go into the forest. That is the daring man. There are two sorts of courage. One is the courage of facing the cannon. And the other is the courage of spiritual conviction. An Emperor who invaded India was told by his teacher to go and see some of the sages there. After a long search for one, he found a very old man sitting on a block of stone. The Emperor talked with him a little and became very much impressed by his wisdom. He asked the sage to go to his country with him. "No," said the sage, "I am quite satisfied with my forest here." Said the Emperor, "I will give you money, position, wealth. I am the Emperor of the world." "No," replied the man, "I don't care for those things." The Emperor replied, "If you do not go, I will kill you." The man smiled serenely and said, "That is the most foolish thing you ever said, Emperor. You cannot kill me. Me the sun cannot dry, fire cannot burn, sword cannot kill, for I am the birthless, the deathless, the ever-living omnipotent, omnipresent Spirit." This is spiritual boldness, while the other is the courage of a lion or a tiger. In the Mutiny of 1857 there was a Swami, a very great soul, whom a Mohammedan mutineer stabbed severely. The Hindu mutineers caught and brought the man to the Swami, offering to kill him. But the Swami looked up calmly and said, "My brother, thou art He, thou art He!" and expired. This is another instance. What good is it to talk of the strength of your muscles, of the superiority of your Western institutions, if you cannot make Truth square with your society, if you cannot build up a society into which the highest Truth will fit? What is the good of this boastful talk about your grandeur and greatness, if you stand up and say, "This courage is not practical." Is nothing practical but pounds, shillings, and pence? If so, why boast of your society? That society is the greatest, where the highest truths become practical. That is my opinion; and if society is; not fit for the highest truths, make it so; and the sooner, the better. Stand up, men and women, in this spirit, dare to believe in the Truth, dare to practice the Truth! The world requires a few hundred bold men and women. Practise that boldness which dares know the Truth, which dares show the Truth in life, which does not quake before death, nay, welcomes death, makes a man know that he, is the Spirit, that, in the whole universe, nothing can kill him. Then you will be free. Then you will know yours real Soul. "This Atman is first to be heard, then thoughts about and then meditated upon."

There is a great tendency in modern times to talk too much of work and decry thought. Doing is very good, but that comes from thinking. Little manifestations of energy through the muscles are called work. But where there is no thought, there will be no work. Fill the brain, therefore, with high thoughts, highest ideals, place them day and night before you, and out of that will come great work. Talk not about impurity, but say that we are pure. We have hypnotised ourselves into this thought that we are little, that we are born, and that we are going to die, and into a constant state of fear.

There is a story about a lioness, who was big with young, going about in search of prey; and seeing a flock of sheep, she jumped upon them. She died in the effort; and a little baby lion was born, motherless. It was taken care of by the sheep and the sheep brought it up, and it grew up with them, ate grass, and bleated like the sheep. And although in time it became a big, full-grown lion. It thought it was a sheep. One day another lion came in search of prey and was astonished to find that in the midst of this flock of sheep was a lion, fleeing like the sheep at the approach of danger. He tried to get near the sheep-lion, to tell it that it was not a sheep but a lion; but the poor animal fled at his approach. However, he watched his opportunity and one day found the sheep-lion sleeping. He approached it and said, "You are a lion." "I am a sheep," cried the other lion and could not believe the contrary but bleated. The lion dragged him towards a lake and said, "Look here, here is my reflection and yours." Then came the comparison. It looked at the lion and then at its own reflection, and in a moment came the idea that it was a lion. The lion roared, the bleating was gone. You are lions, you are souls, pure, infinite, and perfect. The might of the universe is within you. "Why weepest thou, my friend? There is neither birth nor death for thee. Why weepest thou? There is no disease nor misery for thee, but thou art like the infinite sky; clouds of various colours come over it, play for a moment, then vanish. But the sky is ever the same eternal blue." Why do we see wickedness? There was a stump of a tree, and in the dark, a thief came that way and said, "That is a policeman." A young man waiting for his beloved saw it and thought that it was his sweetheart. A child who had been told ghost stories took it for a ghost and began to shriek. But all the time it was the stump of a tree. We see the world as we are. Suppose there is a baby in a room with a bag of gold on the table and a thief comes and steals the gold. Would the baby know it was stolen? That which we have inside, we see outside. The baby has no thief inside and sees no thief outside. So with all knowledge. Do not talk of the wickedness of the world and all its sins. Weep that you are bound to see wickedness yet. Weep that you are bound to see sin everywhere, and if you want to help the world, do not condemn it. Do not weaken it more. For what is sin and what is misery, and what are all these, but the results of weakness? The world is made weaker and weaker every day by such teachings. Men are taught from childhood that they are weak and sinners. Teach them that they are all glorious children of immortality, even those who are the weakest in manifestation. Let positive, strong, helpful thought enter into their brains from very childhood. Lay yourselves open to these thoughts, and not to weakening and paralysing ones. Say to your own minds, "I am He, I am He." Let it ring day and night in your minds like a song, and at the point of death declare "I am He." That is the Truth; the infinite strength of the world is yours. Drive out the superstition that has covered your minds. Let us be brave. Know the Truth and practice the Truth. The goal may be distant, but awake, arise, and stop not till the goal is reached.

CHAPTER III
MAYA AND ILLUSION

Delivered in London

Almost all of you have heard of the word Mâyâ. Generally it is used, though incorrectly, to denote illusion, or delusion, or some such thing. But the theory of Maya forms one of the pillars upon which the Vedanta rests; it is, therefore, necessary that it should be properly understood. I ask a little patience of you, for there is a great danger of its being misunderstood. The oldest idea of Maya that we find in Vedic literature is the sense of delusion; but then the real theory had not been reached. We find such passages as, "Indra through his Maya assumed various forms." Here it is true the word Maya means something like magic, and we find various other passages, always taking the same meaning. The word Maya then dropped out of sight altogether. But in the meantime the idea was developing. Later, the question was raised: "Why can't we know this secret of the universe?" And the answer given was very significant: "Because we talk in vain, and because we are satisfied with the things of the senses, and because we are running after desires; therefore, we, as it were, cover the Reality with a mist." Here the word Maya is not used at all, but we get the idea that the cause of our ignorance is a kind of mist that has come between us and the Truth. Much later on, in one of the latest Upanishads, we find the word Maya reappearing, but this time, a transformation has taken place in it, and a mass of new meaning has attached itself to the word. Theories had been propounded and repeated, others had been taken up, until at last the idea of Maya became fixed. We read in the Shvetâshvatara Upanishad, "Know nature to be Maya and the Ruler of this Maya is the Lord Himself." Coming to our philosophers, we find that this word Maya has been manipulated in various fashions, until we come to the great Shankarâchârya. The theory of Maya was manipulated a little by the Buddhists too, but in the hands of the Buddhists it became very much like what is called Idealism, and that is the meaning that is now generally given to the word Maya. When the Hindu says the world is Maya, at once people get the idea that the world is an illusion. This interpretation has some basis, as coming through the Buddhistic philosophers, because there was one section of philosophers who did not believe in the external world at all. But the Maya of the Vedanta, in its last developed form, is neither Idealism nor Realism, nor is it a theory. It is a simple statement of facts — what we are and what we see around us.

As I have told you before, the minds of the people from whom the Vedas came were intent upon following principles, discovering principles. They had no time to work upon details or to wait for them; they wanted to go deep into the heart of things. Something beyond was calling them, as it were, and they could not wait. Scattered through the Upanishads, we find that the details of subjects which we now call modern sciences are often very erroneous, but, at the same time, their principles are correct. For instance, the idea of ether, which is one of the latest theories of modern science, is to be found in our ancient literature in forms much more developed than is the modern scientific theory of ether today, but it was in principle. When they tried to demonstrate the workings of that principle, they made many mistakes. The theory of the all-pervading life principle, of which all life in this universe is but a differing manifestation, was understood in Vedic times; it is found in the Brâhmanas. There is a long hymn in the Samhitâs in praise of Prâna of which all life is but a manifestation. By the by, it may interest some of you to know that there are theories in the Vedic philosophy about the origin of life on this earth very similar to those which have been advanced by some modern European scientists. You, of course, all know that there is a theory that life came from other planets. It is a settled doctrine with some Vedic philosophers that life comes in this way from the moon.

Coming to the principles, we find these Vedic thinkers very courageous and wonderfully bold in propounding large and generalised theories. Their solution of the mystery of the universe, from the external world, was as satisfactory as it could be. The detailed workings of modern science do not bring the question one step nearer to solution, because the principles have failed. If the theory of ether failed in ancient times to give a solution of the mystery of the universe, working out the details of that ether theory would not bring us much nearer to the truth. If the theory of all-pervading life failed as a theory of this universe, it would not mean anything more if worked out in detail, for the details do not change the principle of the universe. What I mean is that in their inquiry into the principle, the Hindu thinkers were as bold, and in some cases, much bolder than the moderns. They made some of the grandest generalizations that have yet been reached, and some still remain as theories, which modern science has yet to get even as theories. For instance, they not only arrived at the ether theory, but went beyond and classified mind also as a still more rarefied ether. Beyond that again, they found a still more rarefied ether. Yet that was no solution, it did not solve the problem. No amount of knowledge of the external world could solve the problem. "But", says the scientist, "we are just beginning to know a little: wait a few thousand years and we shall get the solution." "No," says the Vedantist, for he has proved beyond all doubt that the mind is limited, that it cannot go beyond certain limits — beyond time, space, and causation. As no man can jump out of his own self, so no man can go beyond the limits that have been put upon him by the laws of time and space. Every attempt to solve the laws of causation, time, and space would be futile, because the very attempt would have to be made by taking for granted the existence of these three. What does the statement of the existence of the world mean, then? "This world has no existence." What is meant by that? It means that it has no absolute existence. It exists only in relation to my mind, to your mind, and to the mind of everyone else. We see this world with the five senses but if we had another sense, we would see in it something more. If we had yet another sense, it would appear as something still different. It has, therefore, no real existence; it has no unchangeable, immovable, infinite existence. Nor can it be called non-existence, seeing that it exists, and we slave to work in and through it. It is a mixture of existence and non-existence.

Coming from abstractions to the common, everyday details of our lives, we find that our whole life is a contradiction, a mixture of existence and non-existence. There is this contradiction in knowledge. It seems that man can know everything, if he only wants to know; but before he has gone a few steps, he finds an adamantine wall which he cannot pass. All his work is in a circle, and he cannot go beyond that circle. The problems which are nearest and dearest to him are impelling him on and calling, day and night, for a solution, but he cannot solve them, because he cannot go beyond his intellect. And yet that desire is implanted strongly in him. Still we know that the only good is to be obtained by controlling and checking it. With every breath, every impulse of our heart asks us to be selfish. At the same time, there is some power beyond us which says that it is unselfishness alone which is good. Every child is a born optimist; he dreams golden dreams. In youth he becomes still more optimistic. It is hard for a young man to believe that there is such a thing as death, such a thing as defeat or degradation. Old age comes, and life is a mass of ruins. Dreams have vanished into the air, and the man becomes a pessimist. Thus we go from one extreme to another, buffeted by nature, without knowing where we are going. It reminds me of a celebrated song in the Lalita Vistara, the biography of Buddha. Buddha was born, says the book, as the saviour of mankind, but he forgot himself in the luxuries of his palace. Some angels came and sang a song to rouse him. And the burden of the whole song is that we are floating down the river of life which is continually changing with no stop and no rest. So are our lives, going on and on without knowing any rest. What are we to do? The man who has enough to eat and drink is an optimist, and he avoids all mention of misery, for it frightens him. Tell not to him of the sorrows and the sufferings of the world; go to him and tell that it is all good. "Yes, I am safe," says he. "Look at me! I have a nice house to live in. I do not fear cold and hunger; therefore do not bring these horrible pictures before me." But, on the other hand, there are others dying of cold and hunger. If you go and teach them that it is all good, they will not hear you. How can they wish others to be happy when they are miserable? Thus we are oscillating between optimism and pessimism.

Then, there is the tremendous fact of death. The whole world is going towards death; everything dies. All our progress, our vanities, our reforms, our luxuries, our wealth, our knowledge, have that one end — death. That is all that is certain. Cities come and go, empires rise and fall, planets break into pieces and crumble into dust, to be blown about by the atmospheres of other planets. Thus it has been going on from time without beginning. Death is the end of everything. Death is the end of life, of beauty, of wealth, of power, of virtue too. Saints die and sinners die, kings die and beggars die. They are all going to death, and yet this tremendous clinging on to life exists. Somehow, we do not know why, we cling to life; we cannot give it up. And this is Maya.

The mother is nursing a child with great care; all her soul, her life, is in that child. The child grows, becomes a man, and perchance becomes a blackguard and a brute, kicks her and beats her every day; and yet the mother clings to the child; and when her reason awakes, she covers it up with the idea of love. She little thinks that it is not love, that it is something which has got hold of her nerves, which she cannot shake off; however she may try, she cannot shake off the bondage she is in. And this is Maya.

We are all after the Golden Fleece. Every one of us thinks that this will be his. Every reasonable man sees that his chance is, perhaps, one in twenty millions, yet everyone struggles for it. And this is Maya.

Death is stalking day and night over this earth of ours, but at the same time we think we shall live eternally. A question was once asked of King Yudhishthira, "What is the most wonderful thing on this earth?" And the king replied, "Every day people are dying around us, and yet men think they will never die." And this is Maya.

These tremendous contradictions in our intellect, in our knowledge, yea, in all the facts of our life face us on all sides. A reformer arises and wants to remedy the evils that are existing in a certain nation; and before they have been remedied, a thousand other evils arise in another place. It is like an old house that is falling; you patch it up in one place and the ruin extends to another. In India, our reformers cry and preach against the evils of enforced widowhood. In the West, non-marriage is the great evil. Help the unmarried on one side; they are suffering. Help the widows on the other; they are suffering. It is like chronic rheumatism: you drive from the head, and it goes to the body; you drive it from there, and it goes to the feet. Reformers arise and preach that learning, wealth, and culture should not be in the hands of a select few; and they do their best to make them accessible to all. These may bring more happiness to some, but, perhaps, as culture comes, physical happiness lessens. The knowledge of happiness brings the knowledge of unhappiness. Which way then shall we go? The least amount of material prosperity that we enjoy is causing the same amount of misery elsewhere. This is the law. The young, perhaps, do not see it clearly, but those who have lived long enough and those who have struggled enough will understand it. And this is Maya. These things are going on, day and night, and to find a solution of this problem is impossible. Why should it be so? It is impossible to answer this, because the question cannot be logically formulated. There is neither how nor why in fact; we only know that it is and that we cannot help it. Even to grasp it, to draw an exact image of it in our own mind, is beyond our power. How can we solve it then?

Maya is a statement of the fact of this universe, of how it is going on. People generally get frightened when these things are told to them. But bold we must be. Hiding facts is not the way to find a remedy. As you all know, a hare hunted by dogs puts its head down and thinks itself safe; so, when we run into optimism; we do just like the hare, but that is no remedy. There are objections against this, but you may remark that they are generally from people who possess many of the good things of life. In this country (England) it is very difficult to become a pessimist. Everyone tells me how wonderfully the world is going on, how progressive; but what he himself is, is his own world. Old questions arise: Christianity must be the only true religion of the world because Christian nations are prosperous! But that assertion contradicts itself, because the prosperity of the Christian nation depends on the misfortune of non-Christian nations. There must be some to prey on. Suppose the whole world were to become Christian, then the Christian nations would become poor, because there would be no non-Christian nations for them to prey upon. Thus the argument kills itself. Animals are living upon plants, men upon animals and, worst of all, upon one another, the strong upon the weak. This is going on everywhere. And this is Maya. What solution do you find for this? We hear every day many explanations, and are told that in the long run all will be good. Taking it for granted that this is possible, why should there be this diabolical way of doing good? Why cannot good be done through good, instead of through these diabolical methods? The descendants of the human beings of today will be happy; but why must there be all this suffering now? There is no solution. This is Maya.

Again, we often hear that it is one of the features of evolution that it eliminates evil, and this evil being continually eliminated from the world, at last only good will remain. That is very nice to hear, and it panders to the vanity of those who have enough of this world's goods, who have not a hard struggle to face every clay and are not being crushed under the wheel of this so-called evolution. It is very good and comforting indeed to such fortunate ones. The common herd may surfer, but they do not care; let them die, they are of no consequence. Very good, yet this argument is fallacious from beginning to end. It takes for granted, in the first place, that manifested good and evil in this world are two absolute realities. In the second place, it make, at still worse assumption that the amount of good is an increasing quantity and the amount of evil is a decreasing quantity. So, if evil is being eliminated in this way by what they call evolution, there will come a time when all this evil will be eliminated and what remains will be all good. Very easy to say, but can it be proved that evil is a lessening quantity? Take, for instance, the man who lives in a forest, who does not know how to cultivate the mind, cannot read a book, has not heard of such a thing as writing. If he is severely wounded, he is soon all right again; while we die if we get a scratch. Machines are making things cheap, making for progress and evolution, but millions are crushed, that one may become rich; while one becomes rich, thousands at the same time become poorer and poorer, and whole masses of human beings are made slaves. That way it is going on. The animal man lives in the senses. If he does not get enough to eat, he is miserable; or if something happens to his body, he is miserable. In the senses both his misery and his happiness begin and end. As soon as this man progresses, as soon as his horizon of happiness increases, his horizon of unhappiness increases proportionately. The man in the forest does not know what it is to be jealous, to be in the law courts, to pay taxes, to be blamed by society, to be ruled over day and night by the most tremendous tyranny that human diabolism ever invented, which pries into the secrets of every human heart. He does not know how man becomes a thousand times more diabolical than any other animal, with all his vain knowledge and with all his pride. Thus it is that, as we emerge out of the senses, we develop higher powers of enjoyment, and at the same time we have to develop higher powers of suffering too. The nerves become finer and capable off more suffering. In every society, we often find that the ignorant, common man, when abused, does not feel much, but he feels a good thrashing. But the gentleman cannot bear a single word of abuse; he has become so finely nerved. Misery has increased with his susceptibility to happiness. This does not go much to prove the evolutionist's case. As we increase our power to be happy, we also increase our power to suffer, and sometimes I am inclined to think that if we increase our power to become happy in arithmetical progression, we shall increase, on the other hand, our power to become miserable in geometrical progression. We who are progressing know that the more we progress, the more avenues are opened to pain as well as to pleasure. And this is Maya.

Thus we find that Maya is not a theory for the explanation of the world; it is simply a statement of facts as they exist, that the very basis of our being is contradiction, that everywhere we have to move through this tremendous contradiction, that wherever there is good, there must also be evil, and wherever there is evil, there must be some good, wherever there is life, death must follow as its shadow, and everyone who smiles will have to weep, and vice versa. Nor can this state of things be remedied. We may verily imagine that there will be a place where there will be only good and no evil, where we shall only smile and never weep. This is impossible in the very nature of things; for the conditions will remain the same. Wherever there is the power of producing a smile in us, there lurks the power of producing tears. Wherever there is the power of producing happiness, there lurks somewhere the power of making us miserable.

Thus the Vedanta philosophy is neither optimistic nor pessimistic. It voices both these views and takes things as they are. It admits that this world is a mixture of good and evil, happiness and misery, and that to increase the one, one must of necessity increase the other. There will never be a perfectly good or bad world, because the very idea is a contradiction in terms. The great secret revealed by this analysis is that good and bad are not two cut-and-dried, separate existences. There is not one thing in this world of ours which you can label as good and good alone, and there is not one thing in the universe which you can label as bad and bad alone. The very same phenomenon which is appearing to be good now, may appear to be bad tomorrow. The same thing which is producing misery in one, may produce happiness in another. The fire that burns the child, may cook a good meal for a starving man. The same nerves that carry the sensations of misery carry also the sensations of happiness. The only way to stop evil, therefore, is to stop good also; there is no other way. To stop death, we shall have to stop life also. Life without death and happiness without misery are contradictions, and neither can be found alone, because each of them is but a different manifestation of the same thing. What I thought to be good yesterday, I do not think to be good now. When I look back upon my life and see what were my ideals at different times, I final this to be so. At one time my ideal was to drive a strong pair of horses; at another time I thought, if I could make a certain kind of sweetmeat, I should be perfectly happy; later I imagined that I should be entirely satisfied if I had a wife and children and plenty of money. Today I laugh at all these ideals as mere childish nonsense.

The Vedanta says, there must come a time when we shall look back and laugh at the ideals which make us afraid of giving up our individuality. Each one of us wants to keep this body for an indefinite time, thinking we shall be very happy, but there will come a time when we shall laugh at this idea. Now, if such be the truth, we are in a state of hopeless contradiction — neither existence nor non-existence, neither misery nor happiness, but a mixture of them. What, then, is the use of Vedanta and all other philosophies and religions? And, above all, what is the use of doing good work? This is a question that comes to the mind. If it is true that you cannot do good without doing evil, and whenever you try to create happiness there will always be misery, people will ask you, "What is the use of doing good?" The answer is in the first place, that we must work for lessening misery, for that is the only way to make ourselves happy. Every one of us finds it out sooner or later in our lives. The bright ones find it out a little earlier, and the dull ones a little later. The dull ones pay very dearly for the discovery and the bright ones less dearly. In the second place, we must do our part, because that is the only way of getting out of this life of contradiction. Both the forces of good and evil will keep the universe alive for us, until we awake from our dreams and give up this building of mud pies. That lesson we shall have to learn, and it will take a long, long time to learn it.

Attempts have been made in Germany to build a system of philosophy on the basis that the Infinite has become the finite. Such attempts are also made in England. And the analysis of the position of these philosophers is this, that the Infinite is trying to express itself in this universe, and that there will come a time when the Infinite will succeed in doing so. It is all very well, and we have used the words Infinite and manifestation and expression, and so on, but philosophers naturally ask for a logical fundamental basis for the statement that the finite can fully express the Infinite. The Absolute and the Infinite can become this universe only by limitation. Everything must be limited that comes through the senses, or through the mind, or through the intellect; and for the limited to be the unlimited is simply absurd and can never be. The Vedanta, on the other hand, says that it is true that the Absolute or the Infinite is trying to express itself in the finite, but there will come a time when it will find that it is impossible, and it will then have to beat a retreat, and this beating a retreat means renunciation which is the real beginning of religion. Nowadays it is very hard even to talk of renunciation. It was said of me in America that I was a man who came out of a land that had been dead and buried for five thousand years, and talked of renunciation. So says, perhaps, the English philosopher. Yet it is true that that is the only path to religion. Renounce and give up. What did Christ say? "He that loseth his life for my sake shall find it." Again and again did he preach renunciation as the only way to perfection. There comes a time when the mind awakes from this long and dreary dream — the child gives up its play and wants to go back to its mother. It finds the truth of the statement, "Desire is never satisfied by the enjoyment of desires, it only increases the more, as fire, when butter is poured upon it."

This is true of all sense-enjoyments, of all intellectual enjoyments, and of all the enjoyments of which the human mind is capable. They are nothing, they are within Maya, within this network beyond which we cannot go. We may run therein through infinite time and find no end, and whenever we struggle to get a little enjoyment, a mass of misery falls upon us. How awful is this! And when I think of it, I cannot but consider that this theory of Maya, this statement that it is all Maya, is the best and only explanation. What an amount of misery there is in this world; and if you travel among various nations you will find that one nation attempts to cure its evils by one means, and another by another. The very same evil has been taken up by various races, and attempts have been made in various ways to check it, yet no nation has succeeded. If it has been minimised at one point, a mass of evil has been crowded at another point. Thus it goes. The Hindus, to keep up a high standard of chastity in the race, have sanctioned child-marriage, which in the long run has degraded the race. At the same time, I cannot deny that this child-marriage makes the race more chaste. What would you have? If you want the nation to be more chaste, you weaken men and women physically by child-marriage. On the other hand, are you in England any better off? No, because chastity is the life of a nation. Do you not find in history that the first death-sign of a nation has been unchastity? When that has entered, the end of the race is in sight. Where shall we get a solution of these miseries then? If parents select husbands and wives for their children, then this evil is minimised. The daughters of India are more practical than sentimental. But very little of poetry remains in their lives. Again, if people select their own husbands and wives, that does not seem to bring much happiness. The Indian woman is generally very happy; there are not many cases of quarrelling between husband and wife. On the other hand in the United States, where the greatest liberty obtains, the number of unhappy homes and marriages is large. Unhappiness is here, there, and everywhere. What does it show? That, after all, not much happiness has been gained by all these ideals. We all struggle for happiness and as soon as we get a little happiness on one side, on the other side there comes unhappiness.

Shall we not work to do good then? Yes, with more zest than ever, but what this knowledge will do for us is to break down our fanaticism. The Englishman will no more be a fanatic and curse the Hindu. He will learn to respect the customs of different nations. There will be less of fanaticism and more of real work. Fanatics cannot work, they waste three-fourths of their energy. It is the level-headed, calm, practical man who works. So, the power to work will increase from this idea. Knowing that this is the state of things, there will be more patience. The sight of misery or of evil will not be able to throw us off our balance and make us run after shadows. Therefore, patience will come to us, knowing that the world will have to go on in its own way. If, for instance, all men have become good, the animals will have in the meantime evolved into men, and will have to pass through the same state, and so with the plants. But only one thing is certain; the mighty river is rushing towards the ocean, and all the drops that constitute the stream will in time be drawn into that boundless ocean. So, in this life, with all its miseries and sorrows, its joys and smiles and tears, one thing is certain, that all things are rushing towards their goal, and it is only a question of time when you and I, and plants and animals, and every particles of life that exists must reach the Infinite Ocean of Perfection, must attain to Freedom, to God.

Let me repeat, once more, that the Vedantic position is neither pessimism nor optimism. It does not say that this world is all evil or all good. It says that our evil is of no less value than our good, and our good of no more value than our evil. They are bound together. This is the world, and knowing this, you work with patience. What for? Why should we work? If this is the state of things, what shall we do? Why not become agnostics? The modern agnostics also know there is no solution of this problem, no getting out of this evil of Maya, as we say in our language; therefore they tell us to be satisfied and enjoy life. Here, again, is a mistake, a tremendous mistake, a most illogical mistake. And it is this. What do you mean by life? Do you mean only the life of the senses? In this, every one of us differs only slightly from the brutes. I am sure that no one is present here whose life is only in the senses. Then, this present life means something more than that. Our feelings, thoughts, and aspirations are all part and parcel of our life; and is not the struggle towards the area, ideal, towards perfection, one of the most important components of what we call life? According to the agnostics, we must enjoy life as it is. But this life means, above all, this search after the ideal; the essence of life is going towards perfection. We must have that, and, therefore, we cannot be agnostics or take the world as it appears. The agnostic position takes this life, minus the ideal component, to be all that exists. And this, the agnostic claims, cannot be reached, therefore he must give up the search. This is what is called Maya — this nature, this universe.

All religions are more or less attempts to get beyond nature — the crudest or the most developed, expressed through mythology or symbology, stories of gods, angels or demons, or through stories of saints or seers, great men or prophets, or through the abstractions of philosophy — all have that one object, all are trying to get beyond these limitations. In one word, they are all struggling towards freedom. Man feels, consciously or unconsciously, that he is bound; he is not what he wants to be. It was taught to him at the very moment he began to look around. That very instant he learnt that he was bound, and be also found that there was something in him which wanted to fly beyond, where the body could not follow, but which was as yet chained down by this limitation. Even in the lowest of religious ideas, where departed ancestors and other spirits — mostly violent and cruel, lurking about the houses of their friends, fond of bloodshed and strong drink — are worshipped, even there we find that one common factor, that of freedom. The man who wants to worship the gods sees in them, above all things, greater freedom than in himself. If a door is closed, he thinks the gods can get through it, and that walls have no limitations for them. This idea of freedom increases until it comes to the ideal of a Personal God, of which the central concept is that He is a Being beyond the limitation of nature, of Maya. I see before me, as it were, that in some of those forest retreats this question is being, discussed by those ancient sages of India; and in one of them, where even the oldest and the holiest fail to reach the solutions a young man stands up in the midst of them, and declares, "Hear, ye children of immortality, hear, who live in the highest places, I have found the way. By knowing Him who is beyond darkness we can go beyond death."

This Maya is everywhere. It is terrible. Yet we have to work through it. The man who says that he will work when the world has become all good and then he will enjoy bliss is as likely to succeed as the man who sits beside the Ganga and says, "I will ford the river when all the water has run into the ocean." The way is not with Maya, but against it. This is another fact to learn. We are not born as helpers of nature, but competitors with nature. We are its bond-masters, but we bind ourselves down. Why is this house here? Nature did not build it. Nature says, go and live in the forest. Man says, I will build a house and fight with nature, and he does so. The whole history of humanity is a continuous fight against the so-called laws of nature, and man gains in the end. Coming to the internal world, there too the same fight is going on, this fight between the animal man and the spiritual man, between light and darkness; and here too man becomes victorious. He, as it were, cuts his way out of nature to freedom.

We see, then, that beyond this Maya the Vedantic philosophers find something which is not bound by Maya; and if we can get there, we shall not be bound by Maya. This idea is in some form or other the common property of all religions. But, with the Vedanta, it is only the beginning of religion and not the end. The idea of a Personal God, the Ruler and Creator of this universe, as He has been styled, the Ruler of Maya, or nature, is not the end of these Vedantic ideas; it is only the beginning. The idea grows and grows until the Vedantist finds that He who, he thought, was standing outside, is he himself and is in reality within. He is the one who is free, but who through limitation thought he was bound.

CHAPTER IV
MAYA AND THE EVOLUTION OF THE CONCEPTION OF GOD

Delivered in London, 20th October 1896

We have seen how the idea of Mâyâ, which forms, as it were, one of the basic doctrines of the Advaita Vedanta, is, in its germs, found even in the Samhitâs, and that in reality all the ideas which are developed in the Upanishads are to be found already in the Samhitas in some form or other. Most of you are by this time familiar with the idea of Maya, and know that it is sometimes erroneously explained as illusion, so that when the universe is said to be Maya, that also has to be explained as being illusion. The translation of the word is neither happy nor correct. Maya is not a theory; it is simply a statement of facts about the universe as it exists, and to understand Maya we must go back to the Samhitas and begin with the conception in the germ.

We have seen how the idea of the Devas came. At the same time we know that these Devas were at first only powerful beings, nothing more. Most of you are horrified when reading the old scriptures, whether of the Greeks, the Hebrews, the Persians, or others, to find that the ancient gods sometimes did things which, to us, are very repugnant. But when we read these books, we entirely forget that we are persons of the nineteenth century, and these gods were beings existing thousands of years ago. We also forget that the people who worshipped these gods found nothing incongruous in their characters, found nothing to frighten them, because they were very much like themselves. I may also remark that that is the one great lesson we have to learn throughout our lives. In judging others we always judge them by our own ideals. That is not as it should be. Everyone must be judged according to his own ideal, and not by that of anyone else. In our dealings with our fellow-beings we constantly labour under this mistake, and I am of opinion that the vast majority of our quarrels with one another arise simply from this one cause that we are always trying to judge others' gods by our own, others' ideals by our ideals, and others' motives by our motives. Under certain circumstances I might do a certain thing, and when I see another person taking the same course I think he has also the same motive actuating him, little dreaming that although the effect may be the same, yet many other causes may produce the same thing. He may have performed the action with quite a different motive from that which impelled me to do it. So in judging of those ancient religions we must not take the standpoint to which we incline, but must put ourselves into the position of thought and life of those early times.

The idea of the cruel and ruthless Jehovah in the Old Testament has frightened many — but why? What right have they to assume that the Jehovah of the ancient Jews must represent the conventional idea of the God of the present day? And at the same time, we must not forget that there will come men after us who will laugh at our ideas of religion and God in the same way that we laugh at those of the ancients. Yet, through all these various conceptions runs the golden thread of unity, and it is the purpose of the Vedanta to discover this thread. "I am the thread that runs through all these various ideas, each one of which is; like a pearl," says the Lord Krishna; and it is the duty of Vedanta to establish this connecting thread, how ever incongruous or disgusting may seem these ideas when judged according to the conceptions of today. These ideas, in the setting of past times, were harmonious and not more hideous than our present ideas. It is only when we try to take them out of their settings and apply to our own present circumstances that the hideousness becomes obvious. For the old surroundings are dead and gone. Just as the ancient Jew has developed into the keen, modern, sharp Jew, and the ancient Aryan into the intellectual Hindu similarly Jehovah has grown, and Devas have grown.

The great mistake is in recognising the evolution of the worshippers, while we do not acknowledge the evolution of the Worshipped. He is not credited with the advance that his devotees have made.

That is to say, you and I, representing ideas, have grown; these gods also, as representing ideas, have grown. This may seem somewhat curious to you — that God can grow. He cannot. He is unchangeable. In the same sense the real man never grows. But man's ideas of God are constantly changing and expanding. We shall see later on how the real man behind each one of these human manifestations is immovable, unchangeable, pure, and always perfect; and in the same way the idea that we form of God is a mere manifestation, our own creation. Behind that is the real God who never changes, the ever pure, the immutable. But the manifestation is always changing revealing the reality behind more and more. When it reveals more of the fact behind, it is called progression, when it hides more of the fact behind, it is called retrogression. Thus, as we grow, so the gods grow. From the ordinary point of view, just as we reveal ourselves as we evolve, so the gods reveal themselves.

We shall now be in a position to understand the theory of Maya. In all the regions of the world the one question they propose to discuss is this: Why is there disharmony in the universe? Why is there this evil in the universe? We do not find this question in the very inception of primitive religious ideas, because the world did not appear incongruous to the primitive man. Circumstances were not inharmonious for him; there was no dash of opinions; to him there was no antagonism of good and evil. There was merely a feeling in his own heart of something which said yea, and something which said nay. The primitive man was a man of impulse. He did what occurred to him, and tried to bring out through his muscles whatever thought came into his mind, and he never stopped to judge, and seldom tried to check his impulses. So with the gods, they were also creatures of impulse. Indra comes and shatters the forces of the demons. Jehovah is pleased with one person and displeased with another, for what reason no one knows or asks. The habit of inquiry had not then arisen, and whatever he did was regarded as right. There was no idea of good or evil. The Devas did many wicked things in our sense of the word; again and again Indra and other gods committed very wicked deeds, but to the worshippers of Indra the ideas of wickedness and evil did not occur, so they did not question them.

With the advance of ethical ideas came the fight. There arose a certain sense in man, called in different languages and nations by different names. Call it the voice of God, or the result of past education, or whatever else you like, but the effect was this that it had a checking power upon the natural impulses of man. There is one impulse in our minds which says, do. Behind it rises another voice which says, do not. There is one set of ideas in our mind which is always struggling to get outside through the channels of the senses, and behind that, although it may be thin and weak, there is an infinitely small voice which says, do not go outside. The two beautiful Sanskrit words for these phenomena are Pravritti and Nivritti, "circling forward" and "circling inward". It is the circling forward which usually governs our actions. Religion begins with this circling inward. Religion begins with this "do not". Spirituality begins with this "do not". When the "do not" is not there, religion has not begun. And this "do not" came, causing men's ideas to grow, despite the fighting gods which they had worshipped.

A little love awoke in the hearts of mankind. It was very small indeed, and even now it is not much greater. It was at first confined to a tribe embracing perhaps members of the same tribe; these gods loved their tribes and each god was a tribal god, the protector of that tribe. And sometimes the members of a tribe would think of themselves as the descendants of their god, just as the clans in different nations think that they are the common descendants of the man who was the founder of the clan. There were in ancient times, and are even now, some people who claim to be descendants not only of these tribal gods, but also of the Sun and the Moon. You read in the ancient Sanskrit books of the great heroic emperors of the solar and the lunar dynasties. They were first worshippers of the Sun and the Moon, and gradually came to think of themselves as descendants of the god of the Sun of the Moon, and so forth. So when these tribal ideas began to grow there came a little love, some slight idea of duty towards each other, a little social organisation. Then, naturally, the idea came: How can we live together without bearing and forbearing? How can one man live with another without having some time or other to check his impulses, to restrain himself, to forbear from doing things which his mind would prompt him to do? It is impossible. Thus comes the idea of restraint. The whole social fabric is based upon that idea of restraint, and we all know that the man or woman who has not learnt the great lesson of bearing and forbearing leads a most miserable life.

Now, when these ideas of religion came, a glimpse of something higher, more ethical, dawned upon the intellect of mankind. The old gods were found to be incongruous — these boisterous, fighting, drinking, beef-eating gods of the ancients — whose delight was in the smell of burning flesh and libations of strong liquor. Sometimes Indra drank so much that he fell upon the ground and talked unintelligibly. These gods could no longer be tolerated. The notion had arisen of inquiring into motives, and the gods had to come in for their share of inquiry. Reason for such-and-such actions was demanded and the reason was wanting. Therefore man gave up these gods, or rather they developed higher ideas concerning them. They took a survey, as it were, of all the actions and qualities of the gods and discarded those which they could not harmonise, and kept those which they could understand, and combined them, labelling them with one name, Deva-deva, the God of gods. The god to be worshipped was no more a simple symbol of power; something more was required than that. He was an ethical god; he loved mankind, and did good to mankind. But the idea of god still remained. They increased his ethical significance, and increased also his power. He became the most ethical being in the universe, as well as almost almighty.

But all this patchwork would not do. As the explanation assumed greater proportions, the difficulty which it sought to solve did the same. If the qualities of the god increased in arithmetical progression, the difficulty and doubt increased in geometrical progression. The difficulty of Jehovah was very little beside the difficulty of the God of the universe, and this question remains to the present day. Why under the reign of an almighty and all-loving God of the universe should diabolical things be allowed to remain? Why so much more misery than happiness, and so much more wickedness than good? We may shut our eyes to all these things, but the fact still remains that this world is a hideous world. At best, it is the hell of Tantalus. Here we are with strong impulses and stronger cravings for sense-enjoyments, but cannot satisfy them. There rises a wave which impels us forward in spite of our own will, and as soon as we move one step, comes a blow. We are all doomed to live here like Tantalus. Ideals come into our head far beyond the limit of our sense-ideals, but when we seek to express them, we cannot do so. On the other hand, we are crushed by the surging mass around us. Yet if I give up all ideality and merely struggle through this world, my existence is that of a brute, and I degenerate and degrade myself. Neither way is happiness. Unhappiness is the fate of those who are content to live in this world, born as they are. A thousand times greater misery is the fate of those who dare to stand forth for truth and for higher things and who dare to ask for something higher than mere brute existence here. These are facts; but there is no explanation — there cannot be any explanation. But the Vedanta shows the way out. You must bear in mind that I have to tell you facts that will frighten you sometimes, but if you remember what I say, think of it, and digest it, it will be yours, it will raise you higher, and make you capable of understanding and living in truth.

Now, it is a statement of fact that this world is a Tantalus's hell, that we do not know anything about this universe, yet at the same time we cannot say that we do not know. I cannot say that this chain exists, when I think that I do not know it. It may be an entire delusion of my brain. I may be dreaming all the time. I am dreaming that I am talking to you, and that you are listening to me. No one can prove that it is not a dream. My brain itself may be a dream, and as to that no one has ever seen his own brain. We all take it for granted. So it is with everything. My own body I take for granted. At the same time

I cannot say, I do not know. This standing between knowledge and ignorance, this mystic twilight, the mingling of truth and falsehood — and where they meet — no one knows. We are walking in the midst of a dream. Half sleeping, half waking, passing all our lives in a haze; this is the fate of everyone of us. This is the fate of all sense-knowledge. This is the fate of all philosophy, of all boasted science, of all boasted human knowledge. This is the universe.

What you call matter, or spirit, or mind, or anything else you may like to call them, the fact remains the same: we cannot say that they are, we cannot say that they are not. We cannot say they are one, we cannot say they are many. This eternal play of light and darkness — indiscriminate, indistinguishable, inseparable — is always there. A fact, yet at the same time not a fact; awake and at the same time asleep. This is a statement of facts, and this is what is called Maya. We are born in this Maya, we live in it, we think in it, we dream in it. We are philosophers in it, we are spiritual men in it, nay, we are devils in this Maya, and we are gods in this Maya. Stretch your ideas as far as you can make them higher and higher, call them infinite or by any other name you please, even these ideas are within this Maya. It cannot be otherwise, and the whole of human knowledge is a generalization of this Maya trying to know it as it appears to be. This is the work of Nâma-Rupa — name and form. Everything that has form, everything that calls up an idea in your mind, is within Maya; for everything that is bound by the laws of time, space, and causation is within Maya.

Let us go back a little to those early ideas of God and see what became of them. We perceive at once that the idea of some Being who is eternally loving us — eternally unselfish and almighty, ruling this universe — could not satisfy. "Where is the just, merciful God?" asked the philosopher. Does He not see millions and millions of His children perish, in the form of men and animals; for who can live one moment here without killing others? Can you draw a breath without destroying thousands of lives? You live, because, millions die. Every moment of your life, every breath that you breathe, is death to thousands; every movement that you make is death to millions. Every morsel that you eat is death to millions. Why should they die? There is an old sophism that they are very low existences. Supposing they are — which is questionable, for who knows whether the ant is greater than the man, or the man than the ant — who can prove one way or the other? Apart from that question, even taking it for granted that these are very low beings, still why should they die? If they are low, they have more reason to live. Why not? Because they live more in the senses, they feel pleasure and pain a thousandfold more than you or I can do. Which of us eats a dinner with the same gusto as a dog or wolf? None, because our energies are not in the senses; they are in the intellect, in the spirit. But in animals, their whole soul is in the senses, and they become mad and enjoy things which we human beings never dream of, and the pain is commensurate with the pleasure. Pleasure and pain are meted out in equal measure. If the pleasure felt by animals is so much keener than that felt by man, it follows that the animals' sense of pain is as keen, if not keener than man's. So the fact is, the pain and misery men feel in dying is intensified a thousandfold in animals, and yet we kill them without troubling ourselves about their misery. This is Maya. And if we suppose there is a Personal God like a human being, who made everything, these so-called explanations and theories which try to prove that out of evil comes good are not sufficient. Let twenty thousand good things come, but why should they come from evil? On that principle, I might cut the throats of others because I want the full pleasure of my five senses. That is no reason. Why should good come through evil? The question remains to be answered, and it cannot be answered. The philosophy of India was compelled to admit this.

The Vedanta was (and is) the boldest system of religion. It stopped nowhere, and it had one advantage. There was no body of priests who sought to suppress every man who tried to tell the truth. There was always absolute religious freedom. In India the bondage of superstition is a social one; here in the West society is very free. Social matters in India are very strict, but religious opinion is free. In England a man may dress any way he likes, or eat what he lilies — no one objects; but if he misses attending church, then Mrs. Grundy is down on him. He has to conform first to what society says on religion, and then he may think of the truth. In India, on the other hand, if a man dines with one who does not belong to his own caste, down comes society with all its terrible powers and crushes him then and there. If he wants to dress a little differently from the way in which his ancestor dressed ages ago, he is done for. I have heard of a man who was cast out by society because he went several miles to see the first railway train. Well, we shall presume that was not true! But in religion, we find atheists, materialists, and Buddhists, creeds, opinions, and speculations of every phase and variety, some of a most startling character, living side by side. Preachers of all sects go about reaching and getting adherents, and at the very gates of the temples of gods, the Brâhmins — to their credit be it said — allow even the materialists to stand and give forth their opinions.

Buddha died at a ripe old age. I remember a friend of mine, a great American scientist, who was fond of reading his life. He did not like the death of Buddha, because he was not crucified. What a false idea! For a man to be great he must be murdered! Such ideas never prevailed in India. This great Buddha travelled all over India, denouncing her gods and even the God of the universe, and yet he lived to a good old age. For eighty years he lived, and had converted half the country.

Then, there were the Chârvâkas, who preached horrible things, the most rank, undisguised materialism, such as in the nineteenth century they dare not openly preach. These Charvakas were allowed to preach from temple to temple, and city to city, that religion was all nonsense, that it was priestcraft, that the Vedas were the words and writings of fools, rogues, and demons, and that there was neither God nor an eternal soul. If there was a soul, why did it not come back after death drawn by the love of wife and child. Their idea was that if there was a soul it must still love after death, and want good things to eat and nice dress. Yet no one hurt these Charvakas.

Thus India has always had this magnificent idea of religious freedom, and you must remember that freedom is the first condition of growth. What you do not make free, will never grow. The idea that you can make others grow and help their growth, that you can direct and guide them, always retaining for yourself the freedom of the teacher, is nonsense, a dangerous lie which has retarded the growth of millions and millions of human beings in this world. Let men have the light of liberty. That is the only condition of growth.

We, in India, allowed liberty in spiritual matters, and we have a tremendous spiritual power in religious thought even today. You grant the same liberty in social matters, and so have a splendid social organisation. We have not given any freedom to the expansion of social matters, and ours is a cramped society. You have never given any freedom in religious matters but with fire and sword have enforced your beliefs, and the result is that religion is a stunted, degenerated growth in the European mind. In India, we have to take off the shackles from society; in Europe, the chains must be taken from the feet of spiritual progress. Then will come a wonderful growth and development of man. If we discover that there is one unity running through all these developments, spiritual, moral, and social, we shall find that religion, in the fullest sense of the word, must come into society, and into our everyday life. In the light of Vedanta you will Understand that all sciences are but manifestations of religion, and so is everything that exists in this world.

We see, then, that through freedom the sciences were built; and in them we have two sets of opinions, the one the materialistic and denouncing, and the other the positive and constructive. It is a most curious fact that in every society you find them. Supposing there is an evil in society, you will find immediately one group rise up and denounce it in vindictive fashion, which sometimes degenerates into fanaticism. There are fanatics in every society, and women frequently join in these outcries, because of their impulsive nature. Every fanatic who gets up and denounces something can secure a following. It is very easy to break down; a maniac can break anything he likes, but it would be hard for him to build up anything. These fanatics may do some good, according to their light, but much morn harm. Because social institutions are not made in a day, and to change them means removing the cause. Suppose there is an evil; denouncing it will not remove it, but you must go to work at the root. First find out the cause, then remove it, and the effect will be removed also. Mere outcry not produce any effect, unless indeed it produces misfortune.

There are others who had sympathy in their hearts and who understood the idea that we must go deep into the cause, these were the great saints. One fact you must remember, that all the great teachers of the world have declared that they came not to destroy but to fulfil. Many times his has not been understood, and their forbearance has been thought to be an unworthy compromise with existing popular opinions. Even now, you occasionally hear that these prophets and great teachers were rather cowardly, and dared not say and do what they thought was right; but that was not so. Fanatics little understand the infinite power of love in the hearts of these great sages who looked upon the inhabitants of this world as their children. They were the real fathers, the real gods, filled with infinite sympathy and patience for everyone; they were ready to bear and forbear. They knew how human society should grow, and patiently slowly, surely, went on applying their remedies, not by denouncing and frightening people, but by gently and kindly leading them upwards step by step. Such were the writers of the Upanishads. They knew full well how the old ideas of God were not reconcilable with the advanced ethical ideas of the time; they knew full well that what the atheists were preaching contained a good deal of truth, nay, great nuggets of truth; but at the same time, they understood that those who wished to sever the thread that bound the beads, who wanted to build a new society in the air, would entirely fail.

We never build anew, we simply change places; we cannot have anything new, we only change the position of things. The seed grows into the tree, patiently and gently; we must direct our energies towards the truth and fulfil the truth that exists, not try to make new truths. Thus, instead of denouncing these old ideas of God as unfit for modern times, the ancient sages began to seek out the reality that was in them. The result was the Vedanta philosophy, and out of the old deities, out of the monotheistic God, the Ruler of the universe, they found yet higher and higher ideas in what is called the Impersonal Absolute; they found oneness throughout the universe.

He who sees in this world of manifoldness that One running through all, in this world of death he who finds that One Infinite Life, and in this world of insentience and ignorance he who finds that One Light and Knowledge, unto him belongs eternal peace. Unto none else, unto none else.

CHAPTER V
MAYA AND FREEDOM

Delivered in London, 22nd October 1896

"Trailing clouds of glory we come," says the poet. Not all of us come as trailing clouds of glory however; some of us come as trailing black fogs; there can be no question about that. But every one of us comes into this world to fight, as on a battlefield. We come here weeping to fight our way, as well as we can, and to make a path for ourselves through this infinite ocean of life; forward we go, having long ages behind us and an immense expanse beyond. So on we go, till death comes and takes us off the field — victorious or defeated, we do not know. And this is Mâyâ.

Hope is dominant in the heart of childhood. The whole world is a golden vision to the opening eyes of the child; he thinks his will is supreme. As he moves onward, at every step nature stands as an adamantine wall, barring his future progress. He may hurl himself against it again and again, striving to break through. The further he goes, the further recedes the ideal, till death comes, and there is release, perhaps. And this is Maya.

A man of science rises, he is thirsting after knowledge. No sacrifice is too great, no struggle too hopeless for him. He moves onward discovering secret after secret of nature, searching out the secrets from her innermost heart, and what for? What is it all for? Why should we give him glory? Why should he acquire fame? Does not nature do infinitely more than any human being can do? — and nature is dull, insentient. Why should it be glory to imitate the dull, the insentient? Nature can hurl a thunderbolt of any magnitude to any distance. If a man can do one small part as much, we praise him and laud him to the skies. Why? Why should we praise him for imitating nature, imitating death, imitating dullness imitating insentience? The force of gravitation can pull to pieces the biggest mass that ever existed; yet it is insentient. What glory is there in imitating the insentient? Yet we are all struggling after that. And this is maya.

The senses drag the human soul out. Man is seeking for pleasure and for happiness where it can never be found. For countless ages we are all taught that this is futile and vain, there is no happiness here. But we cannot learn; it is impossible for us to do so, except through our own experiences. We try them, and a blow comes. Do we learn then? Not even then. Like moths hurling themselves against the flame, we are hurling ourselves again and again into sense-pleasures, hoping to find satisfaction there. We return again and again with freshened energy; thus we go on, till crippled and cheated we die. And this is Maya.

So with our intellect. In our desire to solve the mysteries of the universe, we cannot stop our questioning, we feel we must know and cannot believe that no knowledge is to be gained. A few steps, and there arises the wall of beginningless and endless time which we cannot surmount. A few steps, and there appears a wall of boundless space which cannot be surmounted, and the whole is irrevocably bound in by the walls of cause and effect. We cannot go beyond them. Yet we struggle, and still have to struggle. And this is Maya.

With every breath, with every pulsation of the heart with every one of our movements, we think we are free, and the very same moment we are shown that we are not. Bound slaves, nature's bond-slaves, in body, in mind, in all our thoughts, in all our feelings. And this is Maya.

There was never a mother who did not think her child was a born genius, the most extraordinary child that was ever born; she dotes upon her child. Her whole soul is in the child. The child grows up, perhaps becomes a drunkard, a brute, ill-treats the mother, and the more he ill-treats her, the more her love increases. The world lauds it as the unselfish love of the mother, little dreaming that the mother is a born slave, she cannot help it. She would a thousand times rather throw off the burden, but she cannot. So she covers it with a mass of flowers, which she calls wonderful love. And this is Maya.

We are all like this in the world. A legend tells how once Nârada said to Krishna, "Lord, show me Maya." A few days passed away, and Krishna asked Narada to make a trip with him towards a desert, and after walking for several miles, Krishna said, "Narada, I am thirsty; can you fetch some water for me?" "I will go at once, sir, and get you water." So Narada went. At a little distance there was a village; he entered the village in search of water and knocked at a door, which was opened by a most beautiful young girl. At the sight of her he immediately forgot that his Master was waiting for water, perhaps dying for the want of it. He forgot everything and began to talk with the girl. All that day he did not return to his Master. The next day, he was again at the house, talking to the girl. That talk ripened into love; he asked the father for the daughter, and they were married and lived there and had children. Thus twelve years passed. His father-in-law died, he inherited his property. He lived, as he seemed to think, a very happy life with his wife and children, his fields and his cattle and so forth. Then came a flood. One night the river rose until it overflowed its banks and flooded the whole village. Houses fell, men and animals were swept away and drowned, and everything was floating in the rush of the stream. Narada had to escape. With one hand be held his wife, and with the other two of his children; another child was on his shoulders, and he was trying to ford this tremendous flood. After a few steps he found the current was too strong, and the child on his shoulders fell and was borne away. A cry of despair came from Narada. In trying to save that child, he lost his grasp upon one of the others, and it also was lost. At last his wife, whom he clasped with all his might, was torn away by the current, and he was thrown on the bank, weeping and wailing in bitter lamentation. Behind him there came a gentle voice, "My child, where is the water? You went to fetch a pitcher of water, and I am waiting for you; you have been gone for quite half an hour." "Half an hour! " Narada exclaimed. Twelve whole years had passed through his mind, and all these scenes had happened in half an hour! And this is Maya.

In one form or another, we are all in it. It is a most difficult and intricate state of things to understand. It has been preached in every country, taught everywhere, but only believed in by a few, because until we get the experiences ourselves we cannot believe in it. What does it show? Something very terrible. For it is all futile. Time, the avenger of everything, comes, and nothing is left. He swallows up the saint and the sinner, the king and the peasant, the beautiful and the ugly; he leaves nothing. Everything is rushing towards that one goal destruction. Our knowledge, our arts, our sciences, everything is rushing towards it. None can stem the tide, none can hold it back for a minute. We may try to forget it, in the same way that persons in a plague-striker city try to create oblivion by drinking, dancing, and other vain attempts, and so becoming paralysed. So we are trying to forget, trying to create oblivion by all sorts of sense-pleasures. And this is Maya.

Two ways have been proposed. One method, which everyone knows, is very common, and that is: "It may be very true, but do not think of it. 'Make hay while the sun shines,' as the proverb says. It is all true, it is a fact, but do not mind it. Seize the few pleasures you can, do what little you can, do not look at tile dark side of the picture, but always towards the hopeful, the positive side." There is some truth in this, but there is also a danger. The truth is that it is a good motive power. Hope and a positive ideal are very good motive powers for our lives, but there is a certain danger in them. The danger lies in our giving up the struggle in despair. Such is the case with those who preach, "Take the world as it is, sit down as calmly and comfortably as you can and be contented with all these miseries. When you receive blows, say they are not blows but flowers; and when you are driven about like slaves, say that you are free. Day and night tell lies to others and to your own souls, because that is the only way to live happily." This is what is called practical wisdom, and never was it more prevalent in the world than in this nineteenth century; because never were harder blows hit than at the present time, never was competition keener, never were men so cruel to their fellow-men as now; and, therefore, must this consolation be offered. It is put forward in the strongest way at the present time; but it fails, as it always must fail. We cannot hide a carrion with roses; it is impossible. It would not avail long; for soon the roses would fade, and the carrion would be worse than ever before. So with our lives. We may try to cover our old and festering sores with cloth of gold, but there comes a day when the cloth of gold is removed, and the sore in all its ugliness is revealed.

Is there no hope then? True it is that we are all slaves of Maya, born in Maya, and live in Maya. Is there then no way out, no hope? That we are all miserable, that this world is really a prison, that even our so-called trailing beauty is but a prison-house, and that even our intellects and minds are prison-houses, have been known for ages upon ages. There has never been a man, there has never been a human soul, who has not felt this sometime or other, however he may talk. And the old people feel it most, because in them is the accumulated experience of a whole life, because they cannot be easily cheated by the lies of nature. Is there no way out? We find that with all this, with this terrible fact before us, in the midst of sorrow and suffering, even in this world where life and death are synonymous, even here, there is a still small voice that is ringing through all ages, through every country, and in every heart: "This My Maya is divine, made up of qualities, and very difficult to cross. Yet those that come unto Me, cross the river of life." "Come unto Me all ye that labour and are heavy laden and I will give you rest." This is the voice that is leading us forward. Man has heard it, and is hearing it all through the ages. This voice comes to men when everything seems to be lost and hope has fled, when man's dependence on his own strength has been crushed down and everything seems to melt away between his fingers, and life is a hopeless ruin. Then he hears it. This is called religion.

On the one side, therefore, is the bold assertion that this is all nonsense, that this is Maya, but along with it there is the most hopeful assertion that beyond Maya, there is a way out. On the other hand, practical men tell us, "Don't bother your heads about such nonsense as religion and metaphysics. Live here; this is a very bad world indeed, but make the best of it." Which put in plain language means, live a hypocritical, lying life, a life of continuous fraud, covering all sores in the best way you can. Go on putting patch after patch, until everything is lost, and you are a mass of patchwork. This is what is called practical life. Those that are satisfied with this patchwork will never come to religion. Religion begins with a tremendous dissatisfaction with the present state of things, with our lives, and a hatred, an intense hatred, for this patching up of life, an unbounded disgust for fraud and lies. He alone can be religious who dares say, as the mighty Buddha once said under the Bo-tree, when this idea of practicality appeared before him and he saw that it was nonsense, and yet could not find a way out. When the temptation came to him to give up his search after truth, to go back to the world and live the old life of fraud, calling things by wrong names, telling lies to oneself and to everybody, he, the giant, conquered it and said, "Death is better than a vegetating ignorant life; it is better to die on the battle-field than to live a life of defeat." This is the basis of religion. When a man takes this stand, he is on the way to find the truth, he is on the way to God. That determination must be the first impulse towards becoming religious. I will hew out a way for myself. I will know the truth or give up my life in the attempt. For on this side it is nothing, it is gone, it is vanishing every day. The beautiful, hopeful, young person of today is the veteran of tomorrow. Hopes and joys and pleasures will die like blossoms with tomorrow's frost. That is one side; on the other, there are the great charms of conquest, victories over all the ills of life, victory over life itself, the conquest of the universe. On that side men can stand. Those who dare, therefore, to struggle for victory, for truth, for religion, are in the right way; and that is what the Vedas preach: Be not in despair, the way is very difficult, like walking on the edge of a razor; yet despair not, arise, awake, and find the ideal, the goal.

Now all these various manifestations of religion, in whatever shape and form they have come to mankind, have this one common central basis. It is the preaching of freedom, the way out of this world. They never came to reconcile the world and religion, but to cut the Gordian knot, to establish religion in its own ideal, and not to compromise with the world. That is what every religion preaches, and the duty of the Vedanta is to harmonise all these aspirations, to make manifest the common ground between all the religions of the world, the highest as well as the lowest. What we call the most arrant superstition and the highest philosophy really have a common aim in that they both try to show the way out of the same difficulty, and in most cases this way is through the help of someone who is not himself bound by the laws of nature in one word, someone who is free. In spite of all the difficulties and differences of opinion about the nature of the one free agent, whether he is a Personal God, or a sentient being like man, whether masculine, feminine, or neuter — and the discussions have been endless — the fundamental idea is the same. In spite of the almost hopeless contradictions of the different systems, we find the golden thread of unity running through them all, and in this philosophy, this golden thread has been traced revealed little by little to our view, and the first step to this revelation is the common ground that all are advancing towards freedom.

One curious fact present in the midst of all our joys and sorrows, difficulties and struggles, is that we are surely journeying towards freedom. The question was practically this: "What is this universe? From what does it arise? Into what does it go?" And the answer was: "In freedom it rises, in freedom it rests, and into freedom it melts away." This idea of freedom you cannot relinquish. Your actions, your very lives will be lost without it. Every moment nature is proving us to be slaves and not free. Yet, simultaneously rises the other idea, that still we are free At every step we are knocked down, as it were, by Maya, and shown that we are bound; and yet at the same moment, together with this blow, together with this feeling that we are bound, comes the other feeling that we are free. Some inner voice tells us that we are free. But if we attempt to realise that freedom, to make it manifest, we find the difficulties almost insuperable Yet, in spite of that it insists on asserting itself inwardly, "I am free, I am free." And if you study all the various religions of the world you will find this idea expressed. Not only religion — you must not take this word in its narrow sense — but the whole life of society is the assertion of that one principle of freedom. All movements are the assertion of that one freedom. That voice has been heard by everyone, whether he knows it or not, that voice which declares, "Come unto Me all ye that labour and are heavy laden." It may not be in the same language or the same form of speech, but in some form or other, that voice calling for freedom has been with us. Yes, we are born here on account of that voice; every one of our movements is for that. We are all rushing towards freedom, we are all following that voice, whether we know it or not; as the children of the village were attracted by the music of the flute-player, so we are all following the music of the voice without knowing it.

We are ethical when we follow that voice. Not only the human soul, but all creatures, from the lowest to the highest have heard the voice and are rushing towards it; and in the struggle are either combining with each other or pushing each other out of the way. Thus come competition, joys, struggles, life, pleasure, and death, and the whole universe is nothing but the result of this mad struggle to reach the voice. This is the manifestation of nature.

What happens then? The scene begins to shift. As soon as you know the voice and understand what it is, the whole scene changes. The same world which was the ghastly battle-field of Maya is now changed into something good and beautiful. We no longer curse nature, nor say that the world is horrible and that it is all vain; we need no longer weep and wail. As soon as we understand the voice, we see the reassert why this struggle should be here, this fight, this competition, this difficulty, this cruelty, these little pleasures and joys; we see that they are in the nature of things, because without them there would be no going towards the voice, to attain which we are destined, whether we know it or not. All human life, all nature, therefore, is struggling to attain to freedom. The sun is moving towards the goal, so is the earth in circling round the sun, so is the moon in circling round the earth. To that goal the planet is moving, and the air is blowing. Everything is struggling towards that. The saint is going towards that voice — he cannot help it, it is no glory to him. So is the sinner. The charitable man is going straight towards that voice, and cannot be hindered; the miser is also going towards the same destination: the greatest worker of good hears the same voice within, and he cannot resist it, he must go towards the voice; so with the most arrant idler. One stumbles more than another, and him who stumbles more we call bad, him who stumbles less we call good. Good and bad are never two different things, they are one and the same; the difference is not one of kind, but of degree.

Now, if the manifestation of this power of freedom is really governing the whole universe — applying that to religion, our special study — we find this idea has been the one assertion throughout. Take the lowest form of religion where there is the worship of departed ancestors or certain powerful and cruel gods; what is the prominent idea about the gods or departed ancestors? That they are superior to nature, not bound by its restrictions. The worshipper has, no doubt, very limited ideas of nature. He himself cannot pass through a wall, nor fly up into the skies, but the gods whom he worships can do these things. What is meant by that, philosophically? That the assertion of freedom is there, that the gods whom he worships are superior to nature as he knows it. So with those who worship still higher beings. As the idea of nature expands, the idea of the soul which is superior to nature also expands, until we come to what we call monotheism, which holds that there is Maya (nature), and that there is some Being who is the Ruler of this Maya.

Here Vedanta begins, where these monotheistic ideas first appear. But the Vedanta philosophy wants further explanation. This explanation — that there is a Being beyond all these manifestations of Maya, who is superior to and independent of Maya, and who is attracting us towards Himself, and that we are all going towards Him — is very good, says the Vedanta, but yet the perception is not clear, the vision is dim and hazy, although it does not directly contradict reason. Just as in your hymn it is said, "Nearer my God to Thee," the same hymn would be very good to the Vedantin, only he would change a word, and make it, "Nearer my God to me." The idea that the goal is far off, far beyond nature, attracting us all towards it, has to be brought nearer and nearer, without degrading or degenerating it. The God of heaven becomes the God in nature, and the God in nature becomes the God who is nature, and the God who is nature becomes the God within this temple of the body, and the God dwelling in the temple of the body at last becomes the temple itself, becomes the soul and man — and there it reaches the last words it can teach. He whom the sages have been seeking in all these places is in our own hearts; the voice that you heard was right, says the Vedanta, but the direction you gave to the voice was wrong. That ideal of freedom that you perceived was correct, but you projected it outside yourself, and that was your mistake. Bring it nearer and nearer, until you find that it was all the time within you, it was the Self of your own self. That freedom was your own nature, and this Maya never bound you. Nature never has power over you. Like a frightened child you were dreaming that it was throttling you, and the release from this fear is the goal: not only to see it intellectually, but to perceive it, actualise it, much more definitely than we perceive this world.

Then we shall know that we are free. Then, and then alone, will all difficulties vanish, then will all the perplexities of heart be smoothed away, all crookedness made straight, then will vanish the delusion of manifoldness and nature; and Maya instead of being a horrible, hopeless dream, as it is now will become beautiful, and this earth, instead of being a prison-house, will become our playground, and even dangers and difficulties, even all sufferings, will become deified and show us their real nature, will show us that behind everything, as the substance of everything, He is standing, and that He is the one real Self.

CHAPTER VI
THE ABSOLUTE AND MANIFESTATION

Delivered in London, 1896

The one question that is most difficult to grasp in understanding the Advaita philosophy, and the one question that will be asked again and again and that will always remain is: How has the Infinite, the Absolute, become the finite? I will now take up this question, and, in order to illustrate it, I will use a figure.

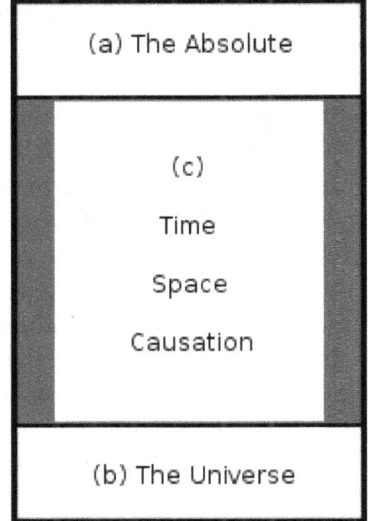

Here is the Absolute (a), and this is the universe (b). The Absolute has become the universe. By this is not only meant the material world, but the mental world, the spiritual world — heavens and earths, and in fact, everything that exists. Mind is the name of a change, and body the name of another change, and so on, and all these changes compose our universe. This Absolute (a) has become the universe (b) by coming through time, space, and causation (c). This is the central idea of Advaita. Time, space, and causation are like the glass through which the Absolute is seen, and when It is seen on the lower side, It appears as the universe. Now we at once gather from this that in the Absolute there is neither time, space, nor causation. The idea of time cannot be there, seeing that there is no mind, no thought. The idea of space cannot be there, seeing that there is no external change. What you call motion and causation cannot exist where there is only One. We have to understand this, and impress it on our minds, that what we call causation begins after, if we may be permitted to say so, the degeneration of the Absolute into the phenomenal, and not before; that our will, our desire and all these things always come after that. I think Schopenhauer's philosophy makes a mistake in its interpretation of Vedanta, for it seeks to make the will everything. Schopenhauer makes the will stand in the place of the Absolute. But the absolute cannot be presented as will, for will is something changeable and phenomenal, and over the line, drawn above time, space, and causation, there is no change, no motion; it is only below the line that external motion and internal motion, called thought begin. There can be no will on the other side, and will therefore, cannot be the cause of this universe. Coming nearer, we see in our own bodies that will is not the cause of every movement. I move this chair; my will is the cause of this movement, and this will becomes manifested as muscular motion at the other end. But the same power that moves the chair is moving the heart, the lungs, and so on, but not through will. Given that the power is the same, it only becomes will when it rises to the plane of consciousness, and to call it will before it has risen to this plane is a misnomer. This makes a good deal of confusion in Schopenhauer's philosophy.

A stone falls and we ask, why? This question is possible only on the supposition that nothing happens without a cause. I request you to make this very clear in your minds, for whenever we ask why anything happens, we are taking for granted that everything that happens must have a why, that is to say, it must have been preceded by something else which acted as the cause. This precedence and succession are what we call the law of causation. It means that everything in the universe is by turn a cause and an effect. It is the cause of certain things which come after it, and is itself the effect of something else which has preceded it. This is called the law of causation and is a necessary condition of all our thinking. We believe that every particle in the universe, whatever it be, is in relation to every other particle. There has been much discussion as to how this idea arose. In Europe, there have been intuitive philosophers who believed that it was constitutional in humanity, others have believed it came from experience, but the question has never been settled. We shall see later on what the Vedanta has to say about it. But first we have to understand this that the very asking of the question "why" presupposes that everything round us has been preceded by certain things and will be succeeded by certain other things. The other belief involved in this question is that nothing in the universe is independent, that everything is acted upon by something outside itself. Interdependence is the law of the whole universe. In asking what caused the Absolute, what an error we are making! To ask this question we have to suppose that the Absolute also is bound by something, that It is dependent on something; and in making this supposition, we drag the Absolute down to the level of the universe. For in the Absolute there is neither time, space, nor causation; It is all one. That which exists by itself alone cannot have any cause. That which is free cannot have any cause; else it would not be free, but bound. That which has relativity cannot be free. Thus we see the very question, why the Infinite became the finite, is an impossible one, for it is self-contradictory. Coming from subtleties to the logic of our common plane, to common sense, we can see this from another side, when we seek to know how the Absolute has become the relative. Supposing we knew the answer, would the Absolute remain the Absolute? It would have become relative. What is meant by knowledge in our common-sense idea? It is only something that has become limited by our mind, that we know, and when it is beyond our mind, it is not knowledge. Now if the Absolute becomes limited by the mind, It is no more Absolute; It has become finite. Everything limited by the mind becomes finite. Therefore to know the Absolute is again a contradiction in terms. That is why this question has never been answered, because if it were answered, there would no more be an Absolute. A God known is no more God; He has become finite like one of us. He cannot be known He is always the Unknowable One.

But what Advaita says is that God is more than knowable. This is a great fact to learn. You must not go home with the idea that God is unknowable in the sense in which agnostics put it. For instance, here is a chair, it is known to us. But what is beyond ether or whether people exist there or not is possibly unknowable. But God is neither known nor unknowable in this sense. He is something still higher than known; that is what is meant by God being unknown and unknowable. The expression is not used in the sense in which it may be said that some questions are unknown ant unknowable. God is more than known. This chair is known, but God is intensely more than that because in and through Him we have to know this chair itself. He is the Witness, the eternal Witness of all knowledge. Whatever we know we have to know in and through Him. He is the Essence of our own Self. He is the Essence of this ego, this I and we cannot know anything excepting in and through that I. Therefore you have to know everything in and through the Brahman. To know the chair you have to know it in and through God. Thus God is infinitely nearer to us than the chair, but yet He is infinitely higher. Neither known, nor unknown, but something infinitely higher than either. He is your Self. "Who would live a second, who would breathe a second in this universe, if that Blessed One were not filling it?" Because in and through Him we breathe, in and through Him we exist. Not the He is standing somewhere and making my blood circulate. What is meant is that He is the Essence of all this, the Soul of my soul. You cannot by any possibility say you know Him; it would be degrading Him. You cannot get out of yourself, so you cannot know Him. Knowledge is objectification. For instance, in memory you are objectifying many things, projecting them out of yourself. All memory, all the things which I have seen and which I know are in my mind. The pictures, the impressions of all these things, are in my mind, and when I would try to think of them, to know them, the first act of knowledge would be to project them outside. This cannot be done with God, because He is the Essence of our souls, we cannot project Him outside ourselves. Here is one of the profoundest passages in Vedanta: "He that is the Essence of your soul, He is the Truth, He is the Self, thou art That, O Shvetaketu." This is what is meant by "Thou art God." You cannot describe Him by any other language. All attempts of language, calling Him father, or brother, or our dearest friend, are attempts to objectify God, which cannot be done. He is the Eternal Subject of everything. I am the subject of this chair; I see the chair; so God is the Eternal Subject of my soul. How can you objectify Him, the Essence of your souls, the Reality of everything? Thus, I would repeat to you once more, God is neither knowable nor unknowable, but something infinitely higher than either. He is one with us, and that which is one with us is neither knowable nor unknowable, as our own self. You cannot know your own self; you cannot move it out and make it an object to look at, because you are that and cannot separate yourself from it. Neither is it unknowable, for what is better known than yourself? It is really the centre of our knowledge. In exactly the same sense, God is neither unknowable nor known, but infinitely higher than both; for He is our real Self.

First, we see then that the question, "What caused the Absolute?" is a contradiction in terms; and secondly, we find that the idea of God in the Advaita is this Oneness; and, therefore, we cannot objectify Him, for we are always living and moving in Him, whether we know it or not. Whatever we do is always through Him. Now the question is: What are time, space, and causation? Advaita means non-duality; there are no two, but one. Yet we see that here is a proposition that the Absolute is manifesting Itself as many, through the veil of time, space, and causation. Therefore it seems that here are two, the Absolute and Mâyâ (the sum total of time, space, and causation). It seems apparently very convincing that there are two. To this the Advaitist replies that it cannot be called two. To have two, we must have two absolute independent existences which cannot be caused. In the first place time, space, and causation cannot be said to be independent existences. Time is entirely a dependent existence; it changes with every change of our mind. Sometimes in dream one imagines that one has lived several years, at other times several months were passed as one second. So, time is entirely dependent on our state of mind. Secondly, the idea of time vanishes altogether, sometimes. So with space. We cannot know what space is. Yet it is there, indefinable, and cannot exist separate from anything else. So with causation.

The one peculiar attribute we find in time, space, and causation is that they cannot exist separate from other things. Try to think of space without colour, or limits, or any connection with the things around — just abstract space. You cannot; you have to think of it as the space between two limits or between three objects. It has to be connected with some object to have any existence. So with time; you cannot have any idea of abstract time, but you have to take two events, one preceding and the other succeeding, and join the two events by the idea of succession. Time depends on two events, just as space has to be related to outside objects. And the idea of causation is inseparable from time and space. This is the peculiar thing about them that they have no independent existence. They have not even the existence which the chair or the wall has. They are as shadows around everything which you cannot catch. They have no real existence; yet they are not non-existent, seeing that through them all things are manifesting as this universe. Thus we see, first, that the combination of time, space, and causation has neither existence nor non-existence. Secondly, it sometimes vanishes. To give an illustration, there is a wave on the ocean. The wave is the same as the ocean certainly, and yet we know it is a wave, and as such different from the ocean. What makes this difference? The name and the form, that is, the idea in the mind and the form. Now, can we think of a wave-form as something separate from the ocean? Certainly not. It is always associated with the ocean idea. If the wave subsides, the form vanishes in a moment, and yet the form was not a delusion. So long as the wave existed the form was there, and you were bound to see the form. This is Maya.

The whole of this universe, therefore, is, as it were, a peculiar form; the Absolute is that ocean while you and I, and suns and stars, and everything else are various waves of that ocean. And what makes the waves different? Only the form, and that form is time, space, and causation, all entirely dependent on the wave. As soon as the wave goes, they vanish. As soon as the individual gives up this Maya, it vanishes for him and he becomes free. The whole struggle is to get rid of this clinging on to time, space, and causation, which are always obstacles in our way. What is the theory of evolution? What are the two factors? A tremendous potential power which is trying to express itself, and circumstances which are holding it down, the environments not allowing it to express itself. So, in order to fight with these environments, the power is taking new bodies again and again. An amoeba, in the struggle, gets another body and conquers some obstacles, then gets another body and so on, until it becomes man. Now, if you carry this idea to its logical conclusion, there must come a time when that power that was in the amoeba and which evolved as man will have conquered all the obstructions that nature can bring before it and will thus escape from all its environments. This idea expressed in metaphysics will take this form; there are two components in every action, the one the subject, the other the object and the one aim of life is to make the subject master of the object. For instance, I feel unhappy because a man scolds me. My struggle will be to make myself strong enough to conquer the environment, so that he may scold and I shall not feel. That is how we are all trying to conquer. What is meant by morality? Making the subject strong by attuning it to the Absolute, so that finite nature ceases to have control over us. It is a logical conclusion of our philosophy that there must come a time when we shall have conquered all the environments, because nature is finite.

Here is another thing to learn. How do you know that nature is finite? You can only know this through metaphysics. Nature is that Infinite under limitations. Therefore it is finite. So, there must come a time when we shall have conquered all environments. And how are we to conquer them? We cannot possibly conquer all the objective environments. We cannot. The little fish wants to fly from its enemies in the water. How does it do so? By evolving wings and becoming a bird. The fish did not change the water or the air; the change was in itself. Change is always subjective. All through evolution you find that the conquest of nature comes by change in the subject. Apply this to religion and morality, and you will find that the conquest of evil comes by the change in the subjective alone. That is how the Advaita system gets its whole force, on the subjective side of man. To talk of evil and misery is nonsense, because they do not exist outside. If I am immune against all anger, I never feel angry. If I am proof against all hatred, I never feel hatred.

This is, therefore, the process by which to achieve that conquest — through the subjective, by perfecting the subjective. I may make bold to say that the only religion which agrees with, and even goes a little further than modern researches, both on physical and moral lines is the Advaita, and that is why it appeals to modern scientists so much. They find that the old dualistic theories are not enough for them, do not satisfy their necessities. A man must have not only faith, but intellectual faith too. Now, in this later part of the nineteenth century, such an idea as that religion coming from any other source than one's own hereditary religion must be false shows that there is still weakness left, and such

ideas must be given up. I do not mean that such is the case in this country alone, it is in every country, and nowhere more than in my own. This Advaita was never allowed to come to the people. At first some monks got hold of it and took it to the forests, and so it came to be called the "Forest Philosophy". By the mercy of the Lord, the Buddha came and preached it to the masses, and the whole nation became Buddhists. Long after that, when atheists and agnostics had destroyed the nation again, it was found out that Advaita was the only way to save India from materialism.

Thus has Advaita twice saved India from materialism Before the Buddha came, materialism had spread to a fearful extent, and it was of a most hideous kind, not like that of the present day, but of a far worse nature. I am a materialist in a certain sense, because I believe that there is only One. That is what the materialist wants you to believe; only he calls it matter and I call it God. The materialists admit that out of this matter all hope, and religion, and everything have come. I say, all these have come out of Brahman. But the materialism that prevailed before Buddha was that crude sort of materialism which taught, "Eat, drink, and be merry; there is no God, soul or heaven; religion is a concoction of wicked priests." It taught the morality that so long as you live, you must try to live happily; eat, though you have to borrow money for the food, and never mind about repaying it. That was the old materialism, and that kind of philosophy spread so much that even today it has got the name of "popular philosophy". Buddha brought the Vedanta to light, gave it to the people, and saved India. A thousand years after his death a similar state of things again prevailed. The mobs, the masses, and various races, had been converted to Buddhism; naturally the teachings of the Buddha became in time degenerated, because most of the people were very ignorant. Buddhism taught no God, no Ruler of the universe, so gradually the masses brought their gods, and devils, and hobgoblins out again, and a tremendous hotchpotch was made of Buddhism in India. Again materialism came to the fore, taking the form of licence with the higher classes and superstition with the lower. Then Shankaracharya arose and once more revivified the Vedanta philosophy. He made it a rationalistic philosophy. In the Upanishads the arguments are often very obscure. By Buddha the moral side of the philosophy was laid stress upon, and by Shankaracharya, the intellectual side. He worked out, rationalised, and placed before men the wonderful coherent system of Advaita.

Materialism prevails in Europe today. You may pray for the salvation of the modern sceptics, but they do not yield, they want reason. The salvation of Europe depends on a rationalistic religion, and Advaita — the non-duality, the Oneness, the idea of the Impersonal God — is the only religion that can have any hold on any intellectual people. It comes whenever religion seems to disappear and irreligion seems to prevail, and that is why it has taken ground in Europe and America.

I would say one thing more in connection with this philosophy. In the old Upanishads we find sublime poetry; their authors were poets. Plato says, inspiration comes to people through poetry, and it seems as if these ancient Rishis, seers of Truth, were raised above humanity to show these truths through poetry. They never preached, nor philosophised, nor wrote. Music came out of their hearts. In Buddha we had the great, universal heart and infinite patience, making religion practical and bringing it to everyone's door. In Shankaracharya we saw tremendous intellectual power, throwing the scorching light of reason upon everything. We want today that bright sun of intellectuality joined with the heart of Buddha, the wonderful infinite heart of love and mercy. This union will give us the highest philosophy. Science and religion will meet and shake hands. Poetry and philosophy will become friends. This will be the religion of the future, and if we can work it out, we may be sure that it will be for all times and peoples. This is the one way that will prove acceptable to modern science, for it has almost come to it. When the scientific teacher asserts that all things are the manifestation of one force, does it not remind you of the God of whom you hear in the Upanishads: "As the one fire entering into the universe expresses itself in various forms, even so that One Soul is expressing Itself in every soul and yet is infinitely more besides?" Do you not see whither science is tending? The Hindu nation proceeded through the study of the mind, through metaphysics and logic. The European nations start from external nature, and now they too are coming to the same results. We find that searching through the mind we at last come to that Oneness, that Universal One, the Internal Soul of everything, the Essence and Reality of everything, the Ever-Free, the Ever-blissful, the Ever-Existing. Through material science we come to the same Oneness. Science today is telling us that all things are but the manifestation of one energy which is the sum total of everything which exists, and the trend of humanity is towards freedom and not towards bondage. Why should men be moral? Because through morality is the path towards freedom, and immorality leads to bondage.

Another peculiarity of the Advaita system is that from its very start it is non-destructive. This is another glory, the boldness to preach, "Do not disturb the faith of any, even of those who through ignorance have attached themselves to lower forms of worship." That is what it says, do not disturb, but help everyone to get higher and higher; include all humanity. This philosophy preaches a God who is a sum total. If you seek a universal religion which can apply to everyone, that religion must not be composed of only the parts, but it must always be their sum total and include all degrees of religious development.

This idea is not clearly found in any other religious system. They are all parts equally struggling to attain to the whole. The existence of the part is only for this. So, from the very first, Advaita had no antagonism with the various sects existing in India. There are dualists existing today, and their number is by far the largest in India, because dualism naturally appeals to less educated minds. It is a very convenient, natural, common-sense explanation of the universe. But with these dualists, Advaita has no quarrel. The one thinks that God is outside the universe, somewhere in heaven, and the other, that He is his own Soul, and that it will be a blasphemy to call Him anything more distant. Any idea of separation would be terrible. He is the nearest of the near. There is no word in any language to express this nearness except the word Oneness. With any other idea the Advaitist is not satisfied just as the dualist is shocked with the concept of the Advaita, and thinks it blasphemous. At the same time the Advaitist knows that these other ideas must be, and so has no quarrel with the dualist who is on the right road. From his standpoint, the dualist will have to see many. It is a constitutional necessity of his standpoint. Let him have it. The Advaitist knows that whatever may be his theories, he is going to the same goal as he himself. There he differs entirely from dualist who is forced by his point of view to believe that all differing views are wrong. The dualists all the world over naturally believe in a Personal God who is purely anthropomorphic, who like a great potentate in this world is pleased with some and displeased with others. He is arbitrarily pleased with some people or races and showers blessing upon them. Naturally the dualist comes to the conclusion that God has favourites, and he hopes to be one of them. You will find that in almost every religion is the idea: "We are the favourites of our God, and only by believing as we do, can you be taken into favour with Him." Some dualists are so narrow as to insist that only the few that have been predestined to the favour of God can be saved; the rest may try ever so hard, but they cannot be accepted. I challenge you to show me one dualistic religion which has not more or less of this exclusiveness. And, therefore, in the nature of things, dualistic religions are bound to fight and quarrel with each other, and this they have ever been doing. Again, these dualists win the popular favour by appealing to the vanity of the uneducated. They like to feel that they enjoy exclusive privileges. The dualist thinks you cannot be moral until you have a God with a rod in His hand, ready to punish you. The unthinking masses are generally dualists, and they, poor fellows, have been persecuted for thousands of years in every country; and their idea of salvation is, therefore, freedom from the fear of punishment. I was asked by a clergyman in America, "What! you have no Devil in your religion? How can that be?"

But we find that the best and the greatest men that have been born in the world have worked with that high impersonal idea. It is the Man who said, "I and my Father are One", whose power has descended unto millions. For thousands of years it has worked for good. And we know that the same Man, because he was a nondualist, was merciful to others. To the masses who could not conceive of anything higher than a Personal God, he said, "Pray to your Father in heaven." To others who could grasp a higher idea, he said, "I am the vine, ye are the branches," but to his disciples to whom he revealed himself more fully, he proclaimed the highest truth, "I and my Father are One."

It was the great Buddha, who never cared for the dualist gods, and who has been called an atheist and materialist, who yet was ready to give up his body for a poor goat. That Man set in motion the highest moral ideas any nation can have. Whenever there is a moral code, it is ray of light from that Man. We cannot force the great hearts of the world into narrow limits, and keep them there, especially at this time in the history of humanity when there is a degree of intellectual development such as was never dreamed of even a hundred years ago, when a wave of scientific knowledge has arisen which nobody, even fifty years ago, would have dreamed of. By trying to force people into narrow limits you degrade them into animals and unthinking masses. You kill their moral life. What is now wanted is a combination of the greatest heart with the highest intellectuality, of infinite love with infinite knowledge. The Vedantist gives no other attributes to God except these three — that He is Infinite Existence, Infinite Knowledge, and Infinite Bliss, and he regards these three as One. Existence without knowledge and love cannot be; knowledge without love and love without knowledge cannot be. What we want is the harmony of Existence, Knowledge, and Bliss Infinite. For that is our goal. We want harmony, not one-sided development. And it is possible to have the intellect of a Shankara with the heart of a Buddha. I hope we shall all struggle to attain to that blessed combination.

CHAPTER VII
GOD IN EVERYTHING

Delivered in London, 27th October 1896

We have seen how the greater portion of our life must of necessity be filled with evils, however we may resist, and that this mass of evil is practically almost infinite for us. We have been struggling to remedy this since the beginning of time, yet everything remains very much the same. The more we discover remedies, the more we find ourselves beset by subtler evils. We have also seen that all religions propose a God, as the one way of escaping these difficulties. All religions tell us that if you take the world as it is, as most practical people would advise us to do in this age, then nothing would be left to us but evil. They further assert that there is something beyond this world. This life in the five senses, life in the material world, is not all; it is only a small portion, and merely superficial. Behind and beyond is the Infinite in which there is no more evil. Some people call It God, some Allah, some Jehovah, Jove, and so on. The Vedantin calls It Brahman.

The first impression we get of the advice given by religions is that we had better terminate our existence. To the question how to cure the evils of life, the answer apparently is, give up life. It reminds one of the old story. A mosquito settled on the head of a man, and a friend, wishing to kill the mosquito, gave it such a blow that he killed both man and mosquito. The remedy of evil seems to suggest a similar course of action. Life is full of ills, the world is full of evils; that is a fact no one who is old enough to know the world can deny.

But what is remedy proposed by all the religions? That this world is nothing. Beyond this world is something which is very real. Here comes the difficulty. The remedy seems to destroy everything. How can that be a remedy? Is there no way out then? The Vedanta says that what all the religions advance is perfectly true, but it should be properly understood. Often it is misunderstood, because the religions are not very clear in their meaning. What we really want is head and heart combined. The heart is great indeed; it is through the heart that come the great inspirations of life. I would a hundred times rather have a little heart and no brain, than be all brains and no heart. Life is possible, progress is possible for him who has heart, but he who has no heart and only brains dies of dryness.

At the same time we know that he who is carried along by his heart alone has to undergo many ills, for now and then he is liable to tumble into pitfalls. The combination of heart and head is what we want. I do not mean that a man should compromise his heart for his brain or vice versa, but let everyone have an infinite amount of heart and feeling, and at the same time an infinite amount of reason. Is there any limit to what we want in this world? Is not the world infinite? There is room for an infinite amount of feeling, and so also for an infinite amount of culture and reason. Let them come together without limit, let them be running together, as it were, in parallel lines each with the other.

Most of the religions understand the fact, but the error into which they all seem to fall is the same; they are carried away by the heart, the feelings. There is evil in the world, give up the world; that is the great teaching, and the only teaching, no doubt. Give up the world. There cannot be two opinions that to understand the truth everyone of us has to give up error. There cannot be two opinions that everyone of us in order to have good must give up evil; there cannot be two opinions that everyone of us to have life must give up what is death.

And yet, what remains to us, if this theory involves giving up the life of the senses, the life as we know it? And what else do we mean by life? If we give this up, what remains?

We shall understand this better, when, later on, we come to the more philosophical portions of the Vedanta. But for the present I beg to state that in Vedanta alone we find a rational solution of the problem. Here I can only lay before you what the Vedanta seeks to teach, and that is the deification of the world. The Vedanta does not in reality denounce the world. The ideal of renunciation nowhere attains such a height as in the teachings of the Vedanta. But, at the same time, dry suicidal advice is not intended; it really means deification of the world — giving up the world as we think of it, as we know it, as it appears to us — and to know what it really is. Deify it; it is God alone. We read at the commencement of one of the oldest of the Upanishads, "Whatever exists in this universe is to be covered with the Lord."

We have to cover everything with the Lord Himself, not by a false sort of optimism, not by blinding our eyes to the evil, but by really seeing God in everything. Thus we have to give up the world, and when the world is given up, what remains? God. What is meant? You can have your wife; it does not mean that you are to abandon her, but that you are to see God in the wife. Give up your children; what does that mean? To turn them out of doors, as some human brutes do in every country? Certainly not. That is diabolism; it is not religion. But see God in your children. So, in everything. In life and in death, in happiness and in misery, the Lord is equally present. The whole world is full of the Lord. Open your eyes and see Him. This is what Vedanta teaches. Give up the world which you have conjectured, because your conjecture was based upon a very partial experience, upon very poor reasoning, and upon your own weakness. Give it up; the world we have been thinking of so long, the world to which we have been clinging so long, is a false world of our own creation. Give that up; open your eyes and see that as such it never existed; it was a dream, Maya. What existed was the Lord Himself. It is He who is in the child, in the wife, and in the husband; it is He who is in the good and in the bad; He is in the sin and in the sinner; He is in life and in death.

A tremendous assertion indeed! Yet that is the theme which the Vedanta wants to demonstrate, to teach, and to preach. This is just the opening theme.

Thus we avoid the dangers of life and its evils. Do not desire anything. What makes us miserable? The cause of all miseries from which we suffer is desire. You desire something, and the desire is not fulfilled; the result is distress. If there is no desire, there is no suffering. But here, too, there is the danger of my being misunderstood. So it is necessary to explain what I mean by giving up desire and becoming free from all misery. The walls have no desire and they never suffer. True, but they never evolve. This chair has no desires, it never suffers; but it is always a chair. There is a glory in happiness, there is a glory in suffering. If I may dare to say so, there is a utility in evil too. The great lesson in misery we all know. There are hundreds of things we have done in our lives which we wish we had never done, but which, at the same time, have been great teachers. As for me, I am glad I have done something good and many things bad; glad I have done something right, and glad I have committed many errors, because every one of them has been a great lesson. I, as I am now, am the resultant of all I have done, all I have thought. Every action and thought have had their effect, and these effects are the sum total of my progress.

We all understand that desires are wrong, but what is meant by giving up desires? How could life go on? It would be the same suicidal advice, killing the desire and the man too. The solution is this. Not that you should not have property, not that you should not have things which are necessary and things which are even luxuries. Have all that you want, and more, only know the truth and realise it. Wealth does not belong to anybody. Have no idea of proprietorship, possessorship. You are nobody, nor am I, nor anyone else. All belongs to the Lord, because the opening verse told us to put the Lord in everything. God is in the wealth that you enjoy. He is in the desire that rises in your mind. He is in the things you buy to satisfy your desire; He is in your beautiful attire, in your beautiful ornaments. This is the line of thought. All will be metamorphosed as soon as you begin to see things in that light. If you put God in your every movement, in your conversation, in your form, in everything, the whole scene changes, and the world, instead of appearing as one of woe and misery, will become a heaven.

"The kingdom of heaven is within you," says Jesus; so says the Vedanta, and every great teacher. "He that hath eyes to see, let him see, and he that hath ears to hear, let him hear." The Vedanta proves that the truth for which we have been searching all this time is present, and was all the time with us. In our ignorance, we thought we had lost it, and went about the world crying and weeping, struggling to find the truth, while all along it was dwelling in our own hearts. There alone can we find it.

If we understand the giving up of the world in its old, crude sense, then it would come to this: that we must not work, that we must be idle, sitting like lumps of earth, neither thinking nor doing anything, but must become fatalists, driven about by every circumstance, ordered about by the laws of nature, drifting from place to place. That would be the result. But that is not what is meant. We must work. Ordinary mankind, driven everywhere by false desire, what do they know of work? The man propelled by his own feelings and his own senses, what does he know about work? He works, who is not propelled by his own desires, by any selfishness whatsoever. He works, who has no ulterior motive in view. He works, who has nothing to gain from work.

Who enjoys the picture, the seller or the seer? The seller is busy with his accounts, computing what his gain will be, how much profit he will realise on the picture. His brain is full of that. He is looking at the hammer, and watching the bids. He is intent on hearing how fast the bids are rising. That man is enjoying the picture who has gone there without any intention of buying or selling. He looks at the picture and enjoys it. So this whole universe is a picture, and when these desires have vanished, men will enjoy the world, and then this buying and selling and these foolish ideas of possession will be ended. The money-lender gone, the buyer gone, the seller gone, this world remains the picture, a beautiful painting. I never read of any more beautiful conception of God than the following: "He is the Great Poet, the Ancient Poet; the whole universe is His poem, coming in verses and rhymes and rhythms, written in infinite bliss." When we have given up desires, then alone shall we be able to read and enjoy this universe of God. Then everything will become deified. Nooks and corners, by-ways and shady places, which we thought dark and unholy, will be all deified. They will all reveal their true nature, and we shall smile at ourselves and think that all this weeping and crying has been but child's play, and we were only standing by, watching.

So, do your work, says the Vedanta. It first advises us how to work — by giving up — giving up the apparent, illusive world. What is meant by that? Seeing God everywhere. Thus do you work. Desire to live a hundred years, have all earthly desires, if you wish, only deify them, convert them into heaven. Have the desire to live a long life of helpfulness, of blissfulness and activity on this earth. Thus working, you will find the way out. There is no other way. If a man plunges headlong into foolish luxuries of the world without knowing the truth, he has missed his footing, he cannot reach the goal. And if a man curses the world, goes into a forest, mortifies his flesh, and kills himself little by little by starvation, makes his heart a barren waste, kills out all feelings, and becomes harsh, stern, and dried-up, that man also has missed the way. These are the two extremes, the two mistakes at either end. Both have lost the way, both have missed the goal.

So work, says the Vedanta, putting God in everything, and knowing Him to be in everything. Work incessantly, holding life as something deified, as God Himself, and knowing that this is all we have to do, this is all we should ask for. God is in everything, where else shall we go to find Him? He is already in every work, in every thought, in every feeling. Thus knowing, we must work — this is the only way, there is no other. Thus the effects of work will not bind us. We have seen how false desires are the cause of all the misery and evil we suffer, but when they are thus deified, purified, through God, they bring no evil, they bring no misery. Those who have not learnt this secret will have to live in a demoniacal world until they discover it. Many do not know what an infinite mine of bliss is in them, around them, everywhere; they have not yet discovered it. What is a demoniacal world? The Vedanta says, ignorance.

We are dying of thirst sitting on the banks of the mightiest river. We are dying of hunger sitting near heaps of food. Here is the blissful universe, yet we do not find it. We are in it all the time, and we are always mistaking it. Religion proposes to find this out for us. The longing for this blissful universe is in all hearts. It has been the search of all nations, it is the one goal of religion, and this ideal is expressed in various languages in different religions. It is only the difference of language that makes all these apparent divergences. One expresses a thought in one way, another a little differently, yet perhaps each is meaning exactly what the other is expressing in a different language.

More questions arise in connection with this. It is very easy to talk. From my childhood I have heard of seeing God everywhere and in everything, and then I can really enjoy the world, but as soon as I mix with the world, and get a few blows from it, the idea vanishes. I am walking in the street thinking that God is in every man, and a strong man comes along and gives me a push and I fall flat on the footpath. Then I rise up quickly with clenched fist, the blood has rushed to my head, and the reflection goes. Immediately I have become mad. Everything is forgotten; instead of encountering God I see the devil. Ever since we were born we have been told to see God in all. Every religion teaches that — see God in everything and everywhere. Do you not remember in the New Testament how Christ says so? We have all been taught that; but it is when we come to the practical side, that the difficulty begins. You all remember how in Æsop's Fables a fine stag is looking at his form reflected in a lake and is saying to his young one, "How powerful I am, look at my splendid head, look at my limbs, how strong and muscular they are; and how swiftly I can run." In the meantime he hears the barking of dogs in the distance, and immediately takes to his heels, and after he has run several miles, he comes back panting. The young one says, "You just told me how strong you were, how was it that when the dog barked, you ran away?" "Yes, my son; but when the dogs bark all my confidence vanishes." Such is the case with us. We think highly of humanity, we feel ourselves strong and valiant, we make grand resolves; but when the "dogs" of trial and temptation bark, we are like the stag in the fable. Then, if such is the case, what is the use of teaching all these things? There is the greatest use. The use is this, that perseverance will finally conquer. Nothing can be done in a day.

"This Self is first to be heard, then to be thought upon, and then meditated upon." Everyone can see the sky, even the very worm crawling upon the earth sees the blue sky, but how very far away it is! So it is with our ideal. It is far away, no doubt, but at the same time, we know that we must have it. We must even have the highest ideal. Unfortunately in this life, the vast majority of persons are groping through this dark life without any ideal at all. If a man with an ideal makes a thousand mistakes, I am sure that the man without an ideal makes fifty thousand. Therefore, it is better to have an ideal. And this ideal we must hear about as much as we can, till it enters into our hearts, into our brains, into our very veins, until it tingles in every drop of our blood and permeates every pore in our body. We must meditate upon it. "Out of the fullness of the heart the mouth speaketh," and out of the fullness of the heart the hand works too.

It is thought which is the propelling force in us. Fill the mind with the highest thoughts, hear them day after day, think them month after month. Never mind failures; they are quite natural, they are the beauty of life, these failures. What would life be without them? It would not be worth having if it were not for struggles. Where would be the poetry of life? Never mind the struggles, the mistakes. I never heard a cow tell a lie, but it is only a cow — never a man. So never mind these failures, these little backslidings; hold the ideal a thousand times, and if you fail a thousand times, make the attempt once more. The ideal of man is to see God in everything. But if you cannot see Him in everything, see Him in one thing, in that thing which you like best, and then see Him in another. So on you can go. There is infinite life before the soul. Take your time and you will achieve your end.

"He, the One, who vibrates more quickly than mind, who attains to more speed than mind can ever do, whom even the gods reach not, nor thought grasps, He moving, everything moves. In Him all exists. He is moving. He is also immovable. He is near and He is far. He is inside everything. He is outside everything, interpenetrating everything. Whoever sees in every being that same Atman, and whoever sees everything in that Atman, he never goes far from that Atman. When all life and the whole universe are seen in this Atman, then alone man has attained the secret. There is no more delusion for him. Where is any more misery for him who sees this Oneness in the universe?"

This is another great theme of the Vedanta, this Oneness of life, this Oneness of everything. We shall see how it demonstrates that all our misery comes through ignorance, and this ignorance is the idea of manifoldness, this separation between man and man, between nation and nation, between earth and moon, between moon and sun. Out of this idea of separation between atom and atom comes all misery. But the Vedanta says this separation does not exist, it is not real. It is merely apparent, on the surface. In the heart of things there is Unity still. If you go below the surface, you find that Unity between man and man, between races and races, high and low, rich and poor, gods and men, and men and animals. If you go deep enough, all will be seen as only variations of the One, and he who has attained to this conception of Oneness has no more delusion. What can delude him? He knows the reality of everything, the secret of everything. Where is there any more misery for him? What does he desire? He has traced the reality of everything to the Lord, the Centre, the Unity of everything, and that is Eternal Existence, Eternal Knowledge, Eternal Bliss. Neither death nor disease, nor sorrow, nor misery, nor discontent is there. All is Perfect Union and Perfect Bliss. For whom should he mourn then? In the Reality, there is no death, there is no misery; in the Reality, there is no one to mourn for, no one to be sorry for. He has penetrated everything, the Pure One, the Formless, the Bodiless, the Stainless. He the Knower, He the Great Poet, the Self-Existent, He who is giving to everyone what he deserves. They grope in darkness who worship this ignorant world, the world that is produced out of ignorance, thinking of it as Existence, and those who live their whole lives in this world, and never find anything better or higher, are groping in still greater darkness. But he who knows the secret of nature, seeing That which is beyond nature through the help of nature, he crosses death, and through the help of That which is beyond nature, he enjoys Eternal Bliss. "Thou sun, who hast covered the Truth with thy golden disc, do thou remove the veil, so that I may see the Truth that is within thee. I have known the Truth that is within thee, I have known what is the real meaning of thy rays and thy glory and have seen That which shines in thee; the Truth in thee I see, and That which is within thee is within me, and I am That."

CHAPTER VIII
REALISATION

Delivered in London, 29th October 1896

I will read to you from one of the Upanishads. It is called the Katha Upanishad. Some of you, perhaps, have read the translation by Sir Edwin Arnold, called the Secret of Death. In our last [i.e. a previous] lecture we saw how the inquiry which started with the origin of the world, and the creation of the universe, failed to obtain a satisfactory answer from without, and how it then turned inwards. This book psychologically takes up that suggestion, questioning into the internal nature of man. It was first asked who created the external world, and how it came into being. Now the question is: What is that in man; which makes him live and move, and what becomes of that when he dies? The first philosophers studied the material substance, and tried to reach the ultimate through that. At the best, they found a personal governor of the universe, a human being immensely magnified, but yet to all intents and purposes a human being. But that could not be the whole of truth; at best, it could be only partial truth. We see this universe as human beings, and our God is our human explanation of the universe.

Suppose a cow were philosophical and had religion it would have a cow universe, and a cow solution of the problem, and it would not be possible that it should see our God. Suppose cats became philosophers, they would see a cat universe and have a cat solution of the problem of the universe, and a cat ruling it. So we see from this that our explanation of the universe is not the whole of the solution. Neither does our conception cover the whole of the universe. It would be a great mistake to accept that tremendously selfish position which man is apt to take. Such a solution of the universal problem as we can get from the outside labours under this difficulty that in the first place the universe we see is our own particular universe, our own view of the Reality. That Reality we cannot see through the senses; we cannot comprehend It. We only know the universe from the point of view of beings with five senses. Suppose we obtain another sense, the whole universe must change for us. Suppose we had a magnetic sense, it is quite possible that we might then find millions and millions of forces in existence which we do not now know, and for which we have no present sense or feeling. Our senses are limited, very limited indeed; and within these limitations exists what we call our universe; and our God is the solution of that universe, but that cannot be the solution of the whole problem. But man cannot stop there. He is a thinking being and wants to find a solution which will comprehensively explain all the universes. He wants to see a world which is at once the world of men, and of gods, and of all possible beings, and to find a solution which will explain all phenomena.

We see, we must first find the universe which includes all universes; we must find something which, by itself, must be the material running through all these various planes of existence, whether we apprehend it through the senses or not. If we could possibly find something which we could know as the common property of the lower as well as of the higher worlds, then our problem would be solved. Even if by the sheer force of logic alone we could understand that there must be one basis of all existence, then our problem might approach to some sort of solution; but this solution certainly cannot be obtained only through the world we see and know, because it is only a partial view of the whole.

Our only hope then lies in penetrating deeper. The early thinkers discovered that the farther they were from; the centre, the more marked were the variations and differentiations; and that the nearer they approached the centre, the nearer they were to unity. The nearer we are to the centre of a circle, the nearer we are to the common ground in which all the radii meet; and the farther we are from the centre, the more divergent is our radial line from the others. The external world is far away from the centre, and so there is no common ground in it where all the phenomena of existence can meet. At best, the external world is but one part of the whole of phenomena. There are other parts, the mental, the moral, and the intellectual — the various planes of existence — and to take up only one, and find a solution of the whole out of that one, is simply impossible. We first, therefore, want to find somewhere a centre from which, as it were, all the other planes of existence start, and standing there we should try to find a solution. That is the proposition. And where is that centre? It is within us. The ancient sages penetrated deeper and deeper until they found that in the innermost core of the human soul is the centre of the whole universe. All the planes gravitate towards that one point. That is the common ground, and standing there alone can we find a common solution. So the question who made this world is not very philosophical, nor does its solution amount to anything.

This the Katha Upanishad speaks in very figurative language. There was, in ancient times, a very rich man, who made a certain sacrifice which required that he should give away everything that he had. Now, this man was not sincere. He wanted to get the fame and glory of having made the sacrifice, but he was only giving things which were of no further use to him — old cows, barren, blind, and lame. He had a boy called Nachiketas. This boy saw that his father was not doing what was right, that he was breaking his vow; but he did not know what to say to him. In India, father and mother are living gods to their children. And so the boy approached the father with the greatest respect and humbly inquired of him, "Father, to whom are you going to give me? For your sacrifice requires that everything shall be given away." The father was very much vexed at this question and replied, "What do you mean, boy? A father giving away his own son?" The boy asked the question a second and a third time, and then the angry father answered, "Thee I give unto Death (Yama)." And the story goes on to say that the boy went to Yama, the god of death. Yama was the first man who died. He went to heaven and became the governor of all the Pitris; all the good people who die, go, and live with him for a long time. He is a very pure and holy person, chaste and good, as his name (Yama) implies.

So the boy went to Yama's world. But even gods are sometimes not at home, and three days this boy had to wait there. After the third day Yama returned. "O learned one," said Yama, "you have been waiting here for three days without food, and you are a guest worthy of respect. Salutation to thee, O Brahmin, and welfare to me! I am very sorry I was not at home. But for that I will make amends. Ask three boons, one for each day." And the boy asked, "My first boon is that my father's anger against me may pass away; that he will be kind to me and recognise me when you allow me to depart." Yama granted this fully. The next boon was that he wanted to know about a certain sacrifice which took people to heaven. Now we have seen that the oldest idea which we got in the Samhitâ portion of the Vedas was only about heaven where they had bright bodies and lived with the fathers. Gradually other ideas came, but they were not satisfying; there was still need for something higher. Living in heaven would not be very different from life in this world. At best, it would only be a very healthy rich man's life, with plenty of sense-enjoyments and a sound body which knows no disease. It would be this material world, only a little more refined; and we have seen the difficulty that the external material world can never solve the problem. So no heaven can solve the problem. If this world cannot solve the problem, no multiplication of this world can do so, because

we must always remember that matter is only an infinitesimal part of the phenomena of nature. The vast part of phenomena which we actually see is not matter. For instance, in every moment of our life what a great part is played by thought and feeling, compared with the material phenomena outside! How vast is this internal world with its tremendous activity! The sense-phenomena are very small compared with it. The heaven solution commits this mistake; it insists that the whole of phenomena is only in touch, taste, sight, etc. So this idea of heaven did not give full satisfaction to all. Yet Nachiketas asks, as the second boon, about some sacrifice through which people might attain to this heaven. There was an idea in the Vedas that these sacrifices pleased the gods and took human beings to heaven.

In studying all religions you will notice the fact that whatever is old becomes holy. For instance, our forefathers in India used to write on birch bark, but in time they learnt how to make paper. Yet the birch bark is still looked upon as very holy. When the utensils in which they used to cook in ancient times were improved upon, the old ones became holy; and nowhere is this idea more kept up than in India. Old methods, which must be nine or ten thousand years old, as of rubbing two sticks together to make fire, are still followed. At the time of sacrifice no other method will do. So with the other branch of the Asiatic Aryans. Their modern descendants still like to obtain fire from lightning, showing that they used to get fire in this way. Even when they learnt other customs, they kept up the old ones, which then became holy. So with the Hebrews. They used to write on parchment. They now write on paper, but parchment is very holy. So with all nations. Every rite which you now consider holy was simply an old custom, and the Vedic sacrifice were of this nature. In course of time, as they found better methods of life, their ideas were much improved; still these old forms remained, and from time to time they were practiced and received a holy significance.

Then, a body of men made it their business to carry on these sacrifices. These were the priests, who speculated on the sacrifices, and the sacrifices became everything to them. The gods came to enjoy the fragrance of the sacrifices, and it was considered that everything in this world could be got by the power of sacrifices. If certain oblations were made, certain hymns chanted, certain peculiar forms of altars made, the gods would grant everything. So Nachiketas asks by what form of sacrifice can a man go to heaven. The second boon was also readily granted by Yama who promised that this sacrifice should henceforth be named after Nachiketas.

Then the third boon comes, and with that the Upanishad proper begins. The boy said, "There is this difficulty: when a man dies some say he is, others that he is not. Instructed by you I desire to understand this." But Yama was frightened. He had been very glad to grant the other two boons. Now he said, "The gods in ancient times were puzzled on this point. This subtle law is not easy to understand. Choose some other boon, O Nachiketas, do not press me on this point, release me."

The boy was determined, and said, "What you have said is true, O Death, that even the gods had doubts on this point, and it is no easy matter to understand. But I cannot obtain another exponent like you and there is no other boon equal to this."

Death said, "Ask for sons and grandsons who will live one hundred years, many cattle, elephants, gold, and horses. Ask for empire on this earth and live as many ears as you like. Or choose any other boon which you think equal to these — wealth and long life. Or be thou a king, O Nachiketas, on the wide earth. I will make thee the enjoyer of all desires. Ask for all those desires which are difficult to obtain in the world. These heavenly maidens with chariots and music, which are not to be obtained by man, are yours. Let them serve you. O Nachiketas, but do not question me as to what comes after death."

Nachiketas said, "These are merely things of a day, O Death, they wear away the energy of all the sense-organs. Even the longest life is very short. These horses and chariots, dances and songs, may remain with Thee. Man cannot be satisfied by wealth. Can we retain wealth when we behold Thee? We shall live only so long as Thou desires". Only the boon which I have asked is chosen by me."

Yama was pleased with this answer and said, "Perfection is one thing and enjoyment another; these two having different ends, engage men differently. He who chooses perfection becomes pure. He who chooses enjoyment misses his true end. Both perfection and enjoyment present themselves to man; the wise man having examined both distinguishes one from the other. He chooses perfection as being superior to enjoyment, but the foolish man chooses enjoyment for the pleasure of his body. O Nachiketas, having thought upon the things which are only apparently desirable, thou hast wisely abandoned them." Death then proceeded to teach Nachiketas.

We now get a very developed idea of renunciation and Vedic morality, that until one has conquered the desires for enjoyment the truth will not shine in him. So long as these vain desires of our senses are clamouring and as it were dragging us outwards every moment, making us slaves to everything outside — to a little colour, a little taste, a little touch — notwithstanding all our pretensions, how can the truth express itself in our hearts?

Yama said, "That which is beyond never rises before the mind of a thoughtless child deluded by the folly of riches. 'This world exists, the other does not,' thinking thus they come again and again under my power. To understand this truth is very difficult. Many, even hearing it continually, do not understand it, for the speaker must be wonderful, so must be the hearer. The teacher must be wonderful, so must be the taught. Neither is the mind to be disturbed By vain arguments, for it is no more a question of argument, it is a question of fact." We have always heard that every religion insists on our having faith. We have been taught to believe blindly. Well, this idea of blind faith is objectionable, no doubt, but analysing it, we find that behind it is a very great truth. What it really means is what we read now. The mind is not to be ruffled by vain arguments, because argument will not help us to know God. It is a question of fact, and not of argument. All argument and reasoning must be based upon certain perceptions. Without these, there cannot be any argument. Reasoning is the method of comparison between certain facts which we have already perceived. If these perceived facts are not there already, there cannot be any reasoning. If this is true of external phenomena, why should it not be so of the internal? The chemist takes certain chemicals and certain results are produced. This is a fact; you see it, sense it, and make that the basis on which to build all your chemical arguments. So with the physicists, so with all other sciences. All knowledge must stand on perception of certain facts, and upon that we have to build our reasoning. But, curiously enough the vast majority of mankind think, especially at the present time, that no such perception is possible in religion, that religion can only be apprehended by vain arguments. Therefore we are told not to disturb the mind by vain arguments. Religion is a question of fact, not of talk. We have to analyse our own souls and to find what is there. We have to understand it and to realise what is understood. That is religion. No amount of talk will make religion. So the question whether there is a God or not can never be proved by argument, for the arguments are as much on one side as on the other. But if there is a God, He is in our own hearts. Have you ever seen Him? The question as to whether this world exists or not has not yet been decided, and the debate between the idealists and the realists is endless. Yet we know that the world exists, that it goes on. We only change the meaning of words. So, with all the questions of life, we must come to facts. There are certain religious facts which, as in external science, have to be perceived, and upon them religion will be built. Of course, the extreme claim that you must believe every dogma of a religion is degrading to the human mind. The man who asks you to believe everything, degrades himself, and, if you believe, degrades you too. The sages of the world have only the right to tell us that they have analysed their minds and have found these facts, and if we do the same we shall also believe, and not before. That is all that there is in religion. But you must always remember this, that as a matter of fact 99.9 per cent of those who attack religion have never analysed their minds, have never struggled to get at the facts. So their arguments do not have any weight against religion, any more than the words of a blind man who cries out, "You are all fools who believe in the sun," would affect us.

This is one great idea to learn and to hold on to, this idea of realisation. This turmoil and fight and difference in religions will cease only when we understand that religion is not in books and temples. It is an actual perception. Only the man who has actually perceived God and soul has religion. There is no real difference between the highest ecclesiastical giant who can talk by the volume, and the lowest, most ignorant materialist. We are all atheists; let us confess it. Mere intellectual assent does not make us religious. Take a Christian, or a Mohammedan, or a follower of any other religion in the world. Any man who truly realised the truth of the Sermon on the Mount would be perfect, and become a god immediately. Yet it is said that there are many millions of Christians in the world. What is meant is that mankind may at some time try to realise that Sermon. Not one in twenty millions is a real Christian.

So, in India, there are said to be three hundred millions of Vedantins. But if there were one in a thousand who had actually realised religion, this world would soon be greatly changed. We are all atheists, and yet we try to fight the man who admits it. We are all in the dark; religion is to us a mere intellectual assent, a mere talk, a mere nothing. We often consider a man religious who can talk well. But this is not religion. "Wonderful methods of joining words, rhetorical powers, and explaining texts of the books in various ways — these are only for the enjoyment of the learned, and not religion." Religion comes when that actual realisation in our own souls begins. That will be the dawn of religion; and then alone we shall be moral. Now we are not much more moral than the animals. We are only held down by the whips of society. If society said today, "I will not punish you if you steal", we should just make a rush for each other's property. It is the policeman that makes us moral. It is social opinion that makes us moral, and really we are little better than animals. We understand how much this is so in the secret of our own hearts. So let us not be hypocrites. Let us confess that we are not religious and have no right to look down on others. We are all brothers and we shall be truly moral when we have realised religion.

If you have seen a certain country, and a man forces you to say that you have not seen it, still in your heart of hearts you know you have. So, when you see religion and God in a more intense sense than you see this external world, nothing will be able to shake your belief. Then you have real faith. That is what is meant by the words in your Gospel, "He who has faith even as a grain of mustard seed." Then you will know the Truth because you have become the Truth.

This is the watchword of the Vedanta — realise religion, no talking will do. But it is done with great difficulty. He has hidden Himself inside the atom, this Ancient One who resides in the inmost recess of every human heart. The sages realised Him through the power of introspection, and got beyond both joy and misery, beyond what we call virtue and vice, beyond good and bad deeds, beyond being and non-being; he who has seen Him has seen the Reality. But what then about heaven? It was the idea of happiness minus unhappiness. That is to say, what we want is the joys of this life minus its sorrows. That is a very good idea, no doubt; it comes naturally; but it is a mistake throughout, because there is no such thing as absolute good, nor any such thing as absolute evil.

You have all heard of that rich man in Rome who learnt one day that he had only about a million pounds of his property left; he said, "What shall I do tomorrow?" and forthwith committed suicide. A million pounds was poverty to him. What is joy, and what is sorrow? It is a vanishing quantity, continually vanishing. When I was a child I thought if I could be a cabman, it would be the very acme of happiness for me to drive about. I do not think so now. To what joy will you cling? This is the one point we must all try to understand, and it is one of the last superstitions to leave us. Everyone's idea of pleasure is different. I have seen a man who is not happy unless he swallows a lump of opium every day. He may dream of a heaven where the land is made of opium. That would be a very bad heaven for me. Again and again in Arabian poetry we read of heaven with beautiful gardens, through which rivers run. I lived much of my life in a country where there is too much water; many villages are flooded and thousands of lives are sacrificed every year. So, my heaven would not have gardens through which rivers flow; I would have a land where very little rain falls. Our pleasures are always changing. If a young man dreams of heaven, he dreams of a heaven where he will have a beautiful wife. When that same man becomes old he does not want a wife. It is our necessities which make our heaven, and the heaven changes with the change of our necessities. If we had a heaven like that desired by those to whom sense-enjoyment is the very end of existence, then we would not progress. That would be the most terrible curse we could pronounce on the soul. Is this all we can come to? A little weeping and dancing, and then to die like a dog! What a curse you pronounce on the head of humanity when you long for these things! That is what you do when you cry after the joys of this world, for you do not know what true joy is. What philosophy insists on is not to give up joys, but to know what joy really is. The Norwegian heaven is a tremendous fighting place where they all sit before Odin; they have a wild boar hunt, and then they go to war and slash each other to pieces. But in some way or other, after a few hours of such fighting, the wounds are all healed up, and they go into a hall where the boar has been roasted, and have a carousal. And then the wild boar takes form again, ready to be hunted the next day. That is much the same thing as our heaven, not a whit worse, only our ideas may be a little more refined. We want to hunt wild boars, and get to a place where all enjoyments will continue, just as the Norwegian imagines that the wild boar is hunted and eaten every day, and recovers the next day.

Now, philosophy insists that there is a joy which is absolute, which never changes. That joy cannot be the joys and pleasures we have in this life, and yet Vedanta shows that everything that is joyful in this life is but a particle of that real joy, because that is the only joy there is. Every moment really we are enjoying the absolute bliss, though covered up, misunderstood, and caricatured. Wherever there is any blessing, blissfulness, or joy, even the joy of the thief in stealing, it is that absolute bliss coming out, only it has become obscured, muddled up, as it were, with all sorts of extraneous conditions, and misunderstood. But to understand that, we have to go through the negation, and then the positive side will begin. We have to give up ignorance and all that is false, and then truth will begin to reveal itself to us. When we have grasped the truth, things which we gave up at first will take new shape and form, will appear to us in a new light, and become deified. They will have become sublimated, and then we shall understand them in their true light. But to understand them, we have first to get a glimpse of truth; we must give them up at first, and then we get them back again, deified. We have to give up all our miseries and sorrows, all our little joys.

"That which all the Vedas declare, which is proclaimed by all penances, seeking which men lead lives of continence, I will tell you in one word — it is 'Om'." You will find this word "Om" praised very much in the Vedas, and it is held to be very sacred.

Now Yama answers the question: "What becomes of a man when the body dies?" "This Wise One never dies, is never born, It arises from nothing, and nothing arises from It. Unborn, Eternal, Everlasting, this Ancient One can never be destroyed with the destruction of the body. If the slayer thinks he can slay, or if the slain thinks he is slain, they both do not know the truth, for the Self neither slays nor is slain." A most tremendous position. I should like to draw your attention to the adjective in the first line, which is "wise". As we proceed we shall find that the ideal of the Vedanta is that all wisdom and all purity are in the soul already, dimly expressed or better expressed — that is all the difference. The difference between man and man, and all things in the whole creation, is not in kind but only in degree. The background, the reality, of everyone is that same Eternal, Ever Blessed, Ever Pure, and Ever Perfect One. It is the Atman, the Soul, in the saint and the sinner, in the happy and the miserable, in the beautiful and the ugly, in men and in animals; it is the same throughout. It is the shining One. The difference is caused by the power of expression. In some It is expressed more, in others less, but this difference of expression has no effect upon the Atman. If in their dress one man shows more of his body than another, it does not make any difference in their bodies; the difference is in their dress. We had better remember here that throughout the Vedanta philosophy, there is no such thing as good and bad, they are not two different things; the same thing is good or bad, and the difference is only in degree. The very thing I call pleasurable today, tomorrow under better circumstances I may call pain. The fire that warms us can also consume us; it is not the fault of the fire. Thus, the Soul being pure and perfect, the man who does evil is giving the lie unto himself, he does not know the nature of himself. Even in the murderer the pure Soul is there; It dies not. It was his mistake; he could not manifest It; he had covered It up. Nor in the man who thinks that he is killed is the Soul killed; It is eternal. It can never be killed, never destroyed. "Infinitely smaller than the smallest, infinitely larger than the largest, this Lord of all is present in the depths of every human heart. The sinless, bereft of all misery, see Him through the mercy of the Lord; the Bodiless, yet dwelling in the body; the Spaceless, yet seeming to occupy space; Infinite, Omnipresent: knowing such to be the Soul, the sages never are miserable."

"This Atman is not to be realised by the power of speech, nor by a vast intellect, nor by the study of their Vedas." This is a very bold utterance. As I told you before, the sages were very bold thinkers, and never stopped at anything. You will remember that in India these Vedas are regarded in a much higher light than even the Christians regard their Bible. Your idea of revelation is that a man was inspired by God; but in India the idea is that things exist because they are in the Vedas. In and through the Vedas the whole creation has come. All that is called knowledge is in the Vedas. Every word is sacred and eternal, eternal as the soul, without beginning and without end. The whole of the Creator's mind is in this book, as it were. That is the light in which the Vedas are held. Why is this thing moral? Because the Vedas say so. Why is that thing immoral? Because the Vedas say so. In spite of that, look at the boldness of these sages whom proclaimed that the truth is not to be found by much study of the Vedas. "With whom the Lord is pleased, to that man He expresses Himself." But then, the objection may be advanced that this is something like partisanship. But at Yama explains, "Those who are evil-doers, whose minds area not peaceful, can never see the Light. It is to those who are true in heart, pure in deed, whose senses are controlled, that this Self manifests Itself."

Here is a beautiful figure. Picture the Self to be then rider and this body the chariot, the intellect to be the charioteer, mind the reins, and the senses the horses. He whose horses are well broken, and whose reins are strong and kept well in the hands of the charioteer (the intellect) reaches the goal which is the state of Him, the Omnipresent. But the man whose horses (the senses) are not controlled, nor the reins (the mind) well managed, goes to destruction. This Atman in all beings does not manifest Himself to the eyes or the senses, but those whose minds have become purified and refined realise Him. Beyond all sound, all sight, beyond form, absolute, beyond all taste and touch, infinite, without beginning and without end, even beyond nature, the Unchangeable; he who realises Him, frees himself from the jaws of death. But it is very difficult. It is, as it were, walking on the edge of a razor; the way is long and perilous, but struggle on, do not despair. Awake, arise, and stop not till the goal is reached.

The one central idea throughout all the Upanishads is that of realisation. A great many questions will arise from time to time, and especially to the modern man. There will be the question of utility, there will be various other questions, but in all we shall find that we are prompted by our past associations. It is association of ideas that has such a tremendous power over our minds. To those who from childhood have always heard of a Personal God and the personality of the mind, these ideas will of course appear very stern and harsh, but if they listen to them and think over them, they will become part of their lives and will no longer frighten them. The great question that generally arises is the utility of philosophy. To that there can be only one answer: if on the utilitarian ground it is good for men to seek for pleasure, why should not those whose pleasure is in religious speculation seek for that? Because sense-enjoyments please many, they seek for them, but there may be others whom they do not please, who want higher enjoyment. The dog's pleasure is only in eating and drinking. The dog cannot understand the pleasure of the scientist who gives up everything, and, perhaps, dwells on the top of a mountain to observe the position of certain stars. The dogs may smile at him and think he is a madman. Perhaps this poor scientist never had money enough to marry even, and lives very simply. May be, the dog laughs at him. But the scientist says, "My dear dog, your pleasure is only in the senses which you enjoy, and you know nothing beyond; but for me this is the most enjoyable life, and if you have the right to seek your pleasure in your own way, so have I in mine." The mistake is that we want to tie the whole world down to our own plane of thought and to make our mind the measure of the whole universe. To you, the old sense-things are, perhaps, the greatest pleasure, but it is not necessary that my pleasure should be the same, and when you insist upon that, I differ from you. That is the difference between the worldly utilitarian and the religious man. The first man says, "See how happy I am. I get money, but do not bother my head about religion. It is too unsearchable, and I am happy without it." So far, so good; good for all utilitarians. But this world is terrible. If a man gets happiness in any way excepting by injuring his fellow-beings, godspeed him; but when this man comes to me and says, "You too must do these things, you will be a fool if you do not," I say, "You are wrong, because the very things, which are pleasurable to you, have not the slightest attraction for me. If I had to go after a few handfuls of gold, my life would not be worth living! I should die." That is the answer the religious man would make. The fact is that religion is possible only for those who have finished with these lower things. We must have our own experiences, must have our full run. It is only when we have finished this run that the other world opens.

The enjoyments of the senses sometimes assume

another phase which is dangerous and tempting. You will always hear the idea — in very old times, in every religion — that a time will come when all the miseries of life wills cease, and only its joys and pleasures will remain, and this earth will become a heaven. That I do not believe. This earth will always remain this same world. It is a most terrible thing to say, yet I do not see my way out of it. The misery in the world is like chronic rheumatism in the body; drive it from one part and it goes to another, drive it from there and you will feel it somewhere else. Whatever you do, it is still there. In olden times people lived in forests, and ate each other; in modern times they do not eat each other's flesh, but they cheat one another. Whole countries and cities are ruined by cheating. That does not show much progress. I do not see that what you call progress in the world is other than the multiplication of desires. If one thing is obvious to me it is this that desires bring all misery; it is the state of the beggar, who is always begging for something, and unable to see anything without the wish to possess it, is always longing, longing for more. If the power to satisfy our desires is increased in arithmetical progression, the power of desire is increased in geometrical progression. The sum total of happiness and misery in this world is at least the same throughout. If a wave rises in the ocean it makes a hollow somewhere. If happiness comes to one man, unhappiness comes to another or, perhaps, to some animal. Men are increasing in numbers and some animals are decreasing; we are killing them off, and taking their land ; we are taking all means of sustenance from them. How can we say, then, that happiness is increasing? The strong race eats up the weaker, but do you think that the strong race will be very happy? No; they will begin to kill each other. I do not see on practical grounds how this world can become a heaven. Facts are against it. On theoretical grounds also, I see it cannot be.

Perfection is always infinite. We are this infinite already, and we are trying to manifest that infinity. You and I, and all beings, are trying to manifest it. So far it is all right. But from this fact some German philosophers have started a peculiar theory — that this manifestation will become higher and higher until we attain perfect manifestation, until we have become perfect beings. What is meant by perfect manifestation? Perfection means infinity, and manifestation means limit, and so it means that we shall become unlimited limiteds, which is self-contradictory. Such a theory may please children; but it is poisoning their minds with lies, and is very bad for religion. But we know that this world is a degradation, that man is a degradation of God, and that Adam fell. There is no religion today that does not teach that man is a degradation. We have been degraded down to the animal, and are now going up, to emerge out of this bondage. But we shall never be able entirely to manifest the Infinite here. We shall struggle hard, but there will come a time when we shall find that it is impossible to be perfect here, while we are bound by the senses. And then the march back to our original state of Infinity will be sounded.

This is renunciation. We shall have to get out of the difficulty by reversing the process by which we got in, and then morality and charity will begin. What is the watchword of all ethical codes? "Not I, but thou", and this "I" is the outcome of the Infinite behind, trying to manifest Itself on the outside world. This little "I" is the result, and it will have to go back and join the Infinite, its own nature. Every time you say, "Not I, my brother, but thou", you are trying to go back, and every time you say "I, and not thou", you take the false step of trying to manifest the Infinite through the sense-world. That brings struggles and evils into the world, but after a time renunciation must come, eternal renunciation. The little "I" is dead and gone. Why care so much for this little life? All these vain desires of living and enjoying this life, here or in some other place, bring death.

If we are developed from animals, the animals also may be degraded men. How do you know it is not so? You have seen that the proof of evolution is simply this: you find a series of bodies from the lowest to the highest rising in a gradually ascending scale. But from that how can you insist that it is always from the lower upwards, and never from the higher downwards? The argument applies both ways, and if anything is true, I believe it is that the series is repeating itself in going up and down. How can you have evolution without involution? Our struggle for the higher life shows that we have been degraded from a high state. It must be so, only it may vary as to details. I always cling to the idea set forth with one voice by Christ, Buddha, and the Vedanta, that we must all come to perfection in time, but only by giving up this imperfection. This world is nothing. It is at best only a hideous caricature, a shadow of the Reality. We must go to the Reality. Renunciation will take us to It. Renunciation is the very basis of our true life; every moment of goodness and real life that we enjoy is when we do not think of ourselves. This little separate self must die. Then we shall find that we are in the Real, and that Reality is God, and He is our own true nature, and He is always in us and with us. Let us live in Him and stand in Him. It is the only joyful state of existence. Life on the plane of the Spirit is the only life, and let us all try to attain to this realisation.

CHAPTER IX
UNITY IN DIVERSITY

Delivered in London, 3rd November 1896

"The Self-existent One projected the senses outwards and, therefore, a man looks outward, not within himself. A certain wise one, desiring immortality, with inverted senses, perceived the Self within." As I have already said, the first inquiry that we find in the Vedas was concerning outward things, and then a new idea came that the reality of things is not to be found in the external world; not by looking outwards, but by turning the eyes, as it is literally expressed, inwards. And the word used for the Soul is very significant: it is He who has gone inward, the innermost reality of our being, the heart centre, the core, from which, as it were, everything comes out; the central sun of which the mind, the body, the sense-organs, and everything else we have are but rays going outwards. "Men of childish intellect, ignorant persons, run after desires which are external, and enter the trap of far-reaching death, but the wise, understanding immortality, never seek for the Eternal in this life of finite things." The same idea is here made clear that in this external world, which is full of finite things, it is impossible to see and find the Infinite. The Infinite must be sought in that alone which is infinite, and the only thing infinite about us is that which is within us, our own soul. Neither the body, nor the mind, not even our thoughts, nor the world we see around us, are infinite. The Seer, He to whom they all belong, the Soul of man, He who is awake in the internal man, alone is infinite, and to seek for the Infinite Cause of this whole universe we must go there. In the Infinite Soul alone we can find it. "What is here is there too, and what is there is here also. He who sees the manifold goes from death to death." We have seen how at first there was the desire to go to heaven. When these ancient Aryans became dissatisfied with the world around them, they naturally thought that after death they would go to some place where there would be all happiness without any misery; these places they multiplied and called Svargas — the word may be translated as heavens — where there would be joy for ever, the body would become perfect, and also the mind, and there they would live with their forefathers. But as soon as philosophy came, men found that this was impossible and absurd. The very idea of an infinite in place would be a contradiction in terms, as a place must begin and continue in time. Therefore they had to give up that idea. They found out that the gods who lived in these heavens had once been human beings on earth, who through their good works had become gods, and the godhoods, as they call them, were different states, different positions; none of the gods spoken of in the Vedas are permanent individuals.

For instance, Indra and Varuna are not the names of certain persons, but the names of positions as governors and so on. The Indra who had lived before is not the same person as the Indra of the present day; he has passed away, and another man from earth has filled his place. So with all the other gods

These are certain positions, which are filled successively by human souls who have raised themselves to the condition of gods, and yet even they die. In the old Rig-Veda we find the word "immortality" used with regard to these gods, but later on it is dropped entirely, for they found that immortality which is beyond time and space cannot be spoken of with regard to any physical form, however subtle it may be. However fine it may be, it must have a beginning in time and space, for the necessary factors that enter into the make-up of form are in space. Try to think of a form without space: it is impossible. Space is one of the materials, as it were, which make up the form, and this is continually changing Space and time are in Maya, and this idea is expressed in the line — "What is hole, that is there too." If there are these gods, they must be bound by the same laws that apply here, and all laws involve destruction and renewal again and again. These laws are moulding matter into different forms, and crushing them out again. Everything born must die; and so, if there are heavens, the same laws must hold good there.

In this world we find that all happiness is followed by misery as its shadow. Life has its shadow, death. They must go together, because they are not contradictory, not two separate existences, but different manifestations of the same unit, life and death, sorrow and happiness, good and evil. The dualistic conception that good and evil are two separate entities, and that they are both going on eternally is absurd on the face of it. They are the diverse manifestations of one and the same fact, one time appearing as bad, and at another time as good. The difference does not exist in kind, but only in degree. They differ from each other in degree of intensity. We find as a fact that the same nerve systems carry good and bad sensations alike, and when the nerves are injured, neither sensation comes to us. If a certain nerve is paralysed, we do not get the pleasurable feelings that used to come along that wires and at the same time we do not get the painful feelings either. They are never two, but the same. Again. the same thing produces pleasure and pain at different times of life. The same phenomenon will produce pleasure in one, and pain in another. The eating of meat produces pleasure to a man, but pain to the animal which is eaten. There has never been anything which gives pleasure to all alike. Some are pleased, others displeased. So on it will go. Therefore, this duality of existence is denied. And what follows? I told you in my last lecture that we can never have ultimately everything good on this earth and nothing bad. It may have disappointed and frightened some of you, but I cannot help it, and I am open to conviction when I am shown to the contrary; but until that can be proved to me, and I can find that it is true, cannot say so.

The general argument against my statement, and apparently a very convincing one, is this that in the course of evolution, all that is evil in what we see around us is gradually being eliminated, and the result is that if this elimination continues for millions of years, a time will come when all the evil will have been extirpated, and the good alone will remain. This is apparently a very sound argument. Would to God it were true! But there is a fallacy in it, and it is this that it takes for granted that both good and evil are things that are eternally fixed. It takes for granted that there is a definite mass of evil, which may be represented by a hundred, and likewise of good, and that this mass of evil is being diminished every day, leaving only the good. But is it so? The history of the world shows that evil is a continuously increasing quantity, as well as good. Take the lowest man; he lives in the forest. His sense of enjoyment is very small, and so also is his power to suffer. His misery is entirely on the sense-plane. If he does not get plenty of food, he is miserable; but give him plenty of food and freedom to rove and to hunt, and he is perfectly happy. His happiness consists only in the senses, and so does his misery also. But if that man increases in knowledge, his happiness will increase, the intellect will open to him, and his sense-enjoyment will evolve into intellectual enjoyment. He will feel pleasure in reading a beautiful poem, and a mathematical problem will be of absorbing interest to him. But, with these, the inner nerves will become more and more susceptible to miseries of mental pain, of which the savage does not think. Take a very simple illustration. In Tibet there is no marriage, and there is no jealousy, yet we know that marriage is a much higher state. The Tibetans have not known the wonderful enjoyment, the blessing of chastity, the happiness of having a chaste, virtuous wife, or a chaste, virtuous husband. These people cannot feel that. And similarly they do not feel the intense jealousy of the chaste wife or husband, or the misery caused by unfaithfulness on either side, with all the heart-burnings and sorrows which believers in chastity experience. On one side, the latter gain happiness, but on the other, they suffer misery too.

Take your country which is the richest in the world, and which is more luxurious than any other, and see how intense is the misery, how many more lunatics you have, compared with other races, only because the desires are so keen. A man must keep up a high standard of living, and the amount of money he spends in one year would be a fortune to a man in India. You cannot preach to him of simple living because society demands so much of him. The wheel of society is rolling on; it stops not for the widow's tears or the orphans' wails. This is the state of things everywhere. Your sense of enjoyment is developed, your society is very much more beautiful than some others. You have so many more things to enjoy. But those who have fewer have much less misery. You can argue thus throughout, the higher the ideal you have in the brain, the greater is your enjoyment, and the more profound your misery. One is like the shadow of the other. That the evils are being eliminated may be true, but if so, the good also must be dying out. But are not evils multiplying fast, and good diminishing, if I may so put it? If good increases in arithmetical progression, evil increase in geometrical progression. And this is Maya. This is neither optimism nor pessimism. Vedanta does not take he position that this world is only a miserable one. That would be untrue. At the same time, it is a mistake to say that this world is full of happiness and blessings. So it is useless to tell children that this world is all good, all flowers, all milk and honey. That is what we have all dreamt. At the same time it is erroneous to think, because one man has suffered more than another, that all is evil. It is this duality, this play of good and evil that makes our world of experiences. At the same time the Vedanta says, "Do not think that good and evil are two, are two separate essences, for they are one and the same thing, appearing in different degrees and in different guises and producing differences of feeling in the same mind." So, the first thought of the Vedanta is the finding of unity in the external; the One Existence manifesting Itself, however different It may appear in manifestation. Think of the old crude theory of the Persians — two gods creating this world, the good god doing everything that is good, and the bad one, everything bad. On the very face of it, you see the absurdity, for if it be carried out, every law of nature must have two parts, one of which is manipulated by one god, and then he goes away and the other god manipulates the other part. There the difficulty comes that both are working in the same world, and these two gods keep themselves in harmony by injuring one portion and doing good to another. This is a crude case, of course, the crudest way of expressing the duality of existence. But, take the more advanced, the more abstract theory that this world is partly good and partly bad. This also is absurd, arguing from the same standpoint. It is the law of unity that gives us our food, and it is the same law that kills many through accidents or misadventure.

We find, then, that this world is neither optimistic nor pessimistic; it is a mixture of both, and as we go on we shall find that the whole blame is taken away from nature and put upon our own shoulders. At the same time the Vedanta shows the way out, but not by denial of evil, because it analyses boldly the fact as it is and does not seek to conceal anything. It is not hopeless; it is not agnostic. It finds out a remedy, but it wants to place that remedy on adamantine foundations: not by shutting the child's mouth and blinding its eyes with something which is untrue, and which the child will find out in a few days. I remember when I was young, a young man's father died and left him poorly off, with a large family to support, and he found that his father's friends were unwilling to help him. He had a conversation with a clergyman who offered this consolation,

"Oh, it is all good, all is sent for our good." That is the old method of trying to put a piece of gold leaf on an old sore. It is a confession of weakness, of absurdity. The young man went away, and six months afterwards a son was born to the clergyman, and he gave a thanksgiving party to which the young man was invited. The clergyman prayed, "Thank God for His mercies." And the young man stood up and said, "Stop, this is all misery." The clergyman asked, "Why?" "Because when my father died you said it was good, though apparently evil; so now, this is apparently good, but really evil." Is this the way to cure the misery of the world? Be good and have mercy on those who suffer. Do not try to patch it up, nothing will cure this world; go beyond it.

This is a world of good and evil. Wherever there is good, evil follows, but beyond and behind all these manifestations, all these contradictions, the Vedanta finds out that Unity. It says, "Give up what is evil and give up what is good." What remains then? Behind good and evil stands something which is yours, the real you, beyond every evil, and beyond every good too, and it is that which is manifesting itself as good and bad. Know that first, and then and then alone you will be a true optimist, and not before; for then you will be able to control everything. Control these manifestations and you will be at liberty to manifest the real "you". First be master of yourself, stand up and be free, go beyond the pale of these laws, for these laws do not absolutely govern you, they are only part of your being. First find out that you are not the slave of nature, never were and never will be; that this nature, infinite as you may think it, is only finite, a drop in the ocean, and your Soul is the ocean; you are beyond the stars, the sun, and the. They are like mere bubbles compared with your infinite being. Know that, and you will control both good and evil. Then alone the whole vision will change and you will stand up and say, "How beautiful is good and how wonderful is evil!"

That is what the Vedanta teaches. It does not propose any slipshod remedy by covering wounds with gold leaf and the more the wound festers, putting on more gold leaf. This life is a hard fact; work your way through it boldly, though it may be adamantine; no matter, the soul is stronger. It lays no responsibility on little gods; for you are the makers of your own fortunes. You make yourselves suffer, you make good and evil, and it is you who put your hands before your eyes and say it is dark. Take your hands away and see the light; you are effulgent, you are perfect already, from the very beginning. We now understand the verse: "He goes from death to death who sees the many here." See that One and be free.

How are we to see it? This mind, so deluded, so weak, so easily led, even this mind can be strong and may catch a glimpse of that knowledge, that Oneness, which saves us from dying again and again. As rain falling upon a mountain flows in various streams down the sides of the mountain, so all the energies which you see here are from that one Unit. It has become manifold falling upon Maya. Do not run after the manifold; go towards the One. "He is in all that moves; He is in all that is pure; He fills the universe; He is in the sacrifice; He is the guest in the house; He is in man, in water, in animals, in truth; He is the Great One. As fire coming into this world is manifesting itself in various forms, even so, that one Soul of the universe is manifesting Himself in all these various forms. As air coming into this universe manifests itself in various forms, even so, the One Soul of all souls, of all beings, is manifesting Himself in all forms." This is true for you when you have understood this Unity, and not before Then is all optimism, because He is seen everywhere. The question is that if all this be true that that Pure One — the Self, the Infinite — has entered all this, how is it that He suffers, how is it that He becomes miserable, impure? He does not, says the Upanishad. "As the sun is the cause of the eyesight of every being, yet is not made defective by the defect in any eye, even so the Self of all is not affected by the miseries of the body, or by any misery that is around you." I may have some disease and see everything yellow, but the sun is not affected by it. "He is the One, the Creator of all, the Ruler of all, the Internal Soul of every being — He who makes His Oneness manifold. Thus sages who realise Him as the Soul of their souls, unto them belongs eternal peace; unto none else, unto none else. He who in this world of evanescence finds Him who never changes, he who in this universe of death finds that One Life, he who in this manifold finds that Oneness, and all those who realise Him as the Soul of their souls, to them belongs eternal peace; unto none else, unto none else. Where to find Him in the external world, where to find Him in the suns, and moons, and stars? There the sun cannot illumine, nor the moon, nor the stars, the flash of lightning cannot illumine the place; what to speak of this mortal fire? He shining, everything else shines. It is His light that they have borrowed, and He is shining through them." Here is another beautiful simile. Those of you who have been in India and have seen how the banyan tree comes from one root and spreads itself far around, will understand this. He is that banyan tree; He is the root of all and has branched out until He has become this universe, and however far He extends, every one of these trunks and branches is connected.

Various heavens are spoken of in the Brâhmana portions of the Vedas, but the philosophical teaching of the Upanishads gives up the idea of going to heaven. Happiness is not in this heaven or in that heaven, it is in the soul; places do not signify anything. Here is another passage which shows the different states of realisation "In the heaven of the forefathers, as a man sees things in a dream, so the Real Truth is seen." As in dreams we see things hazy and not so distinct, so we see the Reality there. There is another heaven called the Gandharva, in which it is still less clear; as a man sees his own reflection in the water, so is the Reality seen there. The highest heaven, of which the Hindus conceive is called the Brahmaloka; and in this, the Truth is seen much more clearly, like light and shade, but not yet quite distinctly. But as a man sees his own face in a mirror, perfect, distinct, and clear, so is the Truth shining in the soul of man. The highest heaven, therefore, is in our own souls; the greatest temple of worship is the human soul, greater than all heavens, says the Vedanta; for in no heaven anywhere, can we understand the reality as distinctly and clearly as in this life, in our own soul. Changing places does not help one much. I thought while I was in India that the cave would give me clearer vision. I found it was not so. Then I thought the forest would do so, then, Varanasi. But the same difficulty existed everywhere, because we make our own worlds. If I am evil, the whole world is evil to me. That is what the Upanishad says. And the same thing applies to all worlds. If I die and go to heaven, I should find the same, for until I am pure it is no use going to caves, or forests, or to Varanasi, or to heaven, and if I have polished my mirror, it does not matter where I live, I get the Reality just as It is. So it is useless, running hither and thither, and spending energy in vain, which should be spent only in polishing the mirror. The same idea is expressed again: "None sees Him, none sees His form with the eyes. It is in the mind, in the pure mind, that He is seen, and this immortality is gained."

Those who were at the summer lectures on Râja-Yoga will be interested to know that what was taught then was a different kind of Yoga. The Yoga which we are now considering consists chiefly in controlling the senses. When the senses are held as slaves by the human soul, when they can no longer disturb the mind, then the Yogi has reached the goal. "When all vain desires of the heart have been given up, then this very mortal becomes immortal, then he becomes one with God even here. When all the knots of the heart are cut asunder, then the mortal becomes immortal, and he enjoys Brahman here." Here, on this earth, nowhere else.

A few words ought to be said here. You will generally hear that this Vedanta, this philosophy and other Eastern systems, look only to something beyond, letting go the enjoyments and struggle of this life. This idea is entirely wrong. It is only ignorant people who do not know anything of Eastern thought, and never had brain enough to understand anything of its real teaching, that tell you so. On the contrary, we read in our scriptures that our philosophers do not want to go to other worlds, but depreciate them as places where people weep and laugh for a little while only and then die. As long as we are weak we shall have to go through these experiences; but whatever is true, is here, and that is the human soul. And this also is insisted upon, that by committing suicide, we cannot escape the inevitable; we cannot evade it. But the right path is hard to find. The Hindu is just as practical as the Western, only we differ in our views of life. The one says, build a good house, let us have good clothes and food, intellectual culture, and so on, for this is the whole of life; and in that he is immensely practical. But the Hindu says, true knowledge of the world means knowledge of the soul, metaphysics; and he wants to enjoy that life. In America there was a great agnostic, a very noble man, a very good man, and a very fine speaker. He lectured on religion, which he said was of no use; why bother our heads about other worlds? He employed this simile; we have an orange here, and we want to squeeze all the juice out of it. I met him once and said, "I agree with you entirely. I have some fruit, and I too want to squeeze out the juice. Our difference lies in the choice of the fruit. You want an orange, and I prefer a mango. You think it is enough to live here and eat and drink and have a little scientific knowledge; but you have no right to say that that will suit all tastes. Such a conception is nothing to me. If I had only to learn how an apple falls to the ground, or how an electric current shakes my nerves, I would commit suicide. I want to understand the heart of things, the very kernel itself. Your study is the manifestation of life, mine is the life itself. My philosophy says you must know that and drive out from your mind all thoughts of heaven and hell and all other superstitions, even though they exist in the same sense that this world exists. I must know the heart of this life, its very essence, what it is, not only how it works and what are its manifestations. I want the why of everything, I leave the how to children. As one of your countrymen said, 'While I am smoking a cigarette, if I were to write a book, it would be the science of the cigarette.' It is good and great to be scientific, God bless them in their search; but when a man says that is all, he is talking foolishly, not caring to know the raison d'être of life, never studying existence itself. I may argue that all your knowledge is nonsense, without a basis. You are studying the manifestations of life, and when I ask you what life is, you say you do not know. You are welcome to your study, but leave me to mine."

I am practical, very practical, in my own way. So your idea that only the West is practical is nonsense. You are practical in one way, and I in another. There are different types of men and minds. If in the East a man is told that he will find out the truth by standing on one leg all his life, he will pursue that method. If in the West men hear that there is a gold mine somewhere in an uncivilised country, thousands will face the dangers there, in the hope of getting the gold; and, perhaps, only one succeeds. The same men have heard that they have souls but are content to leave the care of them to the church. The first man will not go near the savages, he says it may be dangerous. But if we tell him that on the top of a high mountain lives a wonderful sage who can give him knowledge of the soul, he tries to climb up to him, even if he be killed in the attempt. Both types of men are practical, but the mistake lies in regarding this world as the whole of life. Yours is the vanishing point of enjoyment of the senses — there is nothing permanent in it, it only brings more and more misery — while mine brings eternal peace.

I do not say your view is wrong, you are welcome to it. Great good and blessing come out of it, but do not, therefore, condemn my view. Mine also is practical in its own way. Let us all work on our own plans. Would to God all of us were equally practical on both sides. I have seen some scientists who were equally practical, both as scientists and as spiritual men, and it is my great hope that in course of time the whole of humanity will be efficient in the same manner. When a kettle of water is coming to the boil, if you watch the phenomenon, you find first one bubble rising, and then another and so on, until at last they all join, and a tremendous commotion takes place. This world is very similar. Each individual is like a bubble, and the nations, resemble many bubbles. Gradually these nations are joining, and I am sure the day will come when separation will vanish and that Oneness to which we are all going will become manifest. A time must come when every man will be as intensely practical in the scientific world as in the spiritual, and then that Oneness, the harmony of Oneness, will pervade the whole world. The whole of mankind will become Jivanmuktas — free whilst living. We are all struggling towards that one end through our jealousies and hatreds, through our love and co-operation. A tremendous stream is flowing towards the ocean carrying us all along with it; and though like straws and scraps of paper we may at times float aimlessly about, in the long run we are sure to join the Ocean of Life and Bliss.

CHAPTER X
THE FREEDOM OF THE SOUL

Delivered in London, 5th November 1896

The Katha Upanishad, which we have been studying, was written much later than that to which we now turn — the Chhândogya. The language is more modern, and the thought more organised. In the older Upanishads the language is very archaic, like that of the hymn portion of the Vedas, and one has to wade sometimes through quite a mass of unnecessary things to get at the essential doctrines. The ritualistic literature about which I told you which forms the second division of the Vedas, has left a good deal of its mark upon this old Upanishad, so that more than half of it is still ritualistic. There is, however, one great gain in studying the very old Upanishads. You trace, as it were, the historical growth of spiritual ideas. In the more recent Upanishads, the spiritual ideas have been collected and brought into one place; as in the Bhagavad Gitâ, for instance, which we may, perhaps, look upon as the last of the Upanishads, you do not find any inkling of these ritualistic ideas. The Gita is like a bouquet composed of the beautiful flowers of spiritual truths collected from the Upanishads. But in the Gita you cannot study the rise of the spiritual ideas, you cannot trace them to their source. To do that, as has been pointed out by many, you must study the Vedas. The great idea of holiness that has been attached to these books has preserved them, more than any other book in the world, from mutilation. In them, thoughts at their highest and at their lowest have all been preserved, the essential and the non-essential, the most ennobling teachings and the simplest matters of detail stand side by side; for nobody has dared to touch them. Commentators came and tried to smooth them down and to bring out wonderful new ideas from the old things; they tried to find spiritual ideas in even the most ordinary statements, but the texts remained, and as such, they are the most wonderful historical study. We all know that in the scriptures of every religion changes were made to suit the growing spirituality of later times; one word was changed here and another put in there, and so on. This, probably, has not been done with the Vedic literature, or if ever done, it is almost imperceptible. So we have this great advantage, we are able to study thoughts in their original significance, to note how they developed, how from materialistic ideas finer and finer spiritual ideas are evolved, until they attained their greatest height in the Vedanta. Descriptions of some of the old manners and customs are also there, but they do not appear much in the Upanishads. The language used is peculiar, terse, mnemonic.

The writers of these books simply jotted down these lines as helps to remember certain facts which they supposed were already well known. In a narrative, perhaps, which they are telling, they take it for granted that it is well known to everyone they are addressing. Thus a great difficulty arises, we scarcely know the real meaning of any one of these stories, because the traditions have nearly died out, and the little that is left of them has been very much exaggerated. Many new interpretations have been put upon them, so that when you find them in the Purânas they have already become lyrical poems. Just as in the West, we find this prominent fact in the political development of Western races that they cannot bear absolute rule, that they are always trying to prevent any one man from ruling over them, and are gradually advancing to higher and higher democratic ideas, higher and higher ideas of physical liberty, so, in Indian metaphysics, exactly the same phenomenon appears in the development of spiritual life. The multiplicity of gods gave place to one God of the universe, and in the Upanishads there is a rebellion even against that one God. Not only was the idea of many governors of the universe ruling their destinies unbearable, but it was also intolerable that there should be one person ruling this universe. This is the first thing that strikes us. The idea grows and grows, until it attains its climax. In almost all of the Upanishads, we find the climax coming at the last, and that is the dethroning of this God of the universe. The personality of God vanishes, the impersonality comes. God is no more a person, no more a human being, however magnified and exaggerated, who rules this universe, but He has become an embodied principle in every being, immanent in the whole universe. It would be illogical to go from the Personal God to the Impersonal, and at the same time to leave man as a person. So the personal man is broken down, and man as principle is built up. The person is only a phenomenon, the principle is behind it. Thus from both sides, simultaneously, we find the breaking down of personalities and the approach towards principles, the Personal God approaching the Impersonal, the personal man approaching the Impersonal Man. Then come the succeeding stages of the gradual convergence of the two advancing lines of the Impersonal God and the Impersonal Man. And the Upanishads embody the stages through which these two lines at last become one, and the last word of each Upanishad is, "Thou art That". There is but One Eternally Blissful Principle, and that One is manifesting Itself as all this variety.

Then came the philosophers. The work of the Upanishads seems to have ended at that point; the next was taken up by the philosophers. The framework was given them by the Upanishads, and they had to fill in the details. So, many questions would naturally arise. Taking for granted that there is but One Impersonal Principle which is manifesting Itself in all these manifold forms, how is it that the One becomes many? It is another way of putting the same old question which in its crude form comes into the human heart as the inquiry into the cause of evil and so forth. Why does evil exist in the world, and what is its cause? But the same question has now become refined, abstracted. No more is it asked from the platform of the senses why we are unhappy, but from the platform of philosophy. How is it that this One Principle becomes manifold? And the answer, as we have seen, the best answer that India has produced is the theory of Maya which says that It really has not become manifold, that It really has not lost any of Its real nature. Manifoldness is only apparent. Man is only apparently a person, but in reality he is the Impersonal Being. God is a person only apparently, but really He is the Impersonal Being.

Even in this answer there have been succeeding stages, and philosophers have varied in their opinions. All Indian philosophers did not admit this theory of Maya. Possibly most of them did not. There are dualists, with a crude sort of dualism, who would not allow the question to be asked, but stifled it at its very birth. They said, "You have no right to ask such a question, you have no right to ask for an explanation; it is simply the will of God, and we have to submit to it quietly. There is no liberty for the human soul. Everything is predestined — what we shall do, have, enjoy, and suffer; and when suffering comes, it is our duty to endure it patiently; if we do not, we shall be punished all the more. How do we know that? Because the Vedas say so." And thus they have their texts and their meanings and they want to enforce them.

There are others who, though not admitting the Maya theory, stand midway. They say that the whole of this creation forms, as it were, the body of God. God is the Soul of all souls and of the whole of nature. In the case of individual souls, contraction comes from evil doing. When a man does anything evil, his soul begins to contract and his power is diminished and goes on decreasing, until he does good works, when it expands again. One idea seems to be common in all the Indian systems, and I think, in every system in the world, whether they know it or not, and that is what I should call the divinity of man. There is no one system in the world, no real religion, which does not hold the idea that the human soul, whatever it be, or whatever its relation to God, is essentially pure and perfect, whether expressed in the language of mythology, allegory, or philosophy. Its real nature is blessedness and power, not weakness and misery. Somehow or other this misery has come. The crude systems may call it a personified evil, a devil, or an Ahriman, to explain how this misery came. Other systems may try to make a God and a devil in one, who makes some people miserable and others happy, without any reason whatever. Others again, more thoughtful, bring in the theory of Maya and so forth. But one fact stands out clearly, and it is with this that we have to deal. After all, these philosophical ideas and systems are but gymnastics of the mind, intellectual exercises. The one great idea that to me seems to be clear, and comes out through masses of superstition in every country and in every religion, is the one luminous idea that man is divine, that divinity is our nature.

Whatever else comes is a mere superimposition, as the Vedanta calls it. Something has been superimposed, but that divine nature never dies. In the most degraded as well as in the most saintly it is ever present. It has to be called out, and it will work itself out. We have to ask and it will manifest itself. The people of old knew that fire lived in the flint and in dry wood, but friction was necessary to call it out. So this fire of freedom and purity is the nature of every soul, and not a quality, because qualities can be acquired and therefore can be lost. The soul is one with Freedom, and the soul is one with Existence, and the soul is one with Knowledge. The Sat-Chit-Ânanda — Existence-Knowledge-Bliss Absolute — is the nature, the birthright of the Soul, and all the manifestations that we see are Its expressions, dimly or brightly manifesting Itself. Even death is but a manifestation of that Real Existence. Birth and death, life and decay, degeneration and regeneration — are all manifestations of that Oneness. So, knowledge, however it manifests itself, either as ignorance or as learning, is but the manifestation of that same Chit, the essence of knowledge; the difference is only in degree, and not in kind. The difference in knowledge between the lowest worm that crawls under our feet and the highest genius that the world may produce is only one of degree, and not of kind. The Vedantin thinker boldly says that the enjoyments in this life, even the most degraded joys, are but manifestations of that One Divine Bliss, the Essence of the Soul.

This idea seems to be the most prominent in Vedanta, and, as I have said, it appears to me that every religion holds it. I have yet to know the religion which does not. It is the one universal idea working through all religions. Take the Bible for instance. You find there the allegorical statement that the first man Adam was pure, and that his purity was obliterated by his evil deeds afterwards. It is clear from this allegory that they thought that the nature of the primitive man was perfect. The impurities that we see, the weaknesses that we feel, are but superimpositions on that nature, and the subsequent history of the Christian religion shows that they also believe in the possibility, nay, the certainty of regaining that old state. This is the whole history of the Bible, Old and New Testaments together. So with the Mohammedans: they also believed in Adam and the purity of Adam, and through Mohammed the way was opened to regain that lost state. So with the Buddhists: they believe in the state called Nirvana which is beyond this relative world. It is exactly the same as the Brahman of the Vedantins, and the whole system of the Buddhists is founded upon the idea of regaining that lost state of Nirvana. In every system we find this doctrine present, that you cannot get anything which is not yours already. You are indebted to nobody in this universe. You claim your own birthright, as it has been most poetically expressed by a great Vedantin philosopher, in the title of one of his books — "The attainment of our own empire". That empire is ours; we have lost it and we have to regain it. The Mâyâvâdin, however, says that this losing of the empire was a hallucination; you never lost it. This is the only difference.

Although all the systems agree so far that we had the empire, and that we have lost it, they give us varied advice as to how to regain it. One says that you must perform certain ceremonies, pay certain sums of money to certain idols, eat certain sorts of food, live in a peculiar fashion to regain that empire. Another says that if you weep and prostrate yourselves and ask pardon of some Being beyond nature, you will regain that empire. Again, another says if you love such a Being with all your heart, you will regain that empire. All this varied advice is in the Upanishads. As I go on, you will find it so. But the last and the greatest counsel is that you need not weep at all. You need not go through all these ceremonies, and need not take any notice of how to regain your empire, because you never lost it. Why should you go to seek for what you never lost? You are pure already, you are free already. If you think you are free, free you are this moment, and if you think you are bound, bound you will be. This is a very bold statement, and as I told you at the beginning of this course, I shall have to speak to you very boldly. It may frighten you now, but when you think over it, and realise it in your own life, then you will come to know that what I say is true. For, supposing that freedom is not your nature, by no manner of means can you become free. Supposing you were free and in some way you lost that freedom, that shows that you were not free to begin with. Had you been free, what could have made you lose it? The independent can never be made dependent; if it is really dependent, its independence was a hallucination.

Of the two sides, then, which will you take? If you say that the soul was by its own nature pure and free, it naturally follows that there was nothing in this universe which could make it bound or limited. But if there was anything in nature which could bind the soul, it naturally follows that it was not free, and your statement that it was free is a delusion. So if it is possible for us to attain to freedom, the conclusion is inevitable that the soul is by its nature free. It cannot be otherwise. Freedom means independence of anything outside, and that means that nothing outside itself could work upon it as a cause. The soul is causeless, and from this follow all the great ideas that we have. You cannot establish the immortality of the soul, unless you grant that it is by its nature free, or in other words, that it cannot be acted upon by anything outside. For death is an effect produced by some outside cause. I drink poison and I die, thus showing that my body can be acted upon by something outside that is called poison. But if it be true that the soul is free, it naturally follows that nothing can affect it, and it can never die. Freedom, immortality, blessedness, all depend upon the soul being beyond the law of causation, beyond this Maya. Of these two which will you take? Either make the first a delusion, or make the second a delusion. Certainly I will make the second a delusion. It is more consonant with all my feelings and aspirations. I am perfectly aware that I am free by nature, and I will not admit that this bondage is true and my freedom a delusion.

This discussion goes on in all philosophies, in some form or other. Even in the most modern philosophies you find the same discussion arising. There are two parties. One says that there is no soul, that the idea of soul is a delusion produced by the repeated transit of particles or matter, bringing about the combination which you call the body or brain; that the impression of freedom is the result of the vibrations and motions and continuous transit of these particles. There were Buddhistic sects who held the same view and illustrated it by this example: If young take a torch and whirl it round rapidly, there will be a circle of light. That circle does not really exist, because the torch is changing place every moment. We are but bundles of little particles, which in their rapid whirling produce the delusion of a permanent soul. The other party states that in the rapid succession of thought, matter occurs as a delusion, and does not really exist. So we see one side claiming that spirit is a delusion and the other, that matter is a delusion. Which side will you take? Of course, we will take the spirit and deny matter. The arguments are similar for both, only on the spirit side the argument is little stronger. For nobody has ever seen what matter is. We can only feel ourselves. I never knew a man who could feel matter outside of himself. Nobody was ever able to jump outside of himself. Therefore the argument is a little stronger on the side of the spirit. Secondly, the spirit theory explains the universe, whiles materialism does not. Hence the materialistic explanation is illogical. If you boil down all the philosophies and analyse them, you will find that they are reduced to one; or the other of these two positions. So here, too, in a more intricate form, in a more philosophical form, we find the same question about natural purity and freedom. Ones side says that the first is a delusion, and the other, that the second is a delusion. And, of course, we side with the second, in believing that our bondage is a delusion.

The solution of the Vedanta is that we are not bound, we are free already. Not only so, but to say or to think that we are bound is dangerous — it is a mistake, it is self-hypnotism. As soon as you say, "I am bound," "I am weak," "I am helpless," woe unto you; you rivet one more chain upon yourself. Do not say it, do not think it. I have heard of a man who lived in a forest and used to repeat day and night, "Shivoham" — I am the Blessed One — and one day a tiger fell upon him and dragged him away to kill him; people on the other side of the river saw it, and heard the voice so long as voice remained in him, saying, "Shivoham" — even in the very jaws of the tiger. There have been many such men. There have been cases of men who, while being cut to pieces, have blessed their enemies. "I am He, I am He; and so art thou. I am pure and perfect and so are all my enemies. You are He, and so am I." That is - the position of strength. Nevertheless, there are great and wonderful things in the religions of the dualists; wonderful is the idea of the Personal God apart from nature, whom we worship and love. Sometimes this idea is very soothing. But, says the Vedanta, the soothing is something like the effect that comes from an opiate, not natural. It brings weakness in the long run, and what this world wants today, more than it ever did before, is strength. It is weakness, says the Vedanta, which is the cause of all misery in this world. Weakness is the one cause of suffering. We become miserable because we are weak. We lie, steal, kill, and commit other crimes, because we are weak. We suffer because we are weak. We die because we are weak. Where there is nothing to weaken us, there is no death nor sorrow. We are miserable through delusion. Give up the delusion, and the whole thing vanishes. It is plain and simple indeed. Through all these philosophical discussions and tremendous mental gymnastics we come to this one religious idea, the simplest in the whole world.

The monistic Vedanta is the simplest form in which you can put truth. To teach dualism was a tremendous mistake made in India and elsewhere, because people did not look at the ultimate principles, but only thought of the process which is very intricate indeed. To many, these tremendous philosophical and logical propositions were alarming. They thought these things could not be made universal, could not be followed in everyday practical life, and that under the guise of such a philosophy much laxity of living would arise.

But I do not believe at all that monistic ideas preached to the world would produce immorality and weakness. On the contrary, I have reason to believe that it is the only remedy there is. If this be the truth, why let people drink ditch water when the stream of life is flowing by? If this be the truth, that they are all pure, why not at this moment teach it to the whole world? Why not teach it with the voice of thunder to every man that is born, to saints and sinners, men, women, and children, to the man on the throne and to the man sweeping the streets?

It appears now a very big and a very great undertaking; to many it appears very startling, but that is because of superstition, nothing else. By eating all sorts of bad and indigestible food, or by starving ourselves, we are incompetent to eat a good meal. We have listened to words of weakness from our childhood. You hear people say that they do not believe in ghosts, but at the same time, there are very few who do not get a little creepy sensation in the dark. It is simply superstition. So with all religious superstitions There are people in this country who, if I told them there was no such being as the devil, will think all religion is gone. Many people have said to me, how can there be religion without a devil? How can there be religion without someone to direct us? How can we live without being ruled by somebody? We like to be so treated, because we have become used to it. We are not happy until we feel we have been reprimanded by somebody every day. The same superstition! But however terrible it may seem now, the time will come when we shall look back, each one of us, and smile at every one of those superstitions which covered the pure and eternal soul, and repeat with gladness, with truth, and with strength, I am free, and was free, and always will be free. This monistic idea will come out of Vedanta, and it is the one idea that deserves to live. The scriptures may perish tomorrow. Whether this idea first flashed into the brains of Hebrews or of people living in the Arctic regions, nobody cares. For this is the truth and truth is eternal; and truth itself teaches that it is not the special property of any individual or nation. Men, animals, and gods are all common recipients of this one truth. Let them all receive it. Why make life miserable? Why let people fall into all sorts of superstitions? I will give ten thousand lives, if twenty of them will give up their superstition. Not only in this country, but in the land of its very birth, if you tell people this truth, they are frightened. They say, "This idea is for Sannyâsins who give up the world and live in forests; for them it is all right. But for us poor householders, we must all have some sort of fear, we must have ceremonies," and so on.

Dualistic ideas have ruled the world long enough, and this is the result. Why not make a new experiment? It may take ages for all minds to receive monism, but why not begin now? If we have told it to twenty persons in our lives, we have done a great work.

There is one idea which often militates against it. It is this. It is all very well to say, "I am the Pure, the Blessed," but I cannot show it always in my life. That is true; the ideal is always very hard. Every child that is born sees the sky overhead very far away, but is that any reason why we should not look towards the sky? Would it mend matters to go towards superstition? If we cannot get nectar, would it mend matters for us to drink poison? Would it be any help for us, because we cannot realise the truth immediately, to go into darkness and yield to weakness and superstition?

I have no objection to dualism in many of its forms. I like most of them, but I have objections to every form of teaching which inculcates weakness. This is the one question I put to every man, woman, or child, when they are in physical, mental, or spiritual training. Are you strong? Do you feel strength? — for I know it is truth alone that gives strength. I know that truth alone gives life, and nothing but going towards reality will make us strong, and none will reach truth until he is strong. Every system, therefore, which weakens the mind, makes one superstitious, makes one mope, makes one desire all sorts of wild impossibilities, mysteries, and superstitions, I do not like, because its effect is dangerous. Such systems never bring any good; such things create morbidity in the mind, make it weak, so weak that in course of time it will be almost impossible to receive truth or live up to it. Strength, therefore, is the one thing needful. Strength is the medicine for the world's disease. Strength is the medicine which the poor must have when tyrannised over by the rich. Strength is the medicine that the ignorant must have when oppressed by the learned; and it is the medicine that sinners must have when tyrannised over by other sinners; and nothing gives such strength as this idea of monism. Nothing makes us so moral as this idea of monism. Nothing makes us work so well at our best and highest as when all the responsibility is thrown upon ourselves. I challenge everyone of you. How will you behave if I put a little baby in your hands? Your whole life will be changed for the moment; whatever you may be, you must become selfless for the time being. You will give up all your criminal ideas as soon as responsibility is thrown upon you — your whole character will change. So if the whole responsibility is thrown upon our own shoulders, we shall be at our highest and best; when we have nobody to grope towards, no devil to lay our blame upon, no Personal God to carry our burdens, when we are alone responsible, then we shall rise to our highest and best. I am responsible for my fate, I am the bringer of good unto myself, I am the bringer of evil. I am the Pure and Blessed One. We must reject all thoughts that assert the contrary. "I have neither death nor fear, I have neither caste nor creed, I have neither father nor mother nor brother, neither friend nor foe, for I am Existence, Knowledge, and Bliss Absolute; I am the

Blissful One, I am the Blissful One. I am not bound either by virtue or vice, by happiness or misery. Pilgrimages and books and ceremonials can never bind me. I have neither hunger nor thirst; the body is not mine, nor am I subject to the superstitions and decay that come to the body, I am Existence, Knowledge, and Bliss Absolute; I am the Blissful One, I am the Blissful One."

This, says the Vedanta, is the only prayer that we should have. This is the only way to reach the goal, to tell ourselves, and to tell everybody else, that we are divine. And as we go on repeating this, strength comes. He who falters at first will get stronger and stronger, and the voice will increase in volume until the truth takes possession of our hearts, and courses through our veins, and permeates our bodies. Delusion will vanish as the light becomes more and more effulgent, load after load of ignorance will vanish, and then will come a time when all else has disappeared and the Sun alone shines.

CHAPTER XI
THE COSMOS

The Macrocosm

Delivered in New York, 19th January 1896

The flowers that we see all around us are beautiful, beautiful is the rising of the morning sun, beautiful are the variegated hues of nature. The whole universe is beautiful, and man has been enjoying it since his appearance on earth. Sublime and awe-inspiring are the mountains; the gigantic rushing rivers rolling towards the sea, the trackless deserts, the infinite ocean, the starry heavens — all these are awe-inspiring, sublime, and beautiful indeed. The whole mass of existence which we call nature has been acting on the human mind since time immemorial. It has been acting on the thought of man, and as its reaction has come out the question: What are these, whence are they? As far back as the time of the oldest portion of that most ancient human composition, the Vedas, we find the same question asked: "Whence is this? When there was neither aught nor naught, and darkness was hidden in darkness, who projected this universe? How? Who knows the secret?" And the question has come down to us at the present time. Millions of attempts have been made to answer it, yet millions of times it will have to be answered again. It is not that each answer was a failure; every answer to this question contained a part of truth, and this truth gathers strength as time rolls on. I will try to present before you the outline of the answer that I have gathered from the ancient philosophers of India; in harmony with modern knowledge.

We find that in this oldest of questions a few points had been already solved. The first is that there was a time when there was "neither aught nor naught", when this world did not exist; our mother earth with the seas and oceans, the rivers, and mountains, cities and villages human races, animals, plants, birds, and planets and luminaries, all this infinite variety of creation, had no existence. Are we sure of that? We will try to trace how this conclusion is arrived at. What does man see around him? Take a little plant. He puts a seed in the ground, and later, he finds a plant peep out, lift itself slowly above the ground, and grow and grow, till it becomes a gigantic tree. Then it dies, leaving only the seed. It completes the circle — it comes out of the seed, becomes the tree, and ends in the seed again. Look at a bird, how from the egg it springs, lives its life, and then dies, leaving other eggs, seeds of future birds. So with the animals, so with man. Everything in nature begins, as it were, from certain seeds, certain rudiments, certain fine forms, and becomes grosser and grosser, and develops, going on that way for a certain time, and then again goes back to that fine form, and subsides. The raindrop in which the beautiful sunbeam is playing was drawn in the form of vapour from the ocean, went far away into the air, and reached a region where it changed into water, and dropped down in its present form — to be converted into vapour again. So with everything in nature by which we are surrounded. We know that the huge mountains are being worked upon by glaciers and rivers, which are slowly but surely pounding them and pulverising them into sand, that drifts away into the ocean where it settles down on its bed, layer after layer, becoming hard as rocks, once more to be heaped up into mountains of a future generation. Again they will be pounded and pulverised, and thus the course goes on. From sand rise these mountains; unto sand they go.

If it be true that nature is uniform throughout, if it be true, and so far no human experience has contradicted it, that the same method under which a small grain of sand is created, works in creating the gigantic suns and stars and all this universe, if it be true that the whole of this universe is built on exactly the same plan as the atom, if it be true that the same law prevails throughout the universe, then, as it has been said in the Vedas, "Knowing one lump of clay we know the nature of all the clay that is in the universe." Take up a little plant and study its life, and we know the universe as it is. If we know one grain of sand, we understand the secret of the whole universe. Applying this course of reasoning to phenomena, we find, in the first place, that everything is almost similar at the beginning and the end. The mountain comes from the sand, and goes back to the sand; the river comes out of vapour, and goes back to vapour; plant life comes from the seed, and goes back to the seed; human life comes out of human germs, and goes back to human germs. The universe with its stars and planets has come out of a nebulous state and must go back to it. What do we learn from this? That the manifested or the grosser state is the effect, and the finer state the cause. Thousands of years ago, it was demonstrated by Kapila, the great father of all philosophy, that destruction means going back to the cause. If this table here is destroyed, it will go back to its cause, to those fine forms and particles which, combined, made this form which we call a table. If a man dies, he will go back to the elements which gave him his body; if this earth dies, it will go back to the elements which gave it form. This is what is called destruction, going back to the cause. Therefore we learn that the effect is the same as the cause, not different. It is only in another form. This glass is an effect, and it had its cause, and this cause is present in this form. A certain amount of the material called glass plus the force in the hands of the manufacturer, are the causes, the instrumental and the material, which, combined, produced this form called a glass. The force which was in the hands of the manufacturer is present in the glass as the power of adhesion, without which the particles would fall apart; and the glass material is also present. The glass is only a manifestation of these fine causes in a new shape, and if it be broken to pieces, the force which was present in the form of adhesion will go back and join its own element, and the particles of glass will remain the same until they take new forms.

Thus we find that the effect is never different from the cause. It is only that this effect is a reproduction of the cause in a grosser form. Next, we learn that all these particular forms which we call plants, animals, or men are being repeated ad infinitum, rising and falling. The seed produces the tree. The tree produces the seed, which again comes up as another tree, and so on and on; there is no end to it. Water-drops roll down the mountains into the ocean, and rise again as vapour, go back to the mountains and again come down to the ocean. So, rising and falling, the cycle goes on. So with all lives, so with all existence that we can see, feel, hear, or imagine. Everything that is within the bounds of our knowledge is proceeding in the same way, like breathing in and breathing out in the human body. Everything in creation goes on in this form, one wave rising, another falling, rising again, falling again. Each wave has its hollow, each hollow has its wave. The same law must apply to the universe taken as a whole, because of its uniformity. This universe must be resolved into its causes; the sun, moon, stars, and earth, the body and mind, and everything in this universe must return to their finer causes, disappear, be destroyed as it were. But they will live in the causes as fine forms. Out of these fine forms they will emerge again as new earths, suns, moons, and stars.

There is one fact more to learn about this rising and falling. The seed comes out of the tree; it does not immediately become a tree, but has a period of inactivity, or rather, a period of very fine unmanifested action. The seed has to work for some time beneath the soil. It breaks into pieces, degenerates as it were, and regeneration comes out of that degeneration. In the beginning, the whole of this universe has to work likewise for a period in that minute form, unseen and unmanifested, which is called chaos, and; out of that comes a new projection. The whole period of one manifestation of this universe — its going down into the finer form, remaining there for some time, and coming out again — is, in Sanskrit, called a Kalpa or a Cycle. Next comes a very important question especially for modern; times. We see that the finer forms develop slowly and slowly, and gradually becomes grosser and grosser. We have seen that the cause is the same as the effect, and the effect is only the cause in another form. Therefore this whole universe cannot be produced out of nothing. Nothing comes without a cause, and the cause is the effect in another form.

Out of what has this universe been produced then? From a preceding fine universe. Out of what has men been produced? The preceding fine form. Out of what has the tree been produced? Out of the seed; the whole of the tree was there in the seed. It comes out and becomes manifest. So, the whole of this universe has been created out of this very universe existing in a minute form. It has been made manifest now. It will go back to that minute form, and again will be made manifest. Now we find that the fine forms slowly come out and become grosser and grosser until they reach their limit, and when they reach their limit they go back further and further, becoming finer and finer again. This coming out of the fine and becoming gross, simply changing the arrangements of its parts, as it were, is what in modern times called evolution. This is very true, perfectly true; we see it in our lives. No rational man can possibly quarrel with these evolutionists. But we have to learn one thing more. We have to go one step further, and what is that? That every evolution is preceded by an involution. The seed is the father of the tree, but another tree was itself the father of the seed. The seed is the fine form out of which the big tree comes, and another big tree was the form which is involved in that seed. The whole of this universe was present in the cosmic fine universe. The little cell, which becomes afterwards the man, was simply the involved man and becomes evolved as a man. If this is clear, we have no quarrel with the evolutionists, for we see that if they admit this step, instead of their destroying religion, they will be the greatest supporters of it.

We see then, that nothing can be created out of nothing. Everything exists through eternity, and will exist through eternity. Only the movement is in succeeding waves and hollows, going back to fine forms, and coming out into gross manifestations. This involution and evolution is going on throughout the whole of nature. The whole series of evolution beginning with the lowest manifestation of life and reaching up to the highest, the most perfect man, must have been the involution of something else. The question is: The involution of what? What was involved? God. The evolutionist will tell you that your idea that it was God is wrong. Why? Because you see God is intelligent, but we find that intelligence develops much later on in the course of evolution. It is in man and the higher animals that we find intelligence, but millions of years have passed in this world before this intelligence came. This objection of the evolutionists does not hold water, as we shall see by applying our theory. The tree comes out of the seed, goes back to the seed; the beginning and the end are the same. The earth comes out of its cause and returns to it. We know that if we can find the beginning we can find the end. E converso, if we find the end we can find the beginning. If that is so, take this whole evolutionary series, from the protoplasm at one end to the perfect man at the other, and this whole series is one life. In the end we find the perfect man, so in the beginning it must have been the same. Therefore, the protoplasm was the involution of the highest intelligence. You may not see it but that involved intelligence is what is uncoiling itself until it becomes manifested in the most perfect man. That can be mathematically demonstrated. If the law of conservation of energy is true, you cannot get anything out of a machine unless you put it in there first. The amount of work that you get out of an engine is exactly the same as you have put into it in the form of water and coal, neither more nor less. The work I am doing now is just what I put into me, in the shape of air, food, and other things. It is only a question of change and manifestation. There cannot be added in the economy of this universe one particle of matter or one foot-pound of force, nor can one particle of matter or one foot-pound of force be taken out. If that be the case, what is this intelligence? If it was not present in the protoplasm, it must have come all of a sudden, something coming out of nothing, which is absurd. It, therefore, follows absolutely that the perfect man, the free man, the God-man, who has gone beyond the laws of nature, and transcended everything, who has no more to go through this process of evolution, through birth and death, that man called the "Christ-man" by the Christians, and the "Buddha-man" by the Buddhists, and the "Free" by the Yogis — that perfect man who is at one end of the chain of evolution was involved in the cell of the protoplasm, which is at the other end of the same chain.

Applying the same reason to the whole of the universe, we see that intelligence must be the Lord of creation, the cause. What is the most evolved notion that man has of this universe? It is intelligence, the adjustment of part to part, the display of intelligence, of which the ancient design theory was an attempt at expression. The beginning was, therefore, intelligence. At the beginning that intelligence becomes involved, and in the end that intelligence gets evolved. The sum total of the intelligence displayed in the universe must, therefore, be the involved universal intelligence unfolding itself. This universal intelligence is what we call God. Call it by any other name, it is absolutely certain that in the beginning there is that Infinite cosmic intelligence. This cosmic intelligence gets involved, and it manifests, evolves itself, until it becomes the perfect man, the "Christ-man," the "Buddha-man." Then it goes back to its own source. That is why all the scriptures say, "In Him we live and move and have our being." That is why all the scriptures preach that we come from God and go back to God. Do not be frightened by theological terms; if terms frighten you, you are not fit to be philosophers. This cosmic intelligence is what the theologians call God.

I have been asked many times, "Why do you use that old word, God? " Because it is the best word for our purpose; you cannot find a better word than that, because all the hopes, aspirations, and happiness of humanity have been centred in that word. It is impossible now to change the word. Words like these were first coined by great saints who realised their import and understood their meaning. But as they become current in society, ignorant people take these words, and the result is that they lose their spirit and glory. The word God has been used from time immemorial, and the idea of this cosmic intelligence, and all that is great and holy, is associated with it. Do you mean to say that because some fool says it is not all right, we should throw it away? Another man may come and say, "Take my word," and another again, "Take my word." So there will be no end to foolish words. Use the old word, only use it in the true spirit, cleanse it of superstition, and realise fully what this great ancient word means. If you understand the power of the laws of association, you will know that these words are associated with innumerable majestic and powerful ideas; they have been used and worshipped by millions of human souls and associated by them with all that is highest and best, all that is rational, all that is lovable, and all that is great and grand in human nature. And they come as suggestions of these associations, and cannot be given up. If I tried to express all these by only telling you that God created the universe, it would have conveyed no meaning to you. Yet, after all this struggle, we have come back to Him, the Ancient and Supreme One.

We now see that all the various forms of cosmic energy, such as matter, thought, force, intelligence and so forth, are simply the manifestations of that cosmic intelligence, or, as we shall call it henceforth, the Supreme Lord. Everything that you see, feel, or hear, the whole universe, is His creation, or to be a little more accurate, is His projection; or to be still more accurate, is the Lord Himself. It is He who is shining as the sun and the stars, He is the mother earth. He is the ocean Himself. He comes as gentle showers, He is the gentle air that we breathe in, and He it is who is working as force in the body. He is the speech that is uttered, He is the man who is talking. He is the audience that is here. He is the platform on which I stand, He is the light that enables me to see your faces. It is all He. He Himself is both the material and the efficient cause of this universe, and He it is that gets involved in the minute cell, and evolves at the other end and becomes God again. He it is that comes down and becomes the lowest atom, and slowly unfolding His nature, rejoins Himself. This is the mystery of the universe. "Thou art the man, Thou art the woman, Thou art the strong man walking in the pride of youth, Thou art the old man tottering on crutches, Thou art in everything. Thou art everything, O Lord." This is the only solution of the Cosmos that satisfies the human intellect. In one word, we are born of Him, we live in Him, and unto Him we return.

CHAPTER XII
THE COSMOS

The Microcosm

Delivered in New York, 26th January 1896

The human mind naturally wants to get outside, to peer out of the body, as it were, through the channels of the organs. The eye must see, the ear must hear, the senses must sense the external world — and naturally the beauties and sublimities of nature captivate the attention of man first. The first questions that arose in the human soul were about the external world. The solution of the mystery was asked of the sky, of the stars, of the heavenly bodies, of the earth, of the rivers, of the mountains, of the ocean; and in all ancient religions we find traces of how the groping human mind at first caught at everything external. There was a river-god, a sky-god, a cloud-god, a rain-god; everything external, all of which we now call the powers of nature, became metamorphosed, transfigured, into wills, into gods, into heavenly messengers. As the question went deeper and deeper, these external manifestations failed to satisfy the human mind, and finally the energy turned inward, and the question was asked of man's own soul. From the macrocosm the question was reflected back to the microcosm; from the external world the question was reflected to the internal. From analysing the external nature, man is led to analyse the internal; this questioning of the internal man comes with a higher state of civilisation, with a deeper insight into nature, with a higher state of growth.

The subject of discussion this afternoon is this internal man. No question is so near and dear to man's heart as that of the internal man. How many millions of times, in how many countries has this question been asked! Sages and kings, rich and poor, saints and sinners, every man, every woman, all have from time to time asked this question. Is there nothing permanent in this evanescent human life? Is there nothing, they have asked, which does not die away when this body dies? Is there not something living when this frame crumbles into dust? Is there not something which survives the fire which burns the body into ashes? And if so, what is its destiny? Where does it go? Whence did it come? These questions have been asked again and again, and so long as this creation lasts, so long as there are human brains to think, this question will have to be asked. Yet, it is not that the answer did not come; each time the answer came, and as time rolls on, the answer will gain strength more and more. The question was answered once for all thousands of years ago, and through all subsequent time it is being restated, reillustrated, made clearer to our intellect. What we have to do, therefore, is to make a restatement of the answer. We do not pretend to throw any new light on those all-absorbing problems, but only to put before you the ancient truth in the language of modern times, to speak the thoughts of the ancients in the language of the moderns, to speak the thoughts of the philosophers in the language of the people, to speak the thoughts of the angels in the language of man, to speak the thoughts of God in the language of poor humanity, so that man will understand them; for the same divine essence from which the ideas emanated is ever present in man, and, therefore, he can always understand them.

I am looking at you. How many things are necessary for this vision? First, the eyes. For if I am perfect in every other way, and yet have no eyes, I shall not be able to see you. Secondly, the real organ of vision. For the eyes are not the organs. They are but the instruments of vision, and behind them is the real organ, the nerve centre in the brain. If that centre be injured, a man may have the clearest pair of eyes, yet he will not be able to see anything. So, it is necessary that this centre, or the real organ, be there. Thus, with all our senses. The external ear is but the instrument for carrying the vibration of sound inward to the centre. Yet, that is not sufficient. Suppose in your library you are intently reading a book, and the clock strikes, yet you do not hear it. The sound is there, the pulsations in the air are there, the ear and the centre are also there, and these vibrations have been carried through the ear to the centre, and yet you do not hear it. What is wanting? The mind is not there. Thus we see that the third thing necessary is, that the mind must be there. First the external instruments, then the organ to which this external instrument will carry the sensation, and lastly the organ itself must be joined to the mind. When the mind is not joined to the organ, the organ and the ear may take the impression, and yet we shall not be conscious of it. The mind, too, is only the carrier; it has to carry the sensation still forward, and present it to the intellect. The intellect is the determining faculty and decides upon what is brought to it. Still this is not sufficient. The intellect must carry it forward and present the whole thing before the ruler in the body, the human soul, the king on the throne. Before him this is presented, and then from him comes the order, what to do or what not to do; and the order goes down in the same sequence to the intellect, to the mind, to the organs, and the organs convey it to the instruments, and the perception is complete.

The instruments are in the external body, the gross body of man; but the mind and the intellect are not. They are in what is called in Hindu philosophy the finer body; and what in Christian theology you read of as the spiritual body of man; finer, very much finer than the body, and yet not the soul. This soul is beyond them all. The external body perishes in a few years; any simple cause may disturb and destroy it. The finer body is not so easily perishable; yet it sometimes degenerates, and at other times becomes strong. We see how, in the old man, the mind loses its strength, how, when the body is vigorous, the mind becomes vigorous, how various medicines and drugs affect it, how everything external acts on it, and how it reacts on the external world. Just as the body has its progress and decadence, so also has the mind, and, therefore, the mind is not the soul, because the soul can neither decay nor degenerate. How can we know that? How can we know that there is something behind this mind? Because knowledge which is self-illuminating and the basis of intelligence cannot belong to dull, dead matter. Never was seen any gross matter which had intelligence as its own essence. No dull or dead matter can illumine itself. It is intelligence that illumines all matter. This hall is here only through intelligence because, as a hall, its existence would be unknown unless some intelligence built it. This body is not self-luminous; if it were, it would be so in a dead man also. Neither can the mind nor the spiritual body be self-luminous. They are not of the essence of intelligence. That which is self-luminous cannot decay. The luminosity of that which shines through a borrowed light comes and goes; but that which is light itself, what can make that come and go, flourish and decay? We see that the moon waxes and wanes, because it shines through the borrowed light of the sun. If a lump of iron is put into the fire and made red-hot, it glows and shines, but its light will vanish, because it is borrowed. So, decadence is possible only of that light which is borrowed and is not of its own essence.

Now we see that the body, the external shape, has no light as its own essence, is not self-luminous, and cannot know itself; neither can the mind. Why not? Because the mind waxes and wanes, because it is vigorous at one time and weak at another, because it can be acted upon by anything and everything.

Therefore the light which shines through the mind is not its own. Whose is it then? It must belong to that which has it as its own essence, and as such, can never decay or die, never become stronger or weaker; it is self-luminous, it is luminosity itself. It cannot be that the soul knows, it is knowledge. It cannot be that the soul has existence, but it is existence. It cannot be that the soul is happy, it is happiness itself. That which is happy has borrowed its happiness; that which has knowledge has received its knowledge; and that which has relative existence has only a reflected existence. Wherever there are qualities these qualities have been reflected upon the substance, but the soul has not knowledge, existence, and blessedness as its qualities, they are the essence of the soul.

Again, it may be asked, why shall we take this for granted? Why shall we admit that the soul has knowledge, blessedness, existence, as its essence, and has not borrowed them? It may be argued, why not say that the soul's luminosity, the soul's blessedness, the soul's knowledge, are borrowed in the same way as the luminosity of the body is borrowed from the mind? The fallacy of arguing in this way will be that there will be no limit. From whom were these borrowed? If we say from some other source, the same question will be asked again. So, at last we shall have to come to one who is self-luminous; to make matters short then, the logical way is to stop where we get self-luminosity, and proceed no further.

We see, then, that this human being is composed first of this external covering, the body; secondly, the finer body, consisting of mind, intellect, and egoism. Behind them is the real Self of man. We have seen that all the qualities and powers of the gross body are borrowed from the mind, and the mind, the finer body, borrows its powers and luminosity from the soul, standing behind.

A great many questions now arise about the nature of this soul. If the existence of the soul is drawn from the argument that it is self-luminous, that knowledge, existence, blessedness are its essence, it naturally follows that this soul cannot have been created. A self-luminous existence, independent of any other existence, could never have been the outcome of anything. It always existed; there was never a time when it did not exist, because if the soul did not exist, where was time? Time is in the soul; it is when the soul reflects its powers on the mind and the mind thinks, that time comes. When there was no soul, certainly there was no thought, and without thought, there was no time. How can the soul, therefore, be said to be existing in time, when time itself exists in the soul? It has neither birth nor death, but it is passing through all these various stages. It is manifesting slowly and gradually from lower to higher, and so on. It is expressing its own grandeur, working through the mind on the body; and through the body it is grasping the external world and understanding it. It takes up a body and uses it; and when that body has failed and is used up, it takes another body; and so on it goes.

Here comes a very interesting question, that question which is generally known as the reincarnation of the soul. Sometimes people get frightened at the idea, and superstition is so strong that thinking men even believe that they are the outcome of nothing, and then, with the grandest logic, try to deduce the theory that although they have come out of zero, they will be eternal ever afterwards. Those that come out of zero will certainly have to go back to zero. Neither you, nor I nor anyone present, has come out of zero, nor will go back to zero. We have been existing eternally, and will exist, and there is no power under the sun or above the sun which can undo your or my existence or send us back to zero. Now this idea of reincarnation is not only not a frightening idea, but is most essential for the moral well-being of the human race. It is the only logical conclusion that thoughtful men can arrive at. If you are going to exist in eternity hereafter, it must be that you have existed through eternity in the past: it cannot be otherwise. I will try to answer a few objections that are generally brought against the theory. Although many of you will think they are very silly objections, still we have to answer them, for sometimes we find that the most thoughtful men are ready to advance the silliest ideas. Well has it been said that there never was an idea so absurd that it did not find philosophers to defend it. The first objection is, why do we not remember our past? Do we remember all our past in this life? How many of you remember what you did when you were babies? None of you remember your early childhood, and if upon memory depends your existence, then this argument proves that you did not exist as babies, because you do not remember your babyhood. It is simply unmitigated nonsense to say that our existence depends on our remembering it. Why should we remember the past? That brain is gone, broken into pieces, and a new brain has been manufactured. What has come to this brain is the resultant, the sum total of the impressions acquired in our past, with which the mind has come to inhabit the new body.

I, as I stand here, am the effect, the result, of all the infinite past which is tacked on to me. And why is it necessary for me to remember all the past? When a great ancient sage, a seer, or a prophet of old, who came face to face with the truth, says something, these modern men stand up and say, "Oh, he was a fool!" But just use another name, "Huxley says it, or Tyndall"; then it must be true, and they take it for granted. In place of ancient superstitions they have erected modern superstitions, in place of the old Popes of religion they have installed modern Popes of science. So we see that this objection as to memory is not valid, and that is about the only serious objection that is raised against this theory. Although we have seen that it is not necessary for the theory that there shall be the memory of past lives, yet at the same time, we are in a position to assert that there are instances which show that this memory does come, and that each one of us will get back this memory in that life in which he will become free. Then alone you will find that this world is but a dream; then alone you will realise in the soul of your soul that you are but actors and the world is a stage; then alone will the idea of non-attachment come to you with the power of thunder; then all this thirst for enjoyment, this clinging on to life and this world will vanish for ever; then the mind will see dearly as daylight how many times all these existed for you, how many millions of times you had fathers and mothers, sons and daughters, husbands and wives, relatives and friends, wealth and power. They came and went. How many times you were on the topmost crest of the wave, and how many times you were down at the bottom of despair! When memory will bring all these to you, then alone will you stand as a hero and smile when the world frowns upon you. Then alone will you stand up and say. "I care not for thee even, O Death, what terrors hast thou for me?" This will come to all.

Are there any arguments, any rational proofs for this reincarnation of the soul? So far we have been giving the negative side, showing that the opposite arguments to disprove it are not valid. Are there any positive proofs? There are; and most valid ones, too. No other theory except that of reincarnation accounts for the wide divergence that we find between man and man in their powers to acquire knowledge. First, let us consider the process by means of which knowledge is acquired. Suppose I go into the street and see a dog. How do I know it is a dog? I refer it to my mind, and in my mind are groups of all my past experiences, arranged and pigeon-holed, as it were. As soon as a new impression comes, I take it up and refer it to some of the old pigeon-holes, and as soon as I find a group of the same impressions already existing, I place it in that group, and I am satisfied. I know it is a dog, because it coincides with the impressions already there. When I do not find the cognates of this new experience inside, I become dissatisfied. When, not finding the cognates of an impression, we become dissatisfied, this state of the mind is called "ignorance"; but, when, finding the cognates of an impression already existing, we become satisfied, this is called "knowledge". When one apple fell, men became dissatisfied. Then gradually they found out the group. What was the group they found? That all apples fell, so they called it "gravitation". Now we see that without a fund of already existing experience, any new experience would be impossible, for there would be nothing to which to refer the new impression. So, if, as some of the European philosophers think, a child came into the world with what they call tabula rasa, such a child would never attain to any degree of intellectual power, because he would have nothing to which to refer his new experiences. We see that the power of acquiring knowledge varies in each individual, and this shows that each one of us has come with his own fund of knowledge. Knowledge can only be got in one way, the way of experience; there is no other way to know. If we have not experienced it in this life, we must have experienced it in other lives. How is it that the fear of death is everywhere? A little chicken is just out of an egg and an eagle comes, and the chicken flies in fear to its mother. There is an old explanation (I should hardly dignify it by such a name). It is called instinct. What makes that little chicken just out of the egg afraid to die? How is it that as soon as a duckling hatched by a hen comes near water, it jumps into it and swims? It never swam before, nor saw anything swim. People call it instinct. It is a big word, but it leaves us where we were before. Let us study this phenomenon of instinct. A child begins to play on the piano. At first she must pay attention to every key she is fingering, and as she goes on and on for months and years, the playing becomes almost involuntary, instinctive. What was first done with conscious will does not require later on an effort of the will. This is not yet a complete proof. One half remains, and that is that almost all the actions which are now instinctive can be brought under the control of the will. Each muscle of the body can be brought under control. This is perfectly well known. So the proof is complete by this double method, that what we now call instinct is degeneration of voluntary actions; therefore, if the analogy applies to the whole of creation, if all nature is uniform, then what is instinct in lower animals, as well as in men, must be the degeneration of will.

Applying the law we dwelt upon under macrocosm that each involution presupposes an evolution, and each evolution an involution, we see that instinct is involved reason. What we call instinct in men or animals must therefore be involved, degenerated, voluntary actions, and voluntary actions are impossible without experience. Experience started that knowledge, and that knowledge is there. The fear of death, the duckling taking to the water and all involuntary actions in the human being which have become instinctive, are the results of past experiences. So far we have proceeded very clearly, and so far the latest science is with us. But here comes one more difficulty. The latest scientific men are coming back to the ancient sages, and as far as they have done so, there is perfect agreement. They admit that each man and each animal is born with a fund of experience, and that all these actions in the mind are the result of past experience. "But what," they ask, "is the use of saying that that experience belongs to the soul? Why not say it belongs to the body, and the body alone? Why not say it is hereditary transmission?" This is the last question. Why not say that all the experience with which I am born is the resultant effect of all the past experience of my ancestors? The sum total of the experience from the little protoplasm up to the highest human being is in me, but it has come from body to body in the course of hereditary transmission. Where will the difficulty be? This question is very nice, and we admit some part of this hereditary transmission. How far? As far as furnishing the material. We, by our past actions, conform ourselves to a certain birth in a certain body, and the only suitable material for that body comes from the parents who have made themselves fit to have that soul as their offspring.

The simple hereditary theory takes for granted the most astonishing proposition without any proof, that mental experience can be recorded in matters, that mental experience can be involved in matter. When I look at you in the lake of my mind there is a wave. That wave subsides, but it remains in fine form, as an impression. We understand a physical impression remaining in the body. But what proof is there for assuming that the mental impression can remain in the body, since the body goes to pieces? What carries it? Even granting it were possible for each mental impression to remain in the body, that every impression, beginning from the first man down to my father, was in my father's body, how could it be transmitted to me? Through the bioplasmic cell? How could that be? Because the father's body does not come to the child in toto. The same parents may have a number of children; then, from this theory of hereditary transmission, where the impression and the impressed (that is to say, material) are one, it rigorously follows that by the birth of every child the parents must lose a part of their own impressions, or, if the parents should transmit the whole of their impressions, then, after the birth of the first child, their minds would be a vacuum.

Again, if in the bioplasmic cell the infinite amount of impressions from all time has entered, where and how is it? This is a most impossible position, and until these physiologists can prove how and where those impressions live in that cell, and what they mean by a mental impression sleeping in the physical cell, their position cannot be taken for granted. So far it is clear then, that this impression is in the mind, that the mind comes to take its birth and rebirth, and uses the material which is most proper for it, and that the mind which has made itself fit for only a particular kind of body will have to wait until it gets that material. This we understand. The theory then comes to this, that there is hereditary transmission so far as furnishing the material to the soul is concerned. But the soul migrates and manufactures body after body, and each thought we think, and each deed we do, is stored in it in fine forms, ready to spring up again and take a new shape. When I look at you a wave rises in my mind. It dives down, as it were, and becomes finer and finer, but it does not die. It is ready to start up again as a wave in the shape of memory. So all these impressions are in my mind, and when I die the resultant force of them will be upon me. A ball is here, and each one of us takes a mallet in his hands and strikes the ball from all sides; the ball goes from point to point in the room, and when it reaches the door it flies out. What does it carry out with it? The resultant of all these blows. That will give it its direction. So, what directs the soul when the body dies? The resultant, the sum total of all the works it has done, of the thoughts it has thought. If the resultant is such that it has to manufacture a new body for further experience, it will go to those parents who are ready to supply it with suitable material for that body. Thus, from body to body it will go, sometimes to a heaven, and back again to earth, becoming man, or some lower animal. This way it will go on until it has finished its experience, and completed the circle. It then knows its own nature, knows what it is, and ignorance vanishes, its powers become manifest, it becomes perfect; no more is there any necessity for the soul to work through physical bodies, nor is there any necessity for it to work through finer, or mental bodies. It shines in its own light, and is free, no more to be born, no more to die.

We will not go now into the particulars of this. But I will bring before you one more point with regard to this theory of reincarnation. It is the theory that advances the freedom of the human soul. It is the one theory that does not lay the blame of all our weakness upon somebody else, which is a common human fallacy. We do not look at our own faults; the eyes do not see themselves, they see the eyes of everybody else. We human beings are very slow to recognise our own weakness, our own faults, so long as we can lay the blame upon somebody else. Men in general lay all the blame of life on their fellow-men, or, failing that, on God, or they conjure up a ghost, and say it is fate. Where is fate, and who is fate? We reap what we sow. We are the makers of our own fate. None else has the blame, none has the praise. The wind is blowing; those vessels whose sails are unfurled catch it, and go forward on their way, but those which have their sails furled do not catch the wind. Is that the fault of the wind? Is it the fault of the merciful Father, whose wind of mercy is blowing without ceasing, day and night, whose mercy knows no decay, is it His fault that some of us are happy and some unhappy? We make our own destiny. His sun shines for the weak as well as for the strong. His wind blows for saint and sinner alike. He is the Lord of all, the Father of all, merciful, and impartial. Do you mean to say that He, the Lord of creation, looks upon the petty things of our life in the same light as we do? What a degenerate idea of God that would be! We are like little puppies, making life-and-death struggles here, and foolishly thinking that even God Himself will take it as seriously as we do. He knows what the puppies' play means. Our attempts to lay the blame on Him, making Him the punisher, and the rewarder, are only foolish. He neither punishes, nor rewards any. His infinite mercy is open to every one, at all times, in all places, under all conditions, unfailing, unswerving. Upon us depends how we use it. Upon us depends how we utilise it. Blame neither man, nor God, nor anyone in the world. When you find yourselves suffering, blame yourselves, and try to do better.

This is the only solution of the problem. Those that blame others — and, alas! the number of them is increasing every day — are generally miserable with helpless brains; they have brought themselves to that pass through their own mistakes and blame others, but this does not alter their position. It does not serve them in any way. This attempt to throw the blame upon others only weakens them the more. Therefore, blame none for your own faults, stand upon your own feet, and take the whole responsibility upon yourselves. Say, "This misery that I am suffering is of my own doing, and that very thing proves that it will have to be undone by me alone." That which I created, I can demolish; that which is created by some one else I shall never be able to destroy. Therefore, stand up, be bold, be strong. Take the whole responsibility on your own shoulders, and know that you are the creator of your own destiny. All the strength and succour you want is within yourselves. Therefore, make your own future. "Let the dead past bury its dead." The infinite future is before you, and you must always remember that each word, thought, and deed, lays up a store for you and that as the bad thoughts and bad works are ready to spring upon you like tigers, so also there is the inspiring hope that the good thoughts and good deeds are ready with the power of a hundred thousand angels to defend you always and for ever.

CHAPTER XIII
IMMORTALITY

Delivered in America

What question has been asked a greater number of times, what idea has led men more to search the universe for an answer, what question is nearer and dearer to the human heart, what question is more inseparably connected with our existence, than this one, the immortality of the human soul? It has been the theme of poets and sages, of priests and prophets; kings on the throne have discussed it, beggars in the street have dreamt of it. The best of humanity have approached it, and the worst of men have hoped for it. The interest in the theme has not died yet, nor will it die so long as human nature exists. Various answers have been presented to the world by various minds. Thousands, again, in every period of history have given up the discussion, and yet the question remains fresh as ever. Often in the turmoil and struggle of our lives we seem to forget it, but suddenly some one dies — one, perhaps, whom we loved, one near and dear to our hearts is snatched away from us — and the struggle, the din and turmoil of the world around us, cease for a moment, and the soul asks the old questions "What after this?" "What becomes of the soul?"

All human knowledge proceeds out of experience; we cannot know anything except by experience. All our reasoning is based upon generalised experience, all our knowledge is but harmonised experience. Looking around us, what do we find? A continuous change. The plant comes out of the seed, grows into the tree, completes the circle, and comes back to the seed. The animal comes, lives a certain time, dies, and completes the circle. So does man. The mountains slowly but surely crumble away, the rivers slowly but surely dry up, rains come out of the sea, and go back to the sea. Everywhere circles are being completed, birth, growth, development, and decay following each other with mathematical precision. This is our everyday experience. Inside of it all, behind all this vast mass of what we call life, of millions of forms and shapes, millions upon millions of varieties, beginning from the lowest atom to the highest spiritualised man, we find existing a certain unity. Every day we find that the wall that was thought to be dividing one thing and another is being broken down, and all matter is coming to be recognised by modern science as one substance, manifesting in different ways and in various forms; the one life that runs through all like a continuous chain, of which all these various forms represent the links, link after link, extending almost infinitely, but of the same one chain. This is what is called evolution. It is an old, old idea, as old as human society, only it is getting fresher and fresher as human knowledge is progressing. There is one thing more, which the ancients perceived, but which in modern times is not yet so clearly perceived, and that is involution. The seed is becoming the plant; a grain of sand never becomes a plant. It is the father that becomes a child; a lump of clay never becomes the child. From what does this evolution come, is the question. What was the seed? It was the same as the tree. All the possibilities of a future tree are in that seed; all the possibilities of a future man are in the little baby; all the possibilities of any future life are in the germ. What is this? The ancient philosophers of India called it involution. We find then, that every evolution presupposes an involution. Nothing can be evolved which is not already there. Here, again, modern science comes to our help. You know by mathematical reasoning that the sum total of the energy that is displayed in the universe is the same throughout. You cannot take away one atom of matter or one foot-pound of force. You cannot add to the universe one atom of matter or one foot-pound of force. As such, evolution does not come out of zero; then, where does it come from? From previous involution. The child is the man involved, and the man is the child evolved. The seed is the tree involved, and the tree is the seed evolved. All the possibilities of life are in the germ. The problem becomes a little clearer. Add to it the first idea of continuation of life. From the lowest protoplasm to the most perfect human being there is really but one life. Just as in one life we have so many various phases of expression, the protoplasm developing into the baby, the child, the young man, the old man, so, from that protoplasm up to the most perfect man we get one continuous life, one chain. This is evolution, but we have seen that each evolution presupposes an involution. The whole of this life which slowly manifests itself evolves itself from the protoplasm to the perfected human being — the Incarnation of God on earth — the whole of this series is but one life, and the whole of this manifestation must have been involved in that very protoplasm. This whole life, this very God on earth, was involved in it and slowly came out, manifesting itself slowly, slowly, slowly. The highest expression must have been there in the germ state in minute form; therefore this one force, this whole chain, is the involution of that cosmic life which is everywhere. It is this one mass of intelligence which, from the protoplasm up to the most perfected man, is slowly and slowly uncoiling itself. Not that it grows. Take off all ideas of growth from your mind. With the idea of growth is associated something coming from outside, something extraneous, which would give the lie to the truth that the Infinite which lies latent in every life is independent of all external conditions. It can never grow; It was always there, and only manifests Itself.

The effect is the cause manifested. There is no essential difference between the effect and the cause. Take this glass, for instance. There was the material, and the material plus the will of the manufacturer made the glass and these two were its causes and are present in it. In what form is the will present? As adhesion. If the force were not here, each particle would fall away. What is the effect then? It is the same as the cause, only taking; different form, a different composition. When the cause is changed and limited for a time, it becomes the effect We must remember this. Applying it to our idea of life the whole of the manifestation of this one series, from the protoplasm up to the most perfect man, must be the very same thing as cosmic life. First it got involved and became finer; and out of that fine something, which wet the cause, it has gone on evolving, manifesting itself, and becoming grosser.

But the question of immortality is not yet settled. We have seen that everything in this universe is indestructible. There is nothing new; there will be nothing new. The same series of manifestations are presenting themselves alternately like a wheel, coming up and going down. All motion in this universe is in the form of waves, successively rising and falling. Systems after systems are coming out of fine forms, evolving themselves, and taking grosser forms, again melting down, as it were, and going back to the fine forms. Again they rise out of that, evolving for a certain period and slowly going back to the cause. So with all life. Each manifestation of life is coming up and then going back again. What goes down? The form. The form breaks to pieces, but it comes up again. In one sense bodies and forms even are eternal. How? Suppose we take a number of dice and throw them, and they fall in this ratio — 6 — 5 — 3 — 4. We take the dice up and throw them again and again; there must be a time when the same numbers will come again; the same combination must come. Now each particle, each atom, that is in this universe, I take for such a die, and these are being thrown out and combined again and again. All these forms before you are one combination. Here are the forms of a glass, a table, a pitcher of water, and so forth. This is one combination; in time, it will all break. But there must come a time when exactly the same combination comes again, when you will be here, and this form will be here, this subject will be talked, and this pitcher will be here. An infinite number of times this has been, and an infinite number of times this will be repeated. Thus far with the physical forms. What do we find? That even the combination of physical forms is eternally repeated.

A most interesting conclusion that follows from this theory is the explanation of facts such as these: Some of you, perhaps, have seen a man who can read the past life of others and foretell the future. How is it possible for any one to see what the future will be, unless there is a regulated future? Effects of the past will recur in the future, and we see that it is so. You have seen the big Ferris Wheel[1] in Chicago. The wheel revolves, and the little rooms in the wheel are regularly coming one after another; one set of persons gets into these, and after they have gone round the circle, they get out, and a fresh batch of people gets in. Each one of these batches is like one of these manifestations, from the lowest animals to the highest man. Nature is like the chain of the Ferris Wheel, endless and infinite, and these little carriages are the bodies or forms in which fresh batches of souls are riding, going up higher and higher until they become perfect and come out of the wheel. But the wheel goes on. And so long as the bodies are in the wheel, it can be absolutely and mathematically foretold where they will go, but not so of the souls. Thus it is possible to read the past and the future of nature with precision. We see, then, that there is recurrence of the same material phenomena at certain periods, and that the same combinations have been taking place through eternity. But that is not the immortality of the soul. No force can die, no matter can be annihilated. What becomes of it? It goes on changing, backwards and forwards, until it returns to the source from which it came. There is no motion in a straight line. Everything moves in a circle; a straight line, infinitely produced, becomes a circle. If that is the case, there cannot be eternal degeneration for any soul. It cannot be. Everything must complete the circle, and come back to its source. What are you and I and all these souls? In our discussion of evolution and involution, we have seen that you and I must be part of the cosmic consciousness, cosmic life, cosmic mind, which got involved and we must complete the circle and go back to this cosmic intelligence which is God. This cosmic intelligence is what people call Lord, or God, or Christ, or Buddha, or Brahman, what the materialists perceive as force, and the agnostics as that infinite, inexpressible beyond; and we are all parts of that.

This is the second idea, yet this is not sufficient; there will be still more doubts. It is very good to say that there is no destruction for any force. But all the forces and forms that we see are combina-

---

1. An amusement device consisting of a giant power-driven steel wheel, revolvable on its stationary axle, and carrying a number of balanced passenger cars around its rim."— Webster, G. W. G. Ferris erected the first of its kind for the Chicago Exposition of 1893. In India we have a corresponding wooden device very common in fairs. — Ed.

tions. This form before us is a composition of several component parts, and so every force that we see is similarly composite. If you take the scientific idea of force, and call it the sum total, the resultant of several forces, what becomes of your individuality? Everything that is a compound must sooner or later go back to its component parts. Whatever in this universe is the result of the combination of matter or force must sooner or later go back to its components. Whatever is the result of certain causes must die, must be destroyed. It gets broken up, dispersed, and resolved back into its components. Soul is not a force; neither is it thought. It is the manufacturer of thought, but not thought itself; it is the manufacturer of the body, but not the body. Why so? We see that the body cannot be the soul. Why not? Because it is not intelligent. A corpse is not intelligent, nor a piece of meat in a butcher's shop. What do we mean by intelligence? Reactive power. We want to go a little more deeply into this. Here is a pitcher; I see it. How? Rays of light from the pitcher enter my eyes, and make a picture in my retina, which is carried to the brain. Yet there is no vision. What the physiologists call the sensory nerves carry this impression inwards. But up to this there is no reaction. The nerve centre in the brain carries the impression to the mind, and the mind reacts, and as soon as this reaction comes, the pitcher flashes before it. Take a more commonplace example. Suppose you are listening to me intently and a mosquito is sitting on the tip of your nose and giving you that pleasant sensation which mosquitoes can give; but you are so intent on hearing me that you do not feel the mosquito at all. What has happened? The mosquito has bitten a certain part of your skin, and certain nerves are there. They have carried a certain sensation to the brain, and the impression is there, but the mind, being otherwise occupied, does not react, so you are not aware of the presence of the mosquito. When a new impression comes, if the mind does not react, we shall not be conscious of it, but when the reaction comes we feel, we see, we hear, and so forth. With this reaction comes illumination, as the Sâmkhya philosophers call it. We see that the body cannot illuminate, because in the absence of attention no sensation is possible. Cases have been known where, under peculiar conditions, a man who had never learnt a particular language was found able to speak it. Subsequent inquiries proved that the man had, when a child, lived among people who spoke that language and the impressions were left in his brain. These impressions remained stored up there, until through some cause the mind reacted, and illumination came, and then the man was able to speak the language. This shows that the mind alone is not sufficient, that the mind itself is an instrument in the hands of someone. In the case of that boy the mind contained that language, yet he did not know it, but later there came a time when he did. It shows that there is someone besides the mind; and when the boy was a baby, that someone did not use the power; but when the boy grew up, he took advantage of it, and used it. First, here is the body, second the mind, or instrument of thought, and third behind this mind is the Self of man. The Sanskrit word is Atman. As modern philosophers have identified thought with molecular changes in the brain, they do not know how to explain such a case, and they generally deny it. The mind is intimately connected with the brain which dies every time the body changes. The Self is the illuminator, and the mind is the instrument in Its hands, and through that instrument It gets hold of the external instrument, and thus comes perception. The external instruments get hold of the impressions and carry them to the organs, for you must remember always, that the eyes and ears are only receivers — it is the internal organs, the brain centres, which act. In Sanskrit these centres are called Indriyas, and they carry sensations to the mind, and the mind presents them further back to another state of the mind, which in Sanskrit is called Chitta, and there they are organised into will, and all these present them to the King of kings inside, the Ruler on His throne, the Self of man. He then sees and gives His orders. Then the mind immediately acts on the organs, and the organs on the external body. The real Perceiver, the real Ruler, the Governor, the Creator, the Manipulator of all this, is the Self of man.

We see, then, that the Self of man is not the body,

neither is It thought. It cannot be a compound. Why not? Because everything that is a compound can be seen or imagined. That which we cannot imagine or perceive, which we cannot bind together, is not force or matter, cause or effect, and cannot be a compound. The domain of compounds is only so far as our mental universe, our thought universe extends. Beyond this it does not hold good; it is as far as law reigns, and if there is anything beyond law, it cannot be a compound at all. The Self of man being beyond the law of causation, is not a compound. It is ever free and is the Ruler of everything that is within law. It will never die, because death means going back to the component parts, and that which was never a compound can never die. It is sheer nonsense to say It dies.

We are now treading on finer and finer ground, and some of you, perhaps, will be frightened. We have seen that this Self, being beyond the little universe of matter and force and thought, is a simple; and as a simple It cannot die. That which does not die cannot live. For life and death are the obverse and reverse of the same coin. Life is another name for death, and death for life. One particular mode of manifestation is what we call life; another particular mode of manifestation of the same thing is what we call death. When the wave rises on the top it is life; and when it falls into the hollow it is death. If anything is beyond death, we naturally see it must also be beyond life. I must remind you of the first conclusion that the soul of man is part of the cosmic energy that exists, which is God. We now find that it is beyond life and death. You were never born, and you will never die. What is this birth and death that we see around us? This belongs to the body only, because the soul is omnipresent. "How can that be?" you may ask. "So many people are sitting here, and you say the soul is omnipresent?" What is there, I ask, to limit anything that is beyond law, beyond causation? This glass is limited; it is not omnipresent, because the surrounding matter forces it to take that form, does not allow it to expand. It is conditioned be everything around it, and is, therefore, limited. But that which is beyond law, where there is nothing to act upon it, how can

that be limited? It must be omnipresent. You are everywhere in the universe. How is it then that I am born and I am going to die, and all that? That is the talk of ignorance, hallucination of the brain. You were neither born, nor will you die. You have had neither birth, nor will have rebirth, nor life, nor incarnation, nor anything. What do you mean by coming and going? All shallow nonsense. You are everywhere. Then what is this coming and going? It is the hallucination produced by the change of this fine body which you call the mind. That is going on. Just a little speck of cloud passing before the sky. As it moves on and on, it may create the delusion that the sky moves. Sometimes you see a cloud moving before the moon, and you think that the moon is moving. When you are in a train you think the land is flying, or when you are in a boat, you think the water moves. In reality you are neither going nor coming, you are not being born, nor going to be reborn; you are infinite, ever-present, beyond all causation, and ever-free. Such a question is out of place, it is arrant nonsense. How could there be mortality when there was no birth?

One step more we will have to take to come to a logical conclusion. There is no half-way house. You are metaphysicians, and there is no crying quarter. If then we are beyond all law, we must be omniscient, ever-blessed; all knowledge must be in us and all power and blessedness. Certainly. You are the omniscient. Omnipresent being of the universe. But of such beings can there be many? Can there be a hundred thousand millions of omnipresent beings? Certainly not. Then, what becomes of us all? You are only one; there is only one such Self, and that One Self is you. Standing behind this little nature is what we call the Soul. There is only One Being, One Existence, the ever-blessed, the omnipresent, the omniscient, the birthless, deathless. "Through His control the sky expands, through His control the air breathes, through His control the sun shines, and through His control all live. He is the Reality in nature, He is the Soul of your soul, nay, more, you are He, you are one with Him." Wherever there are two, there is fear, there is danger, there is conflict, there is strife. When it is all One, who is there to hate, who is there to struggle with? When it is all He, with whom can you fight? This explains the true nature of life; this explains the true nature of being. This is perfection, and this is God. As long as you see the many, you are under delusion. "In this world of many he who sees the One, in this ever changing world he who sees Him who never changes, as the Soul of his own soul, as his own Self, he is free, he is blessed, he has reached the goal." Therefore know that thou art He; thou art the God of this universe, "Tat Tvam Asi" (That thou art). All these various ideas that I am a man or a woman, or sick or healthy, or strong or weak, or that I hate or I love, or have a little power, are but hallucinations. Away with them! What makes you weak? What makes you fear? You are the One Being in the universe. What frightens you? Stand up then and be free. Know that every thought and word that weakens you in this world is the only evil that exists. Whatever makes men weak and fear is the only evil that should be shunned. What can frighten you? If the suns come down, and the moons crumble into dust, and systems after systems are hurled into annihilation, what is that to you? Stand as a rock; you are indestructible. You are the Self, the God of the universe. Say — "I am Existence Absolute, Bliss Absolute, Knowledge Absolute, I am He," and like a lion breaking its cage, break your chain and be free for ever. What frightens you, what holds you down? Only ignorance and delusion; nothing else can bind you. You are the Pure One, the Ever-blessed.

Silly fools tell you that you are sinners, and you sit down in a corner and weep. It is foolishness, wickedness, downright rascality to say that you are sinners! You are all God. See you not God and call Him man? Therefore, if you dare, stand on that — mould your whole life on that. If a man cuts your throat, do not say no, for you are cutting your own throat. When you help a poor man, do not feel the least pride. That is worship for you, and not the cause of pride. Is not the whole universe you? Where is there any one that is not you? You are the Soul of this universe. You are the sun, moon, and stars, it is you that are shining everywhere. The whole universe is you. Whom are you going to hate or to fight? Know, then, that thou art He, and model your whole life accordingly; and he who knows this and models his life accordingly will no more grovel in darkness.

CHAPTER XIV
THE ATMAN

Delivered in America

Many of you have read Max Müller's celebrated book, Three Lectures on the Vedanta Philosophy, and some of you may, perhaps, have read, in German, Professor Deussen's book on the same philosophy. In what is being written and taught in the West about the religious thought of India, one school of Indian thought is principally represented, that which is called Advaitism, the monistic side of Indian religion; and sometimes it is thought that all the teachings of the Vedas are comprised in that one system of philosophy. There are, however, various phases of Indian thought; and, perhaps, this non-dualistic form is in the minority as compared with the other phases. From the most ancient times there have been various sects of thought in India, and as there never was a formulated or recognised church or any body of men to designate the doctrines which should be believed by each school, people were very free to choose their own form, make their own philosophy and establish their own sects. We, therefore, find that from the most ancient times India was full of religious sects. At the present time, I do not know how many hundreds of sects we have in India, and several fresh ones are coming into existence every year. It seems that the religious activity of that nation is simply inexhaustible.

Of these various sects, in the first place, there can be made two main divisions, the orthodox and the unorthodox. Those that believe in the Hindu scriptures, the Vedas, as eternal revelations of truth, are called orthodox, and those that stand on other authorities, rejecting the Vedas, are the heterodox in India. The chief modern unorthodox Hindu sects are the Jains and the Buddhists. Among the orthodox some declare that the scriptures are of much higher authority than reason; others again say that only that portion of the scriptures which is rational should be taken and the rest rejected.

Of the three orthodox divisions, the Sânkhyas, the Naiyâyikas, and the Mimâmsakas, the former two, although they existed as philosophical schools, failed to form any sect. The one sect that now really covers India is that of the later Mimamsakas or the Vedantists. Their philosophy is called Vedantism. All the schools of Hindu philosophy start from the Vedanta or Upanishads, but the monists took the name to themselves as a speciality, because they wanted to base the whole of their theology and philosophy upon the Vedanta and nothing else. In the course of time the Vedanta prevailed, and all the various sects of India that now exist can be referred to one or other of its schools. Yet these schools are not unanimous in their opinions.

We find that there are three principal variations among the Vedantists. On one point they all agree, and that is that they all believe in God. All these Vedantists also believe the Vedas to be the revealed word of God, not exactly in the same sense, perhaps, as the Christians or the Mohammedans believe, but in a very peculiar sense. Their idea is that the Vedas are an expression of the knowledge of God, and as God is eternal, His knowledge is eternally with Him, and so are the Vedas eternal. There is another common ground of belief: that of creation in cycles, that the whole of creation appears and disappears; that it is projected and becomes grosser and grosser, and at the end of an incalculable period of time it becomes finer and finer, when it dissolves and subsides, and then comes a period of rest. Again it begins to appear and goes through the same process. They postulate the existence of a material which they call Âkâsha, which is something like the ether of the scientists, and a power which they call Prâna. About this Prana they declare that by its vibration the universe is produced. When a cycle ends, all this manifestation of nature becomes finer and finer and dissolves into that Akasha which cannot be seen or felt, yet out of which everything is manufactured.

All the forces that we see in nature, such as gravitation, attraction, and repulsion, or as thought, feeling, and nervous motion — all these various forces resolve into that Prana, and the vibration of the Prana ceases. In that state it remains until the beginning of the next cycle. Prana then begins to vibrate, and that vibration acts upon the Akasha, and all these forms are thrown out in regular succession.

The first school I will tell you about is styled the dualistic school. The dualists believe that God, who is the creator of the universe and its ruler, is eternally separate from nature, eternally separate from the human soul. God is eternal; nature is eternal; so are all souls. Nature and the souls become manifested and change, but God remains the same. According to the dualists, again, this God is personal in that He has qualities, not that He has a body. He has human attributes; He is merciful, He is just, He is powerful, He is almighty, He can be approached, He can be prayed to, He can be loved, He loves in return, and so forth. In one word, He is a human God, only infinitely greater than man; He has none of the evil qualities which men have. "He is the repository of an infinite number of blessed qualities" — that is their definition. He cannot create without materials, and nature is the material out of which He creates the whole universe. There are some non-Vedantic dualists, called "Atomists", who believe that nature is nothing but an infinite number of atoms, and God's will, acting upon these atoms, creates. The Vedantists deny the atomic theory; they say it is perfectly illogical. The indivisible atoms are like geometrical points without parts or magnitude; but something without parts or magnitude, if multiplied an infinite number of times, will remain the same. Anything that has no parts will never make something that has parts; any number of zeros added together will not make one single whole number. So, if these atoms are such that they have no parts or magnitude, the creation of the universe is simply impossible out of such atoms. Therefore, according to the Vedantic dualists, there is what they call indiscrete or undifferentiated nature, and out of that God creates the universe. The vast mass of Indian people are dualists. Human nature ordinarily cannot conceive of anything higher. We find that ninety per cent of the population of the earth who believe in any religion are dualists. All the religions of Europe and Western Asia are dualistic; they have to be. The ordinary man cannot think of anything which is not concrete. He naturally likes to cling to that which his intellect can grasp. That is to say, he can only conceive of higher spiritual ideas by bringing them down to his own level. He can only grasp abstract thoughts by making them concrete. This is the religion of the masses all over the world. They believe in a God who is entirely separate from them, a great king, a high, mighty monarch, as it were. At the same time they make Him purer than the monarchs of the earth; they give Him all good qualities and remove the evil qualities from Him. As if it were ever possible for good to exist without evil; as if there could be any conception of light without a conception of darkness!

With all dualistic theories the first difficulty is, how is it possible that under the rule of a just and merciful God, the repository of an infinite number of good qualities, there can be so many evils in this world? This question arose in all dualistic religions, but the Hindus never invented a Satan as an answer to it. The Hindus with one accord laid the blame on man, and it was easy for them to do so. Why? Because, as I have just now told you, they did not believe that souls were created out of nothing We see in this life that we can shape and form our future every one of us, every day, is trying to shape the morrow; today we fix the fate of the morrow; tomorrow we shall fix the fate of the day after, and so on. It is quite logical that this reasoning can be pushed backward too. If by our own deeds we shape our destiny in the future why not apply the same rule to the past? If, in an infinite chain, a certain number of links are alternately repeated then, if one of these groups of links be explained, we can explain the whole chain. So, in this infinite length of time, if we can cut off one portion and explain that portion and understand it, then, if it be true that nature is uniform, the same explanation must apply to the whole chain of time. If it be true that we are working out our own destiny here within this short space of time if it be true that everything must have a cause as we see it now, it must also be true that that which we are now is the effect of the whole of our past; therefore, no other person is necessary to shape the destiny of mankind but man himself. The evils that are in the world are caused by none else but ourselves. We have caused all this evil; and just as we constantly see misery resulting from evil actions, so can we also see that much of the existing misery in the world is the effect of the past wickedness of man. Man alone, therefore, according to this theory, is responsible. God is not to blame. He, the eternally merciful Father, is not to blame at all. "We reap what we sow."

Another peculiar doctrine of the dualists is, that every soul must eventually come to salvation. No one will be left out. Through various vicissitudes, through various sufferings and enjoyments, each one of them will come out in the end. Come out of what? The one common idea of all Hindu sects is that all souls have to get out of this universe. Neither the universe which we see and feel, nor even an imaginary one, can be right, the real one, because both are mixed up with good and evil. According to the dualists, there is beyond this universe a place full of happiness and good only; and when that place is reached, there will be no more necessity of being born and reborn, of living and dying; and this idea is very dear to them. No more disease there, and no more death. There will be eternal happiness, and they will be in the presence of God for all time and enjoy Him for ever. They believe that all beings, from the lowest worm up to the highest angels and gods, will all, sooner or later, attain to that world where there will be no more misery. But our world will never end; it goes on infinitely, although moving in waves. Although moving in cycles it never ends. The number of souls that are to be saved, that are to be perfected, is infinite. Some are in plants, some are in the lower animals, some are in men, some are in gods, but all of them, even the highest gods, are imperfect, are in bondage. What is the bondage? The necessity of being born and the necessity of dying. Even the highest gods die. What are these gods? They mean certain states, certain offices. For instance, Indra the king of gods, means a certain office; some soul which was very high has gone to fill that post in this cycle, and after this cycle he will be born again as man and come down to this earth, and the man who is very good in this cycle will go and fill that post in the next cycle. So with all these gods; they are certain offices which have been filled alternately by millions and millions of souls, who, after filling those offices, came down and became men. Those who do good works in this world and help others, but with an eye to reward, hoping to reach heaven or to get the praise of their fellow-men, must when they die, reap the benefit of those good works — they become these gods. But that is not salvation; salvation never will come through hope of reward. Whatever man desires the Lord gives him. Men desire power, they desire prestige, they desire enjoyments as gods, and they get these desires fulfilled, but no effect of work can be eternal. The effect will be exhausted after a certain length of time; it may be aeons, but after that it will be gone, and these gods must come down again and become men and get another chance for liberation. The lower animals will come up and become men, become gods, perhaps, then become men again, or go back to animals, until the time when they will get rid of all desire for enjoyment, the thirst for life, this clinging on to the "me and mine". This "me and mine" is the very root of all the evil in the world. If you ask a dualist, "Is your child yours?" he will say, "It is God's. My property is not mine, it is God's." Everything should be held as God's.

Now, these dualistic sects in India are great vegetarians, great preachers of non-killing of animals. But their idea about it is quite different from that of the Buddhist. If you ask a Buddhist, "Why do you preach against killing any animal?" he will answer, "We have no right to take any life;" and if you ask a dualist, "Why do you not kill any animal?" he says, "Because it is the Lord's." So the dualist says that this "me and mine" is to be applied to God and God alone; He is the only "me" and everything is His. When a man has come to the state when he has no "me and mine," when everything is given up to the Lord, when he loves everybody and is ready even to give up his life for an animal, without any desire for reward, then his heart will be purified, and when the heart has been purified, into that heart will come the love of God. God is the centre of attraction for every soul, and the dualist says, "A needle covered up with clay will not be attracted by a magnet, but as soon as the clay is washed off, it will be attracted." God is the magnet and human soul is the needle, and its evil works, the dirt and dust that cover it. As soon as the soul is pure it will by natural attraction come to God and remain with Him for ever, but remain eternally separate. The perfected soul, if it wishes, can take any form; it is able to take a hundred bodies, if it wishes or have none at all, if it so desires. It becomes almost almighty, except that it cannot create; that power belongs to God alone. None, however perfect, can manage the affairs of the universe; that function belongs to God. But all souls, when they become perfect, become happy for ever and live eternally with God. This is the dualistic statement.

One other idea the dualists preach. They protest against the idea of praying to God, "Lord, give me this and give me that." They think that should not be done. If a man must ask some material gift, he should ask inferior beings for it; ask one of these gods, or angels or a perfected being for temporal things. God is only to be loved. It is almost a blasphemy to pray to God, "Lord, give me this, and give me that." According to the dualists, therefore, what a man wants, he will get sooner or later by praying to one of the gods; but if he wants salvation, he must worship God. This is the religion of the masses of India.

The real Vedanta philosophy begins with those known as the qualified non-dualists. They make the statement that the effect is never different from the cause; the effect is but the cause reproduced in another form. If the universe is the effect and God the cause, it must be God Himself — it cannot be anything but that. They start with the assertion that God is both the efficient and the material cause of the universe; that He Himself is the creator, and He Himself is the material out of which the whole of nature is projected. The word "creation" in your language has no equivalent in Sanskrit, because there is no sect in India which believes in creation, as it is regarded in the West, as something coming out of nothing. It seems that at one time there were a few that had some such idea, but they were very quickly silenced. At the present time I do not know of any sect that believes this. What we mean by creation is projection of that which already existed. Now, the whole universe, according to this sect, is God Himself. He is the material of the universe. We read in the Vedas, "As the Urnanâbhi (spider) spins the thread out of its own body, . . . even so the whole universe has come out of the Being."

If the effect is the cause reproduced, the question is: "How is it that we find this material, dull, unintelligent universe produced from a God, who is not material, but who is eternal intelligence? How, if the cause is pure and perfect, can the effect be quite different?" What do these qualified non-dualists say? Theirs is a very peculiar theory. They say that these three existences, God, nature, and the soul, are one. God is, as it were, the Soul, and nature and souls are the body of God. Just as I have a body and I have a soul, so the whole universe and all souls are the body of God, and God is the Soul of souls. Thus, God is the material cause of the universe. The body may be changed — may be young or old, strong or weak — but that does not affect the soul at all. It is the same eternal existence, manifesting through the body. Bodies come and go, but the soul does not change. Even so the whole universe is the body of God, and in that sense it is God. But the change in the universe does not affect God. Out of this material He creates the universe, and at the end of a cycle His body becomes finer, it contracts; at the beginning of another cycle it becomes expanded again, and out of it evolve all these different worlds.

Now both the dualists and the qualified non-dualists admit that the soul is by its nature pure, but through its own deeds it becomes impure. The qualified non-dualists express it more beautifully than the dualists, by saying that the soul's purity and perfection become contracted and again become manifest, and what we are now trying to do is to remanifest the intelligence, the purity, the power which is natural to the soul. Souls have a multitude of qualities, but not that of almightiness or all-knowingness. Every wicked deed contracts the nature of the soul, and every good deed expands it, and these souls, are all parts of God. "As from a blazing fire fly millions of sparks of the same nature, even so from this Infinite Being, God, these souls have come." Each has the same goal. The God of the qualified non-dualists is also a Personal God, the repository of an infinite number of blessed qualities, only He is interpenetrating everything in the universe. He is immanent in everything and everywhere; and when the scriptures say that God is everything, it means that God is interpenetrating everything, not that God has become the wall, but that God is in the wall. There is not a particle, not an atom in the universe where He is not. Souls are all limited; they are not omnipresent. When they get expansion of their powers and become perfect, there is no more birth and death for them; they live with God for ever.

Now we come to Advaitism, the last and, what we think, the fairest flower of philosophy and religion that any country in any age has produced, where human thought attains its highest expression and even goes beyond the mystery which seems to be impenetrable. This is the non-dualistic Vedantism. It is too abstruse, too elevated to be the religion of the masses. Even in India, its birthplace, where it has been ruling supreme for the last three thousand years, it has not been able to permeate the masses. As we go on we shall find that it is difficult for even the most thoughtful man and woman in any country to understand Advaitism. We have made ourselves so weak; we have made ourselves so low. We may make great claims, but naturally we want to lean on somebody else. We are like little, weak plants, always wanting a support. How many times I have been asked for a "comfortable religion!" Very few men ask for the truth, fewer still dare to learn the truth, and fewest of all dare to follow it in all its practical bearings. It is not their fault; it is all weakness of the brain. Any new thought, especially of a high kind, creates a disturbance, tries to make a new channel, as it were, in the brain matter, and that unhinges the system, throws men off their balance.

They are used to certain surroundings, and have to overcome a huge mass of ancient superstitions, ancestral superstition, class superstition, city superstition, country superstition, and behind all, the vast mass of superstition that is innate in every human being. Yet there are a few brave souls in the world who dare to conceive the truth, who dare to take it up, and who dare to follow it to the end.

What does the Advaitist declare? He says, if there is a God, that God must be both the material and the efficient cause of the universe. Not only is He the creator, but He is also the created. He Himself is this universe. How can that be? God, the pure, the spirit, has become the universe? Yes; apparently so. That which all ignorant people see as the universe does not really exist. What are you and I and all these things we see? Mere self-hypnotism; there is but one Existence, the Infinite, the Ever-blessed One. In that Existence we dream all these various dreams. It is the Atman, beyond all, the Infinite, beyond the known, beyond the knowable; in and through That we see the universe. It is the only Reality. It is this table; It is the audience before me; It is the wall; It is everything, minus the name and form. Take away the form of the table, take away the name; what remains is It. The Vedantist does not call It either He or She — these are fictions, delusions of the human brain — there is no sex in the soul. People who are under illusion, who have become like animals, see a woman or a man; living gods do not see men or women. How can they who are beyond everything have any sex idea? Everyone and everything is the Atman — the Self — the sexless, the pure, the ever-blessed. It is the name, the form, the body, which are material, and they make all this difference. If you take away these two differences of name and form, the whole universe is one; there are no two, but one everywhere. You and I are one. There is neither nature, nor God, nor the universe, only that one Infinite Existence, out of which, through name and form, all these are manufactured. How to know the Knower? It cannot be known. How can you see your own Self? You can only reflect yourself. So all this universe is the reflection of that One Eternal Being, the Atman, and as the reflection falls upon good or bad reflectors, so good or bad images are cast up. Thus in the murderer, the reflector is bad and not the Self. In the saint the reflector is pure. The Self — the Atman — is by Its own nature pure. It is the same, the one Existence of the universe that is reflecting Itself from the lowest worm to the highest and most perfect being. The whole of this universe is one Unity, one Existence, physically, mentally, morally and spiritually. We are looking upon this one Existence in different forms and creating all these images upon It. To the being who has limited himself to the condition of man, It appears as the world of man. To the being who is on a higher plane of existence, It may seem like heaven. There is but one Soul in the universe, not two. It neither comes nor goes. It is neither born, nor dies, nor reincarnates. How can It die? Where can It go? All these heavens, all these earths, and all these places are vain imaginations of the mind. They do not exist, never existed in the past, and never will exist in the future.

I am omnipresent, eternal. Where can I go? Where am I not already? I am reading this book of nature. Page after page I am finishing and turning over, and one dream of life after another goes Away. Another page of life is turned over; another dream of life comes, and it goes away, rolling and rolling, and when I have finished my reading, I let it go and stand aside, I throw away the book, and the whole thing is finished. What does the Advaitist preach? He dethrones all the gods that ever existed, or ever will exist in the universe and places on that throne the Self of man, the Atman, higher than the sun and the moon, higher than the heavens, greater than this great universe itself. No books, no scriptures, no science can ever imagine the glory of the Self that appears as man, the most glorious God that ever was, the only God that ever existed, exists, or ever will exist. I am to worship, therefore, none but myself. "I worship my Self," says the Advaitist. To whom shall I bow down? I salute my Self. To whom shall I go for help? Who can help me, the Infinite Being of the universe? These are foolish dreams, hallucinations; who ever helped any one? None. Wherever you see a weak man, a dualist, weeping and wailing for help from somewhere above the skies, it is because he does not know that the skies also are in him. He wants help from the skies, and the help comes. We see that it comes; but it comes from within himself, and he mistakes it as coming from without. Sometimes a sick man lying on his bed may hear a tap on the door. He gets up and opens it and finds no one there. He goes back to bed, and again he hears a tap. He gets up and opens the door. Nobody is there. At last he finds that it was his own heartbeat which he fancied was a knock at the door. Thus man, after this vain search after various gods outside himself, completes the circle, and comes back to the point from which he started — the human soul, and he finds that the God whom he was searching in hill and dale, whom he was seeking in every brook, in every temple, in churches and heavens, that God whom he was even imagining as sitting in heaven and ruling the world, is his own Self. I am He, and He is I. None but I was God, and this little I never existed.

Yet, how could that perfect God have been deluded? He never was. How could a perfect God have been dreaming? He never dreamed. Truth never dreams. The very question as to whence this illusion arose is absurd. Illusion arises from illusion alone. There will be no illusion as soon as the truth is seen. Illusion always rests upon illusion; it never rests upon God, the Truth, the Atman. You are never in illusion; it is illusion that is in you, before you. A cloud is here; another comes and pushes it aside and takes its place. Still another comes and pushes that one away. As before the eternal blue sky, clouds of various hue and colour come, remain for a short time and disappear, leaving it the same eternal blue, even so are you, eternally pure, eternally perfect. You are the veritable Gods of the universe; nay, there are not two — there is but One. It is a mistake to say, "you and I"; say "I". It is I who am eating in millions of mouths; how can I be hungry? It is I who am working through an infinite number of hands; how can I be inactive? It is I who am living the life of the whole universe; where is death for me? I am beyond all life, beyond all death. Where shall I seek for freedom? I am free by my nature. Who can bind me — the God of this universe? The scriptures of the world are but little maps, wanting to delineate my glory, who am the only existence of the universe. Then what are these books to me? Thus says the Advaitist.

"Know the truth and be free in a moment." All the darkness will then vanish. When man has seen himself as one with the Infinite Being of the universe, when all separateness has ceased, when all men and women, an gods and angels, all animals and plants, and the whole universe have melted into that Oneness, then all fear disappears. Can I hurt myself? Can I kill myself? Can I injure myself? Whom to fear? Can you fear yourself? Then will all sorrow disappear. What can cause me sorrow? I am the One Existence of the universe. Then all jealousies will disappear; of whom to be jealous? Of myself? Then all bad feelings disappear. Against whom can I have bad feeling? Against myself? There is none in the universe but I. And this is the one way, says the Vedantist, to Knowledge. Kill out this differentiation, kill out this superstition that there are many. "He who in this world of many sees that One, he who in this mass of insentiency sees that one Sentient Being, he who in this world of shadows catches that Reality, unto him belongs eternal peace, unto none else, unto none else."

These are the salient points of the three steps which Indian religious thought has taken in regard to God. We have seen that it began with the Personal, the extra-cosmic God. It went from the external to the internal cosmic body, God immanent in the universe, and ended in identifying the soul itself with that God, and making one Soul, a unit of all these various manifestations in the universe. This is the last word of the Vedas. It begins with dualism, goes through a qualified monism and ends in perfect monism. We know how very few in this world can come to the last, or even dare believe in it, and fewer still dare act according to it. Yet we know that therein lies the explanation of all ethics, of all morality and all spirituality in the universe. Why is it that every one says, "Do good to others?" Where is the explanation? Why is it that all great men have preached the brotherhood of mankind, and greater men the brotherhood of all lives? Because whether they were conscious of it or not, behind all that, through all their irrational and personal superstitions, was peering forth the eternal light of the Self denying all manifoldness, and asserting that the whole universe is but one.

Again, the last word gave us one universe, which through the senses we see as matter, through the intellect as souls, and through the spirit as God. To the man who throws upon himself veils, which the world calls wickedness and evil, this very universe will change and become a hideous place; to another man, who wants enjoyments, this very universe will change its appearance and become a heaven, and to the perfect man the whole thing will vanish and become his own Self.

Now, as society exists at the present time, all these three stages are necessary; the one does not deny the other, one is simply the fulfilment of the other. The Advaitist or the qualified Advaitist does not say that dualism is wrong; it is a right view, but a lower one. It is on the way to truth; therefore let everybody work out his own vision of this universe, according to his own ideas. Injure none, deny the position of none; take man where he stands and, if you can, lend him a helping hand and put him on a higher platform, but do not injure and do not destroy. All will come to truth in the long run. "When all the desires of the heart will be vanquished, then this very mortal will become immortal" — then the very man will become God.

CHAPTER XV
THE ATMAN: ITS BONDAGE AND FREEDOM

Delivered in America

According to the Advaita philosophy, there is only one thing real in the universe, which it calls Brahman; everything else is unreal, manifested and manufactured out of Brahman by the power of Mâyâ. To reach back to that Brahman is our goal. We are, each one of us, that Brahman, that Reality, plus this Maya. If we can get rid of this Maya or ignorance, then we become what we really are. According to this philosophy, each man consists of three parts — the body, the internal organ or the mind, and behind that, what is called the Âtman, the Self. The body is the external coating and the mind is the internal coating of the Atman who is the real perceiver, the real enjoyer, the being in the body who is working the body by means of the internal organ or the mind.

The Âtman is the only existence in the human body which is immaterial. Because it is immaterial, it cannot be a compound, and because it is not a compound, it does not obey the law of cause and effect, and so it is immortal. That which is immortal can have no beginning because everything with a beginning must have an end. It also follows that it must be formless; there cannot be any form without matter. Everything that has form must have a beginning and an end. We have none of us seen a form which had not a beginning and will not have an end. A form comes out of a combination of force and matter. This chair has a peculiar form, that is to say a certain quantity of matter is acted upon by a certain amount of force and made to assume a particular shape. The shape is the result of a combination of matter and force. The combination cannot be eternal; there must come to every combination a time when it will dissolve. So all forms have a beginning and an end. We know our body will perish;

it had a beginning and it will have an end. But the Self having no form, cannot be bound by the law of beginning and end. It is existing from infinite time; just as time is eternal, so is the Self of man eternal. Secondly, it must be all-pervading. It is only form that is conditioned and limited by space; that which is formless cannot be confined in space. So, according to Advaita Vedanta, the Self, the Atman, in you, in me, in every one, is omnipresent. You are as much in the sun now as in this earth, as much in England as in America. But the Self acts through the mind and the body, and where they are, its action is visible.

Each work we do, each thought we think, produces an impression, called in Sanskrit Samskâra, upon the mind and the sum total of these impressions becomes the tremendous force which is called "character". The character of a man is what he has created for himself; it is the result of the mental and physical actions that he has done in his life. The sum total of the Samskaras is the force which gives a man the next direction after death. A man dies; the body falls away and goes back to the elements; but the Samskaras remain, adhering to the mind which, being made of fine material, does not dissolve, because the finer the material, the more persistent it is. But the mind also dissolves in the long run, and that is what we are struggling for. In this connection, the best illustration that comes to my mind is that of the whirlwind. Different currents of air coming from different directions meet and at the meeting-point become united and go on rotating; as they rotate, they form a body of dust, drawing in bits of paper, straw, etc., at one place, only to drop them and go on to another, and so go on rotating, raising and forming bodies out of the materials which are before them. Even so the forces, called Prâna in Sanskrit, come together and form the body and the mind out of matter, and move on until the body falls down, when they raise other materials to make another body, and when this falls, another rises, and thus the process goes on. Force cannot travel without matter. So when the body falls down, the mind-stuff remains, Prana in the form of Samskaras acting on it; and then it goes on to another point, raises up another whirl from fresh materials, and begins another motion; and so it travels from place to place until the force is all spent; and then it falls down, ended. So when the mind will end, be broken to pieces entirely, without leaving any Samskara, we shall be entirely free, and until that time we are in bondage; until then the Atman is covered by the whirl of the mind, and imagines it is being taken from place to place. When the whirl falls down, the Atman finds that It is all-pervading. It can go where It likes, is entirely free, and is able to manufacture any number of minds or bodies It likes; but until then It can go only with the whirl. This freedom is the goal towards which we are all moving.

Suppose there is a ball in this room, and we each have a mallet in our hands and begin to strike the ball, giving it hundreds of blows, driving it from point to point, until at last it flies out of the room. With what force and in what direction will it go out? These will be determined by the forces that have been acting upon it all through the room. All the different blows that have been given will have their effects. Each one of our actions, mental and physical, is such a blow. The human mind is a ball which is being hit. We are being hit about this room of the world all the time, and our passage out of it is determined by the force of all these blows. In each case, the speed and direction of the ball is determined by the hits it has received; so all our actions in this world will determine our future birth. Our present birth, therefore, is the result of our past. This is one case: suppose I give you an endless chain, in which there is a black link and a white link alternately, without beginning and without end, and suppose I ask you the nature of the chain. At first you will find a difficulty in determining its nature, the chain being infinite at both ends, but slowly you find out it is a chain. You soon discover that this infinite chain is a repetition of the two links, black and white, and these multiplied infinitely become a whole chain. If you know the nature of one of these links, you know the nature of the whole chain, because it is a perfect repetition. All our lives, past, present, and future, form, as it were, an infinite chain, without beginning and without end, each link of which is one life, with two ends, birth and death. What we are and do here is being repeated again and again, with but little variation. So if we know these two links, we shall know all the passages we shall have to pass through in this world. We see, therefore, that our passage into this world has been exactly determined by our previous passages. Similarly we are in this world by our own actions. Just as we go out with the sum total of our present actions upon us, so we see that we come into it with the sum total of our past actions upon us; that which takes us out is the very same thing that brings us in. What brings us in? Our past deeds. What takes us out? Our own deeds here, and so on and on we go. Like the caterpillar that takes the thread from its own mouth and builds its cocoon and at last finds itself caught inside the cocoon, we have bound ourselves by our own actions, we have thrown the network of our actions around ourselves. We have set the law of causation in motion, and we find it hard to get ourselves out of it. We have set the wheel in motion, and we are being crushed under it. So this philosophy teaches us that we are uniformly being bound by our own actions, good or bad.

The Atman never comes nor goes, is never born nor dies. It is nature moving before the Atman, and the reflection of this motion is on the Atman; and the Atman ignorantly thinks it is moving, and not nature. When the Atman thinks that, it is in bondage; but when it comes to find it never moves, that it is omnipresent, then freedom comes. The Atman in bondage is called Jiva. Thus you see that when it is said that the Atman comes and goes, it is said only for facility of understanding, just as for convenience in studying astronomy you are asked to suppose that the sun moves round the earth, though such is not the case. So the Jiva, the soul, comes to higher or lower states. This is the well-known law of reincarnation; and this law binds all creation.

People in this country think it too horrible that man should come up from an animal. Why? What will be the end of these millions of animals? Are they nothing? If we have a soul, so have they; and if they have none, neither have we. It is absurd to say that man alone has a soul, and the animals none. I have seen men worse than animals.

The human soul has sojourned in lower and higher forms, migrating from one to another, according to the Samskaras or impressions, but it is only in the highest form as man that it attains to freedom. The man form is higher than even the angel form, and of all forms it is the highest; man is the highest being in creation, because he attains to freedom.

All this universe was in Brahman, and it was, as it were, projected out of Him, and has been moving on to go back to the source from which it was projected, like the electricity which comes out of the dynamo, completes the circuit, and returns to it. The same is the case with the soul. Projected from Brahman, it passed through all sorts of vegetable and animal forms, and at last it is in man, and man is the nearest approach to Brahman. To go back to Brahman from which we have been projected is the great struggle of life. Whether people know it or not does not matter. In the universe, whatever we see of motion, of struggles in minerals or plants or animals is an effort to come back to the centre and be at rest. There was an equilibrium, and that has been destroyed; and all parts and atoms and molecules are struggling to find their lost equilibrium again. In this struggle they are combining and re-forming, giving rise to all the wonderful phenomena of nature. All struggles and competitions in animal life, plant life, and everywhere else, all social struggles and wars are but expressions of that eternal struggle to get back to that equilibrium.

The going from birth to death, this travelling, is what is called Samsara in Sanskrit, the round of birth and death literally. All creation, passing through this round, will sooner or later become free. The question may be raised that if we all shall come to freedom, why should we struggle to attain it? If every one is going to be free, we will sit down and wait. It is true that every being will become free, sooner or later; no one can be lost. Nothing can come to destruction; everything must come up. If that is so, what is the use of our struggling? In the first place, the struggle is the only means that will bring us to the centre, and in the second place, we do not know why we struggle. We have to. "Of thousands of men some are awakened to the idea that they will become free." The vast masses of mankind are content with material things, but there are some who awake, and want to get back, who have had enough of this playing, down here. These struggle consciously, while the rest do it unconsciously.

The alpha and omega of Vedanta philosophy is to "give up the world," giving up the unreal and taking the real. Those who are enamoured of the world may ask, "Why should we attempt to get out of it, to go back to the centre? Suppose we have all come from God, but we find this world is pleasurable and nice; then why should we not rather try to get more and more of the world? Why should we try to get out of it?" They say, look at the wonderful improvements going on in the world every day, how much luxury is being manufactured for it. This is very enjoyable. Why should we go away, and strive for something which is not this? The answer is that the world is certain to die, to be broken into pieces and that many times we have had the same enjoyments. All the forms which we are seeing now have been manifested again and again, and the world in which we live has been here many times before. I have been here and talked to you many times before. You will know that it must be so, and the very words that you have been listening to now, you have heard many times before. And many times more it will be the same. Souls were never different, the bodies have been constantly dissolving and recurring. Secondly, these things periodically occur. Suppose here are three or four dice, and when we throw them, one comes up five, another four, another three, and another two. If you keep on throwing, there must come times when those very same numbers will recur. Go on throwing, and no matter how long may be the interval, those numbers must come again. It cannot be asserted in how many throws they will come again; this is the law of chance. So with souls and their associations. However distant may be the periods, the same combinations and dissolutions will happen again and again. The same birth, eating and drinking, and then death, come round again and again. Some never find anything higher than the enjoyments of the world, but those who want to soar higher find that these enjoyments are never final, are only by the way.

Every form, let us say, beginning from the little worm and ending in man, is like one of the cars of the Chicago Ferris Wheel which is in motion all the time, but the occupants change. A man goes into a car, moves with the wheel, and comes out. The wheel goes on and on. A soul enters one form, resides in it for a time, then leaves it and goes into another and quits that again for a third. Thus the round goes on till it comes out of the wheel and becomes free.

Astonishing powers of reading the past and the future of a man's life have been known in every country and every age. The explanation is that so long as the Atman is within the realm of causation — though its inherent freedom is not entirely lost and can assert itself, even to the extent of taking the soul out of the causal chain, as it does in the case of men who become free — its actions are greatly influenced by the causal law and thus make it possible for men, possessed with the insight to trace the sequence of effects, to tell the past and the future.

So long as there is desire or want, it is a sure sign that there is imperfection. A perfect, free being cannot have any desire. God cannot want anything. If He desires, He cannot be God. He will be imperfect. So all the talk about God desiring this and that, and becoming angry and pleased by turns is babies' talk, but means nothing. Therefore it has been taught by all teachers, "Desire nothing, give up all desires and be perfectly satisfied."

A child comes into the world crawling and without teeth, and the old man gets out without teeth and crawling. The extremes are alike, but the one has no experience of the life before him, while the other has gone through it all. When the vibrations of ether are very low, we do not see light, it is darkness; when very high, the result is also darkness. The extremes generally appear to be the same, though one is as distant from the other as the poles. The wall has no desires, so neither has the perfect man. But the wall is not sentient enough to desire, while for the perfect man there is nothing to desire. There are idiots who have no desires in this world, because their brain is imperfect. At the same time, the highest state is when we have no desires, but the two are opposite poles of the same existence. One is near the animal, and the other near to God.

CHAPTER XVI
THE REAL AND THE APPARENT MAN

Delivered in New York

Here we stand, and our eyes look forward sometimes miles ahead. Man has been doing that since he began to think. He is always looking forward, looking ahead. He wants to know where he goes even after the dissolution of his body. Various theories have been propounded, system after system has been brought forward to suggest explanations. Some have been rejected, while others have been accepted, and thus it will go on, so long as man is here, so long as man thinks. There is some truth in each of these systems. There is a good deal of what is not truth in all of them. I shall try to place before you the sum and substance, the result, of the inquiries in this line that have been made in India. I shall try to harmonise the various thoughts on the subject, as they have come up from time to time among Indian philosophers. I shall try to harmonise the psychologists and the metaphysicians, and, if possible, I shall harmonise them with modern scientific thinkers also.

The one theme of the Vedanta philosophy is the search after unity. The Hindu mind does not care for the particular; it is always after the general, nay, the universal. "What is that, by knowing which everything else is to be known?" That is the one theme. "As through the knowledge of one lump of clay all that is of clay is known, so, what is that, by knowing which this whole universe itself will be known?" That is the one search. The whole of this universe, according to the Hindu philosophers, can be resolved into one material, which they call Âkâsha. Everything that we see around us, feel, touch, taste, is simply a differentiated manifestation of this Akasha. It is all-pervading, fine. All that we call solids, liquids, or gases, figures, forms, or bodies, the earth, sun, moon, and stars — everything is composed of this Akasha.

What force is it which acts upon this Akasha and manufactures this universe out of it? Along with Akasha exists universal power; all that is power in the universe, manifesting as force or attraction — nay, even as thought — is but a different manifestation of that one power which the Hindus call Prâna. This Prana, acting on Akasha, is creating the whole of this universe. In the beginning of a cycle, this Prana, as it were, sleeps in the infinite ocean of Akasha. It existed motionless in the beginning. Then arises motion in this ocean of Akasha by the action of this Prana, and as this Prana begins to move, to vibrate, out of this ocean come the various celestial systems, suns, moons, stars, earth, human beings, animals, plants, and the manifestations of all the various forces and phenomena. Every manifestation of power, therefore, according to them, is this Prana. Every material manifestation is Akasha. When this cycle will end, all that we call solid will melt away into the next form, the next finer or the liquid form; that will melt into the gaseous, and that into finer and more uniform heat vibrations, and all will melt back into the original Akasha, and what we now call attraction, repulsion, and motion, will slowly resolve into the original Prana. Then this Prana is said to sleep for a period, again to emerge and to throw out all those forms; and when this period will end, the whole thing will subside again. Thus this process of creation is going down, and coming up, oscillating backwards and forwards. In the language of modern science, it is becoming static during one period, and during another period it is becoming dynamic. At one time it becomes potential, and at the next period it becomes active. This alteration has gone on through eternity.

Yet, this analysis is only partial. This much has been known even to modern physical science. Beyond that, the research of physical science cannot reach. But the inquiry does not stop in consequence. We have not yet found that one, by knowing which everything else will be known. We have resolved the whole universe into two components, into what are called matter and energy, or what the ancient philosophers of India called Akasha and Prana. The next step is to resolve this Akasha and the Prana into their origin. Both can be resolved into the still higher entity which is called mind. It is out of mind, the Mahat, the universally existing thought-power, that these two have been produced. Thought is a still finer manifestation of being than either Akasha or Prana. It is thought that splits itself into these two. The universal thought existed in the beginning, and that manifested, changed, evolved itself into these two Akasha and Prana: and by the combination of these two the whole universe has been produced.

We next come to psychology. I am looking at you. The external sensations are brought to me by the eyes; they are carried by the sensory nerves to the brain. The eyes are not the organs of vision. They are but the external instruments, because if the real organ behind, that which carries the sensation to the brain, is destroyed, I may have twenty eyes, yet I cannot see you. The picture on the retina may be as complete as possible, yet I shall not see you. Therefore, the organ is different from its instruments; behind the instruments, the eyes, there must be the organ So it is with all the sensations. The nose is not the sense of smell; it is but the instrument, and behind it is the organ. With every sense we have, there is first the external instrument in the physical body; behind that in the same physical body, there is the organ; yet these are not sufficient. Suppose I am talking to you, and you are listening to me with close attention. Something happens, say, a bell rings; you will not, perhaps, hear the bell ring. The pulsations of that sound came to your ear, struck the tympanum, the impression was carried by the nerve into the brain; if the whole process was complete up to carrying the impulse to the brain, why did you not hear? Something else was wanting — the mind was not attached to the organ. When the mind detaches itself from the organ, the organ may bring any news to it, but the mind will not receive it. When it attaches itself to the organ, then alone is it possible for the mind to receive the news. Yet, even that does not complete the whole. The instruments may bring the sensation from outside, the organs may carry it inside, the mind may attach itself to the organ, and yet the perception may not be complete. One more factor is necessary; there must be a reaction within. With this reaction comes knowledge. That which is outside sends, as it were, the current of news into my brain. My mind takes it up, and presents it to the intellect, which groups it in relation to pre-received impressions and sends a current of reaction, and with that reaction comes perception. Here, then, is the will. The state of mind which reacts is called Buddhi, the intellect. Yet, even this does not complete the whole. One step more is required. Suppose here is a camera and there is a sheet of cloth, and I try to throw a picture on that sheet. What am I to do? I am to guide various rays of light through the camera to fall upon the sheet and become grouped there. Something is necessary to have the picture thrown upon, which does not move. I cannot form a picture upon something which is moving; that something must be stationary, because the rays of light which I throw on it are moving, and these moving rays of light, must be gathered, unified, co-ordinated, and completed upon something which is stationary. Similar is the case with the sensations which these organs of ours are carrying inside and presenting to the mind, and which the mind in its turn is presenting to the intellect. This process will not be complete unless there is something permanent in the background upon which the picture, as it were, may be formed, upon which we may unify all the different impressions. What is it that gives unity to the changing whole of our being? What is it that keeps up the identity of the moving thing moment after moment? What is it upon which all our different impressions are pieced together, upon which the perceptions, as it were, come together, reside, and form a united whole? We have found that to serve this end there must be something, and we also see that that something must be, relatively to the body and mind, motionless. The sheet of cloth upon which the camera throws the picture is, relatively to the rays of light, motionless, else there will be no picture. That is to say, the perceiver must be an individual. This something upon which the mind is painting all these pictures, this something upon which our sensations, carried by the mind and intellect, are placed and grouped and formed into a unity, is what is called the soul of man.

We have seen that it is the universal cosmic mind that splits itself into the Akasha and Prana, and beyond mind we have found the soul in us. In the universe, behind the universal mind, there is a Soul that exists, and it is called God. In the individual it is the soul of man. In this universe, in the cosmos, just as the universal mind becomes evolved into Akasha and Prana, even so, we may find that the Universal Soul Itself becomes evolved as mind. Is it really so with the individual man? Is his mind the creator of his body, and his soul the creator of his mind? That is to say, are his body, his mind, and his soul three different existences or are they three in one or, again, are they different states of existence of the same unit being? We shall gradually try to find an answer to this question. The first step that we have now gained is this: here is this external body, behind this external body are the organs, the mind, the intellect, and behind this is the soul. At the first step, we have found, as it were, that the soul is separate from the body, separate from the mind itself. Opinions in the religious world become divided at this point, and the departure is this. All those religious views which generally pass under the name of dualism hold that this soul is qualified, that it is of various qualities, that all feelings of enjoyment, pleasure, and pain really belong to the soul. The non-dualists deny that the soul has any such qualities; they say it is unqualified.

Let me first take up the dualists, and try to present to you their position with regard to the soul and its destiny; next, the system that contradicts them; and lastly, let us try to find the harmony which non-dualism will bring to us. This soul of man, because it is separate from the mind and body, because it is not composed of Akasha and Prana, must be immortal. Why? What do we mean by mortality? Decomposition. And that is only possible for things that are the result of composition; anything that is made of two or three ingredients must become decomposed. That alone which is not the result of composition can never become decomposed, and, therefore, can never die. It is immortal. It has been existing throughout eternity; it is uncreate. Every item of creation is simply a composition; no one ever saw creation come out of nothing. All that we know of creation is the combination of already existing things into newer forms. That being so, this soul of man, being simple, must have been existing for ever, and it will exist for ever. When this body falls off, the soul lives on. According to the Vedantists, when this body dissolves, the vital forces of the man go back to his mind and the mind becomes dissolved, as it were, into the Prana, and that Prana enters into the soul of man, and the soul of man comes out, clothed, as it were, with what they call the fine body, the mental body, or spiritual body, as you may like to call it. In this body are the Samskâras of the man. What are the Samskaras? This mind is like a lake, and every thought is like a wave upon that lake. Just as in the lake waves rise and then fall down and disappear, so these thought-waves are continually rising in the mind-stuff and then disappearing, but they do not disappear for ever. They become finer and finer, but they are all there, ready to start up at another time when called upon to do so. Memory is simply calling back into waveform some of those thoughts which have gone into that finer state of existence. Thus, everything that we have thought, every action that we have done, is lodged in the mind; it is all there in fine form, and when a man dies, the sum total of these impressions is in the mind, which again works upon a little fine material as a medium. The soul, clothed, as it were, with these impressions and the fine body, passes out, and the destiny of the soul is guided by the resultant of all the different forces represented by the different impressions. According to us, there are three different goals for the soul.

Those that are very spiritual, when they die, follow the solar rays and reach what is called the solar sphere, through which they reach what is called the lunar sphere, and through that they reach what is called the sphere of lightning, and there they meet with another soul who is already blessed, and he guides the new-comer forward to the highest of all spheres, which is called the Brahmaloka, the sphere of Brahmâ. There these souls attain to omniscience and omnipotence, become almost as powerful and all-knowing as God Himself; and they reside there for ever, according to the dualists, or, according to the non-dualists, they become one with the Universal at the end of the cycle. The next class of persons, who have been doing good work with selfish motives, are carried by the results of their good works, when they die, to what is called lunar sphere, where there are various heavens, and there they acquire fine bodies, the bodies of gods. They become gods and live there and enjoy the blessing of heaven for a long period; and after that period is finished, the old Karma is again upon them, and so they fall back again to the earth; they come down through the spheres of air and clouds and all these various regions, and, at last, reach the earth through raindrops. There on the earth they attach themselves to some cereal which is eventually eaten by some man who is fit to supply them with material to make a new body. The last class, namely, the wicked, when they die, become ghosts or demons, and live somewhere midway between the lunar sphere and this earth. Some try to disturb mankind, some are friendly; and after living there for some time they also fall back to the earth and become animals. After living for some time in an animal body they get released, and come back, and become men again, and thus get one more chance to work out their salvation. We see, then, that those who have nearly attained to perfection, in whom only very little of impurity remains, go to the Brahmaloka through the rays of the sun; those who were a middling sort of people, who did some good work here with the idea of going to heaven, go to the heavens in the lunar sphere and there obtain god-bodies; but they have again to become men and so have one more chance to become perfect. Those that are very wicked become ghosts and demons, and then they may have to become animals; after that they become men again and get another chance to perfect themselves. This earth is called the Karma-Bhumi, the sphere of Karma. Here alone man makes his good or bad Karma. When a man wants to go to heaven and does good works for that purpose, he becomes as good and does not as such store up any bad Karma. He just enjoys the effects of the good work he did on earth; and when this good Karma is exhausted, there come, upon him the resultant force of all the evil Karma he had previously stored up in life, and that brings him down again to this earth. In the same way, those that become ghosts remain in that state, not giving rise to fresh Karma, but suffer the evil results of their past misdeeds, and later on remain for a time in an animal body without causing any fresh Karma. When that period is finished, they too become men again. The states of reward and punishment due to good and bad Karmas are devoid of the force generating fresh Karmas; they have only to be enjoyed or suffered. If there is an extraordinarily good or an extraordinarily evil Karma, it bears fruit very quickly. For instance, if a man has been doing many evil things all his life, but does one good act, the result of that good act will immediately appear, but when that result has been gone through, all the evil acts must produce their results also. All men who do certain good and great acts, but the general tenor of whose lives has not been correct, will become gods; and after living for some time in god-bodies, enjoying the powers of gods, they will have again to become men; when the power of the good acts is thus finished, the old evil comes up to be worked out. Those who do extraordinarily evil acts have to put on ghost and devil bodies, and when the effect of those evil actions is exhausted, the little good action which remains associated with them, makes them again become men. The way to Brahmaloka, from which there is no more fall or return, is called the Devayâna, i.e. the way to God; the way to heaven is known as Pitriyâna, i.e. the way to the fathers.

Man, therefore, according to the Vedanta philosophy, is the greatest being that is in the universe, and this world of work the best place in it, because only herein is the greatest and the best chance for him to become perfect. Angels or gods, whatever you may call them, have all to become men, if they want to become perfect. This is the great centre, the wonderful poise, and the wonderful opportunity — this human life.

We come next to the other aspect of philosophy. There are Buddhists who deny the whole theory of the soul that I have just now been propounding. "What use is there," says the Buddhist, "to assume something as the substratum, as the background of this body and mind? Why may we not allow thoughts to run on? Why admit a third substance beyond this organism, composed of mind and body, a third substance called the soul? What is its use? Is not this organism sufficient to explain itself? Why take anew a third something?" These arguments are very powerful. This reasoning is very strong. So far as outside research goes, we see that this organism is a sufficient explanation of itself — at least, many of us see it in that light. Why then need there be a soul as substratum, as a something which is neither mind nor body but stands as a background for both mind and body? Let there be only mind and body. Body is the name of a stream of matter continuously changing. Mind is the name of a stream of consciousness or thought continuously changing. What produces the apparent unity between these two? This unity does not really exist, let us say. Take, for instance, a lighted torch, and whirl it rapidly before you. You see a circle of fire. The circle does not really exist, but because the torch is continually moving, it leaves the appearance of a circle. So there is no unity in this life; it is a mass of matter continually rushing down, and the whole of this matter you may call one unity, but no more. So is mind; each thought is separate from every other thought; it is only the rushing current that leaves behind the illusion of unity; there is no need of a third substance. This universal phenomenon of body and mind is all that really is; do not posit something behind it. You will find that this Buddhist thought has been taken up by certain sects and schools in modern times, and all of them claim that it is new — their own invention. This has been the central idea of most of the Buddhistic philosophies, that this world is itself all-sufficient; that you need not ask for any background at all; all that is, is this sense-universe: what is the use of thinking of something as a support to this universe? Everything is the aggregate of qualities; why should there be a hypothetical substance in which they should inhere? The idea of substance comes from the rapid interchange of qualities, not from something unchangeable which exists behind them. We see how wonderful some of these arguments are, and they appeal easily to the ordinary experience of humanity — in fact, not one in a million can think of anything other than phenomena. To the vast majority of men nature appears to be only a changing, whirling, combining, mingling mass of change. Few of us ever have a glimpse of the calm sea behind. For us it is always lashed into waves; this universe appears to us only as a tossing mass of waves. Thus we find these two opinions. One is that there is something behind both body and mind which is an unchangeable and immovable substance; and the other is that there is no such thing as immovability or unchangeability in the universe; it is all change and nothing but change. The solution of this difference comes in the next step of thought, namely, the non-dualistic.

It says that the dualists are right in finding something behind all, as a background which does not change; we cannot conceive change without there being something unchangeable. We can only conceive of anything that is changeable, by knowing something which is less changeable, and this also must appear more changeable in comparison with something else which is less changeable, and so on and on, until we are bound to admit that there must be something which never changes at all. The whole of this manifestation must have been in a state of non-manifestation, calm and silent, being the balance of opposing forces, so to say, when no force operated, because force acts when a disturbance of the equilibrium comes in. The universe is ever hurrying on to return to that state of equilibrium again. If we are certain of any fact whatsoever, we are certain of this. When the dualists claim that there is a something which does not change, they are perfectly right, but their analysis that it is an underlying something which is neither the body nor the mind, a something separate from both, is wrong. So far as the Buddhists say that the whole universe is a mass of change, they are perfectly right; so long as I am separate from the universe, so long as I stand back and look at something before me, so long as there are two things — the looker-on and the thing looked upon — it will appear always that the universe is one of change, continuously changing all the time. But the reality is that there is both change and changelessness in this universe. It is not that the soul and the mind and the body are three separate existences, for this organism made of these three is really one. It is the same thing which appears as the body, as the mind, and as the thing beyond mind and body, but it is not at the same time all these. He who sees the body does not see the mind even, he who sees the mind does not see that which he calls the soul, and he who sees the soul — for him the body and mind have vanished. He who sees only motion never sees absolute calm, and he who sees absolute calm — for him motion has vanished. A rope is taken for a snake. He who sees the rope as the snake, for him the rope has vanished, and when the delusion ceases and he looks at the rope, the snake has vanished.

There is then but one all-comprehending existence, and that one appears as manifold. This Self or Soul or Substance is all that exists in the universe. That Self or Substance or Soul is, in the language of non-dualism, the Brahman appearing to be manifold by the interposition of name and form. Look at the waves in the sea. Not one wave is really different from the sea, but what makes the wave apparently different? Name and form; the form of the wave and the name which we give to it, "wave". This is what makes it different from the sea. When name and form go, it is the same sea. Who can make any real difference between the wave and the sea? So this whole universe is that one Unit Existence; name and form have created all these various differences. As when the sun shines upon millions of globules of water, upon each particle is seen a most perfect representation of the sun, so the one Soul, the one Self, the one Existence of the universe, being reflected on all these numerous globules of varying names and forms, appears to be various. But it is in reality only one. There is no "I" nor "you"; it is all one. It is either all "I" or all "you". This idea of duality, calf two, is entirely false, and the whole universe, as we ordinarily know it, is the result of this false knowledge. When discrimination comes and man finds there are not two but one, he finds that he is himself this universe. "It is I who am this universe as it now exists, a continuous mass of change. It is I who am beyond all changes, beyond all qualities, the eternally perfect, the eternally blessed."

There is, therefore, but one Atman, one Self, eternally pure, eternally perfect, unchangeable, unchanged; it has never changed; and all these various changes in the universe are but appearances in that one Self.

Upon it name and form have painted all these dreams; it is the form that makes the wave different from the sea. Suppose the wave subsides, will the form remain? No, it will vanish. The existence of the wave was entirely dependent upon the existence of the sea, but the existence of the sea was not at all dependent upon the existence of the wave. The form remains so long as the wave remains, but as soon as the wave leaves it, it vanishes, it cannot remain. This name and form is the outcome of what is called Maya. It is this Maya that is making individuals, making one appear different from another. Yet it has no existence. Maya cannot be said to exist. Form cannot be said to exist, because it depends upon the existence of another thing. It cannot be said as not to exist, seeing that it makes all this difference. According to the Advaita philosophy, then, this Maya or ignorance — or name and form, or, as it has been called in Europe, "time, space, and causality" — is out of this one Infinite Existence showing us the manifoldness of the universe; in substance, this universe is one. So long as any one thinks that there are two ultimate realities, he is mistaken. When he has come to know that there is but one, he is right. This is what is being proved to us every day, on the physical plane, on the mental plane, and also on the spiritual plane. Today it has been demonstrated that you and I, the sun, the moon, and the stars are but the different names of different spots in the same ocean of matter, and that this matter is continuously changing in its configuration. This particle of energy that was in the sun several months ago may be in the human being now; tomorrow it may be in an animal, the day after tomorrow it may be in a plant. It is ever coming and going. It is all one unbroken, infinite mass of matter, only differentiated by names and forms. One point is called the sun; another, the moon; another, the stars; another, man; another, animal; another, plant; and so on. And all these names are fictitious; they have no reality, because the whole is a continuously changing mass of matter. This very same universe, from another standpoint, is an ocean of thought, where each one of us is a point called a particular mind. You are a mind, I am a mind, everyone is a mind; and the very same universe viewed from the standpoint of knowledge, when the eyes have been cleared of delusions, when the mind has become pure, appears to be the unbroken Absolute Being, the ever pure, the unchangeable, the immortal.

What then becomes of all this threefold eschatology of the dualist, that when a man dies he goes to heaven, or goes to this or that sphere, and that the wicked persons become ghosts, and become animals, and so forth? None comes and none goes, says the non-dualist. How can you come and go? You are infinite; where is the place for you to go? In a certain school a number of little children were being examined. The examiner had foolishly put all sorts of difficult questions to the little children. Among others there was this question: "Why does not the earth fall?" His intention was to bring out the idea of gravitation or some other intricate scientific truth from these children. Most of them could not even understand the question, and so they gave all sorts of wrong answers. But one bright little girl answered it with another question: "Where shall it fall?" The very question of the examiner was nonsense on the face of it. There is no up and down in the universe; the idea is only relative. So it is with regard to the soul; the very question of birth and death in regard to it is utter nonsense. Who goes and who comes? Where are you not? Where is the heaven that you are not in already? Omnipresent is the Self of man. Where is it to go? Where is it not to go? It is everywhere. So all this childish dream and puerile illusion of birth and death, of heavens and higher heavens and lower worlds, all vanish immediately for the perfect. For the nearly perfect it vanishes after showing them the several scenes up to Brahmaloka. It continues for the ignorant.

How is it that the whole world believes in going to heaven, and in dying and being born? I am studying a book, page after page is being read and turned over. Another page comes and is turned over. Who changes? Who comes and goes? Not I, but the book. This whole nature is a book before the soul, chapter after chapter is being read and turned over, and every now and then a scene opens. That is read and turned over. A fresh one comes, but the soul is ever the same — eternal. It is nature that is changing, not the soul of man. This never changes. Birth and death are in nature, not in you. Yet the ignorant are deluded; just as we under delusion think that the sun is moving and not the earth, in exactly the same way we think that we are dying, and not nature. These are all, therefore, hallucinations. Just as it is a hallucination when we think that the fields are moving and not the railway train, exactly in the same manner is the hallucination of birth and death. When men are in a certain frame of mind, they see this very existence as the earth, as the sun, the moon, the stars; and all those who are in the same state of mind see the same things. Between you and me there may be millions of beings on different planes of existence. They will never see us, nor we them; we only see those who are in the same state of mind and on the same plane with us. Those musical instruments respond which have the same attunement of vibration, as it were; if the state of vibration, which they call "man-vibration", should be changed, no longer would men be seen here; the whole "man-universe" would vanish, and instead of that, other scenery would come before us, perhaps gods and the god-universe, or perhaps, for the wicked man, devils and the diabolic world; but all would be only different views of the one universe. It is this universe which, from the human plane, is seen as the earth, the sun, the moon, the stars, and all such things — it is this very universe which, seen from the plane of wickedness, appears as a place of punishment. And this very universe is seen as heaven by those who want to see it as heaven. Those who have been dreaming of going to a God who is sitting on a throne, and of standing there praising Him all their lives, when they die, will simply see a vision of what they have in their minds; this very universe will simply change into a vast heaven, with all sorts of winged beings flying about and a God sitting on a throne. These heavens are all of man's own making. So what the dualist says is true, says the Advaitin, but it is all simply of his own making. These spheres and devils and gods and reincarnations and transmigrations are all mythology; so also is this human life. The great mistake that men always make is to think that this life alone is true. They understand it well enough when other things are called mythologies, but are never willing to admit the same of their own position. The whole thing as it appears is mere mythology, and the greatest of all lies is that we are bodies, which we never were nor even can be. It is the greatest of all lies that we are mere men; we are the God of the universe. In worshipping God we have been always worshipping our own hidden Self. The worst lie that you ever tell yourself is that you were born a sinner or a wicked man. He alone is a sinner who sees a sinner in another man. Suppose there is a baby here, and you place a bag of gold on the table. Suppose a robber comes and takes the gold away. To the baby it is all the same; because there is no robber inside, there is no robber outside. To sinners and vile men, there is vileness outside, but not to good men. So the wicked see this universe as a hell, and the partially good see it as heaven, while the perfect beings realise it as God Himself. Then alone the veil falls from the eyes, and the man, purified and cleansed, finds his whole vision changed. The bad dreams that have been torturing him for millions of years, all vanish, and he who was thinking of himself either as a man, or a god, or a demon, he who was thinking of himself as living in low places, in high places, on earth, in heaven, and so on, finds that he is really omnipresent; that all time is in him, and that he is not in time; that all the heavens are in him, that he is not in any heaven; and that all the gods that man ever worshipped are in him, and that he is not in any one of those gods. He was the manufacturer of gods and demons, of men and plants and animals and stones, and the real nature of man now stands unfolded to him as being higher than heaven, more perfect than this universe of ours, more infinite than infinite time, more omnipresent than the omnipresent ether. Thus alone man becomes fearless, and becomes free. Then all delusions cease, all miseries vanish, all fears come to an end for ever. Birth goes away and with it death; pains fly, and with them fly away pleasures; earths vanish, and with them vanish heavens; bodies vanish, and with them vanishes the mind also. For that man disappears the whole universe, as it were. This searching, moving, continuous struggle of forces stops for ever, and that which was manifesting itself as force and matter, as struggles of nature, as nature itself, as heavens and earths and plants and animals and men and angels, all that becomes transfigured into one infinite, unbreakable, unchangeable existence, and the knowing man finds that he is one with that existence. "Even as clouds of various colours come before the sky, remain there for a second and then vanish away," even so before this soul are all these visions coming, of earths and heavens, of the moon and the gods, of pleasures and pains; but they all pass away leaving the one infinite, blue, unchangeable sky. The sky never changes; it is the clouds that change. It is a mistake to think that the sky is changed. It is a mistake to think that we are impure, that we are limited, that we are separate. The real man is the one Unit Existence.

Two questions now arise. The first is: "Is it possible to realise this? So far it is doctrine, philosophy, but is it possible to realise it?" It is. There are men still living in this world for whom delusion has vanished for ever. Do they immediately die after such realisation? Not so soon as we should think. Two wheels joined by one pole are running together. If I get hold of one of the wheels and, with an axe, cut the pole asunder, the wheel which I have got hold of stops, but upon the other wheel is its past momentum, so it runs on a little arid then falls down. This pure and perfect being, the soul, is one wheel, and this external hallucination of body and mind is the other wheel, joined together by the pole of work, of Karma. Knowledge is the axe which will sever the bond between the two, and the wheel of the soul will stop — stop thinking that it is coming and going, living and dying, stop thinking that it is nature and has wants and desires, and will find that it is perfect, desireless. But upon the other wheel, that of the body and mind, will be the momentum of past acts; so it will live for some time, until that momentum of past work is exhausted, until that momentum is worked away, and then the body and mind fall, and the soul becomes free. No more is there any going to heaven and coming back, not even any going to the Brahmaloka, or to any of the highest of the spheres, for where is he to come from, or to go to? The man who has in this life attained to this state, for whom, for a minute at least, the ordinary vision of the world has changed and the reality has been apparent, he is called the "Living Free". This is the goal of the Vedantin, to attain freedom while living.

Once in Western India I was travelling in the desert country on the coast of the Indian Ocean. For days and days I used to travel on foot through the desert, but it was to my surprise that I saw every day beautiful lakes, with trees all round them, and the shadows of the trees upside down and vibrating there. "How wonderful it looks and they call this a desert country!" I said to myself. Nearly a month I travelled, seeing these wonderful lakes and trees and plants. One day I was very thirsty and wanted to have a drink of water, so I started to go to one of these clear, beautiful lakes, and as I approached, it vanished. And with a flash it came to my brain, "This is the mirage about which I have read all my life," and with that came also the idea that throughout the whole of this month, every day, I had been seeing the mirage and did not know it. The next morning I began my march. There was again the lake, but with it came also the idea that it was the mirage and not a true lake. So is it with this universe. We are all travelling in this mirage of the world day after day, month after month, year after year, not knowing that it is a mirage. One day it will break up, but it will come back again: the body has to remain under the power of past Karma, and so the mirage will come back. This world will come back upon us so long as we are bound by Karma: men, women, animals, plants, our attachments and duties, all will come back to us, but not with the same power. Under the influence of the new knowledge the strength of Karma will be broken, its poison will be lost. It becomes transformed, for along with it there comes the idea that we know it now, that the sharp distinction between the reality and the mirage has been known.

This world will not then be the same world as before. There is, however, a danger here. We see in every country people taking up this philosophy and saying, "I am beyond all virtue and vice; so I am not bound by any moral laws; I may do anything I like." You may find many fools in this country at the present time, saying, "I am not bound; I am God Himself; let me do anything I like." This is not right, although it is true that the soul is beyond all laws, physical, mental, or moral. Within law is bondage; beyond law is freedom. It is also true that freedom is of the nature of the soul, it is its birthright: that real freedom of the soul shines through veils of matter in the form of the apparent freedom of man. Every moment of your life you feel that you are free. We cannot live, talk, or breathe for a moment without feeling that we are free; but, at the same time, a little thought shows us that we are like machines and not free. What is true then? Is this idea of freedom a delusion? One party holds that the idea of freedom is a delusion; another says that the idea of bondage is a delusion. How does this happen? Man is really free, the real man cannot but be free. It is when he comes into the world of Maya, into name and form, that he becomes bound. Free will is a misnomer. Will can never be free. How can it be? It is only when the real man has become bound that his will comes into existence, and not before. The will of man is bound, but that which is the foundation of that will is eternally free. So, even in the state of bondage which we call human life or god-life, on earth or in heaven, there yet remains to us that recollection of the freedom which is ours by divine right. And consciously or unconsciously we are all struggling towards it. When a man has attained his own freedom, how can he be bound by any law? No law in this universe can bind him, for this universe itself is his.

He is the whole universe. Either say he is the whole universe or say that to him there is no universe. How can he have then all these little ideas about sex and about country? How can he say, I am a man, I am a woman I am a child? Are they not lies? He knows that they are. How can he say that these are man's rights, and these others are woman's rights? Nobody has rights; nobody separately exists. There is neither man nor woman; the soul is sexless, eternally pure. It is a lie to say that I am a man or a woman, or to say that I belong to this country or that. All the world is my country, the whole universe is mine, because I have clothed myself with it as my body. Yet we see that there are people in this world who are ready to assert these doctrines, and at the same time do things which we should call filthy; and if we ask them why they do so, they tell us that it is our delusion and that they can do nothing wrong. What is the test by which they are to be judged? The test is here.

Though evil and good are both conditioned manifestations of the soul, yet evil is the most external coating, and good is the nearer coating of the real man, the Self. And unless a man cuts through the layer of evil he cannot reach the layer of good, and unless he has passed through both the layers of good and evil he cannot reach the Self. He who reaches the Self, what remains attached to him? A little Karma, a little bit of the momentum of past life, but it is all good momentum. Until the bad momentum is entirely worked out and past impurities are entirely burnt, it is impossible for any man to see and realise truth. So, what is left attached to the man who has reached the Self and seen the truth is the remnant of the good impressions of past life, the good momentum. Even if he lives in the body and works incessantly, he works only to do good; his lips speak only benediction to all; his hands do only good works; his mind can only think good thoughts; his presence is a blessing wherever he goes. He is himself a living blessing. Such a man will, by his very presence, change even the most wicked persons into saints. Even if he does not speak, his very presence will be a blessing to mankind. Can such men do any evil; can they do wicked deeds? There is, you must remember, all the difference of pole to pole between realisation and mere talking. Any fool can talk. Even parrots talk. Talking is one thing, and realising is another. Philosophies, and doctrines, and arguments, and books, and theories, and churches, and sects, and all these things are good in their own way; but when that realisation comes, these things drop away. For instance, maps are good, but when you see the country itself, and look again at the maps, what a great difference you find! So those that have realised truth do not require the ratiocinations of logic and all other gymnastics of the intellect to make them understand the truth; it is to them the life of their lives, concretised, made more than tangible. It is, as the sages of the Vedanta say, "even as a fruit in your hand"; you can stand up and say, it is here. So those that have realised the truth will stand up and say, "Here is the Self". You may argue with them by the year, but they will smile at you; they will regard it all as child's prattle; they will let the child prattle on. They have realised the truth and are full. Suppose you have seen a country, and another man comes to you and tries to argue with you that that country never existed, he may go on arguing indefinitely, but your only attitude of mind towards him must be to hold that the man is fit for a lunatic asylum. So the man of realisation says, "All this talk in the world about its little religions is but prattle; realisation is the soul, the very essence of religion." Religion can be realised. Are you ready? Do you want it? You will get the realisation if you do, and then you will be truly religious. Until you have attained realisation there is no difference between you and atheists. The atheists are sincere, but the man who says that he believes in religion and never attempts to realise it is not sincere.

The next question is to know what comes after realisation. Suppose we have realised this oneness of the universe, that we are that one Infinite Being, and suppose we have realised that this Self is the only Existence and that it is the same Self which is manifesting in all these various phenomenal forms, what becomes of us after that? Shall we become inactive, get into a corner and sit down there and die away? "What good will it do to the world?" That old question! In the first place, why should it do good to the world? Is there any reason why it should? What right has any one to ask the question, "What good will it do to the world?" What is meant by that? A baby likes candies. Suppose you are conducting investigations in connection with some subject of electricity and the baby asks you, "Does it buy candies?" "No" you answer. "Then what good will it do?" says the baby. So men stand up and say, "What good will this do to the world; will it give us money?" "No." "Then what good is there in it?" That is what men mean by doing good to the world. Yet religious realisation does all the good to the world. People are afraid that when they attain to it, when they realise that there is but one, the fountains of love will be dried up, that everything in life will go away, and that all they love will vanish for them, as it were, in this life and in the life to come. People never stop to think that those who bestowed the least thought on their own individualities have been the greatest workers in the world. Then alone a man loves when he finds that the object of his love is not any low, little, mortal thing. Then alone a man loves when he finds that the object of his love is not a clod of earth, but it is the veritable God Himself. The wife will love the husband the more when she thinks that the husband is God Himself. The husband will love the wife the more when he knows that the wife is God Himself. That mother will love the children more who thinks that the children are God Himself. That man will love his greatest enemy who knows that that very enemy is God Himself. That man will love a holy man who knows that the holy man is God Himself, and that very man will also love the unholiest of men because he knows the background of that unholiest of men is even He, the Lord. Such a man becomes a world-mover for whom his little self is dead and God stands in its place. The whole universe will become transfigured to him. That which is painful and miserable will all vanish; struggles will all depart and go. Instead of being a prison-house, where we every day struggle and fight and compete for a morsel of bread, this universe will then be to us a playground. Beautiful will be this universe then! Such a man alone has the right to stand up and say, "How beautiful is this world!" He alone has the right to say that it is all good. This will be the great good to the world resulting from such realisation, that instead of this world going on with all its friction and clashing, if all mankind today realise only a bit of that great truth, the aspect of the whole world will be changed, and, in place of fighting and quarrelling, there would be a reign of peace. This indecent and brutal hurry which forces us to go ahead of every one else will then vanish from the world. With it will vanish all struggle, with it will vanish all hate, with it will vanish all jealousy, and all evil will vanish away for ever. Gods will live then upon this earth. This very earth will then become heaven, and what evil can there be when gods are playing with gods, when gods are working with gods, and gods are loving gods? That is the great utility of divine realisation. Everything that you see in society will be changed and transfigured then. No more will you think of man as evil; and that is the first great gain. No more will you stand up and sneeringly cast a glance at a poor man or woman who has made a mistake. No more, ladies, will you look down with contempt upon the poor woman who walks the street in the night, because you will see even there God Himself. No more will you think of jealousy and punishments. They will all vanish; and love, the great ideal of love, will be so powerful that no whip and cord will be necessary to guide mankind aright.

If one millionth part of the men and women who live in this world simply sit down and for a few minutes say, "You are all God, O ye men and O ye animals and living beings, you are all the manifestations of the one living Deity!" the whole world will be changed in half an hour. Instead of throwing tremendous bomb-shells of hatred into every corner, instead of projecting currents of jealousy and of evil thought, in every country people will think that it is all He. He is all that you see and feel. How can you see evil until there is evil in you? How can you see the thief, unless he is there, sitting in the heart of your heart? How can you see the murderer until you are yourself the murderer? Be good, and evil will vanish for you. The whole universe will thus be changed. This is the greatest gain to society. This is the great gain to the human organism. These thoughts were thought out, worked out amongst individuals in ancient times in India. For various reasons, such as the exclusiveness of the teachers and foreign conquest, those thoughts were not allowed to spread. Yet they are grand truths; and wherever they have been working, man has become divine. My whole life has been changed by the touch of one of these divine men, about whom I am going to speak to you next Sunday; and the time is coming when these thoughts will be cast abroad over the whole world. Instead of living in monasteries, instead of being confined to books of philosophy to be studied only by the learned, instead of being the exclusive possession of sects and of a few of the learned, they will all be sown broadcast over the whole world, so that they may become the common property of the saint and the sinner, of men and women and children, of the learned and of the ignorant. They will then permeate the atmosphere of the world, and the very air that we breathe will say with every one of its pulsations, "Thou art That". And the whole universe with its myriads of suns and moons, through everything that speaks, with one voice will say, "Thou art That".

PRACTICAL VEDANTA AND OTHER LECTURES

PRACTICAL VEDANTA
PART I

Delivered in London, 10th November 1896

I have been asked to say something about the practical position of the Vedanta philosophy. As I have told you, theory is very good indeed, but how are we to carry it into practice? If it be absolutely impracticable, no theory is of any value whatever, except as intellectual gymnastics. The Vedanta, therefore, as a religion must be intensely practical. We must be able to carry it out in every part of our lives. And not only this, the fictitious differentiation between religion and the life of the world must vanish, for the Vedanta teaches oneness — one life throughout. The ideals of religion must cover the whole field of life, they must enter into all our thoughts, and more and more into practice. I will enter gradually on the practical side as we proceed. But this series of lectures is intended to be a basis, and so we must first apply ourselves to theories and understand how they are worked out, proceeding from forest caves to busy streets and cities; and one peculiar feature we find is that many of these thoughts have been the outcome, not of retirement into forests, but have emanated from persons whom we expect to lead the busiest lives — from ruling monarchs.

Shvetaketu was the son of Âruni, a sage, most probably a recluse. He was brought up in the forest, but he went to the city of the Panchâlas and appeared at the court of the king, Pravâhana Jaivali. The king asked him, "Do you know how beings depart hence at death?" "No, sir." "Do you know how they return hither?" "No, sir." "Do you know the way of the fathers and the way of the gods?" "No, sir." Then the king asked other questions. Shvetaketu could not answer them. So the king told him that he knew nothing. The boy went back to his father, and the father admitted that he himself could not answer these questions. It was not that he was unwilling to answer these questions. It was not that he was unwilling to teach the boy, but he did not know these things. So he went to the king and asked to be taught these secrets. The king said that these things had been hitherto known only among kings; the priests never knew them. He, however, proceeded to teach him what he desired to know. In various Upanishads we find that this Vedanta philosophy is not the outcome of meditation in the forests only, but that the very best parts of it were thought out and expressed by brains which were busiest in the everyday affairs of life. We cannot conceive any man busier than an absolute monarch, a man who is ruling over millions of people, and yet, some of these rulers were deep thinkers.

Everything goes to show that this philosophy must be very practical; and later on, when we come to the Bhagavad-Gita — most of you, perhaps, have read it, it is the best commentary we have on the Vedanta philosophy — curiously enough the scene is laid on the battlefield, where Krishna teaches this philosophy to Arjuna; and the doctrine which stands out luminously in every page of the Gita is intense activity, but in the midst of it, eternal calmness. This is the secret of work, to attain which is the goal of the Vedanta. Inactivity, as we understand it in the sense of passivity, certainly cannot be the goal. Were it so, then the walls around us would be the most intelligent; they are inactive. Clods of earth, stumps of trees, would be the greatest sages in the world; they are inactive. Nor does inactivity become activity when it is combined with passion. Real activity, which is the goal of Vedanta, is combined with eternal calmness, the calmness which cannot be ruffled, the balance of mind which is never disturbed, whatever happens. And we all know from our experience in life that that is the best attitude for work.

I have been asked many times how we can work if we do not have the passion which we generally feel for work. I also thought in that way years ago, but as I am growing older, getting more experience, I find it is not true. The less passion there is, the better we work. The calmer we are, the better for us, and the more the amount of work we can do. When we let loose our feelings, we waste so much energy, shatter our nerves, disturb our minds, and accomplish very little work. The energy which ought to have gone out as work is spent as mere feeling, which counts for nothing. It is only when the mind is very calm and collected that the whole of its energy is spent in doing good work. And if you read the lives of the great workers which the world has produced, you will find that they were wonderfully calm men. Nothing, as it were, could throw them off their balance. That is why the man who becomes angry never does a great amount of work, and the man whom nothing can make angry accomplishes so much. The man who gives way to anger, or hatred, or any other passion, cannot work; he only breaks himself to pieces, and does nothing practical. It is the calm, forgiving, equable, well-balanced mind that does the greatest amount of work.

The Vedanta preaches the ideal; and the ideal, as we know, is always far ahead of the real, of the practical, as we may call it. There are two tendencies in human nature: one to harmonise the ideal with the life, and the other to elevate the life to the ideal. It is a great thing to understand this, for the former tendency is the temptation of our lives. I think that I can only do a certain class of work. Most of it, perhaps, is bad; most of it, perhaps, has a motive power of passion behind it, anger, or greed, or selfishness. Now if any man comes to preach to me a certain ideal, the first step towards which is to give up selfishness, to give up self-enjoyment, I think that is impractical. But when a man brings an ideal which can be reconciled with my selfishness, I am glad at once and jump at it. That is the ideal for me. As the word "orthodox" has been manipulated into various forms, so has been the word "practical". "My doxy is orthodoxy; your doxy is heterodoxy." So with practicality. What I think is practical, is to me the only practicality in the world. If I am a shopkeeper, I think shopkeeping the only practical pursuit in the world. If I am a thief, I think stealing is the best means of being practical; others are not practical. You see how we all use this word practical for things we like and can do. Therefore I will ask you to understand that Vedanta, though it is intensely practical, is always so in the sense of the ideal. It does not preach an impossible ideal, however high it be, and it is high enough for an ideal. In one word, this ideal is that you are divine, "Thou art That". This is the essence of Vedanta; after all its ramifications and intellectual gymnastics, you know the human soul to be pure and omniscient, you see that such superstitions as birth and death would be entire nonsense when spoken of in connection with the soul. The soul was never born and will never die, and all these ideas that we are going to die and are afraid to die are mere superstitions. And all such ideas as that we can do this or cannot do that are superstitions. We can do everything. The Vedanta teaches men to have faith in themselves first. As certain religions of the world say that a man who does not believe in a Personal God outside of himself is an atheist, so the Vedanta says, a man who does not believe in himself is an atheist. Not believing in the glory of our own soul is what the Vedanta calls atheism. To many this is, no doubt, a terrible idea; and most of us think that this ideal can never be reached; but the Vedanta insists that it can be realised by every one. There is neither man nor woman or child, nor difference of race or sex, nor anything that stands as a bar to the realisation of the ideal, because Vedanta shows that it is realised already, it is already there.

All the powers in the universe are already ours. It is we who have put our hands before our eyes and cry that it is dark. Know that there is no darkness around us. Take the hands away and there is the light which was from the beginning. Darkness never existed, weakness never existed. We who are fools cry that we are weak; we who are fools cry that we are impure. Thus Vedanta not only insists that the ideal is practical, but that it has been so all the time; and this Ideal, this Reality, is our own nature. Everything else that you see is false, untrue. As soon as you say, "I am a little mortal being," you are saying something which is not true, you are giving the lie to yourselves, you are hypnotising yourselves into something vile and weak and wretched.

The Vedanta recognises no sin, it only recognises error. And the greatest error, says the Vedanta, is to say that you are weak, that you are a sinner, a miserable creature, and that you have no power and you cannot do this and that. Every time you think in that way, you, as it were, rivet one more link in the chain that binds you down, you add one more layer of hypnotism on to your own soul. Therefore, whosoever thinks he is weak is wrong, whosoever thinks he is impure is wrong, and is throwing a bad thought into the world. This we must always bear in mind that in the Vedanta there is no attempt at reconciling the present life — the hypnotised life, this false life which we have assumed — with the ideal; but this false life must go, and the real life which is always existing must manifest itself, must shine out. No man becomes purer and purer, it is a matter of greater manifestation. The veil drops away, and the native purity of the soul begins to manifest itself. Everything is ours already — infinite purity, freedom, love, and power.

The Vedanta also says that not only can this be realised in the depths of forests or caves, but by men in all possible conditions of life. We have seen that the people who discovered these truths were neither living in caves nor forests, nor following the ordinary vocations of life, but men who, we have every reason to believe, led the busiest of lives, men who had to command armies, to sit on thrones, and look to the welfare of millions — and all these, in the days of absolute monarchy, and not as in these days when a king is to a great extent a mere figurehead. Yet they could find time to think out all these thoughts, to realise them, and to teach them to humanity. How much more then should it be practical for us whose lives, compared with theirs, are lives of leisure? That we cannot realise them is a shame to us, seeing that we are comparatively free all the time, having very little to do. My requirements are as nothing compared with those of an ancient absolute monarch. My wants are as nothing compared with the demands of Arjuna on the battlefield of Kurukshetra, commanding a huge army; and yet he could find time in the midst of the din and turmoil of battle to talk the highest philosophy and to carry it into his life also. Surely we ought to be able to do as much in this life of ours — comparatively free, easy, and comfortable. Most of us here have more time than we think we have, if we really want to use it for good. With the amount of freedom we have we can attain to two hundred ideals in this life, if we will, but we must not degrade the ideal to the actual.

One of the most insinuating things comes to us in the shape of persons who apologise for our mistakes and teach us how to make special excuses for all our foolish wants and foolish desires; and we think that their ideal is the only ideal we need have. But it is not so. The Vedanta teaches no such thing. The actual should be reconciled to the ideal, the present life should be made to coincide with life eternal.

For you must always remember that the one central ideal of Vedanta is this oneness. There are no two in anything, no two lives, nor even two different kinds of life for the two worlds. You will find the Vedas speaking of heavens and things like that at first; but later on, when they come to the highest ideals of their philosophy, they brush away all these things. There is but one life, one world, one existence. Everything is that One, the difference is in degree and not in kind. The difference between our lives is not in kind. The Vedanta entirely denies such ideas as that animals are separate from men, and that they were made and created by God to be used for our food.

Some people have been kind enough to start an antivivisection society. I asked a member, "Why do you think, my friend, that it is quite lawful to kill animals for food, and not to kill one or two for scientific experiments?" He replied, "Vivisection is most horrible, but animals have been given to us for food." Oneness includes all animals. If man's life is immortal, so also is the animal's. The difference is only in degree and not in kind. The amoeba and I are the same, the difference is only in degree; and from the standpoint of the highest life, all these differences vanish. A man may see a great deal of difference between grass and a little tree, but if you mount very high, the grass and the biggest tree will appear much the same. So, from the standpoint of the highest ideal, the lowest animal and the highest man are the same. If you believe there is a God, the animals and the highest creatures must be the same. A God who is partial to his children called men, and cruel to his children called brute beasts, is worse than a demon. I would rather die a hundred times than worship such a God. My whole life would be a fight with such a God But there is no difference, and those who say there is, are irresponsible, heartless people who do not know. Here is a case of the word practical used in a wrong sense. I myself may not be a very strict vegetarian, but I understand the ideal. When I eat meat I know it is wrong. Even if I am bound to eat it under certain circumstances, I know it is cruel. I must not drag my ideal down to the actual and apologise for my weak conduct in this way. The ideal is not to eat flesh, not to injure any being, for all animals are my brothers. If you can think of them as your brothers, you have made a little headway towards the brotherhood of all souls, not to speak of the brotherhood of man! That is child's play. You generally find that this is not very acceptable to many, because it teaches them to give up the actual, and go higher up to the ideal. But if you bring out a theory which is reconciled with their present conduct, they regard it as entirely practical.

There is this strongly conservative tendency in human nature: we do not like to move one step forward. I think of mankind just as I read of persons who become frozen in snow; all such, they say, want to go to sleep, and if you try to drag them up, they say, "Let me sleep; it is so beautiful to sleep in the snow", and they die there in that sleep. So is our nature. That is what we are doing all our life, getting frozen from the feet upwards, and yet wanting to sleep. Therefore you must struggle towards the ideal, and if a man comes who wants to bring that ideal down to your level, and teach a religion that does not carry that highest ideal, do not listen to him. To me that is an impracticable religion. But if a man teaches a religion which presents the highest ideal, I am ready for him. Beware when anyone is trying to apologise for sense vanities and sense weaknesses. If anyone wants to preach that way to us, poor, sense-bound clods of earth as we have made ourselves by following that teaching, we shall never progress. I have seen many of these things, have had some experience of the world, and my country is the land where religious sects grow like mushrooms. Every year new sects arise. But one thing I have marked, that it is only those that never want to reconcile the man of flesh with the man of truth that make progress. Wherever there is this false idea of reconciling fleshly vanities with the highest ideals, of dragging down God to the level of man, there comes decay. Man should not be degraded to worldly slavery, but should be raised up to God.

At the same time, there is another side to the question. We must not look down with contempt on others. All of us are going towards the same goal. The difference between weakness and strength is one of degree; the difference between virtue and vice is one of degree, the difference between heaven and hell is one of degree, the difference between life and death is one of degree, all differences in this world are of degree, and not of kind, because oneness is the secret of everything. All is One, which manifests Itself, either as thought, or life, or soul, or body, and the difference is only in degree. As such, we have no right to look down with contempt upon those who are not developed exactly in the same degree as we are. Condemn none; if you can stretch out a helping hand, do so. If you cannot, fold your hands, bless your brothers, and let them go their own way. Dragging down and condemning is not the way to work. Never is work accomplished in that way. We spend our energies in condemning others. Criticism and condemnation is a vain way of spending our energies, for in the long run we come to learn that all are seeing the same thing, are more or less approaching the same ideal, and that most of our differences are merely differences of expression.

Take the idea of sin. I was telling you just now the Vedantic idea of it, and the other idea is that man is a sinner. They are practically the same, only the one takes the positive and the other the negative side. One shows to man his strength and the other his weakness. There may be weakness, says the Vedanta, but never mind, we want to grow. Disease was found out as soon as man was born. Everyone knows his disease; it requires no one to tell us what our diseases are. But thinking all the time that we are diseased will not cure us — medicine is necessary. We may forget anything outside, we may try to become hypocrites to the external world, but in our heart of hearts we all know our weaknesses. But, says the Vedanta, being reminded of weakness does not help much; give strength, and strength does not come by thinking of weakness all the time. The remedy for weakness is not brooding over weakness, but thinking of strength. Teach men of the strength that is already within them. Instead of telling them they are sinners, the Vedanta takes the opposite position, and says, "You are pure and perfect, and what you call sin does not belong to you." Sins are very low degrees of Self-manifestation; manifest your Self in a high degree. That is the one thing to remember; all of us can do that. Never say, "No", never say, "I cannot", for you are infinite. Even time and space are as nothing compared with your nature. You can do anything and everything, you are almighty.

These are the principles of ethics, but we shall now come down lower and work out the details. We shall see how this Vedanta can be carried into our everyday life, the city life, the country life, the national life, and the home life of every nation. For, if a religion cannot help man wherever he may be, wherever he stands, it is not of much use; it will remain only a theory for the chosen few. Religion, to help mankind, must be ready and able to help him in whatever condition he is, in servitude or in freedom, in the depths of degradation or on the heights of purity; everywhere, equally, it should be able to come to his aid. The principles of Vedanta, or the ideal of religion, or whatever you may call it, will be fulfilled by its capacity for performing this great function.

The ideal of faith in ourselves is of the greatest help to us. If faith in ourselves had been more extensively taught and practiced, I am sure a very large portion of the evils and miseries that we have would have vanished. Throughout the history of mankind, if any motive power has been more potent than another in the lives of all great men and women, it is that of faith in themselves. Born with the consciousness that they were to be great, they became great. Let a man go down as low as possible; there must come a time when out of sheer desperation he will take an upward curve and will learn to have faith in himself. But it is better for us that we should know it from the very first. Why should we have all these bitter experiences in order to gain faith in ourselves? We can see that all the difference between man and man is owing to the existence or non-existence of faith in himself. Faith in ourselves will do everything. I have experienced it in my own life, and am still doing so; and as I grow older that faith is becoming stronger and stronger. He is an atheist who does not believe in himself. The old religions said that he was an atheist who did not believe in God. The new religion says that he is the atheist who does not believe in himself. But it is not selfish faith because the Vedanta, again, is the doctrine of oneness. It means faith in all, because you are all. Love for yourselves means love for all, love for animals, love for everything, for you are all one. It is the great faith which will make the world better. I am sure of that. He is the highest man who can say with truth, "I know all about myself." Do you know how much energy, how many powers, how many forces are still lurking behind that frame of yours? What scientist has known all that is in man? Millions of years have passed since man first came here, and yet but one infinitesimal part of his powers has been manifested. Therefore, you must not say that you are weak. How do you know what possibilities lie behind that degradation on the surface? You know but little of that which is within you. For behind you is the ocean of infinite power and blessedness.

"This Âtman is first to be heard of." Hear day and night that you are that Soul. Repeat it to yourselves day and night till it enters into your very veins, till it tingles in every drop of blood, till it is in your flesh and bone. Let the whole body be full of that one ideal, "I am the birthless, the deathless, the blissful, the omniscient, the omnipotent, ever-glorious Soul." Think on it day and night; think on it till it becomes part and parcel of your life. Meditate upon it, and out of that will come work. "Out of the fullness of the heart the mouth speaketh," and out of the fullness of the heart the hand worketh also. Action will come. Fill yourselves with the ideal; whatever you do, think well on it. All your actions will be magnified, transformed, deified, by the very power of the thought. If matter is powerful, thought is omnipotent. Bring this thought to bear upon your life, fill yourselves with the thought of your almightiness, your majesty, and your glory. Would to God no superstitions had been put into your head! Would to God we had not been surrounded from our birth by all these superstitious influences and paralysing ideas of our weakness and vileness! Would to God that mankind had had an easier path through which to attain to the noblest and highest truths! But man had to pass through all this; do not make the path more difficult for those who are coming after you.

These are sometimes terrible doctrines to teach. I know people who get frightened at these ideas, but for those who want to be practical, this is the first thing to learn. Never tell yourselves or others that you are weak. Do good if you can, but do not injure the world. You know in your inmost heart that many of your limited ideas, this humbling of yourself and praying and weeping to imaginary beings are superstitions. Tell me one case where these prayers have been answered. All the answers that came were from your own hearts. You know there are no ghosts, but no sooner are you in the dark than you feel a little creepy sensation. That is so because in our childhood we have had all these fearful ideas put into our heads. But do not teach these things to others through fear of society and public opinion, through fear of incurring the hatred of friends, or for fear of losing cherished superstitions. Be masters of all these. What is there to be taught more in religion than the oneness of the universe and faith in one's self? All the works of mankind for thousands of years past have been towards this one goal, and mankind is yet working it out. It is your turn now and you already know the truth. For it has been taught on all sides. Not only philosophy and psychology, but materialistic sciences have declared it. Where is the scientific man today who fears to acknowledge the truth of this oneness of the universe? Who is there who dares talk of many worlds? All these are superstitions. There is only one life and one world, and this one life and one world is appearing to us as manifold. This manifoldness is like a dream. When you dream, one dream passes away and another comes. You do not live in your dreams. The dreams come one after another, scene after scene unfolds before you. So it is in this world of ninety per cent misery and ten per cent happiness. Perhaps after a while it will appear as ninety per cent happiness, and we shall call it heaven, but a time comes to the sage when the whole thing vanishes, and this world appears as God Himself, and his own soul as God. It is not therefore that there are many worlds, it is not that there are many lives. All this manifoldness is the manifestation of that One. That One is manifesting Himself as many, as matter, spirit, mind, thought, and everything else. It is that One, manifesting Himself as many. Therefore the first step for us to take is to teach the truth to ourselves and to others.

Let the world resound with this ideal, and let superstitions vanish. Tell it to men who are weak and persist in telling it. You are the Pure One; awake and arise, O mighty one, this sleep does not become you. Awake and arise, it does not befit you. Think not that you are weak and miserable. Almighty, arise and awake, and manifest your own nature. It is not fitting that you think yourself a sinner. It is not fitting that you think yourself weak. Say that to the world, say it to yourselves, and see what a practical result comes, see how with an electric flash everything is manifested, how everything is changed. Tell that to mankind, and show them their power. Then we shall learn how to apply it in our daily lives.

To be able to use what we call Viveka (discrimination), to learn how in every moment of our lives, in every one of our actions, to discriminate between what is right and wrong, true and false, we shall have to know the test of truth, which is purity, oneness. Everything that makes for oneness is truth. Love is truth, and hatred is false, because hatred makes for multiplicity. It is hatred that separates man from man; therefore it is wrong and false. It is a disintegrating power; it separates and destroys.

Love binds, love makes for that oneness. You become one, the mother with the child, families with the city, the whole world becomes one with the animals. For love is Existence, God Himself; and all this is the manifestation of that One Love, more or less expressed. The difference is only in degree, but it is the manifestation of that One Love throughout. Therefore in all our actions we have to judge whether it is making for diversity or for oneness. If for diversity we have to give it up, but if it makes for oneness we are sure it is good. So with our thoughts; we have to decide whether they make for disintegration, multiplicity, or for oneness, binding soul to soul and bringing one influence to bear. If they do this, we will take them up, and if not, we will throw them off as criminal.

The whole idea of ethics is that it does not depend on anything unknowable, it does not teach anything unknown, but in the language of the Upanishad, "The God whom you worship as an unknown God, the same I preach unto thee." It is through the Self that you know anything. I see the chair; but to see the chair, I have first to perceive myself and then the chair. It is in and through the Self that the chair is perceived. It is in and through the Self that you are known to me, that the whole world is known to me; and therefore to say this Self is unknown is sheer nonsense. Take off the Self and the whole universe vanishes. In and through the Self all knowledge comes. Therefore it is the best known of all. It is yourself, that which you call I. You may wonder how this I of me can be the I of you. You may wonder how this limited I can be the unlimited Infinite, but it is so. The limited is a mere fiction. The Infinite has been covered up, as it were, and a little of It is manifesting as the I. Limitation can never come upon the unlimited; it is a fiction. The Self is known, therefore, to every one of us — man, woman, or child — and even to animals. Without knowing Him we can neither live nor move, nor have our being; without knowing this Lord of all, we cannot breathe or live a second. The God of the Vedanta is the most known of all and is not the outcome of imagination.

If this is not preaching a practical God, how else could you teach a practical God? Where is there a more practical God than He whom I see before me — a God omnipresent, in every being, more real than our senses? For you are He, the Omnipresent God Almighty, the Soul of your souls, and if I say you are not, I tell an untruth. I know it, whether at all times I realise it or not. He is the Oneness, the Unity of all, the Reality of all life and all existence.

These ideas of the ethics of Vedanta have to be worked out in detail, and, therefore, you must have patience. As I have told you, we want to take the subject in detail and work it up thoroughly, to see how the ideas grow from very low ideals, and how the one great Ideal of oneness has developed and become shaped into the universal love; and we ought to study these in order to avoid dangers. The world cannot find time to work it up from the lowest steps. But what is the use of our standing on higher steps if we cannot give the truth to others coming afterwards? Therefore, it is better to study it in all its workings; and first, it is absolutely necessary to clear the intellectual portion, although we know that intellectuality is almost nothing; for it is the heart that is of most importance. It is through the heart that the Lord is seen, and not through the intellect. The intellect is only the street-cleaner, cleansing the path for us, a secondary worker, the policeman; but the policeman is not a positive necessity for the workings of society. He is only to stop disturbances, to check wrong-doing, and that is all the work required of the intellect. When you read intellectual books, you think when you have mastered them, "Bless the Lord that I am out of them", because the intellect is blind and cannot move of itself, it has neither hands nor feet. It is feeling that works, that moves with speed infinitely superior to that of electricity or anything else. Do you feel? — that is the question. If you do, you will see the Lord: It is the feeling that you have today that will be intensified, deified, raised to the highest platform, until it feels everything, the oneness in everything, till it feels God in itself and in others. The intellect can never do that. "Different methods of speaking words, different methods of explaining the texts of books, these are for the enjoyment of the learned, not for the salvation of the soul" (Vivekachudâmani, 58).

Those of you who have read Thomas a Kempis know how in every page he insists on this, and almost every holy man in the world has insisted on it. Intellect is necessary, for without it we fall into crude errors and make all sorts of mistakes. Intellect checks these; but beyond that, do not try to build anything upon it. It is an inactive, secondary help; the real help is feeling, love. Do you feel for others? If you do, you are growing in oneness. If you do not feel for others, you may be the most intellectual giant ever born, but you will be nothing; you are but dry intellect, and you will remain so. And if you feel, even if you cannot read any book and do not know any language, you are in the right way. The Lord is yours.

Do you not know from the history of the world where the power of the prophets lay? Where was it? In the intellect? Did any of them write a fine book on philosophy, on the most intricate ratiocinations of logic? Not one of them. They only spoke a few words. Feel like Christ and you will be a Christ; feel like Buddha and you will be a Buddha. It is feeling that is the life, the strength, the vitality, without which no amount of intellectual activity can reach God. Intellect is like limbs without the power of locomotion. It is only when feeling enters and gives them motion that they move and work on others. That is so all over the world, and it is a thing which you must always remember. It is one of the most practical things in Vedantic morality, for it is the teaching of the Vedanta that you are all prophets, and all must be prophets. The book is not the proof of your conduct, but you are the proof of the book. How do you know that a book teaches truth? Because you are truth and feel it. That is what the Vedanta says. What is the proof of the Christs and Buddhas of the world? That you and I feel like them. That is how you and I understand that they were true. Our prophet-soul is the proof of their prophet-soul. Your godhead is the proof of God Himself. If you are not a prophet, there never has been anything true of God. If you are not God, there never was any God, and never will be. This, says the Vedanta, is the ideal to follow. Every one of us will have to become a prophet, and you are that already. Only know it. Never think there is anything impossible for the soul. It is the greatest heresy to think so. If there is sin, this is the only sin — to say that you are weak, or others are weak.

PRACTICAL VEDANTA PART II

Delivered in London, 12th November 1896

I will relate to you a very ancient story from the Chhândogya Upanishad, which tells how knowledge came to a boy. The form of the story is very crude, but we shall find that it contains a principle. A young boy said to his mother, "I am going to study the Vedas. Tell me the name of my father and my caste." The mother was not a married woman, and in India the child of a woman who has not been married is considered an outcast; he is not recognised by society and is not entitled to study the Vedas. So the poor mother said, "My child, I do not know your family name; I was in service, and served in different places; I do not know who your father is, but my name is Jabâlâ and your name is Satyakâma." The little child went to a sage and asked to be taken as a student. The sage asked him, "What is the name of your father, and what is your caste?" The boy repeated to him what he had heard from his mother. The sage at once said, "None but a Brâhmin could speak such a damaging truth about himself. You are a Brahmin and I will teach you. You have not swerved from truth." So he kept the boy with him and educated him.

Now come some of the peculiar methods of education in ancient India. This teacher gave Satyakama four hundred lean, weak cows to take care of, and sent him to the forest. There he went and lived for some time. The teacher had told him to come back when the herd would increase to the number of one thousand. After a few years, one day Satyakama heard a big bull in the herd saying to him, "We are a thousand now; take us back to your teacher. I will teach you a little of Brahman." "Say on, sir," said Satyakama. Then the bull said, "The East is a part of the Lord, so is the West, so is the South, so is the North. The four cardinal points are the four parts of Brahman. Fire will also teach you something of Brahman." Fire was a great symbol in those days, and every student had to procure fire and make offerings. So on the following day, Satyakama started for his Guru's house, and when in the evening he had performed his oblation, and worshipped at the fire, and was sitting near it, he heard a voice come from the fire, "O Satyakama." "Speak, Lord," said Satyakama. (Perhaps you may remember a very similar story in the Old Testament, how Samuel heard a mysterious voice.) "O Satyakama, I am come to teach you a little of Brahman. This earth is a portion of that Brahman. The sky and the heaven are portions of It. The ocean is a part of that Brahman." Then the fire said that a certain bird would also teach him something. Satyakama continued his journey and on the next day when he had performed his evening sacrifice a swan came to him and said, "I will teach you something about Brahman. This fire which you worship, O Satyakama, is a part of that Brahman. The sun is a part, the moon is a part, the lightning is a part of that Brahman. A bird called Madgu will tell you more about it." The next evening that bird came, and a similar voice was heard by Satyakama, "I will tell you something about Brahman. Breath is a part of Brahman, sight is a part, hearing is a part, the mind is a part." Then the boy arrived at his teacher's place and presented himself before him with due reverence. No sooner had the teacher seen this disciple than he remarked: "Satyakama, thy face shines like that of a knower of Brahman! Who then has taught thee?" "Beings other than men," replied Satyakama. "But I wish that you should teach me, sir. For I have heard from men like you that knowledge which is learnt from a Guru alone leads to the supreme good." Then the sage taught him the same knowledge which he had received from the gods. "And nothing was left out, yea, nothing was left out."

Now, apart from the allegories of what the bull, the fire, and the birds taught, we see the tendency of the thought and the direction in which it was going in those days. The great idea of which we here see the germ is that all these voices are inside ourselves. As we understand these truths better, we find that the voice is in our own heart, and the student understood that all the time he was hearing the truth; but his explanation was not correct. He was interpreting the voice as coming from the external world, while all the time, it was within him. The second idea that we get is that of making the knowledge of the Brahman practical. The world is always seeking the practical possibilities of religion, and we find in these stories how it was becoming more and more practical every day. The truth was shown through everything with which the students were familiar. The fire they were worshipping was Brahman, the earth was a part of Brahman, and so on.

The next story belongs to Upakosala Kâmalâyana, a disciple of this Satyakama, who went to be taught by him and dwelt with him for some time. Now Satyakama went away on a journey, and the student became very downhearted; and when the teacher's wife came and asked him why he was not eating, the boy said, "I am too unhappy to eat." Then a voice came from the fire he was worshipping, saying "This life is Brahman, Brahman is the ether, and Brahman is happiness. Know Brahman.' "I know, sir," the boy replied, "that life is Brahman, but that It is ether and happiness I do not know." Then it explained that the two words ether and happiness signified one thing in reality, viz. the sentient ether (pure intelligence) that resides in the heart. So, it taught him Brahman as life and as the ether in the heart. Then the fire taught him, "This earth, food, fire, and sun whom you worship, are forms of Brahman. The person that is seen in the sun, I am He. He who knows this and meditates on Him, all his sins vanish and he has long life and becomes happy. He who lives in the cardinal points, the moon, the stars, and the water, I am He. He who lives in this life, the ether, the heavens, and the lightning, I am He." Here too we see the same idea of practical religion. The things which they were worshipping, such as the fire, the sun, the moon, and so forth, and the voice with which they were familiar, form the subject of the stories which explain them and give them a higher meaning. And this is the real, practical side of Vedanta. It does not destroy the world, but it explains it; it does not destroy the person, but explains him; it does not destroy the individuality, but explains it by showing the real individuality. It does not show that this world is vain and does not exist, but it says, "Understand what this world is, so that it may not hurt you." The voice did not say to Upakosala that the fire which he was worshipping, or the sun, or the moon, or the lightning, or anything else, was all wrong, but it showed him that the same spirit which was inside the sun, and moon, and lightning, and the fire, and the earth, was in him, so that everything became transformed, as it were, in the eyes of Upakosala. The fire which was merely a material fire before, in which to make oblations, assumed a new aspect and became the Lord. The earth became transformed, life became transformed, the sun, the moon, the stars, the lightning, everything became transformed and deified. Their real nature was known. The theme of the Vedanta is to see the Lord in everything, to see things in their real nature, not as they appear to be. Then another lesson is taught in the Upanishads: "He who shines through the eyes is Brahman; He is the Beautiful One, He is the Shining One. He shines in all these worlds." A certain peculiar light, a commentator says, which comes to the pure man, is what is meant by the light in the eyes, and it is said that when a man is pure such a light will shine in his eyes, and that light belongs really to the Soul within, which is everywhere. It is the same light which shines in the planets, in the stars, and suns.

I will now read to you some other doctrine of these ancient Upanishads, about birth and death and so on. Perhaps it will interest you. Shvetaketu went to the king of the Panchâlas, and the king asked him, "Do you know where people go when they die? Do you know how they come back? Do you know why the other world does not become full?" The boy replied that he did not know. Then he went to his father and asked him the same questions. The father said, "I do not know," and he went to the king. The king said that this knowledge was never known to the priests, it was only with the kings, and that was the reason why kings ruled the world. This man stayed with the king for some time, for the king said he would teach him. "The other world, O Gautama, is the fire. The sun is its fuel. The rays are the smoke. The day is the flame. The moon is the embers. And the stars are the sparks. In this fire the gods pour libation of faith and from this libation king Soma is born." So on he goes. "You need not make oblation to that little fire: the whole world is that fire, and this oblation, this worship, is continually going on. The gods, and the angels, and everybody is worshipping it. Man is the greatest symbol of fire, the body of man." Here also we see the ideal becoming practical and Brahman is seen in everything. The principle that underlies all these stories is that invented symbolism may be good and helpful, but already better symbols exist than any we can invent. You may invent an image through which to worship God, but a better image already exists, the living man. You may build a temple in which to worship God, and that may be good, but a better one, a much higher one, already exists, the human body.

You remember that the Vedas have two parts, the ceremonial and the knowledge portions. In time ceremonials had multiplied and become so intricate that it was almost hopeless to disentangle them, and so in the Upanishads we find that the ceremonials are almost done away with, but gently, by explaining them. We see that in old times they had these oblations and sacrifices, then the philosophers came, and instead of snatching away the symbols from the hands of the ignorant, instead of taking the negative position, which we unfortunately find so general in modern reforms, they gave them something to take their place. "Here is the symbol of fire," they said. "Very good! But here is another symbol, the earth. What a grand, great symbol! Here is this little temple, but the whole universe is a temple; a man can worship anywhere. There are the peculiar figures that men draw on the earth, and there are the altars, but here is the greatest of altars, the living, conscious human body, and to worship at this altar is far higher than the worship of any dead symbols."

We now come to a peculiar doctrine. I do not understand much of it myself. If you can make something out of it, I will read it to you. When a man dies, who has by meditation purified himself and got knowledge, he first goes to light, then from light to day, from day to the light half of the moon, from that to the six months when the sun goes to the north, from that to the year, from the year to the sun, from the sun to the moon, from the moon to the lightning, and when he comes to the sphere of lightning, he meets a person who is not human, and that person leads him to (the conditioned) Brahman. This is the way of the gods. When sages and wise persons die, they go that way and they do not return. What is meant by this month and year, and all these things, no one understands clearly. Each one gives his own meaning, and some say it is all nonsense. What is meant by going to the world of the moon and of the sun, and this person who comes to help the soul after it has reached the sphere of lightning, no one knows. There is an idea among the Hindus that the moon is a place where life exists, and we shall see how life has come from there. Those that have not attained to knowledge, but have done good work in this life, first go, when they die, through smoke, then to night, then to the dark fifteen days, then to the six months when the sun goes to the south, and from that they go to the region of their forefathers, then to ether, then to the region of the moon, and there become the food of the gods, and later, are born as gods and live there so long as their good works will permit. And when the effect of the good work has been finished, they come back to earth by the same route. They first become ether, and then air, and then smoke, and then mist, then cloud, and then fall upon the earth as raindrops; then they get into food, which is eaten up by human beings, and finally become their children. Those whose works have been very good take birth in good families, and those whose works have been bad take bad births, even in animal bodies. Animals are continually coming to and going from this earth. That is why the earth is neither full nor empty.

Several ideas we can get also from this, and later on, perhaps, we shall be able to understand it better, and we can speculate a little upon what it means. The last part which deals with how those who have been in heaven return, is clearer, perhaps, than the first part; but the whole idea seems to be this that there is no permanent heaven without realising God. Now some people who have not realised God, but have done good work in this world, with the view of enjoying the results, go, when they die, through this and that place, until they reach heaven, and there they are born in the same way as we are here, as children of the gods, and they live there as long as their good works will permit. Out of this comes one basic idea of the Vedanta that everything which has name and form is transient. This earth is transient, because it has name and form, and so the heavens must be transient, because there also name and form remain. A heaven which is eternal will be contradictory in terms, because everything that has name and form must begin in time, exist in time, and end in time. These are settled doctrines of the Vedanta, and as such the heavens are given up.

We have seen in the Samhitâ that the idea of heaven was that it was eternal, much the same as is prevalent among Mohammedans and Christians. The Mohammedans concretise it a little more. They say it is a place where there are gardens, beneath which rivers run. In the desert of Arabia water is very desirable, so the Mohammedan always conceives of his heaven as containing much water. I was born in a country where there are six months of rain every year. I should think of heaven, I suppose, as a dry place, and so also would the English people. These heavens in the Samhita are eternal, and the departed have beautiful bodies and live with their forefathers, and are happy ever afterwards. There they meet with their parents, children, and other relatives, and lead very much the same sort of life as here, only much happier. All the difficulties and obstructions to happiness in this life have vanished, and only its good parts and enjoyments remain. But however comfortable mankind may consider this state of things, truth is one thing and comfort is another. There are cases where truth is not comfortable until we reach its climax. Human nature is very conservative It does something, and having once done that, finds it hard to get out of it. The mind will not receive new thoughts, because they bring discomfort.

In the Upanishads, we see a tremendous departure made. It is declared that these heavens in which men live with the ancestors after death cannot be permanent. Seeing that everything which has name and form must die. If there are heavens with forms, these heavens must vanish in course of time; they may last millions of years, but there must come a time when they will have to go. With this idea came another that these souls must come back to earth, and that heavens are places where they enjoy the results of their good works, and after these effects are finished they come back into this earth life again. One thing is clear from this that mankind had a perception of the philosophy of causation even at the early time. Later on we shall see how our philosophers bring that out in the language of philosophy and logic, but here it is almost in the language of children. One thing you may remark in reading these books that it is all internal perception. If you ask me if this can be practical, my answer is, it has been practical first, and philosophical next. You can see that first these things have been perceived and realised and then written. This world spoke to the early thinkers. Birds spoke to them, animals spoke to them, the sun and the moon spoke to them; and little by little they realised things, and got into the heart of nature. Not by cogitation not by the force of logic, not by picking the brains of others and making a big book, as is the fashion in modern times, not even as I do, by taking up one of their writings and making a long lecture, but by patient investigation and discovery they found out the truth. Its essential method was practice, and so it must be always. Religion is ever a practical science, and there never was nor will be any theological religion. It is practice first, and knowledge afterwards. The idea that souls come back is already there. Those persons who do good work with the idea of a result, get it, but the result is not permanent. There we get the idea of causation very beautifully put forward, that the effect is only commensurate with the cause. As the cause is, so the effect will be. The cause being finite, the effect must be finite. If the cause is eternal the effect can be eternal, but all these causes, doing good work, and all other things, are only finite causes, and as such cannot produce infinite result.

We now come to the other side of the question. As there cannot be an eternal heaven, on the same grounds, there cannot be an eternal hell. Suppose I am a very wicked man, doing evil every minute of my life. Still, my whole life here, compared with my eternal life, is nothing. If there be an eternal punishment, it will mean that there is an infinite effect produced by a finite cause, which cannot be. If I do good all my life, I cannot have an infinite heaven; it would be making the same mistake. But there is a third course which applies to those who have known the Truth, to those who have realised It. This is the only way to get beyond this veil of Mâyâ — to realise what Truth is; and the Upanishads indicate what is meant by realising the Truth.

It means recognising neither good nor bad, but knowing all as coming from the Self; Self is in everything. It means denying the universe; shutting your eyes to it; seeing the Lord in hell as well as in heaven; seeing the Lord in death as well as in life. This is the line of thought in the passage I have read to you; the earth is a symbol of the Lord, the sky is the Lord, the place we fill is the Lord, everything is Brahman. And this is to be seen, realised, not simply talked or thought about. We can see as its logical consequence that when the soul has realised that everything is full of the Lord, of Brahman, it will not care whether it goes to heaven, or hell, or anywhere else; whether it be born again on this earth or in heaven. These things have ceased to have any meaning to that soul, because every place is the same, every place is the temple of the Lord, every place has become holy and the presence of the Lord is all that it sees in heaven, or hell, or anywhere else. Neither good nor bad, neither life nor death — only the one infinite Brahman exists.

According to the Vedanta, when a man has arrived at that perception, he has become free, and he is the only man who is fit to live in this world. Others are not. The man who sees evil, how can he live in this world? His life is a mass of misery. The man who sees dangers, his life is a misery; the man who sees death, his life is a misery. That man alone can live in this world, he alone can say, "I enjoy this life, and I am happy in this life". Who has seen the Truth, and the Truth in everything. By the by, I may tell you that the idea of hell does not occur in the Vedas anywhere. It comes with the Purânas much later. The worst punishment according to the Vedas is coming back to earth, having another chance in this world. From the very first we see the idea is taking the impersonal turn. The ideas of punishment and reward are very material, and they are only consonant with the idea of a human God, who loves one and hates another, just as we do. Punishment and reward are only admissible with the existence of such a God. They had such a God in the Samhita, and there we find the idea of fear entering, but as soon as we come to the Upanishads, the idea of fear vanishes, and the impersonal idea takes its place. It is naturally the hardest thing for man to understand, this impersonal idea, for he is always clinging on to the person. Even people who are thought to be great thinkers get disgusted at the idea of the Impersonal God. But to me it seems so absurd to think of God as an embodied man. Which is the higher idea, a living God, or a dead God? A God whom nobody sees, nobody knows, or a God Known?

The Impersonal God is a living God, a principle. The difference between personal and impersonal is this, that the personal is only a man, and the impersonal idea is that He is the angel, the man, the animal, and yet something more which we cannot see, because impersonality includes all personalities, is the sum total of everything in the universe, and infinitely more besides. "As the one fire coming into the world is manifesting itself in so many forms, and yet is infinitely more besides," so is the Impersonal.

We want to worship a living God. I have seen nothing but God all my life, nor have you. To see this chair you first see God, and then the chair in and through Him He is everywhere saying, "I am". The moment you feel "I am", you are conscious of Existence. Where shall we go to find God if we cannot see Him in our own hearts and in every living being? "Thou art the man, Thou art the woman, Thou art the girl, and Thou art the boy. Thou art the old man tottering with a stick. Thou art the young man walking in the pride of his strength." Thou art all that exists, a wonderful living God who is the only fact in the universe. This seems to many to be a terrible contradiction to the traditional God who lives behind a veil somewhere and whom nobody ever sees. The priests only give us an assurance that if we follow them, listen to their admonitions, and walk in the way they mark out for us — then when we die, they will give us a passport to enable us to see the face of God! What are all these heaven ideas but simply modifications of this nonsensical priestcraft?

Of course the impersonal idea is very destructive, it takes away all trade from the priests, churches, and temples. In India there is a famine now, but there are temples in each one of which there are jewels worth a king's ransom! If the priests taught this Impersonal idea to the people, their occupation would be gone. Yet we have to teach it unselfishly, without priestcraft. You are God and so am I; who obeys whom? Who worships whom? You are the highest temple of God; I would rather worship you than any temple, image, or Bible. Why are some people so contradictory in their thought? They are like fish slipping through our fingers. They say they are hard-headed practical men. Very good. But what is more practical than worshipping here, worshipping you? I see you, feel you, and I know you are God. The Mohammedan says, there is no God but Allah. The Vedanta says, there is nothing that is not God. It may frighten many of you, but you will understand it by degrees. The living God is within you, and yet you are building churches and temples and believing all sorts of imaginary nonsense. The only God to worship is the human soul in the human body. Of course all animals are temples too, but man is the highest, the Taj Mahal of temples. If I cannot worship in that, no other temple will be of any advantage. The moment I have realised God sitting in the temple of every human body, the moment I stand in reverence before every human being and see God in him — that moment I am free from bondage, everything that binds vanishes, and I am free.

This is the most practical of all worship. It has nothing to do with theorising and speculation. Yet it frightens many. They say it is not right. They go on theorising about old ideals told them by their grandfathers, that a God somewhere in heaven had told some one that he was God. Since that time we have only theories. This is practicality according to them, and our ideas are impractical! No doubt, the Vedanta says that each one must have his own path, but the path is not the goal. The worship of a God in heaven and all these things are not bad, but they are only steps towards the Truth and not the Truth itself. They are good and beautiful, and some wonderful ideas are there, but the Vedanta says at every point, "My friend, Him whom you are worshipping as unknown, I worship as thee. He whom you are worshipping as unknown and are seeking for, throughout the universe, has been with you all the time. You are living through Him, and He is the Eternal Witness of the universe" "He whom all the Vedas worship, nay, more, He who is always present in the eternal 'I'. He existing, the whole universe exists. He is the light and life of the universe. If the 'I' were not in you, you would not see the sun, everything would be a dark mass. He shining, you see the world."

One question is generally asked, and it is this that this may lead to a tremendous amount of difficulty. Everyone of us will think, "I am God, and whatever I do or think must be good, for God can do no evil." In the first place, even taking this danger of misinterpretation for granted, can it be proved that on the other side the same danger does not exist? They have been worshipping a God in heaven separate from them, and of whom they are much afraid. They have been born shaking with fear, and all their life they will go on shaking. Has the world been made much better by this? Those who have understood and worshipped a Personal God, and those who have understood and worshipped an Impersonal God, on which side have been the great workers of the world — gigantic workers, gigantic moral powers? Certainly on the Impersonal. How can you expect morality to be developed through fear? It can never be. "Where one sees another, where one hears another, that is Maya. When one does not see another, when one does not hear another, when everything has become the Atman, who sees whom, who perceives whom?" It is all He, and all I, at the same time. The soul has become pure. Then, and then alone we understand what love is. Love cannot come through fear, its basis is freedom. When we really begin to love the world, then we understand what is meant by brotherhood or mankind, and not before.

So, it is not right to say that the Impersonal idea will lead to a tremendous amount of evil in the world, as if the other doctrine never lent itself to works of evil, as if it did not lead to sectarianism deluging the world with blood and causing men to tear each other to pieces. "My God is the greatest God, let us decide it by a free fight." That is the outcome of dualism all over the world. Come out into the broad open light of day, come out from the little narrow paths, for how can the infinite soul rest content to live and die in small ruts? Come out into the universe of Light. Everything in the universe is yours, stretch out your arms and embrace it with love. If you ever felt you wanted to do that, you have felt God.

You remember that passage in the sermon of Buddha, how he sent a thought of love towards the south, the north, the east, and the west, above and below, until the whole universe was filled with this love, so grand, great, and infinite. When you have that feeling, you have true personality. The whole universe is one person; let go the little things. Give up the small for the Infinite, give up small enjoyments for infinite bliss. It is all yours, for the Impersonal includes the Personal. So God is Personal and Impersonal at the same time. And Man, the Infinite, Impersonal Man, is manifesting Himself as person. We the infinite have limited ourselves, as it were, into small parts. The Vedanta says that Infinity is our true nature; it will never vanish, it will abide for ever. But we are limiting ourselves by our Karma, which like a chain round our necks has dragged us into this limitation. Break that chain and be free. Trample law under your feet. There is no law in human nature, there is no destiny, no fate. How can there be law in infinity? Freedom is its watchword. Freedom is its nature, its birthright. Be free, and then have any number of personalities you like. Then we will play like the actor who comes upon the stage and plays the part of a beggar. Contrast him with the actual beggar walking in the streets. The scene is, perhaps, the same in both cases, the words are, perhaps, the same, but yet what difference! The one enjoys his beggary while the other is suffering misery from it. And what makes this difference? The one is free and the other is bound. The actor knows his beggary is not true, but that he has assumed it for play, while the real beggar thinks that it is his too familiar state and that he has to bear it whether he wills it or not. This is the law. So long as we have no knowledge of our real nature, we are beggars, jostled about by every force in nature; and made slaves of by everything in nature; we cry all over the world for help, but help never comes to us; we cry to imaginary beings, and yet it never comes. But still we hope help will come, and thus in weeping, wailing, and hoping, one life is passed, and the same play goes on and on.

Be free; hope for nothing from anyone. I am sure if you look back upon your lives you will find that you were always vainly trying to get help from others which never came. All the help that has come was from within yourselves. You only had the fruits of what you yourselves worked for, and yet you were strangely hoping all the time for help. A rich man's parlour is always full; but if you notice, you do not find the same people there. The visitors are always hoping that they will get something from those wealthy men, but they never do. So are our lives spent in hoping, hoping, hoping, which never comes to an end. Give up hope, says the Vedanta. Why should you hope? You have everything, nay, you are everything. What are you hoping for? If a king goes mad, and runs about trying to find the king of his country, he will never find him, because he is the king himself. He may go through every village and city in his own country, seeking in every house, weeping and wailing, but he will never find him, because he is the king himself. It is better that we know we are God and give up this fool's search after Him; and knowing that we are God we become happy and contented. Give up all these mad pursuits, and then play your part in the universe, as an actor on the stage.

The whole vision is changed, and instead of an eternal prison this world has become a playground; instead of a land of competition it is a land of bliss, where there is perpetual spring, flowers bloom and butterflies flit about. This very world becomes heaven, which formerly was hell. To the eyes of the bound it is a tremendous place of torment, but to the eyes of the free it is quite otherwise. This one life is the universal life, heavens and all those places are here. All the gods are here, the prototypes of man. The gods did not create man after their type, but man created gods. And here are the prototypes, here is Indra, here is Varuna, and all the gods of the universe. We have been projecting our little doubles, and we are the originals of these gods, we are the real, the only gods to be worshipped. This is the view of the Vedanta, and this its practicality. When we have become free, we need not go mad and throw up society and rush off to die in the forest or the cave; we shall remain where we were, only we shall understand the whole thing. The same phenomena will remain, but with a new meaning. We do not know the world yet; it is only through freedom that we see what it is, and understand its nature. We shall see then that this so-called law, or fate, or destiny occupied only an infinitesimal part of our nature. It was only one side, but on the other side there was freedom all the time. We did not know this, and that is why we have been trying to save ourselves from evil by hiding our faces in the ground, like the hunted hare. Through delusion we have been trying to forget our nature, and yet we could not; it was always calling upon us, and all our search after God or gods, or external freedom, was a search after our real nature. We mistook the voice. We thought it was from the fire, or from a god or the sun, or moon, or stars, but at last we have found that it was from within ourselves. Within ourselves is this eternal voice speaking of eternal freedom; its music is eternally going on. Part of this music of the Soul has become the earth, the law, this universe, but it was always ours and always will be. In one word, the ideal of Vedanta is to know man as he really is, and this is its message, that if you cannot worship your brother man, the manifested God, how can you worship a God who is unmanifested?

Do you not remember what the Bible says, "If you cannot love your brother whom you have seen, how can you love God whom you have not seen?" If you cannot see God in the human face, how can you see him in the clouds, or in images made of dull, dead matter, or in mere fictitious stories of our brain? I shall call you religious from the day you begin to see God in men and women, and then you will understand what is meant by turning the left cheek to the man who strikes you on the right. When you see man as God, everything, even the tiger, will be welcome. Whatever comes to you is but the Lord, the Eternal, the Blessed One, appearing to us in various forms, as our father, and mother, and friend, and child — they are our own soul playing with us.

As our human relationships can thus be made divine, so our relationship with God may take any of these forms and we can look upon Him as our father, or mother, or friend, or beloved. Calling God Mother is a higher ideal than calling Him Father; and to call Him Friend is still higher; but the highest is to regard Him as the Beloved. The highest point of all is to see no difference between lover and beloved. You may remember, perhaps, the old Persian story, of how a lover came and knocked at the door of the beloved and was asked, "Who are you?" He answered, "It is I", and there was no response. A second time he came, and exclaimed, "I am here", but the door was not opened. The third time he came, and the voice asked from inside, "Who is there?" He replied, "I am thyself, my beloved", and the door opened. So is the relation between God and ourselves. He is in everything, He is everything. Every man and woman is the palpable, blissful, living God. Who says God is unknown? Who says He is to be searched after? We have found God eternally. We have been living in Him eternally; everywhere He is eternally known, eternally worshipped.

Then comes another idea, that other forms of worship are not errors. This is one of the great points to be remembered, that those who worship God through ceremonials and forms, however crude we may think them to be, are not in error. It is the journey from truth to truth, from lower truth to higher truth. Darkness is less light; evil is less good; impurity is less purity. It must always be borne in mind that we should see others with eyes of love, with sympathy, knowing that they are going along the same path that we have trodden. If you are free, you must know that all will be so sooner or later, and if you are free, how can you see the impermanent? If you are really pure, how do you see the impure? For what is within, is without. We cannot see impurity without having it inside ourselves. This is one of the practical sides of Vedanta, and I hope that we shall all try to carry it into our lives. Our whole life here is to carry this into practice, but the one great point we gain is that we shall work with satisfaction and contentment, instead of with discontent and dissatisfaction, for we know that Truth is within us, we have It as our birthright, and we have only to manifest It, and make It tangible.

PRACTICAL VEDANTA PART III

Delivered in London, 17th November 1896

In the Chhâdogya Upanishad we read that a sage called Nârada came to another called Sanatkumâra, and asked him various questions, of which one was, if religion was the cause of things as they are. And Sanatkumara leads him, as it were, step by step, telling him that there is something higher than this earth, and something higher than that, and so on, till he comes to Âkâsha, ether. Ether is higher than light, because in the ether are the sun and the moon, lightning and the stars; in ether we live, and in ether we die. Then the question arises, if there is anything higher than that, and Sanatkumara tells him of Prâna. This Prana, according to the Vedanta, is the principle of life. It is like ether, an omnipresent principle; and all motion, either in the body or anywhere else, is the work of this Prana. It is greater than Akasha, and through it everything lives. Prana is in the mother, in the father, in the sister, in the teacher, Prana is the knower.

I will read another passage, where Shvetaketu asks his father about the Truth, and the father teaches him different things, and concludes by saying, "That which is the fine cause in all these things, of It are all these things made. That is the All, that is Truth, thou art That, O Shvetaketu." And then he gives various examples. "As a bee, O Shvetaketu, gathers honey from different flowers, and as the different honeys do not know that they are from various trees, and from various flowers, so all of us, having come to that Existence, know not that we have done so. Now, that which is that subtle essence, in It all that exists has its self. It is the True. It is the Self and thou, O Shvetaketu, are That." He gives another example of the rivers running down to the ocean. "As the rivers, when they are in the ocean, do not know that they have been various rivers, even so when we come out of that Existence, we do not know that we are That. O Shvetaketu, thou art That." So on he goes with his teachings.

Now there are two principles of knowledge. The one principle is that we know by referring the particular to the general, and the general to the universal; and the second is that anything of which the explanation is sought is to be explained so far as possible from its own nature. Taking up the first principle, we see that all our knowledge really consists of classifications, going higher and higher. When something happens singly, we are, as it were, dissatisfied. When it can be shown that the same thing happens again and again, we are satisfied and call it law. When we find that one apple falls, we are dissatisfied; but when we find that all apples fall, we call it the law of gravitation and are satisfied. The fact is that from the particular we deduce the general.

When we want to study religion, we should apply this scientific process. The same principle also holds good here, and as a fact we find that that has been the method all through. In reading these books from which I have been translating to you, the earliest idea that I can trace is this principle of going from the particular to the general. We see how the "bright ones" became merged into one principle; and likewise in the ideas of the cosmos we find the ancient thinkers going higher and higher — from the fine elements they go to finer and more embracing elements, and from these particulars they come to one omnipresent ether, and from that even they go to an all embracing force, or Prana; and through all this runs the principle, that one is not separate from the others. It is the very ether that exists in the higher form of Prana, or the higher form of Prana concretes, so to say, and becomes ether; and that ether becomes still grosser, and so on.

The generalization of the Personal God is another case in point. We have seen how this generalization was reached, and was called the sum total of all consciousness. But a difficulty arises — it is an incomplete generalization. We take up only one side of the facts of nature, the fact of consciousness, and upon that we generalise, but the other side is left out. So, in the first place it is a defective generalization. There is another insufficiency, and that relates to the second principle. Everything should be explained from its own nature. There may have been people who thought that every apple that fell to the ground was dragged down by a ghost, but the explanation is the law of gravitation; and although we know it is not a perfect explanation, yet it is much better than the other, because it is derived from the nature of the thing itself, while the other posits an extraneous cause. So throughout the whole range of our knowledge; the explanation which is based upon the nature of the thing itself is a scientific explanation, and an explanation which brings in an outside agent is unscientific.

So the explanation of a Personal God as the creator of the universe has to stand that test. If that God is outside of nature, having nothing to do with nature, and this nature is the outcome of the command of that God and produced from nothing, it is a very unscientific theory, and this has been the weak point of every Theistic religion throughout the ages. These two defects we find in what is generally called the theory of monotheism, the theory of a Personal God, with all the qualities of a human being multiplied very much, who, by His will, created this universe out of nothing and yet is separate from it. This leads us into two difficulties.

As we have seen, it is not a sufficient generalization, and secondly, it is not an explanation of nature from nature. It holds that the effect is not the cause, that the cause is entirely separate from the effect. Yet all human knowledge shows that the effect is but the cause in another form. To this idea the discoveries of modern science are tending every day, and the latest theory that has been accepted on all sides is the theory of evolution, the principle of which is that the effect is but the cause in another form, a readjustment of the cause, and the cause takes the form of the effect. The theory of creation out of nothing would be laughed at by modern scientists.

Now, can religion stand these tests? If there be any religious theories which can stand these two tests, they will be acceptable to the modern mind, to the thinking mind. Any other theory which we ask the modern man to believe, on the authority of priests, or churches, or books, he is unable to accept, and the result is a hideous mass of unbelief. Even in those in whom there is an external display of belief, in their hearts there is a tremendous amount of unbelief. The rest shrink away from religion, as it were, give it up, regarding it as priestcraft only.

Religion has been reduced to a sort of national form. It is one of our very best social remnants; let it remain. But the real necessity which the grandfather of the modern man felt for it is gone; he no longer finds it satisfactory to his reason. The idea of such a Personal God, and such a creation, the idea which is generally known as monotheism in every religion, cannot hold its own any longer. In India it could not hold its own because of the Buddhists, and that was the very point where they gained their victory in ancient times. They showed that if we allow that nature is possessed of infinite power, and that nature can work out all its wants, it is simply unnecessary to insist that there is something besides nature. Even the soul is unnecessary.

The discussion about substance and qualities is very old, and you will sometimes find that the old superstition lives even at the present day. Most of you have read how, during the Middle Ages, and, I am sorry to say, even much later, this was one of the subjects of discussion, whether qualities adhered to substance, whether length, breadth, and thickness adhered to the substance which we call dead matter, whether, the substance remaining, the qualities are there or not. To this our Buddhist says, "You have no ground for maintaining the existence of such a substance; the qualities are all that exist; you do not see beyond them." This is just the position of most of our modern agnostics. For it is this fight of the substance and qualities that, on a higher plane, takes the form of the fight between noumenon and phenomenon. There is the phenomenal world, the universe of continuous change, and there is something behind which does not change; and this duality of existence, noumenon and phenomenon, some hold, is true, and others with better reason claim that you have no right to admit the two, for what we see, feel, and think is only the phenomenon. You have no right to assert there is anything beyond phenomenon; and there is no answer to this. The only answer we get is from the monistic theory of the Vedanta. It is true that only one exists, and that one is either phenomenon or noumenon. It is not true that there are two — something changing, and, in and through that, something which does not change; but it is the one and the same thing which appears as changing, and which is in reality unchangeable. We have come to think of the body, and mind, and soul as many, but really there is only one; and that one is appearing in all these various forms. Take the well-known illustration of the monists, the rope appearing as the snake. Some people, in the dark or through some other cause, mistake the rope for the snake, but when knowledge comes, the snake vanishes and it is found to be a rope. By this illustration we see that when the snake exists in the mind, the rope has vanished, and when the rope exists, the snake has gone. When we see phenomenon, and phenomenon only, around us, the noumenon has vanished, but when we see the noumenon, the unchangeable, it naturally follows that the phenomenon has vanished. Now, we understand better the position of both the realist and the idealist. The realist sees the phenomenon only, and the idealist looks to the noumenon. For the idealist, the really genuine idealist, who has truly arrived at the power of perception, whereby he can get away from all ideas of change, for him the changeful universe has vanished, and he has the right to say it is all delusion, there is no change. The realist at the same time looks at the changeful. For him the unchangeable has vanished, and he has a right to say this is all real.

What is the outcome of this philosophy? It is that the idea of Personal God is not sufficient. We have to get to something higher, to the Impersonal idea. It is the only logical step that we can take. Not that the personal idea would be destroyed by that, not that we supply proof that the Personal God does not exist, but we must go to the Impersonal for the explanation of the personal, for the Impersonal is a much higher generalization than the personal. The Impersonal only can be Infinite, the personal is limited. Thus we preserve the personal and do not destroy it. Often the doubt comes to us that if we arrive at the idea of the Impersonal God, the personal will be destroyed, if we arrive at the idea of the Impersonal man, the personal will be lost. But the Vedantic idea is not the destruction of the individual, but its real preservation. We cannot prove the individual by any other means but by referring to the universal, by proving that this individual is really the universal. If we think of the individual as separate from everything else in the universe, it cannot stand a minute. Such a thing never existed.

Secondly, by the application of the second principle, that the explanation of everything must come out of the nature of the thing, we are led to a still bolder idea, and one more difficult to understand. It is nothing less than this, that the Impersonal Being, our highest generalization, is in ourselves, and we are That. "O Shvetaketu, thou art That." You are that Impersonal Being; that God for whom you have been searching all over the universe is all the time yourself — yourself not in the personal sense but in the Impersonal. The man we know now, the manifested, is personalised, but the reality of this is the Impersonal. To understand the personal we have to refer it to the Impersonal, the particular must be referred to the general, and that Impersonal is the Truth, the Self of man.

There will be various questions in connection with this, and I shall try to answer them as we go on. Many difficulties will arise, but first let us clearly understand the position of monism. As manifested beings we appear to be separate, but our reality is one, and the less we think of ourselves as separate from that One, the better for us. The more we think of ourselves as separate from the Whole, the more miserable we become. From this monistic principle we get at the basis of ethics, and I venture to say that we cannot get any ethics from anywhere else. We know that the oldest idea of ethics was the will of some particular being or beings, but few are ready to accept that now, because it would be only a partial generalization. The Hindus say we must not do this or that because the Vedas say so, but the Christian is not going to obey the authority of the Vedas. The Christian says you must do this and not do that because the Bible says so. That will not be binding on those who do not believe in the Bible. But we must have a theory which is large enough to take in all these various grounds. Just as there are millions of people who are ready to believe in a Personal Creator, there have also been thousands of the brightest minds in this world who felt that such ideas were not sufficient for them, and wanted something higher, and wherever religion was not broad enough to include all these minds, the result was that the brightest minds in society were always outside of religion; and never was this so marked as at the present time, especially in Europe.

To include these minds, therefore, religion must become broad enough. Everything it claims must be judged from the standpoint of reason. Why religions should claim that they are not bound to abide by the standpoint of reason, no one knows. If one does not take the standard of reason, there cannot be any true judgment, even in the case of religions. One religion may ordain something very hideous. For instance, the Mohammedan religion allows Mohammedans to kill all who are not of their religion. It is clearly stated in the Koran, "Kill the infidels if they do not become Mohammedans." They must be put to fire and sword. Now if we tell a Mohammedan that this is wrong, he will naturally ask,

"How do you know that? How do you know it is not good? My book says it is." If you say your book is older, there will come the Buddhist, and say, my book is much older still. Then will come the Hindu, and say, my books are the oldest of all. Therefore referring to books will not do. Where is the standard by which you can compare? You will say, look at the Sermon on the Mount, and the Mohammedan will reply, look at the Ethics of the Koran. The Mohammedan will say, who is the arbiter as to which is the better of the two? Neither the New Testament nor the Koran can be the arbiter in a quarrel between them. There must be some independent authority, and that cannot be any book, but something which is universal; and what is more universal than reason? It has been said that reason is not strong enough; it does not always help us to get at the Truth; many times it makes mistakes, and, therefore, the conclusion is that we must believe in the authority of a church! That was said to me by a Roman Catholic, but I could not see the logic of it. On the other hand I should say, if reason be so weak, a body of priests would be weaker, and I am not going to accept their verdict, but I will abide by my reason, because with all its weakness there is some chance of my getting at truth through it; while, by the other means, there is no such hope at all.

We should, therefore, follow reason and also sympathise with those who do not come to any sort of belief, following reason. For it is better that mankind should become atheist by following reason than blindly believe in two hundred millions of gods on the authority of anybody. What we want is progress, development, realisation. No theories ever made men higher. No amount of books can help us to become purer. The only power is in realisation, and that lies in ourselves and comes from thinking. Let men think. A clod of earth never thinks; but it remains only a lump of earth. The glory of man is that he is a thinking being. It is the nature of man to think and therein he differs from animals. I believe in reason and follow reason having seen enough of the evils of authority, for I was born in a country where they have gone to the extreme of authority.

The Hindus believe that creation has come out of the Vedas. How do you know there is a cow? Because the word cow is in the Vedas. How do you know there is a man outside? Because the word man is there. If it had not been, there would have been no man outside. That is what they say. Authority with a vengeance! And it is not studied as I have studied it, but some of the most powerful minds have taken it up and spun out wonderful logical theories round it. They have reasoned it out, and there it stands — a whole system of philosophy; and thousands of the brightest intellects hare been dedicated through thousands of years to the working out of this theory. Such has been the power of authority, and great are the dangers thereof. It stunts the growth of humanity, and we must not forget that we want growth. Even in all relative truth, more than the truth itself, we want the exercise. That is our life.

The monistic theory has this merit that it is the most rational of all the religious theories that we can conceive of. Every other theory, every conception of God which is partial and little and personal is not rational. And yet monism has this grandeur that it embraces all these partial conceptions of God as being necessary for many. Some people say that this personal explanation is irrational. But it is consoling; they want a consoling religion and we understand that it is necessary for them. The clear light of truth very few in this life can bear, much less live up to. It is necessary, therefore, that this comfortable religion should exist; it helps many souls to a better one. Small minds whose circumference is very limited and which require little things to build them up, never venture to soar high in thought. Their conceptions are very good and helpful to them, even if only of little gods and symbols. But you have to understand the Impersonal, for it is in and through that alone that these others can be explained. Take, for instance, the idea of a Personal God. A man who understands and believes in the Impersonal — John Stuart Mill, for example — may say that a Personal God is impossible, and cannot be proved. I admit with him that a Personal God cannot be demonstrated. But He is the highest reading of the Impersonal that can be reached by the human intellect, and what else is the universe but various readings of the Absolute? It is like a book before us, and each one has brought his intellect to read it, and each one has to read it for himself. There is something which is common in the intellect of all men; therefore certain things appear to be the same to the intellect of mankind. That you and I see a chair proves that there is something common to both our minds. Suppose a being comes with another sense, he will not see the chair at all; but all beings similarly constituted will see the same things. Thus this universe itself is the Absolute, the unchangeable, the noumenon; and the phenomenon constitutes the reading thereof. For you will first find that all phenomena are finite. Every phenomenon that we can see, feel, or think of, is finite, limited by our knowledge, and the Personal God as we conceive of Him is in fact a phenomenon. The very idea of causation exists only in the phenomenal world, and God as the cause of this universe must naturally be thought of as limited, and yet He is the same Impersonal God. This very universe, as we have seen, is the same Impersonal Being read by our intellect. Whatever is reality in the universe is that Impersonal Being, and the forms and conceptions are given to it by our intellects. Whatever is real in this table is that Being, and the table form and all other forms are given by our intellects.

Now, motion, for instance, which is a necessary adjunct of the phenomenal, cannot be predicated of the Universal. Every little bit, every atom inside the universe, is in a constant state of change and motion, but the universe as a whole is unchangeable, because motion or change is a relative thing; we can only think of something in motion in comparison with something which is not moving. There must be two things in order to understand motion. The whole mass of the universe, taken as a unit, cannot move. In regard to what will it move? It cannot be said to change. With regard to what will it change? So the whole is the Absolute; but within it every particle is in a constant state of flux and change. It is unchangeable and changeable at the same time, Impersonal and Personal in one. This is our conception of the universe, of motion and of God, and that is what is meant by "Thou art That". Thus we see that the Impersonal instead of doing away with the personal, the Absolute instead of pulling down the relative, only explains it to the full satisfaction of our reason and heart. The Personal God and all that exists in the universe are the same Impersonal Being seen through our minds. When we shall be rid of our minds, our little personalities, we shall become one with It. This is what is meant by "Thou art That". For we must know our true nature, the Absolute.

The finite, manifested man forgets his source and thinks himself to be entirely separate. We, as personalised, differentiated beings, forget our reality, and the teaching of monism is not that we shall give up these differentiations, but we must learn to understand what they are. We are in reality that Infinite Being, and our personalities represent so many channels through which this Infinite Reality is manifesting Itself; and the whole mass of changes which we call evolution is brought about by the soul trying to manifest more and more of its infinite energy. We cannot stop anywhere on this side of the Infinite; our power, and blessedness, and wisdom, cannot but grow into the Infinite. Infinite power and existence and blessedness are ours, and we have not to acquire them; they are our own, and we have only to manifest them.

This is the central idea of monism, and one that is so hard to understand. From my childhood everyone around me taught weakness; I have been told ever since I was born that I was a weak thing. It is very difficult for me now to realise my own strength, but by analysis and reasoning I gain knowledge of my own strength, I realise it. All the knowledge that we have in this world, where did it come from? It was within us. What knowledge is outside? None. Knowledge was not in matter; it was in man all the time. Nobody ever created knowledge; man brings it from within. It is lying there. The whole of that big banyan tree which covers acres of ground, was in the little seed which was, perhaps, no bigger than one eighth of a mustard seed; all that mass of energy was there confined. The gigantic intellect, we know, lies coiled up in the protoplasmic cell, and why should not the infinite energy? We know that it is so. It may seem like a paradox, but is true. Each one of us has come out of one protoplasmic cell, and all the powers we possess were coiled up there. You cannot say they came from food; for if you heap up food mountains high, what power comes out of it? The energy was there, potentially no doubt, but still there. So is infinite power in the soul of man, whether he knows it or not. Its manifestation is only a question of being conscious of it. Slowly this infinite giant is, as it were, waking up, becoming conscious of his power, and arousing himself; and with his growing consciousness, more and more of his bonds are breaking, chains are bursting asunder, and the day is sure to come when, with the full consciousness of his infinite power and wisdom, the giant will rise to his feet and stand erect. Let us all help to hasten that glorious consummation.

PRACTICAL VEDANTA PART IV

Delivered in London, 18th November 1896

We have been dealing more with the universal so far. This morning I shall try to place before you the Vedantic ideas of the relation of the particular to the universal. As we have seen, in the dualistic form of Vedic doctrines, the earlier forms, there was a clearly defined particular and limited soul for every being. There have been a great many theories about this particular soul in each individual, but the main discussion was between the ancient Vedantists and the ancient Buddhists, the former believing in the individual soul as complete in itself, the latter denying in toto the existence of such an individual soul. As I told you the other day, it is pretty much the same discussion you have in Europe as to substance and quality, one set holding that behind the qualities there is something as substance, in which the qualities inhere; and the other denying the existence of such a substance as being unnecessary, for the qualities may live by themselves. The most ancient theory of the soul, of course, is based upon the argument of self-identity — "I am I" — that the I of yesterday is the I of today, and the I of today will be the I of tomorrow; that in spite of all the changes that are happening to the body, I yet believe that I am the same I. This seems to have been the central argument with those who believed in a limited, and yet perfectly complete, individual soul.

On the other hand, the ancient Buddhists denied the necessity of such an assumption. They brought forward the argument that all that we know, and all that we possibly can know, are simply these changes. The positing of an unchangeable and unchanging substance is simply superfluous, and even if there were any such unchangeable thing, we could never understand it, nor should we ever be able to cognise it in any sense of the word. The same discussion you will find at the present time going on in Europe between the religionists and the idealists on the one side, and the modern positivists and agnostics on the other; one set believing there is something which does not change (of whom the latest representative is your Herbert Spencer), that we catch a glimpse of something which is unchangeable. And the other is represented by the modern Comtists and modern Agnostics. Those of you who were interested a few years ago in the discussions between Herbert Spencer and Frederick Harrison might have noticed that it was the same old difficulty, the one party standing for a substance behind the changeful, and the other party denying the necessity for such an assumption. One party says we cannot conceive of changes without conceiving of something which does not change; the other party brings out the argument that this is superfluous; we can only conceive of something which is changing, and as to the unchanging, we can neither know, feel, nor sense it.

In India this great question did not find its solution in very ancient times, because we have seen that the assumption of a substance which is behind the qualities, and which is not the qualities, can never be substantiated; nay, even the argument from self-identity, from memory, — that I am the I of yesterday because I remember it, and therefore I have been a continuous something — cannot be substantiated. The other quibble that is generally put forward is a mere delusion of words. For instance, a man may take a long series of such sentences as "I do", "I go", "I dream", "I sleep", "I move", and here you will find it claimed that the doing, going, dreaming etc., have been changing, but what remained constant was that "I". As such they conclude that the "I" is something which is constant and an individual in itself, but all these changes belong to the body. This, though apparently very convincing and clear, is based upon the mere play on words. The "I" and the doing, going, and dreaming may be separate in black and white, but no one can separate them in his mind.

When I eat, I think of myself as eating — am identified with eating. When I run, I and the running are not two separate things. Thus the argument from personal identity does not seem to be very strong. The other argument from memory is also weak. If the identity of my being is represented by my memory, many things which I have forgotten are lost from that identity. And we know that people under certain conditions forget their whole past. In many cases of lunacy a man will think of himself as made of glass, or as being an animal. If the existence of that man depends on memory, he has become glass, which not being the case we cannot make the identity of the Self depend on such a flimsy substance as memory. Thus we see that the soul as a limited yet complete and continuing identity cannot be established as separate from the qualities. We cannot establish a narrowed-down, limited existence to which is attached a bunch of qualities.

On the other hand, the argument of the ancient Buddhists seems to be stronger — that we do not know, and cannot know, anything that is beyond the bunch of qualities. According to them, the soul consists of a bundle of qualities called sensations and feelings. A mass of such is what is called the soul, and this mass is continually changing.

The Advaitist theory of the soul reconciles both these positions. The position of the Advaitist is that it is true that we cannot think of the substance as separate from the qualities, we cannot think of change and not-change at the same time; it would be impossible. But the very thing which is the substance is the quality; substance and quality are not two things. It is the unchangeable that is appearing as the changeable. The unchangeable substance of the universe is not something separate from it. The noumenon is not something different from the phenomena, but it is the very noumenon which has become the phenomena. There is a soul which is unchanging, and what we call feelings and perceptions, nay, even the body, are the very soul, seen from another point of view. We have got into the habit of thinking that we have bodies and souls and so forth, but really speaking, there is only one.

When I think of myself as the body, I am only a body; it is meaningless to say I am something else. And when I think of myself as the soul, the body vanishes, and the perception of the body does not remain. None can get the perception of the Self without his perception of the body having vanished, none can get perception of the substance without his perception of the qualities having vanished.

The ancient illustration of Advaita, of the rope being taken for a snake, may elucidate the point a little more. When a man mistakes the rope for a snake, the rope has vanished, and when he takes it for a rope, the snake has vanished, and the rope only remains. The ideas of dual or treble existence come from reasoning on insufficient data, and we read them in books or hear about them, until we come under the delusion that we really have a dual perception of the soul and the body; but such a perception never really exists. The perception is either of the body or of the soul. It requires no arguments to prove it, you can verify it in your own minds.

Try to think of yourself as a soul, as a disembodied something. You will find it to be almost impossible, and those few who are able to do so will find that at the time when they realise themselves as a soul they have no idea of the body. You have heard of, or perhaps have seen, persons who on particular occasions had been in peculiar states of mind, brought about by deep meditation, self-hypnotism, hysteria, or drugs. From their experience you may gather that when they were perceiving the internal something, the external had vanished for them. This shows that whatever exists is one. That one is appearing in these various forms, and all these various forms give rise to the relation of cause and effect. The relation of cause and effect is one of evolution — the one becomes the other, and so on. Sometimes the cause vanishes, as it were, and in its place leaves the effect. If the soul is the cause of the body, the soul, as it were vanishes for the time being, and the body remains; and when the body vanishes, the soul remains. This theory fits the arguments of the Buddhists that were levelled against the assumption of the dualism of body and soul, by denying the duality, and showing that the substance and the qualities are one and the same thing appearing in various forms.

We have seen also that this idea of the unchangeable can be established only as regards the whole, but never as regards the part. The very idea of part comes from the idea of change or motion. Everything that is limited we can understand and know, because it is changeable; and the whole must be unchangeable, because there is no other thing besides it in relation to which change would be possible. Change is always in regard to something which does not change, or which changes relatively less.

According to Advaita, therefore, the idea of the soul as universal, unchangeable, and immortal can be demonstrated as far as possible. The difficulty would be as regards the particular. What shall we do with the old dualistic theories which have such a hold upon us, and which we have all to pass through — these beliefs in limited, little, individual souls?

We have seen that we are immortal with regard to the whole; but the difficulty is, we desire so much to be immortal as parts of the whole. We have seen that we are Infinite, and that that is our real individuality. But we want so much to make these little souls individual. What becomes of them when we find in our everyday experience that these little souls are individuals, with only this reservation that they are continuously growing individuals? They are the same, yet not the same. The I of yesterday is the I of today, and yet not so, it is changed somewhat. Now, by getting rid of the dualistic conception, that in the midst of all these changes there is something that does not change, and taking the most modern of conceptions, that of evolution, we find that the "I" is a continuously changing, expanding entity.

If it be true that man is the evolution of a mollusc, the mollusc individual is the same as the man, only it has to become expanded a great deal. From mollusc to man it has been a continuous expansion towards infinity. Therefore the limited soul can be styled an individual which is continuously expanding towards the Infinite Individual. Perfect individuality will only be reached when it has reached the Infinite, but on this side of the Infinite it is a continuously changing, growing personality. One of the remarkable features of the Advaitist system of Vedanta is to harmonise the preceding systems. In many cases it helped the philosophy very much; in some cases it hurt it. Our ancient philosophers knew what you call the theory of evolution; that growth is gradual, step by step, and the recognition of this led them to harmonise all the preceding systems. Thus not one of these preceding ideas was rejected. The fault of the Buddhistic faith was that it had neither the faculty nor the perception of this continual, expansive growth, and for this reason it never even made an attempt to harmonise itself with the preexisting steps towards the ideal. They were rejected as useless and harmful.

This tendency in religion is most harmful. A man gets a new and better idea, and then he looks back on those he has given up, and forthwith decides that they were mischievous and unnecessary. He never thinks that, however crude they may appear from his present point of view, they were very useful to him, that they were necessary for him to reach his present state, and that everyone of us has to grow in a similar fashion, living first on crude ideas, taking benefit from them, and then arriving at a higher standard. With the oldest theories, therefore, the Advaita is friendly. Dualism and all systems that had preceded it are accepted by the Advaita not in a patronising way, but with the conviction that they are true manifestations of the same truth, and that they all lead to the same conclusions as the Advaita has reached.

With blessing, and not with cursing, should be preserved all these various steps through which humanity has to pass. Therefore all these dualistic systems have never been rejected or thrown out, but have been kept intact in the Vedanta; and the dualistic conception of an individual soul, limited yet complete in itself, finds its place in the Vedanta.

According to dualism, man dies and goes to other worlds, and so forth; and these ideas are kept in the Vedanta in their entirety. For with the recognition of growth in the Advaitist system, these theories are given their proper place by admitting that they represent only a partial view of the Truth.

From the dualistic standpoint this universe can only be looked upon as a creation of matter or force, can only be looked upon as the play of a certain will, and that will again can only be looked upon as separate from the universe. Thus a man from such a standpoint has to see himself as composed of a dual nature, body and soul, and this soul, though limited, is individually complete in itself. Such a man's ideas of immortality and of the future life would necessarily accord with his idea of soul. These phases have been kept in the Vedanta, and it is, therefore, necessary for me to present to you a few of the popular ideas of dualism. According to this theory, we have a body, of course, and behind the body there is what they call a fine body. This fine body is also made of matter, only very fine. It is the receptacle of all our Karma, of all our actions and impressions, which are ready to spring up into visible forms. Every thought that we think, every deed that we do, after a certain time becomes fine, goes into seed form, so to speak, and lives in the fine body in a potential form, and after a time it emerges again and bears its results. These results condition the life of man. Thus he moulds his own life. Man is not bound by any other laws excepting those which he makes for himself. Our thoughts, our words and deeds are the threads of the net which we throw round ourselves, for good or for evil. Once we set in motion a certain power, we have to take the full consequences of it. This is the law of Karma. Behind the subtle body, lives Jiva or the individual soul of man. There are various discussions about the form and the size of this individual soul. According to some, it is very small like an atom; according to others, it is not so small as that; according to others, it is very big, and so on. This Jiva is a part of that universal substance, and it is also eternal; without beginning it is existing, and without end it will exist. It is passing through all these forms in order to manifest its real nature which is purity. Every action that retards this manifestation is called an evil action; so with thoughts. And every action and every thought that helps the Jiva to expand, to manifest its real nature, is good. One theory that is held in common in India by the crudest dualists as well as by the most advanced non-dualists is that all the possibilities and powers of the soul are within it, and do not come from any external source. They are in the soul in potential form, and the whole work of life is simply directed towards manifesting those potentialities.

They have also the theory of reincarnation which says that after the dissolution of this body, the Jiva will have another, and after that has been dissolved, it will again have another, and so on, either here or in some other worlds; but this world is given the preference, as it is considered the best of all worlds for our purpose. Other worlds are conceived of as worlds where there is very little misery, but for that very reason, they argue, there is less chance of thinking of higher things there. As this world contains some happiness and a good deal of misery, the Jiva some time or other gets awakened, as it were, and thinks of freeing itself. But just as very rich persons in this world have the least chance of thinking of higher things, so the Jiva in heaven has little chance of progress, for its condition is the same as that of a rich man, only more intensified; it has a very fine body which knows no disease, and is under no necessity of eating or drinking, and all its desires are fulfilled. The Jiva lives there, having enjoyment after enjoyment, and so forgets all about its real nature. Still there are some higher worlds, where in spite of all enjoyments, its further evolution is possible. Some dualists conceive of the goal as the highest heaven, where souls will live with God for ever. They will have beautiful bodies and will know neither disease nor death, nor any other evil, and all their desires will be fulfilled. From time to time some of them will come back to this earth and take another body to teach human beings the way to God; and the great teachers of the world have been such. They were already free, and were living with God in the highest sphere; but their love and sympathy for suffering humanity was so great that they came and incarnated again to teach mankind the way to heaven.

Of course we know that the Advaita holds that this cannot be the goal or the ideal; bodilessness must be the ideal. The ideal cannot be finite. Anything short of the Infinite cannot be the ideal, and there cannot be an infinite body. That would be impossible, as body comes from limitation. There cannot be infinite thought, because thought comes from limitation. We have to go beyond the body, and beyond thought too, says the Advaita. And we have also seen that, according to Advaita, this freedom is not to be attained, it is already ours. We only forget it and deny it. Perfection is not to be attained, it is already within us. Immortality and bliss are not to be acquired, we possess them already; they have been ours all the time.

If you dare declare that you are free, free you are this moment. If you say you are bound, bound you will remain. This is what Advaita boldly declares. I have told you the ideas of the dualists. You can take whichever you like.

The highest ideal of the Vedanta is very difficult to understand, and people are always quarrelling about it, and the greatest difficulty is that when they get hold of certain ideas, they deny and fight other ideas. Take up what suits you, and let others take up what they need. If you are desirous of clinging to this little individuality, to this limited manhood, remain in it, have all these desires, and be content and pleased with them. If your experience of manhood has been very good and nice, retain it as long as you like; and you can do so, for you are the makers of your own fortunes; none can compel you to give up your manhood. You will be men as long as you like; none can prevent you. If you want to be angels, you will be angels, that is the law. But there may be others who do not want to be angels even. What right have you to think that theirs is a horrible notion? You may be frightened to lose a hundred pounds, but there may be others who would not even wink if they lost all the money they had in the world. There have been such men and still there are. Why do you dare to judge them according to your standard? You cling on to your limitations, and these little worldly ideas may be your highest ideal. You are welcome to them. It will be to you as you wish. But there are others who have seen the truth and cannot rest in these limitations, who have done with these things and want to get beyond. The world with all its enjoyments is a mere mud-puddle for them. Why do you want to bind them down to your ideas? You must get rid of this tendency once for all. Accord a place to everyone.

I once read a story about some ships that were caught in a cyclone in the South Sea Islands, and there was a picture of it in the Illustrated London News. All of them were wrecked except one English vessel, which weathered the storm. The picture showed the men who were going to be drowned, standing on the decks and cheering the people who were sailing through the storm.[2] Be brave and generous like that. Do not drag others down to where you are. Another foolish notion is that if we lose our little individuality, there will be no morality, no hope for humanity. As if everybody had been dying for humanity all the time! God bless you! If in every country there were two hundred men and women really wanting to do good to humanity, the millennium would come in five days. We know how we are dying for humanity! These are all tall talks, and nothing else. The history of the world shows that those who never thought of their little individuality were the greatest benefactors of the human race, and that the more men and women think of themselves, the less are they able to do for others. One is unselfishness, and the other selfishness. Clinging on to little enjoyments, and to desire the continuation and repetition of this state of things is utter selfishness. It arises not from any desire for truth, its genesis is not in kindness for other beings, but in the utter selfishness of the human heart, in the idea,

---

2. H.M.S. Calliope and the American men-of-war at Samoa. — Ed

"I will have everything, and do not care for anyone else." This is as it appears to me. I would like to see more moral men in the world like some of those grand old prophets and sages of ancient times who would have given up a hundred lives if they could by so doing benefit one little animal! Talk of morality and doing good to others! Silly talk of the present time!

I would like to see moral men like Gautama Buddha, who did not believe in a Personal God or a personal soul, never asked about them, but was a perfect agnostic, and yet was ready to lay down his life for anyone, and worked all his life for the good of all, and thought only of the good of all. Well has it been said by his biographer, in describing his birth, that he was born for the good of the many, as a blessing to the many. He did not go to the forest to meditate for his own salvation; he felt that the world was burning, and that he must find a way out. "Why is there so much misery in the world?" — was the one question that dominated his whole life. Do you think we are so moral as the Buddha?

The more selfish a man, the more immoral he is. And so also with the race. That race which is bound down to itself has been the most cruel and the most wicked in the whole world. There has not been a religion that has clung to this dualism more than that founded by the Prophet of Arabia, and there has not been a religion which has shed so much blood and been so cruel to other men. In the Koran there is the doctrine that a man who does not believe these teachings should be killed; it is a mercy to kill him! And the surest way to get to heaven, where there are beautiful houris and all sorts of sense-enjoyments, is by killing these unbelievers. Think of the bloodshed there has been in consequence of such beliefs!

In the religion of Christ there was little of crudeness; there is very little difference between the pure religion of Christ and that of the Vedanta. You find there the idea of oneness; but Christ also preached dualistic ideas to the people in order to give them something tangible to take hold of, to lead them up to the highest ideal. The same Prophet who preached, "Our Father which art in heaven", also preached, "I and my Father are one", and the same Prophet knew that through the "Father in heaven" lies the way to the "I and my Father are one". There was only blessing and love in the religion of Christ; but as soon as crudeness crept in, it was degraded into something not much better than the religion of the Prophet of Arabia. It was crudeness indeed — this fight for the little self, this clinging on to the "I", not only in this life, but also in the desire for its continuance even after death. This they declare to be unselfishness; this the foundation of morality! Lord help us, if this be the foundation of morality! And strangely enough, men and women who ought to know better think all morality will be destroyed if these little selves go and stand aghast at the idea that morality can only stand upon their destruction. The watchword of all well-being, of all moral good is not "I" but "thou". Who cares whether there is a heaven or a hell, who cares if there is a soul or not, who cares if there is an unchangeable or not? Here is the world, and it is full of misery. Go out into it as Buddha did, and struggle to lessen it or die in the attempt. Forget yourselves; this is the first lesson to be learnt, whether you are a theist or an atheist, whether you are an agnostic or a Vedantist, a Christian or a Mohammedan. The one lesson obvious to all is the destruction of the little self and the building up of the Real Self.

Two forces have been working side by side in parallel lines. The one says "I", the other says "not I". Their manifestation is not only in man but in animals, not only in animals but in the smallest worms. The tigress that plunges her fangs into the warm blood of a human being would give up her own life to protect her young. The most depraved man who thinks nothing of taking the lives of his brother men will, perhaps, sacrifice himself without any hesitation to save his starving wife and children. Thus throughout creation these two forces are working side by side; where you find the one, you find the other too. The one is selfishness, the other is unselfishness. The one is acquisition, the other is renunciation. The one takes, the other gives. From the lowest to the highest, the whole universe is the playground of these two forces. It does not require any demonstration; it is obvious to all.

What right has any section of the community to base the whole work and evolution of the universe upon one of these two factors alone, upon competition and struggle? What right has it to base the whole working of the universe upon passion and fight, upon competition and struggle? That these exist we do not deny; but what right has anyone to deny the working of the other force? Can any man deny that love, this "not I", this renunciation is the only positive power in the universe? That other is only the misguided employment of the power of love; the power of love brings competition, the real genesis of competition is in love. The real genesis of evil is in unselfishness. The creator of evil is good, and the end is also good. It is only misdirection of the power of good. A man who murders another is, perhaps, moved to do so by the love of his own child. His love has become limited to that one little baby, to the exclusion of the millions of other human beings in the universe. Yet, limited or unlimited, it is the same love.

Thus the motive power of the whole universe, in what ever way it manifests itself, is that one wonderful thing, unselfishness, renunciation, love, the real, the only living force in existence. Therefore the Vedantist insists upon that oneness. We insist upon this explanation because we cannot admit two causes of the universe. If we simply hold that by limitation the same beautiful, wonderful love appears to be evil or vile, we find the whole universe explained by the one force of love. If not, two causes of the universe have to be taken for granted, one good and the other evil, one love and the other hatred. Which is more logical? Certainly the one-force theory.

Let us now pass on to things which do not possibly belong to dualism. I cannot stay longer with the dualists. I am afraid. My idea is to show that the highest ideal of morality and unselfishness goes hand in hand with the highest metaphysical conception, and that you need not lower your conception to get ethics and morality, but, on the other hand, to reach a real basis of morality and ethics you must have the highest philosophical and scientific conceptions. Human knowledge is not antagonistic to human well-being. On the contrary, it is knowledge alone that will save us in every department of life — in knowledge is worship. The more we know the better for us. The Vedantist says, the cause of all that is apparently evil is the limitation of the unlimited. The love which gets limited into little channels and seems to be evil eventually comes out at the other end and manifests itself as God. The Vedanta also says that the cause of all this apparent evil is in ourselves. Do not blame any supernatural being, neither be hopeless and despondent, nor think we are in a place from which we can never escape unless someone comes and lends us a helping hand. That cannot be, says the Vedanta. We are like silkworms; we make the thread out of our own substance and spin the cocoon, and in course of time are imprisoned inside. But this is not for ever. In that cocoon we shall develop spiritual realisation, and like the butterfly come out free. This network of Karma we have woven around ourselves; and in our ignorance we feel as if we are bound, and weep and wail for help. But help does not come from without; it comes from within ourselves. Cry to all the gods in the universe. I cried for years, and in the end I found that I was helped. But help came from within. And I had to undo what I had done by mistake. That is the only way. I had to cut the net which I had thrown round myself, and the power to do this is within. Of this I am certain that not one aspiration, well-guided or ill-guided in my life, has been in vain, but that I am the resultant of all my past, both good and evil. I have committed many mistakes in my life; but mark you, I am sure of this that without every one of those mistakes I should not be what I am today, and so am quite satisfied to have made them. I do not mean that you are to go home and wilfully commit mistakes; do not misunderstand me in that way. But do not mope because of the mistakes you have committed, but know that in the end all will come out straight. It cannot be otherwise, because goodness is our nature, purity is our nature, and that nature can never be destroyed. Our essential nature always remains the same.

What we are to understand is this, that what we call mistakes or evil, we commit because we are weak, and we are weak because we are ignorant. I prefer to call them mistakes. The word sin, although originally a very good word, has got a certain flavour about it that frightens me. Who makes us ignorant? We ourselves. We put our hands over our eyes and weep that it is dark. Take the hands away and there is light; the light exists always for us, the self-effulgent nature of the human soul. Do you not hear what your modern scientific men say? What is the cause of evolution? Desire. The animal wants to do something, but does not find the environment favourable, and therefore develops a new body. Who develops it? The animal itself, its will. You have developed from the lowest amoeba. Continue to exercise your will and it will take you higher still. The will is almighty. If it is almighty, you may say, why cannot I do everything? But you are thinking only of your little self. Look back on yourselves from the state of the amoeba to the human being; who made all that? Your own will. Can you deny then that it is almighty? That which has made you come up so high can make you go higher still. What you want is character, strengthening of the will.

If I teach you, therefore, that your nature is evil, that you should go home and sit in sackcloth and ashes and weep your lives out because you took certain false steps, it will not help you, but will weaken you all the more, and I shall be showing you the road to more evil than good. If this room is full of darkness for thousands of years and you come in and begin to weep and wail, "Oh the darkness", will the darkness vanish? Strike a match and light comes in a moment. What good will it do you to think all your lives, "Oh, I have done evil, I have made many mistakes"? It requires no ghost to tell us that. Bring in the light and the evil goes in a moment. Build up your character, and manifest your real nature, the Effulgent, the Resplendent, the Ever-Pure, and call It up in everyone that you see. I wish that everyone of us had come to such a state that even in the vilest of human beings we could see the Real Self within, and instead of condemning them, say, "Rise thou effulgent one, rise thou who art always pure, rise thou birthless and deathless, rise almighty, and manifest thy true nature. These little manifestations do not befit thee." This is the highest prayer that the Advaita teaches. This is the one prayer, to remember our true nature, the God who is always within us, thinking of it always as infinite, almighty, ever-good, ever-beneficent, selfless, bereft of all limitations. And because that nature is selfless, it is strong and fearless; for only to selfishness comes fear. He who has nothing to desire for himself, whom does he fear, and what can frighten him? What fear has death for him? What fear has evil for him? So if we are Advaitists, we must think from this moment that our old self is dead and gone. The old Mr., Mrs., and Miss So-and-so are gone, they were mere superstitions, and what remains is the ever-pure, the ever-strong, the almighty, the all-knowing — that alone remains for us, and then all fear vanishes from us. Who can injure us, the omnipresent? All weakness has vanished from us, and our only work is to arouse this knowledge in our fellow beings. We see that they too are the same pure self, only they do not know it; we must teach them, we must help them to rouse up their infinite nature. This is what I feel to be absolutely necessary all over the world. These doctrines are old, older than many mountains possibly. All truth is eternal. Truth is nobody's property; no race, no individual can lay any exclusive claim to it. Truth is the nature of all souls. Who can lay any special claim to it? But it has to be made practical, to be made simple (for the highest truths are always simple), so that it may penetrate every pore of human society, and become the property of the highest intellects and the commonest minds, of the man, woman, and child at the same time. All these ratiocinations of logic, all these bundles of metaphysics, all these theologies and ceremonies may have been good in their own time, but let us try to make things simpler and bring about the golden days when every man will be a worshipper, and the Reality in every man will be the object of worship.

THE WAY TO THE REALISATION OF A UNIVERSAL RELIGION

Delivered in the Universalist Church, Pasadena, California, 28th January 1900

No search has been dearer to the human heart than that which brings to us light from God. No study has taken so much of human energy, whether in times past or present, as the study of the soul, of God, and of human destiny. However immersed we are in our daily occupations, in our ambitions, in our work, in the midst of the greatest of our struggles, sometimes there will come a pause; the mind stops and wants to know something beyond this world. Sometimes it catches glimpses of a realm beyond the senses, and a struggle to get at it is the result. Thus it has been throughout the ages, in all countries. Man has wanted to look beyond, wanted to expand himself; and all that we call progress, evolution, has been always measured by that one search, the search for human destiny, the search for God.

As our social struggles are represented amongst different nations by different social organizations, so is man's spiritual struggle represented by various religions; and as different social organizations are constantly quarrelling, are constantly at war with one another, so these spiritual organisations have been constantly at war with one another, constantly quarrelling. Men belonging to a particular social organisation claim that the right to live only belongs to them; and so long as they can, they want to exercise that right at the cost of the weak. We know that just now there is a fierce struggle of that sort going on in South Africa. Similarly, each religious sect has; claimed the exclusive right to live. And thus we find that though there is nothing that has brought to man more blessings than religion, yet at the same time, there is nothing that has brought more horror than religion. Nothing has made more for peace and love than religion; nothing has engendered fiercer hatred than religion. Nothing has made the brotherhood of man more tangible than religion; nothing has bred more bitter enmity between man and man than religion. Nothing has built more charitable institutions, more hospitals for men, and even for animals, than religion; nothing has deluged the world with more blood than religion. We know, at the same time, that there has always been an undercurrent of thought; there have been always parties of men, philosophers, students of comparative religion who have tried and are still trying to bring about harmony in the midst of all these jarring and discordant sects. As regards certain countries, these attempts have succeeded, but as regards the whole world, they have failed.

There are some religions which have come down to us from the remotest antiquity, which are imbued with the idea that all sects should be allowed to live, that every sect has a meaning, a great idea, imbedded within itself, and, therefore it is necessary for the good of the world and ought to be helped. In modern times the same idea is prevailing and attempts are made from time to time to reduce it to practice. These attempts do not always come up to our expectations, up to the required efficiency. Nay, to our great disappointment, we sometimes find that we are quarrelling all the more.

Now, leaving aside dogmatic study, and taking a common-sense view of the thing, we find at the start that there is a tremendous life-power in all the great religions of the world. Some may say that they are ignorant of this, but ignorance is no excuse. If a man says "I do not know what is going on in the external world, therefore things that are going on in the external world do not exist", that man is inexcusable. Now, those of you that watch the movement of religious thought all over the world are perfectly aware that not one of the great religions of the world has died; not only so, each one of them is progressive. Christians are multiplying, Mohammedans are multiplying, the Hindus are gaining ground, and the Jews also are increasing, and by their spreading all over the world and increasing rapidly, the fold of Judaism is constantly expanding.

Only one religion of the world — an ancient, great religion — has dwindled away, and that is the religion of Zoroastrianism, the religion of the ancient Persians. Under the Mohammedan conquest of Persia about a hundred thousand of these people came and took shelter in India and some remained in ancient Persia. Those that were in Persia, under the constant persecution of the Mohammedans, dwindled down till there are at most only ten thousand; in India there are about eighty thousand of them, but they do not increase. Of course, there is an initial difficulty; they do not convert others to their religion. And then, this handful of persons living in India, with the pernicious custom of cousin marriage, do not multiply. With this single exception, all the great religions are living, spreading, and increasing. We must remember that all the great religions of the world are very ancient, not one has been formed at the present time, and that every religion of the world owes its origin to the country between the Ganga and the Euphrates; not one great religion has arisen in Europe, not one in America, not one; every religion is of Asiatic origin and belongs to that part of the world. If what the modern scientists say is true, that the survival of the fittest is the test, these religions prove by their still living that they are yet fit for some people. There is a reason why they should live, they bring good to many. Look at the Mohammedans, how they are spreading in some places in Southern Asia, and spreading like fire in Africa. The Buddhists are spreading all over Central Asia, all the time. The Hindus, like the Jews, do not convert others; still gradually, other races are coming within Hinduism and adopting the manners and customs of the Hindus and falling into line with them. Christianity, you all know, is spreading — though I am not sure that the results are equal to the energy put forth. The Christians' attempt at propaganda has one tremendous defect — and that is the defect of all Western institutions: the machine consumes ninety per cent of the energy, there is too much machinery. Preaching has always been the business of the Asiatics. The Western people are grand in organisation, social institutions, armies, governments, etc.; but when it comes to preaching religion, they cannot come near the Asiatic, whose business it has been all the time, and he knows it, and he does not use too much machinery.

This then is a fact in the present history of the human race, that all these great religions exist and are spreading and multiplying. Now, there is a meaning, certainly, to this; and had it been the will of an All-wise and All-merciful Creator that one of these religions should exist and the rest should die, it would have become a fact long, long ago. If it were a fact that only one of these religions is true and all the rest are false, by this time it would have covered the whole ground. But this is not so; not one has gained all the ground. All religions sometimes advance — sometimes decline. Now, just think of this: in your own country there are more than sixty millions of people, and only twenty-one millions professing religions of all sorts. So it is not always progress. In every country, probably, if the statistics are taken, you would find that religions are sometimes progressing and sometimes going back. Sects are multiplying all the time. If the claims of a religion that it has all the truth and God has given it all this truth in a certain book were true, why are there so many sects? Fifty years do not pass before there are twenty sects founded upon the same book. If God has put all the truth in certain books, He does not give us those books in order that we may quarrel over texts. That seems to be the fact. Why is it? Even if a book were given by God which contained all the truth about religion, it would not serve the purpose because nobody could understand the book. Take the Bible, for instance, and all the sects that exist amongst Christians; each one puts its own interpretation upon the same text, and each says that it alone understands that text and all the rest are wrong. So with every religion. There are many sects among the Mohammedans and among the Buddhists, and hundreds among the Hindus. Now, I bring these facts before you in order to show you that any attempt to bring all humanity to one method of thinking in spiritual things has been a failure and always will be a failure. Every man that starts a theory, even at the present day, finds that if he goes twenty miles away from his followers, they will make twenty sects. You see that happening all the time. You cannot make all conform to the same ideas: that is a fact, and I thank God that it is so. I am not against any sect. I am glad that sects exist, and I only wish they may go on multiplying more and more. Why? Simply because of this: If you and I and all who are present here were to think exactly the same thoughts, there would be no thoughts for us to think. We know that two or more forces must come into collision in order to produce motion. It is the clash of thought, the differentiation of thought, that awakes thought. Now, if we all thought alike, we would be like Egyptian mummies in a museum looking vacantly at one another's faces — no more than that! Whirls and eddies occur only in a rushing, living stream. There are no whirlpools in stagnant, dead water. When religions are dead, there will be no more sects; it will be the perfect peace and harmony of the grave. But so long as mankind thinks, there will be sects. Variation is the sign of life, and it must be there. I pray that they may multiply so that at last there will be as many sects as human beings, and each one will have his own method, his individual method of thought in religion.

But this thing exists already. Each one of us is thinking in his own way, but his natural course has been obstructed all the time and is still being obstructed. If the sword is not used directly, other means will be used. Just hear what one of the best preachers in New York says: he preaches that the Filipinos should be conquered because that is the only way to teach Christianity to them! They are already Catholics; but he wants to make them Presbyterians, and for this, he is ready to lay all this terrible sin of bloodshed upon his race. How terrible! And this man is one of the greatest preachers of this country, one of the best informed men. Think of the state of the world when a man like that is not ashamed to stand up and utter such arrant nonsense; and think of the state of the world when an audience cheers him! Is this civilisation? It is the old blood-thirstiness of the tiger, the cannibal, the savage, coming out once more under new names, new circumstances. What else can it be? If the state of things is such now, think of the horrors through which the world passed in olden times, when every sect was trying by every means in its power to tear to pieces the other sects. History shows that. The tiger in us is only asleep; it is not dead. When opportunities come, it jumps up and, as of old, uses its claws and fangs. Apart from the sword, apart from material weapons, there are weapons still more terrible — contempt, social hatred, and social ostracism. Now, these are the most terrible of all inflictions that are hurled against persons who do not think exactly in the same way as we do. And why should everybody think just as we do? I do not see any reason. If I am a rational man, I should be glad they do not think just as I do. I do not want to live in a grave-like land; I want to be a man in a world of men. Thinking beings must differ; difference is the first sign of thought. If I am a thoughtful man, certainly I ought to like to live amongst thoughtful persons where there are differences of opinion.

Then arises the question: How can all these varieties be true? If one thing is true, its negation is false. How can contradictory opinions be true at the same time? This is the question which I intend to answer. But I will first ask you: Are all the religions of the world really contradictory? I do not mean the external forms in which great thoughts are clad. I do not mean the different buildings, languages, rituals, books, etc. employed in various religions, but I mean the internal soul of every religion. Every religion has a soul behind it, and that soul may differ from the soul of another religion; but are they contradictory? Do they contradict or supplement each other? — that is the question. I took up the question when I was quite a boy, and have been studying it all my life. Thinking that my conclusion may be of some help to you, I place it before you. I believe that they are not contradictory; they are supplementary. Each religion, as it were, takes up one part of the great universal truth, and spends its whole force in embodying and typifying that part of the great truth. It is, therefore, addition; not exclusion. That is the idea. System after system arises, each one embodying a great idea, and ideals must be added to ideals. And this is the march of humanity. Man never progresses from error to truth, but from truth to truth, from lesser truth to higher truth — but it is never from error to truth. The child may develop more than the father, but was the father inane? The child is the father plus something else. If your present state of knowledge is much greater than it was when you were a child, would you look down upon that stage now? Will you look back and call it inanity? Why, your present stage is the knowledge of the child plus something more.

Then, again, we also know that there may be almost contradictory points of view of the same thing, but they will all indicate the same thing. Suppose a man is journeying towards the sun, and as he advances he takes a photograph of the sun at every stage. When he comes back, he has many photographs of the sun, which he places before us. We see that not two are alike, and yet, who will deny that all these are photographs of the same sun, from different standpoints? Take four photographs of this church from different corners: how different they would look, and yet they would all represent this church. In the same way, we are all looking at truth from different standpoints, which vary according to our birth, education, surroundings, and so on. We are viewing truth, getting as much of it as these circumstances will permit, colouring the truth with our own heart, understanding it with our own intellect, and grasping it with our own mind. We can only know as much of truth as is related to us, as much of it as we are able to receive. This makes the difference between man and man, and occasions sometimes even contradictory ideas; yet we all belong to the same great universal truth.

My idea, therefore, is that all these religions are different forces in the economy of God, working for the good of mankind; and that not one can become dead, not one can be killed. Just as you cannot kill any force in nature, so you cannot kill any one of these spiritual forces. You have seen that each religion is living. From time to time it may retrograde or go forward. At one time, it may be shorn of a good many of its trappings; at another time it may be covered with all sorts of trappings; but all the same, the soul is ever there, it can never be lost. The ideal which every religion represents is never lost, and so every religion is intelligently on the march.

And that universal religion about which philosophers and others have dreamed in every country already exists. It is here. As the universal brotherhood of man is already existing, so also is universal religion. Which of you, that have travelled far and wide, have not found brothers and sisters in every nation? I have found them all over the world. Brotherhood already exists; only there are numbers of persons who fail to see this and only upset it by crying for new brotherhoods. Universal religion, too, is already existing. If the priests and other people that have taken upon themselves the task of preaching different religions simply cease preaching for a few moments, we shall see it is there. They are disturbing it all the time, because it is to their interest. You see that priests in every country are very conservative. Why is it so? There are very few priests who lead the people; most of them are led by the people and are their slaves and servants. If you say it is dry, they say it is so; if you say it is black, they say it is black. If the people advance, the priests must advance. They cannot lag behind. So, before blaming the priests — it is the fashion to blame the priest — you ought to blame yourselves. You only get what you deserve. What would be the fate of a priest who wants to give you new and advanced ideas and lead you forward? His children would probably starve, and he would be clad in rags. He is governed by the same worldly laws as you are. "If you go on," he says, "let us march." Of course, there are exceptional souls, not cowed down by public opinion. They see the truth and truth alone they value. Truth has got hold of them, has got possession of them, as it were, and they cannot but march ahead. They never look backward, and for them there are no people. God alone exists for them, He is the Light before them, and they are following that Light.

I met a Mormon gentleman in this country, who tried to persuade me to his faith. I said, "I have great respect for your opinions, but in certain points we do not agree — I belong to a monastic order, and you believe in marrying many wives. But why don't you go to India to preach?" Then he was astonished. He said, "Why, you don't believe in any marriage at all, and we believe in polygamy, and yet you ask me to go to your country!" I said, "Yes; my countrymen will hear every religious thought wherever it may come from. I wish you would go to India, first, because I am a great believer in sects. Secondly, there are many men in India who are not at all satisfied with any of the existing sects, and on account of this dissatisfaction, they will not have anything to do with religion, and, possibly, you might get some of them." The greater the number of sects, the more chance of people getting religion. In the hotel, where there are all sorts of food, everyone has a chance to get his appetite satisfied. So I want sects to multiply in every country, that more people may have a chance to be spiritual. Do not think that people do not like religion. I do not believe that. The preachers cannot give them what they need. The same man that may have been branded as an atheist, as a materialist, or what not, may meet a man who gives him the truth needed by him, and he may turn out the most spiritual man in the community. We can eat only in our own way. For instance, we Hindus eat with our fingers. Our fingers are suppler than yours, you cannot use your fingers the same way. Not only the food should be supplied, but it should be taken in your own particular way. Not only must you have the spiritual ideas, but they must come to you according to your own method. They must speak your own language, the language of your soul, and then alone they will satisfy you. When the man comes who speaks my language and gives truth in my language, I at once understand it and receive it for ever. This is a great fact.

Now from this we see that there are various grades and types of human minds and what a task religions take upon them! A man brings forth two or three doctrines and claims that his religion ought to satisfy all humanity. He goes out into the world, God's menagerie, with a little cage in hand, and says, "God and the elephant and everybody has to go into this. Even if we have to cut the elephant into pieces, he must go in." Again, there may be a sect with a few good ideas. Its followers say, "All men must come in! " "But there is no room for them." "Never mind! Cut them to pieces; get them in anyhow; if they don't get in, why, they will be damned." No preacher, no sect, have I ever met that pauses and asks, "Why is it that people do not listen to us?" Instead, they curse the people and say, "The people are wicked." They never ask, "How is it that people do not listen to my words? Why cannot I make them see the truth? Why cannot I speak in their language? Why cannot I open their eyes?" Surely, they ought to know better, and when they find people do not listen to them, if they curse anybody, it should be themselves. But it is always the people's fault! They never try to make their sect large enough to embrace every one.

Therefore we at once see why there has been so much narrow-mindedness, the part always claiming to be the whole; the little, finite unit always laying claim to the infinite. Think of little sects, born within a few hundred years out of fallible human brains, making this arrogant claim of knowledge of the whole of God's infinite truth! Think of the arrogance of it! If it shows anything, it is this, how vain human beings are. And it is no wonder that such claims have always failed, and, by the mercy of the Lord, are always destined to fail. In this line the Mohammedans were the best off; every step forward was made with the sword — the Koran in the one hand and the sword in the other: "Take the Koran, or you must die; there is no alternative! " You know from history how phenomenal was their success; for six hundred years nothing could resist them, and then there came a time when they had to cry halt. So will it be with other religions if they follow the same methods. We are such babes! We always forget human nature. When we begin life, we think that our fate will be something extraordinary, and nothing can make us disbelieve that. But when we grow old, we think differently. So with religions. In their early stages, when they spread a. little, they get the idea that they can change the minds of the whole human race in a few years, and go on killing and massacring to make converts by force; then they fail, and begin to understand better. We see that these sects did not succeed in what they started out to do, which was a great blessing. Just think if one of those fanatical sects had succeeded all over the world, where would man be today? Now, the Lord be blessed that they did not succeed! Yet, each one represents a great truth; each religion represents a particular excellence — something which is its soul. There is an old story which comes to my mind: There were some ogresses who used to kill people and do all sorts of mischief; but they themselves could not be killed, until someone found out that their souls were in certain birds, and so long as the birds were safe nothing could destroy the ogresses. So, each one of us has, as it were, such a bird, where our soul is; has an ideal, a mission to perform in life. Every human being is an embodiment of such an ideal, such a mission. Whatever else you may lose, so long as that ideal is not lost, and that mission is not hurt, nothing can kill you. Wealth may come and go, misfortunes may pile mountains high, but if you have kept the ideal entire, nothing can kill you. You may have grown old, even a hundred years old, but if that mission is fresh and young in your heart, what can kill you? But when that ideal is lost and that mission is hurt, nothing can save you. All the wealth, all the power of the world will not save you. And what are nations but multiplied individuals? So, each nation has a mission of its own to perform in this harmony of races; and so long as that nation keeps to that ideal, that nation nothing can kill; but if that nation gives up its mission in life and goes after something else, its life becomes short, and it vanishes.

And so with religions. The fact that all these old religions are living today proves that they must have kept that mission intact; in spite of all their mistakes, in spite of all difficulties, in spite of all quarrels, in spite of all the incrustation of forms and figures, the heart of every one of them is sound — it is a throbbing, beating, living heart. They have not lost, any one of them, the great mission they came for. And it is splendid to study that mission. Take Mohammedanism, for instance. Christian people hate no religion in the world so much as Mohammedanism. They think it is the very worst form of religion that ever existed. As soon as a man becomes a Mohammedan, the whole of Islam receives him as a brother with open arms, without making any distinction, which no other religion does. If one of your American Indians becomes a Mohammedan, the Sultan of Turkey would have no objection to dine with him. If he has brains, no position is barred to him. In this country, I have never yet seen a church where the white man and the negro can kneel side by side to pray. Just think of that: Islam makes its followers all equal — so, that, you see, is the peculiar excellence of Mohammedanism. In many places in the Koran you find very sensual ideas of life. Never mind. What Mohammedanism comes to preach to the world is this practical brotherhood of all belonging to their faith. That is the essential part of the Mohammedan religion; and all the other ideas about heaven and of life etc. are not Mohammedanism. They are accretions.

With the Hindus you will find one national idea — spirituality. In no other religion, in no other sacred books of the world, will you find so much energy spent in defining the idea of God. They tried to define the ideal of soul so that no earthly touch might mar it. The spirit must be divine; and spirit understood as spirit must not be made into a man. The same idea of unity, of the realisation of God, the omnipresent, is preached throughout. They think it is all nonsense to say that He lives in heaven, and all that. It is a mere human, anthropomorphic idea. All the heaven that ever existed is now and here. One moment in infinite time is quite as good as any other moment. If you believe in a God, you can see Him even now. We think religion begins when you have realised something. It is not believing in doctrines, nor giving intellectual assent, nor making declarations. If there is a God, have you seen Him? If you say "no", then what right have you to believe in Him? If you are in doubt whether there is a God, why do you not struggle to see Him? Why do you not renounce the world and spend the whole of your life for this one object? Renunciation and spirituality are the two great ideas of India, and it is because India clings to these ideas that all her mistakes count for so little.

With the Christians, the central idea that has been preached by them is the same: "Watch and pray, for the kingdom of Heaven is at hand" — which means, purify your minds and be ready! And that spirit never dies. You recollect that the Christians are, even in the darkest days, even in the most superstitious Christian countries, always trying to prepare themselves for the coming of the Lord, by trying to help others, building hospitals, and so on. So long as the Christians keep to that ideal, their religion lives.

Now an ideal presents itself to my mind. It may be only a dream. I do not know whether it will ever be realised in this world, but sometimes it is better to dream a dream, than die on hard facts. Great truths, even in a dream are good, better than bad facts. So, let us dream a dream.

You know that there are various grades of mind. You may be a matter-of-fact, common-sense rationalist: you do not care for forms and ceremonies; you want intellectual, hard, ringing facts, and they alone will satisfy you. Then there are the Puritans, the Mohammedans, who will not allow a picture or a statue in their place of worship. Very well! But there is another man who is more artistic. He wants a great deal of art — beauty of lines and curves, the colours, flowers, forms; he wants candles, lights, and all the insignia and paraphernalia of ritual, that he may see God. His mind takes God in those forms, as yours takes Him through the intellect. Then, there is the devotional man, whose soul is crying for God: he has no other idea but to worship God, and to praise Him. Then again, there is the philosopher, standing outside all these, mocking at them. He thinks, "What nonsense they are! What ideas about God!"

They may laugh at one another, but each one has a place in this world. All these various minds, all these various types are necessary. If there ever is going to be an ideal religion, it must be broad and large enough to supply food for all these minds. It must supply the strength of philosophy to the philosopher, the devotee's heart to the worshipper; to the ritualist, it will give all that the most marvellous symbolism can convey; to the poet, it will give as much of heart as he can take in, and other things besides. To make such a broad religion, we shall have to go back to the time when religions began and take them all in.

Our watchword, then, will be acceptance, and not exclusion. Not only toleration, for so-called toleration is often blasphemy, and I do not believe in it. I believe in acceptance. Why should I tolerate? Toleration means that I think that you are wrong and I am just allowing you to live. Is it not a blasphemy to think that you and I are allowing others to live? I accept all religions that were in the past, and worship with them all; I worship God with every one of them, in whatever form they worship Him. I shall go to the mosque of the Mohammedan; I shall enter the Christian's church and kneel before the crucifix; I shall enter the Buddhistic temple, where I shall take refuge in Buddha and in his Law. I shall go into the forest and sit down in meditation with the Hindu, who is trying to see the Light which enlightens the heart of every one.

Not only shall I do all these, but I shall keep my heart open for all that may come in the future. Is God's book finished? Or is it still a continuous revelation going on? It is a marvellous book — these spiritual revelations of the world. The Bible, the Vedas, the Koran, and all other sacred books are but so many pages, and an infinite number of pages remain yet to be unfolded. I would leave it open for all of them. We stand in the present, but open ourselves to the infinite future. We take in all that has been in the past, enjoy the light of the present, and open every window of the heart for all that will come in the future. Salutation to all the prophets of the past, to all the great ones of the present, and to all that are to come in the future!

THE IDEAL OF A UNIVERSAL RELIGION

How It Must Embrace Different Types Of Minds And Methods

Wheresoever our senses reach, or whatsoever our minds imagine, we find therein the action and reaction of two forces, the one counteracting the other and causing the constant play of the mixed phenomena that we see around us, and of those which we feel in our minds. In the external world, the action of these opposite forces is expressing itself as attraction and repulsion, or as centripetal and centrifugal forces; and in the internal, as love and hatred, good and evil. We repel some things, we attract others. We are attracted by one, we are repelled by another. Many times in our lives we find that without any reason whatsoever we are, as it were, attracted towards certain persons; at other times, similarly, we are repelled by others. This is patent to all, and the higher the field of action, the more potent, the more remarkable, are the influences of these opposite forces. Religion is the highest plane of human thought and life, and herein we find that the workings of these two forces have been most marked. The intensest love that humanity has ever known has come from religion, and the most diabolical hatred that humanity has known has also come from religion. The noblest words of peace that the world has ever heard have come from men on the religious plane, and the bitterest denunciation that the world has ever known has been uttered by religious men. The higher the object of any religion and the finer its organisation, the more remarkable are its activities. No other human motive has deluged the world with blood so much as religion; at the same time, nothing has brought into existence so many hospitals and asylums for the poor; no other human influence has taken such care, not only of humanity, but also of the lowest of animals, as religion has done. Nothing makes us so cruel as religion, and nothing makes us so tender as religion. This has been so in the past, and will also, in all probability, be so in the future. Yet out of the midst of this din and turmoil, this strife and struggle, this hatred and jealousy of religions and sects, there have arisen, from time to time, potent voices, drowning all this noise — making themselves heard from pole to pole, as it were — proclaiming peace and harmony. Will it ever come?

Is it possible that there should ever reign unbroken harmony in this plane of mighty religious struggle. The world is exercised in the latter part of this century by the question of harmony; in society, various plans are being proposed, and attempts are made to carry them into practice; but we know how difficult it is to do so. People find that it is almost impossible to mitigate the fury of the struggle of life, to tone down the tremendous nervous tension that is in man. Now, if it is so difficult to bring harmony and peace to the physical plane of life — the external, gross, and outward side of it — then a thousand times more difficult is it to bring peace and harmony to rule over the internal nature of man. I would ask you for the time being to come out of the network of words. We have all been hearing from childhood of such things as love, peace, charity, equality, and universal brotherhood; but they have become to us mere words without meaning, words which we repeat like parrots, and it has become quite natural for us to do so. We cannot help it. Great souls, who first felt these great ideas in their hearts, manufactured these words; and at that time many understood their meaning. Later on, ignorant people have taken up those words to play with them and made religion a mere play upon words, and not a thing to be carried into practice. It becomes "my father's religion", "our nation's religion", "our country's religion", and so forth. It becomes only a phase of patriotism to profess any religion, and patriotism is always partial. To bring harmony into religion must always be difficult. Yet we will consider this problem of the harmony of religions.

We see that in every religion there are three parts — I mean in every great and recognised religion. First, there is the philosophy which presents the whole scope of that religion, setting forth its basic principles, the goal and the means of reaching it. The second part is mythology, which is philosophy made concrete. It consists of legends relating to the lives of men, or of supernatural beings, and so forth. It is the abstractions of philosophy concretised in the more or less imaginary lives of men and supernatural beings. The third part is the ritual. This is still more concrete and is made up of forms and ceremonies, various physical attitudes, flowers and incense, and many other things, that appeal to the senses. In these consists the ritual. You will find that all recognised religions have these three elements. Some lay more stress on one, some on another. Let us now take into consideration the first part, philosophy. Is there one universal philosophy? Not yet. Each religion brings out its own doctrines and insists upon them as being the only true ones. And not only does it do that, but it thinks that he who does not believe in them must go to some horrible place. Some will even draw the sword to compel others to believe as they do. This is not through wickedness, but through a particular disease of the human brain called fanaticism. They are very sincere, these fanatics, the most sincere of human beings; but they are quite as irresponsible as other lunatics in the world. This disease of fanaticism is one of the most dangerous of all diseases. All the wickedness of human nature is roused by it. Anger is stirred up, nerves are strung high, and human beings become like tigers.

Is there any mythological similarity, is there any mythological harmony, any universal mythology accepted by all religions? Certainly not. All religions have their own mythology, only each of them says, "My stories are not mere myths." Let us try to understand the question by illustration. I simply mean to illustrate, I do not mean criticism of any religion. The Christian believes that God took the shape of a dove and came down to earth; to him this is history, and not mythology. The Hindu believes that God is manifested in the cow. Christians say that to believe so is mere mythology, and not history, that it is superstition. The Jews think that if an image be made in the form of a box, or a chest, with an angel on either side, then it may be placed in the Holy of Holies; it is sacred to Jehovah; but if the image be made in the form of a beautiful man or woman, they say, "This is a horrible idol; break it down! " This is our unity in mythology! If a man stands up and says, "My prophet did such and such a wonderful thing", others will say, "That is only superstition", but at the same time they say that their own prophet did still more wonderful things, which they hold to be historical. Nobody in the world, as far as I have seen, is able to make out the fine distinction between history and mythology, as it exists in the brains of these persons. All such stories, to whatever religion they may belong, are really mythological, mixed up occasionally, it may be with, a little history.

Next come the rituals. One sect has one particular form of ritual and thinks that that is holy, while the rituals of another sect are simply arrant superstition. If one sect worships a peculiar sort of symbol, another sect says, "Oh, it is horrible!" Take, for instance, a general form of symbol. The phallus symbol is certainly a sexual symbol, but gradually that aspect of it has been forgotten, and it stands now as a symbol of the Creator. Those nations which have this as their symbol never think of it as the phallus; it is just a symbol, and there it ends. But a man from another race or creed sees in it nothing but the phallus, and begins to condemn it; yet at the same time he may be doing something which to the so-called phallic worshippers appears most horrible. Let me take two points for illustration, the phallus symbol and the sacrament of the Christians. To the Christians the phallus is horrible, and to the Hindus the Christian sacrament is horrible. They say that the Christian sacrament, the killing of a man and the eating of his flesh and the drinking of his blood to get the good qualities of that man, is cannibalism. This is what some of the savage tribes do; if a man is brave, they kill him and eat his heart, because they think that it will give them the qualities of courage and bravery possessed by that man. Even such a devout Christian as Sir John Lubbock admits this and says that the origin of this Christian symbol is in this savage idea. The Christians, of course, do not admit this view of its origin; and what it may imply never comes to their mind. It stands for holy things, and that is all they want to know. So even in rituals there is no universal symbol, which can command general recognition and acceptance. Where then is any universality? How is it possible then to have a universal form of religion? That, however, already exists. And let us see what it is.

We all hear about universal brotherhood, and how societies stand up especially to preach this. I remember an old story. In India, taking wine is considered very bad. There were two brothers who wished, one night, to drink wine secretly; and their uncle, who was a very orthodox man was sleeping in a room quite close to theirs. So, before they began to drink, they said to each other, "We must be very silent, or uncle will wake up." When they were drinking, they continued repeating to each other "Silence! Uncle will wake up", each trying to shout the other down. And, as the shouting increased, the uncle woke up, came into the room, and discovered the whole thing. Now, we all shout like these drunken men," Universal brotherhood! We are all equal, therefore let us make a sect." As soon as you make a sect you protest against equality, and equality is no more. Mohammedans talk of universal brotherhood, but what comes out of that in reality? Why, anybody who is not a Mohammedan will not be admitted into the brotherhood; he will more likely have his throat cut. Christians talk of universal brotherhood; but anyone who is not a Christian must go to that place where he will be eternally barbecued.

And so we go on in this world in our search after universal brotherhood and equality. When you hear such talk in the world, I would ask you to be a little reticent, to take care of yourselves, for, behind all this talk is often the intensest selfishness. "In the winter sometimes a thunder-cloud comes up; it roars and roars, but it does not rain; but in the rainy season the clouds speak not, but deluge the world with water." So those who are really workers, and really feel at heart the universal brotherhood of man, do not talk much, do not make little sects for universal brotherhood; but their acts, their movements, their whole life, show out clearly that they in truth possess the feeling of brotherhood for mankind, that they have love and sympathy for all. They do not speak, they do and they live. This world is too full of blustering talk. We want a little more earnest work, and less talk.

So far we see that it is hard to find any universal features in regard to religion, and yet we know that they exist. We are all human beings, but are we all equal? Certainly not. Who says we are equal? Only the lunatic. Are we all equal in our brains, in our powers, in our bodies? One man is stronger than another, one man has more brain power than another. If we are all equal, why is there this inequality? Who made it? We. Because we have more or less powers, more or less brain, more or less physical strength, it must make a difference between us. Yet we know that the doctrine of equality appeals to our heart. We are all human beings; but some are men, and some are women. Here is a black man, there is a white man; but all are men, all belong to one humanity. Various are our faces; I see no two alike, yet we are all human beings. Where is this one humanity? I find a man or a woman, either dark or fair; and among all these faces I know that there is an abstract humanity which is common to all. I may not find it when I try to grasp it, to sense it, and to actualise it, yet I know for certain that it is there. If I am sure of anything, it is of this humanity which is common to us all. It is through this generalised entity that I see you as a man or a woman. So it is with this universal religion, which runs through all the various religions of the world in the form of God; it must and does exist through eternity. "I am the thread that runs through all these pearls," and each pearl is a religion or even a sect thereof. Such are the different pearls, and the Lord is the thread that runs through all of them; only the majority of mankind are entirely unconscious of it.

Unity in variety is the plan of the universe. We are all men, and yet we are all distinct from one another. As a part of humanity I am one with you, and as Mr. So-and-so I am different from you. As a man you are separate from the woman; as a human being you are one with the woman. As a man you are separate from the animal, but as living beings, man, woman, animal, and plant are all one; and as existence, you are one with the whole universe. That universal existence is God, the ultimate Unity in the universe. In Him we are all one. At the same time, in manifestation, these differences must always remain. In our work, in our energies, as they are being manifested outside, these differences must always remain. We find then that if by the idea of a universal religion it is meant that one set of doctrines should be believed in by all mankind it is wholly impossible. It can never be, there can never be a time when all faces will be the same. Again, if we expect that there will be one universal mythology, that is also impossible; it cannot be. Neither can there be one universal ritual. Such a state of things can never come into existence; if it ever did, the world would be destroyed, because variety is the first principle of life. What makes us formed beings? Differentiation. Perfect balance would be our destruction. Suppose the amount of heat in this room, the tendency of which is towards equal and perfect diffusion, gets that kind of diffusion, then for all practical purposes that heat will cease to be. What makes motion possible in this universe? Lost balance. The unity of sameness can come only when this universe is destroyed, otherwise such a thing is impossible. Not only so, it would be dangerous to have it. We must not wish that all of us should think alike. There would then be no thought to think. We should be all alike, as the Egyptian mummies in a museum, looking at each other without a thought to think. It is this difference, this differentiation, this losing of the balance between us, which is the very soul of our progress, the soul of all our thought. This must always be.

What then do I mean by the ideal of a universal religion? I do not mean any one universal philosophy, or any one universal mythology, or any one universal ritual held alike by all; for I know that this world must go on working, wheel within wheel, this intricate mass of machinery, most complex, most wonderful. What can we do then? We can make it run smoothly, we can lessen the friction, we can grease the wheels, as it were. How? By recognising the natural necessity of variation. Just as we have recognised unity by our very nature, so we must also recognise variation. We must learn that truth may be expressed in a hundred thousand ways, and that each of these ways is true as far as it goes. We must learn that the same thing can be viewed from a hundred different standpoints, and yet be the same thing. Take for instance the sun. Suppose a man standing on the earth looks at the sun when it rises in the morning; he sees a big ball. Suppose he starts on a journey towards the sun and takes a camera with him, taking photographs at every stage of his journey, until he reaches the sun. The photographs of each stage will be seen to be different from those of the other stages; in fact, when he gets back, he brings with him so many photographs of so many different suns, as it would appear; and yet we know that the same sun was photographed by the man at the different stages of his progress. Even so is it with the Lord. Through high philosophy or low, through the most exalted mythology or the grossest, through the most refined ritualism or arrant fetishism, every sect, every soul, every nation, every religion, consciously or unconsciously, is struggling upward, towards God; every vision of truth that man has, is a vision of Him and of none else. Suppose we all go with vessels in our hands to fetch water from a lake. One has a cup, another a jar, another a bucket, and so forth, and we all fill our vessels. The water in each case naturally takes the form of the vessel carried by each of us. He who brought the cup has the water in the form of a cup; he who brought the jar — his water is in the shape of a jar, and so forth; but, in every case, water, and nothing but water, is in the vessel. So it is in the case of religion; our minds are like these vessels, and each one of us is trying to arrive at the realisation of God. God is like that water filling these different vessels, and in each vessel the vision of God comes in the form of the vessel. Yet He is One. He is God in every case. This is the only recognition of universality that we can get.

So far it is all right theoretically. But is there any way of practically working out this harmony in religions? We find that this recognition that all the various views of religion are true has been very very old. Hundreds of attempts have been made in India, in Alexandria, in Europe, in China, in Japan, in Tibet, and lastly in America, to formulate a harmonious religious creed, to make all religions come together in love. They have all failed, because they did not adopt any practical plan. Many have admitted that all the religions of the world are right, but they show no practical way of bringing them together, so as to enable each of them to maintain its own individuality in the conflux. That plan alone is practical, which does not destroy the individuality of any man in religion and at the same time shows him a point of union with all others. But so far, all the plans of religious harmony that have been tried, while proposing to take in all the various views of religion, have, in practice, tried to bind them all down to a few doctrines, and so have produced more new sects, fighting, struggling, and pushing against each other.

I have also my little plan. I do not know whether it will work or not, and I want to present it to you for discussion. What is my plan? In the first place I would ask mankind to recognise this maxim, "Do not destroy". Iconoclastic reformers do no good to the world. Break not, pull not anything down, but build. Help, if you can; if you cannot, fold your hands and stand by and see things go on. Do not injure, if you cannot render help. Say not a word against any man's convictions so far as they are sincere. Secondly, take man where he stands, and from there give him a lift. If it be true that God is the centre of all religions, and that each of us is moving towards Him along one of these radii, then it is certain that all of us must reach that centre. And at the centre, where all the radii meet, all our differences will cease; but until we reach there, differences there must be. All these radii converge to the same centre. One, according to his nature, travels along one of these lines, and another, along another; and if we all push onward along our own lines, we shall surely come to the centre, because, "All roads lead to Rome". Each of us is naturally growing and developing according to his own nature; each will in time come to know the highest truth for after all, men must teach themselves. What can you and I do? Do you think you can teach even a child? You cannot. The child teaches himself. Your duty is to afford opportunities and to remove obstacles. A plant grows. Do you make the plant grow? Your duty is to put a hedge round it and see that no animal eats up the plant, and there your duty ends. The plant grows of itself. So it is in regard to the spiritual growth of every man. None can teach you; none can make a spiritual man of you. You have to teach yourself; your growth must come from inside.

What can an external teacher do? He can remove the obstructions a little, and there his duty ends. Therefore help, if you can; but do not destroy. Give up all ideas that you can make men spiritual. It is impossible. There is no other teacher to you than your own soul. Recognise this. What comes of it? In society we see so many different natures. There are thousands and thousands of varieties of minds and inclinations. A thorough generalisation of them is impossible, but for our practical purpose it is sufficient to have them characterised into four classes. First, there is the active man, the worker; he wants to work, and there is tremendous energy in his muscles and his nerves. His aim is to work — to build hospitals, do charitable deeds, make streets, to plan and to organise. Then there is the emotional man who loves the sublime and the beautiful to an excessive degree. He loves to think of the beautiful, to enjoy the aesthetic side of nature, and adore Love and the God of Love. He loves with his whole heart the great souls of all times, the prophets of religions, and the Incarnations of God on earth; he does not care whether reason can or cannot prove that Christ or Buddha existed; he does not care for the exact date when the Sermon on the Mount was preached, or for the exact moment of Krishna's birth; what he cares for is their personalities, their lovable figures. Such is his ideal. This is the nature of the lover, the emotional man. Then, there is the mystic whose mind wants to analyse its own self, to understand the workings of the human mind, what the forces are that are working inside, and how to know, manipulate, and obtain control over them. This is the mystical mind. Then, there is the philosopher who wants to weigh everything and use his intellect even beyond the possibilities of all human philosophy.

Now a religion, to satisfy the largest proportion of mankind, must be able to supply food for all these various types of minds; and where this capability is wanting, the existing sects all become one-sided. Suppose you go to a sect which preaches love and emotion. They sing and weep, and preach love. But as soon as you say, "My friend, that is all right, but I want something stronger than this — a little reason and philosophy; I want to understand things step by step and more rationally", they say, "Get out"; and they not only ask you to get out but would send you to the other place, if they could. The result is that that sect can only help people of an emotional turn of mind. They not only do not help others, but try to destroy them; and the most wicked part of the whole thing is that they will not only not help others, but do not believe in their sincerity. Again, there are philosophers who talk of the wisdom of India and the East and use big psychological terms, fifty syllables long, but if an ordinary man like me goes to them and says, "Can you tell me anything to make me spiritual?", the first thing they would do would be to smile and say, "Oh, you are too far below us in your reason. What can you understand about spirituality?" These are high-up philosophers. They simply show you the door. Then there are the mystical sects who speak all sorts of things about different planes of existence, different states of mind, and what the power of the mind can do, and so on; and if you are an ordinary man and say, "Show me anything good that I can do; I am not much given to speculation; can you give me anything that will suit me?", they will smile and say, "Listen to that fool; he knows nothing, his existence is for nothing." And this is going on everywhere in the world. I would like to get extreme exponents of all these different sects, and shut them up in a room, and photograph their beautiful derisive smiles!

This is the existing condition of religion, the existing condition of things. What I want to propagate is a religion that will be equally acceptable to all minds; it must be equally philosophic, equally emotional, equally mystic, and equally conducive to action. If professors from the colleges come, scientific men and physicists, they will court reason. Let them have it as much as they want. There will be a point beyond which they will think they cannot go, without breaking with reason. They will say, "These ideas of God and salvation are superstitious, guise them up! " I say, "Mr. Philosopher, this body of yours is a bigger superstition. Give it up, don't go home to dinner or to your philosophic chair. Give up the body, and if you cannot, cry quarter and sit down." For religion must be able to show how to realise the philosophy that teaches us that this world is one, that there is but one Existence in the universe. Similarly, if the mystic comes, we must welcome him, be ready to give him the science of mental analysis, and practically demonstrate it before him. And if emotional people come, we must sit, laugh, and weep with them in the name of the Lord; we must "drink the cup of love and become mad". If the energetic worker comes, we must work with him, with all the energy that we have. And this combination will be the ideal of the nearest approach to a universal religion. Would to God that all men were so constituted that in their minds all these elements of philosophy, mysticism, emotion, and of work were equally present in full! That is the ideal, my ideal of a perfect man. Everyone who has only one or two of these elements of character, I consider "one-sided; and this world is almost full of such "one-sided" men, with knowledge of that one road only in which they move; and anything else is dangerous and horrible to them. To become harmoniously balanced in all these four directions is my ideal of religion. And this religion is attained by what we, in India, call Yoga — union. To the worker, it is union between men and the whole of humanity; to the mystic, between his lower and Higher Self; to the lover, union between himself and the God of Love; and to the philosopher; it is the union of all existence. This is what is meant by Yoga. This is a Sanskrit term, and these four divisions of Yoga have in Sanskrit different names. The man who seeks after this kind of union is called a Yogi. The worker is called the Karma-Yogi. He who seeks the union through love is called the Bhakti-Yogi. He who seeks it through mysticism is called the Râja-Yogi. And he who seeks it through philosophy is called the Jnâna-Yogi So this word Yogi comprises them all.

Now first of all let me take up Râja-Yoga. What is this Raja-Yoga, this controlling of the mind? In this country you are associating all sorts of hobgoblins with the word Yoga, I am afraid. Therefore, I must start by telling you that it has nothing to do with such things. No one of these Yogas gives up reason, no one of them asks you to be hoodwinked, or to deliver your reason into the hands of priests of any type whatsoever. No one of them asks that you should give your allegiance to any superhuman messenger. Each one of them tells you to cling to your reason to hold fast to it. We find in all beings three sorts of instruments of knowledge. The first is instinct, which you find most highly developed in animals; this is the lowest instrument of knowledge. What is the second instrument of knowledge? Reasoning. You find that most highly developed in man. Now in the first place, instinct is an inadequate instrument; to animals, the sphere of action is very limited, and within that limit instinct acts. When you come to man, you see it is largely developed into reason. The sphere of action also has here become enlarged. Yet even reason is still very insufficient. Reason can go only a little way and then it stops, it cannot go any further; and if you try to push it, the result is helpless confusion, reason itself becomes unreasonable. Logic becomes argument in a circle. Take, for instance, the very basis of our perception, matter and force. What is matter? That which is acted upon by force. And force? That which acts upon matter. You see the complication, what the logicians call see-saw, one idea depending on the other, and this again depending on that. You find a mighty barrier before reason, beyond which reasoning cannot go; yet it always feels impatient to get into the region of the Infinite beyond. This world, this universe which our senses feel, or our mind thinks, is but one atom, so to say, of the Infinite, projected on to the plane of consciousness; and within that narrow limit, defined by the network of consciousness, works our reason, and not beyond. Therefore, there must be some other instrument to take us beyond, and that instrument is called inspiration. So instinct, reason, and inspiration are the three instruments of knowledge. Instinct belongs to animals, reason to man, and inspiration to Godmen. But in all human beings are to be found, in a more or less developed condition, the germs of all these three instruments of knowledge. To have these mental instruments evolved, the germs must be there. And this must also be remembered that one instrument is a development of the other, and therefore does not contradict it. It is reason that develops into inspiration, and therefore inspiration does not contradict reason, but fulfils it. Things which reason cannot get at are brought to light by inspiration; and they do not contradict reason. The old man does not contradict the child, but fulfils the child. Therefore you must always bear in mind that the great danger lies in mistaking the lower form of instrument to be the higher. Many times instinct is presented before the world as inspiration, and then come all the spurious claims for the gift of prophecy. A fool or a semi-lunatic thinks that the confusion going on in his brain is inspiration, and he wants men to follow him. The most contradictory irrational nonsense that has been preached in the world is simply the instinctive jargon of confused lunatic brains trying to pass for the language of inspiration.

The first test of true teaching must be, that the teaching should not contradict reason. And you may see that such is the basis of all these Yogas. We take the Raja-Yoga, the psychological Yoga, the psychological way to union. It is a vast subject, and I can only point out to you now the central idea of this Yoga. We have but one method of acquiring knowledge. From the lowest man to the highest Yogi, all have to use the same method; and that method is what is called concentration. The chemist who works in his laboratory concentrates all the powers of his mind, brings them into one focus, and throws them on the elements; and the elements stand analysed, and thus his knowledge comes. The astronomer has also concentrated the powers of his mind and brought them into one focus; and he throws them on to objects through his telescope; and stars and systems roll forward and give up their secrets to him. So it is in every case — with the professor in his chair, the student with his book — with every man who is working to know. You are hearing me, and if my words interest you, your mind will become concentrated on them; and then suppose a clock strikes, you will not hear it, on account of this concentration; and the more you are able to concentrate your mind, the better you will understand me; and the more I concentrate my love and powers, the better I shall be able to give expression to what I want to convey to you. The more this power of concentration, the more knowledge is acquired, because this is the one and only method of acquiring knowledge. Even the lowest shoeblack, if he gives more concentration, will black shoes better; the cook with concentration will cook a meal all the better. In making money, or in worshipping God, or in doing anything, the stronger the power of concentration, the better will that thing be done. This is the one call, the one knock, which opens the gates of nature, and lets out floods of light. This, the power of concentration, is the only key to the treasure-house of knowledge. The system of Raja-Yoga deals almost exclusively with this. In the present state of our body we are so much distracted, and the mind is frittering away its energies upon a hundred sorts of things. As soon as I try to calm my thoughts and concentrate my mind upon any one object of knowledge, thousands of undesired impulses rush into the brain, thousands of thoughts rush into the mind and disturb it. How to check it and bring the mind under control is the whole subject of study in Raja-Yoga.

Now take Karma-Yoga, the attainment of God through work. It is evident that in society there are many persons who seem to be born for some sort of activity or other, whose minds cannot be concentrated on the plane of thought alone, and who have but one idea, concretised in work, visible and tangible. There must be a science for this kind of life too. Each one of us is engaged in some work, but the majority of us fritter away the greater portion of our energies, because we do not know the secret of work. Karma-Yoga explains this secret and teaches where and how to work, how to employ to the greatest advantage the largest part of our energies in the work that is before us. But with this secret we must take into consideration the great objection against work, namely that it causes pain. All misery and pain come from attachment. I want to do work, I want to do good to a human being; and it is ninety to one that that human being whom I have helped will prove ungrateful and go against me; and the result to me is pain. Such things deter mankind from working; and it spoils a good portion of the work and energy of mankind, this fear of pain and misery. Karma-Yoga teaches us how to work for work's sake, unattached, without caring who is helped, and what for. The Karma-Yogi works because it is his nature, because he feels that it is good for him to do so, and he has no object beyond that. His position in this world is that of a giver, and he never cares to receive anything. He knows that he is giving, and does not ask for anything in return and, therefore, he eludes the grasp of misery. The grasp of pain, whenever it comes, is the result of the reaction of "attachment".

There is then the Bhakti-Yoga for the man of emotional nature, the lover. He wants to love God, he relies upon and uses all sorts of rituals, flowers, incense, beautiful buildings, forms and all such things. Do you mean to say they are wrong? One fact I must tell you. It is good for you to remember, in this country especially, that the world's great spiritual giants have all been produced only by those religious sects which have been in possession of very rich mythology and ritual. All sects that have attempted to worship God without any form or ceremony have crushed without mercy everything that is beautiful and sublime in religion. Their religion is a fanaticism at best, a dry thing. The history of the world is a standing witness to this fact. Therefore do not decry these rituals and mythologies. Let people have them; let those who so desire have them. Do not exhibit that unworthy derisive smile, and say, "They are fools; let them have it." Not so; the greatest men I have seen in my life, the most wonderfully developed in spirituality, have all come through the discipline of these rituals. I do not hold myself worthy to sit at their feet, and for me to criticise them! How do I know how these ideas act upon the human minds which of them I am to accept and which to reject? We are apt to criticise everything in the world: without sufficient warrant. Let people have all the mythology they want, with its beautiful inspirations; for you must always bear in mind that emotional natures do not care for abstract definitions of the truth. God to them is something tangible, the only thing that is real; they feel, hear, and see Him, and love Him. Let them have their God. Your rationalist seems to them to be like the fool who, when he saw a beautiful statue, wanted to break it to find out of what material it was made. Bhakti-Yoga: teaches them how to love, without any ulterior motives, loving God and loving the good because it is good to do so, not for going to heaven, nor to get children, wealth, or anything else. It teaches them that love itself is the highest recompense of love — that God Himself is love. It teaches them to pay all kinds of tribute to God as the Creator, the Omnipresent, Omniscient, Almighty Ruler, the Father and the Mother. The highest phrase that can express Him, the highest idea that the human mind can conceive of Him, is that He is the God of Love. Wherever there is love, it is He. "Wherever there is any love, it is He, the Lord is present there." Where the husband kisses the wife, He is there in the kiss; where the mother kisses the child, He is there in the kiss; where friends clasp hands, He, the Lord, is present as the God of Love. When a great man loves and wishes to help mankind, He is there giving freely His bounty out of His love to mankind. Wherever the heart expands, He is there manifested. This is what the Bhakti-Yoga teaches.

We lastly come to the Jnana-Yogi, the philosopher, the thinker, he who wants to go beyond the visible. He is the man who is not satisfied with the little things of this world. His idea is to go beyond the daily routine of eating, drinking, and so on; not even the teaching of thousands of books will satisfy him. Not even all the sciences will satisfy him; at the best, they only bring this little world before him. What else will give him satisfaction? Not even myriads of systems of worlds will satisfy him; they are to him but a drop in the ocean of existence. His soul wants to go beyond all that into the very heart of being, by seeing Reality as It is; by realising It, by being It, by becoming one with that Universal Being. That is the philosopher. To say that God is the Father or the Mother, the Creator of this universe, its Protector and Guide, is to him quite inadequate to express Him. To him, God is the life of his life, the soul of his soul. God is his own Self. Nothing else remains which is other than God. All the mortal parts of him become pounded by the weighty strokes of philosophy and are brushed away. What at last truly remains is God Himself.

Upon the same tree there are two birds, one on the top, the other below. The one on the top is calm, silent, and majestic, immersed in his own glory; the one on the lower branches, eating sweet and bitter fruits by turns, hopping from branch to branch, is becoming happy and miserable by turns. After a time the lower bird eats an exceptionally bitter fruit and gets disgustful and looks up and sees the other bird, that wondrous one of golden plumage, who eats neither sweet nor bitter fruit, who is neither happy nor miserable, but calm, Self-centred, and sees nothing beyond his Self. The lower bird longs for this condition but soon forgets it, and again begins to eat the fruits. In a little while, he eats another exceptionally bitter fruit, which makes him feel miserable, and he again looks up, and tries to get nearer to the upper bird. Once more he forgets and after a time he looks up, and so on he goes again and again, until he comes very near to the beautiful bird and sees the reflection of light from his plumage playing around his own body, and he feels a change and seems to melt away; still nearer he comes, and everything about him melts away, and at last he understands this wonderful change. The lower bird was, as it were, only the substantial-looking shadow, the reflection of the higher; he himself was in essence the upper bird all the time. This eating of fruits, sweet and bitter, this lower, little bird, weeping and happy by turns, was a vain chimera, a dream: all along, the real bird was there above, calm and silent, glorious and majestic, beyond grief, beyond sorrow. The upper bird is God, the Lord of this universe; and the lower bird is the human soul, eating the sweet and bitter fruits of this world. Now and then comes a heavy blow to the soul. For a time, he stops the eating and goes towards the unknown God, and a flood of light comes. He thinks that this world is a vain show. Yet again the senses drag him down, and he begins as before to eat the sweet and bitter fruits of the world. Again an exceptionally hard blow comes. His heart becomes open again to divine light; thus gradually he approaches God, and as he gets nearer and nearer, he finds his old self melting away. When he has come near enough, he sees that he is no other than God, and he exclaims, "He whom I have described to you as the Life of this universe, as present in the atom, and in suns and moons — He is the basis of our own life, the Soul of our soul. Nay, thou art That." This is what this Jnana-Yoga teaches. It tells man that he is essentially divine. It shows to mankind the real unity of being, and that each one of us is the Lord God Himself, manifested on earth. All of us, from the lowest worm that crawls under our feet to the highest beings to whom we look up with wonder and awe — all are manifestations of the same Lord.

Lastly, it is imperative that all these various Yogas should be carried out in, practice; mere theories about them will not do any good. First we have to hear about them, then we have to think about them. We have to reason the thoughts out, impress them on our minds, and we have to meditate on them, realise them, until at last they become our whole life. No longer will religion remain a bundle of ideas or theories, nor an intellectual assent; it will enter into our very self. By means of intellectual assent we may today subscribe to many foolish things, and change our minds altogether tomorrow. But true religion never changes. Religion is realisation; not talk, nor doctrine, nor theories, however beautiful they may be. It is being and becoming, not hearing or acknowledging; it is the whole soul becoming changed into what it believes. That is religion.

THE OPEN SECRET

Delivered at Los Angeles, Calif., 5th January 1900

Whichever way we turn in trying to understand things in their reality, if we analyse far enough, we find that at last we come to a peculiar state of things, seemingly a contradiction: something which our reason cannot grasp and yet is a fact. We take up something — we know it is finite; but as soon as we begin to analyse it, it leads us beyond our reason, and we never find an end to all its qualities, its possibilities, its powers, its relations. It has become infinite. Take even a common flower, that is finite enough; but who is there that can say he knows all about the flower? There is no possibility of anyone's getting to the end of the knowledge about that one flower. The flower has become infinite — the flower which was finite to begin with. Take a grain of sand. Analyse it. We start with the assumption that it is finite, and at last we find that it is not, it is infinite; all the same, we have looked upon it as finite. The flower is similarly treated as a finite something.

So with all our thoughts and experiences, physical and mental. We begin, we may think, on a small scale, and grasp them as little things; but very soon they elude our knowledge and plunge into the abyss of the infinite. And the greatest and the first thing perceived is ourselves. We are also in the same dilemma about existence. We exist. We see we are finite beings. We live and die. Our horizon is narrow. We are here, limited, confronted by the universe all around. Nature can crush us out of existence in a moment. Our little bodies are just held together, ready to go to pieces at a moment's notice. We know that. In the region of action how powerless we are! Our will is being thwarted at every turn. So many things we want to do, and how few we can do! There is no limit to our willing. We can will everything, want everything, we can desire to go to the dogstar. But how few of our desires can be accomplished! The body will not allow it. Well, nature is against the accomplishment of our will. We are weak. What is true of the flower, of the grain of sand, of the physical world, and of every thought, is a hundredfold more true of ourselves. We are also in the same dilemma of existence, being finite and infinite at the same time. We are like waves in the ocean; the wave is the ocean and yet not the ocean. There is not any part of the wave of which you cannot say, "It is the ocean." The name "ocean" applies to the wave and equally to every other part of the ocean, and yet it is separate from the ocean. So in this infinite ocean of existence we are like wavelets. At the same time, when we want really to grasp ourselves, we cannot — we have become the infinite.

We seem to be walking in dreams. Dreams are all right in a dream-mind; but as soon as you want to grasp one of them, it is gone. Why? Not that it was false, but because it is beyond the power of reason, the power of the intellect to comprehend it. Everything in this life is so vast that the intellect is nothing in comparison with it. It refuses to be bound by the laws of the intellect! It laughs at the bondage the intellect wants to spread around it. And a thousandfold more so is this the case with the human soul. "We ourselves"— this is the greatest mystery of the universe.

How wonderful it all is! Look at the human eye. How easily it can be destroyed, and yet the biggest suns exist only because your eyes see them. The world exists because your eyes certify that it exists. Think of that mystery! These poor little eyes! A strong light, or a pin, can destroy them. Yet the most powerful engines of destruction, the most powerful cataclysms, the most wonderful of existences, millions of suns and stars and moons and earth — all depend for their existence upon, and have to be certified by, these two little things! They say, "Nature, you exist", and we believe nature exists. So with all our senses.

What is this? Where is weakness? Who is strong? What is great and what is small? What is high and what is low in this marvellous interdependence of existence where the smallest atom is necessary for the existence of the whole? Who is great and who is small? It is past finding out! And why? Because none is great and none is small. All things are interpenetrated by that infinite ocean; their reality is that infinite; and whatever there is on the surface is but that infinite. The tree is infinite; so is everything that you see or feel — every grain of sand, every thought, every soul, everything that exists, is infinite. Infinite is finite and finite infinite. This is our existence.

Now, that may be all true, but all this feeling after the Infinite is at present mostly unconscious. It is not that we have forgotten that infinite nature of ours: none can ever do that. Who can ever think that he can be annihilated? Who can think that he will die? None can. All our relation to the Infinite works in us unconsciously. In a manner, therefore, we forget our real being, and hence all this misery comes.

In practical daily life we are hurt by small things; we are enslaved by little beings. Misery comes because we think we are finite — we are little beings. And yet, how difficult it is to believe that we are infinite beings! In the midst of all this misery and trouble, when a little thing may throw me off my balance, it must be my care to believe that I am infinite. And the fact is that we are, and that consciously or unconsciously we are all searching after that something which is infinite; we are always seeking for something that is free.

There was never a human race which did not have a religion and worship some sort of God or gods. Whether the God or gods existed or not is no question; but what is the analysis of this psychological phenomenon? Why is all the world trying to find, or seeking for, a God? Why? Because in spite of all this bondage, in spite of nature and this tremendous energy of law grinding us down, never allowing us to turn to any side — wherever we go, whatever we want to do, we are thwarted by this law, which is everywhere — in spite of all this, the human soul never forgets its freedom and is ever seeking it. The search for freedom is the search of all religions; whether they know it or not, whether they can formulate it well or ill, the idea is there. Even the lowest man, the most ignorant, seeks for something which has power over nature's laws. He wants to see a demon, a ghost, a god — somebody who can subdue nature, for whom nature is not almighty, for whom there is no law. "Oh, for somebody who can break the law!" That is the cry coming from the human heart. We are always seeking for someone who breaks the law. The rushing engine speeds along the railway track; the little worm crawls out of its way. We at once say, "The engine is dead matter, a machine; and the worm is alive," because the worm attempted to break the law. The engine, with all its power and might, can never break the law. It is made to go in any direction man wants, and it cannot do otherwise; but the worm, small and little though it was, attempted to break the law and avoid the danger. It tried to assert itself against law, assert its freedom; and there was the sign of the future God in it.

Everywhere we see this assertion of freedom, this freedom of the soul. It is reflected in every religion in the shape of God or gods; but it is all external yet — for those who only see the gods outside. Man decided that he was nothing. He was afraid that he could never be free; so he went to seek for someone outside of nature who was free. Then he thought that there were many and many such free beings, and gradually he merged them all into one God of gods and Lord of lords. Even that did not satisfy him. He came a little closer to truth, a little nearer; and then gradually found that whatever he was, he was in some way connected with the God of gods and Lord of lords; that he, though he thought himself bound and low and weak, was somehow connected with that God of gods. Then visions came to him; thought arose and knowledge advanced. And he began to come nearer and nearer to that God, and at last found out that God and all the gods, this whole psychological phenomenon connected with the search for an all-powerful free soul, was but a reflection of his own idea of himself. And then at last he discovered that it was not only true that "God made man after His own image", but that it was also true that man made God after his own image. That brought out the idea of divine freedom. The Divine Being was always within, the nearest of the near. Him we had ever been seeking outside, and at last found that He is in the heart of our hearts. You may know the story of the man who mistook his own heartbeat for somebody knocking at the door, and went to the door and opened it, but found nobody there, so he went back. Again he seemed to hear a knocking at the door, but nobody was there. Then he understood that it was his own heartbeat, and he had misinterpreted it as a knocking at the door. Similarly, man after his search finds out that this infinite freedom that he was placing in imagination all the time in the nature outside is the internal subject, the eternal Soul of souls; this Reality, he himself.

Thus at last he comes to recognise this marvellous duality of existence: the subject, infinite and finite in one — the Infinite Being is also the same finite soul. The Infinite is caught, as it were, in the meshes of the intellect and apparently manifests as finite beings, but the reality remains unchanged.

This is, therefore, true knowledge: that the Soul of our souls, the Reality that is within us, is That which is unchangeable, eternal, ever-blessed, ever-free. This is the only solid ground for us to stand upon.

This, then, is the end of all death, the advent of all immortality, the end of all misery. And he who sees that One among the many, that One unchangeable in the universe of change, he who sees Him as the Soul of his soul, unto him belongs eternal peace — unto none else.

And in the midst of the depths of misery and degradation, the Soul sends a ray of light, and man wakes up and finds that what is really his, he can never lose. No, we can never lose what is really ours. Who can lose his being? Who can lose his very existence? If I am good, it is the existence first, and then that becomes coloured with the quality of goodness. If I am evil, it is the existence first, and that becomes coloured with the quality of badness. That existence is first, last, and always; it is never lost, but ever present.

Therefore, there is hope for all. None can die; none can be degraded for ever. Life is but a playground, however gross the play may be. However we may receive blows, and however knocked about we may be, the Soul is there and is never injured. We are that Infinite.

Thus sang a Vedantin, "I never had fear nor doubt. Death never came to me. I never had father or mother: for I was never born. Where are my foes? — for I am All. I am the Existence and Knowledge and Bliss Absolute. I am It. I am It. Anger and lust and jealousy, evil thoughts and all these things, never came to me; for I am the Existence, the Knowledge, the Bliss Absolute. I am It. I am It."

That is the remedy for all disease, the nectar that cures death. Here we are in this world, and our nature rebels against it. But let us repeat, "I am It; I am It. I have no fear, nor doubt, nor death. I have no sex, nor creed, nor colour. What creed can I have? What sect is there to which I should belong? What sect can hold me? I am in every sect!"

However much the body rebels, however much the mind rebels, in the midst of the uttermost darkness, in the midst of agonising tortures, in the uttermost despair, repeat this, once, twice, thrice, ever more. Light comes gently, slowly, but surely it comes.

Many times I have been in the jaws of death, starving, footsore, and weary; for days and days I had had no food, and often could walk no farther; I would sink down under a tree, and life would seem ebbing away. I could not speak, I could scarcely think, but at last the mind reverted to the idea: "I have no fear nor death; I never hunger nor thirst. I am It! I am It! The whole of nature cannot crush me; it is my servant. Assert thy strength, thou Lord of lords and God of gods! Regain thy lost empire! Arise and walk and stop not!" And I would rise up, reinvigorated, and here am I, living, today. Thus, whenever darkness comes, assert the reality and everything adverse must vanish. For, after all, it is but a dream. Mountain-high though the difficulties appear, terrible and gloomy though all things seem, they are but Mâyâ. Fear not — it is banished. Crush it, and it vanishes. Stamp upon it, and it dies. Be not afraid. Think not how many times you fail. Never mind. Time is infinite. Go forward: assert yourself again and again, and light must come. You may pray to everyone that was ever born, but who will come to help you? And what of the way of death from which none knows escape? Help thyself out by thyself. None else can help thee, friend. For thou alone art thy greatest enemy, thou alone art thy greatest friend. Get hold of the Self, then. Stand up. Don't be afraid. In the midst of all miseries and all weakness, let the Self come out, faint and imperceptible though it be at first. You will gain courage, and at last like a lion you will roar out, "I am It! I am It!" "I am neither a man, nor a woman, nor a god, nor a demon; no, nor any of the animals, plants, or trees. I am neither poor nor rich, neither learned nor ignorant. All these things are very little compared with what I am: for I am It! I am It! Behold the sun and the moon and the stars: I am the light that is shining in them! I am the beauty of the fire! I am the power in the universe! For, I am It! I am It!

"Whoever thinks that I am little makes a mistake, for the Self is all that exists. The sun exists because I declare it does, the world exists because I declare it does. Without me they cannot remain, for I am Existence, Knowledge, and Bliss Absolute — ever happy, ever pure, ever beautiful. Behold, the sun is the cause of our vision, but is not itself ever affected by any defect in the eyes of any one; even so I am. I am working through all organs, working through everything, but never does the good and evil of work attach to me. For me there is no law, nor Karma. I own the laws of Karma. I ever was and ever am.

"My real pleasure was never in earthly things — in husband, wife, children, and other things. For I am like the infinite blue sky: clouds of many colours pass over it and play for a second; they move off, and there is the same unchangeable blue. Happiness and misery, good and evil, may envelop me for a moment, veiling the Self; but I am still there. They pass away because they are changeable. I shine, because I am unchangeable. If misery comes, I know it is finite, therefore it must die. If evil comes, I know it is finite, it must go. I alone am infinite and untouched by anything. For I am the Infinite, that Eternal, Changeless Self." — So sings one of our poets.

Let us drink of this cup, this cup that leads to everything that is immortal, everything that is unchangeable. Fear not. Believe not that we are evil, that we are finite,. that we can ever die. It is not true.

"This is to be heard of, then to be thought upon, and then to be meditated upon." When the hands work,. the mind should repeat, "I am It. I am It." Think of it, dream of it, until it becomes bone of your bones and; flesh of your flesh, until all the hideous dreams of littleness, of weakness, of misery, and of evil, have entirely vanished, and no more then can the Truth be hidden from you even for a moment.

THE WAY TO BLESSEDNESS

I shall tell you a story from the Vedas tonight. The Vedas are the sacred scriptures of the Hindus and are a vast collection of literature, of which the last part is called the Vedanta, meaning the end of the Vedas. It deals with the theories contained in them, and more especially the philosophy with which we are concerned. It is written in archaic Sanskrit, and you must remember it was written thousands of years ago. There was a certain man who wanted to make a big sacrifice. In the religion of the Hindus, sacrifice plays a great part. There are various sorts of sacrifices. They make altars and pour oblations into the fire, and repeat various hymns and so forth; and at the end of the sacrifice they make a gift to the Brahmins and the poor. Each sacrifice has its peculiar gift. There was one sacrifice, where everything a man possessed had to be given up. Now this man, though rich, was miserly, and at the same time wanted to get a great name for having done this most difficult sacrifice. And when he did this sacrifice, instead of giving up everything he had, he gave away only his blind, lame, and old cows that would never more give milk. But he had a son called Nachiketas, a bright young boy, who, observing the poor gifts made by his father, and pondering on the demerit that was sure to accrue to him thereby, resolved to make amends for them by making a gift of himself. So he went to his father and said, "And to whom will you give me?" The father did not answer the boy, and the boy asked a second and a third time, when the father got vexed and said, "Thee I give unto Yama, thee I give unto Death." And the boy went straight to the kingdom of Yama. Yama was not at home, so he waited there. After three days Yama came and said to him, "O Brahmin, thou art my guest, and thou hast been here for three days without any food. I salute thee, and in order to repay thee for this trouble, I will grant thee three boons." Then the boy asked the first boon, "May my father's anger against me get calmed down," and the second boon was that he wanted to know about a certain sacrifice. And then came the third boon. "When a man dies, the question arises: What becomes of him: Some people say he ceases to exist. Others say that he exists. Please tell me what the answer is. This is the third boon that I want." Then Death answered, "The gods in ancient times tried to unravel the mystery; this mystery is so fine that it is hard to know. Ask for some other boon: do not ask this one. Ask for a long life of a hundred years. Ask for cattle and horses, ask for great kingdoms. Do not press me to answer this. Whatever man desires for his enjoyment, ask all that and I will fulfil it, but do not want to know this secret." "No sir," said the boy, man is not to be satisfied with wealth; if wealth were wanted, we should "get it, if we have only seen you. We shall also live so long as you rule. What decaying mortal, living in the world below and possessed of knowledge, having gained the company of the undecaying and the immortal, will delight in long life, knowing the nature of the pleasure produced by song and sport? Therefore, tell me this secret about the great hereafter, I do not want anything else; that is what Nachiketas wants, the mystery of death." Then the God of death was pleased. We have been saying in the last two or three lectures that this Jnâna prepares the mind. So you see here that the first preparation is that a man must desire nothing else but the truth, and truth for truth's sake. See how this boy rejected all these gifts which Death offered him; possessions, property, wealth, long life, and everything he was ready to sacrifice for this one idea, knowledge only, the truth. Thus alone can truth come. The God of death became pleased. "Here are two ways," he said, "one of enjoyment, the other of blessedness. These two in various ways draw mankind. He becomes a sage who, of these two, takes up that which leads to blessedness, and he degenerates who takes up the road to enjoyment. I praise you, Nachiketas; you have not asked for desire. In various ways I tempted you towards the path of enjoyment; you resisted them all, you have known that knowledge is much higher than a life of enjoyment.

"You have understood that the man who lives in ignorance and enjoys, is not different from the brute beast. Yet there are many who, though steeped in ignorance, in the pride of their hearts, think that they are great sages and go round and round in many crooked ways, like the blind led by the blind. This truth, Nachiketas, never shines in the heart of those who are like ignorant children, deluded by a few lumps of earth. They do not understand this world, nor the other world. They deny this and the other one, and thus again and again come under my control. Many have not even the opportunity to hear about it; and many, though hearing, cannot know it, because the teacher must be wonderful; so must he be wonderful too unto whom the knowledge is carried. If the speaker is a man who is not highly advanced, then even a hundred times heard, and a hundred times taught, the truth never illumines the soul. Do not disturb your mind by vain arguments, Nachiketas; this truth only becomes effulgent in the heart which has been made pure. He who cannot be seen without the greatest difficulty, He who is hidden, He who has entered the cave of the heart of hearts — the Ancient One — cannot be seen with the external eyes; seeing Him with the eyes of the soul, one gives up both pleasure and pain. He who knows this secret gives up all his vain desires, and attains this superfine perception, and thus becomes ever blessed. Nachiketas, that is the way to blessedness. He is beyond all virtue, beyond all vice, beyond all duties, beyond all non-duties, beyond all existence, beyond all that is to be; he who knows this, alone knows. He whom all the Vedas seek, to see whom men undergo all sorts of asceticism, I will tell you His name: It is Om. This eternal Om is the Brahman, this is the immortal One; he who knows the secret of this — whatever he desires is his. This Self of man, Nachiketas, about which you seek to know, is never born, and never dies. Without beginning, ever existing, this Ancient One is not destroyed, when the body is destroyed. If the slayer thinks that he can slay, and if the slain man thinks he is slain, both are mistaken, for neither can the Self kill, nor can It be killed. Infinitely smaller than the smallest particle, infinitely greater than the greatest existence, the Lord of all lives in the cave of the heart of every being. He who has become sinless sees Him in all His glory, through the mercy of the same Lord. (We find that the mercy of God is one of the causes of God-realisation.) Sitting He goes far, lying He goes everywhere; who else but men of purified and subtle understanding are qualified to know the God in whom all conflicting attributes meet? Without body, yet living in the body, untouched, yet seemingly in contact, omnipresent — knowing the Âtman to be such, the sage gives up all misery. This Atman is not to be attained by the study of the Vedas, nor by the highest intellect, nor by much learning. Whom the Atman seeks, he gets the Atman; unto him He discloses His glory. He who is continuously doing evil deeds, he whose mind is not calm, he who cannot meditates he who is always disturbed and fickle — he cannot understand and realise this Atman who has entered the cave of the heart. This body, O Nachiketas, is the chariot, the organs of the senses are the horses, the mind is the reins, the intellect is the charioteer, and the soul is the rider in the chariot. When the soul joins himself with the charioteer, Buddhi or intellect, and then through it with the mind, the reins, and through it again with the organs, the horses, he is said to be the enjoyer; he perceives, he works, he acts. He whose mind is not under control, and who has no discrimination, his senses are not controllable like vicious horses in the hands of a driver. But he who has discrimination, whose mind is controlled, his organs are always controllable like good horses in the hands of a driver. He who has discrimination, whose mind is always in the way to understand truth, who is always pure — he receives that truth, attaining which there is no rebirth. This,

O Nachiketas, is very difficult, the way is long, and it is hard to attain. It is only those who have attained the finest perception that can see it, that can understand it. Yet do not be frightened. Awake, be up and doing. Do not stop till you have reached the goal. For the sages say that the task is very difficult, like walking on the edge of a razor. He who is beyond the senses, beyond all touch, beyond all form, beyond all taste, the Unchangeable, the Infinite, beyond even intelligence, the Indestructible — knowing Him alone, we are safe from the jaws of death."

So far, we see that Yama describes the goal that is to be attained. The first idea that we get is that birth, death, misery, and the various tossings about to which we are subject in the world can only be overcome by knowing that which is real. What is real? That which never changes, the Self of man, the Self behind the universe. Then, again, it is said that it is very difficult to know Him. Knowing does not mean simply intellectual assent, it means realisation. Again and again we have read that this Self is to be seen, to be perceived. We cannot see it with the eyes; the perception for it has to become superfine. It is gross perception by which the walls and books are perceived, but the perception to discern the truth has to be made very fine, and that is the whole secret of this knowledge. Then Yama says that one must be very pure. That is the way to making the perception superfine; and then he goes on to tell us other ways. That self-existent One is far removed from the organs. The organs or instruments see outwards, but the self-existing One, the Self, is seen inwards. You must remember the qualification that is required: the desire to know this Self by turning the eyes inwards. All these beautiful things that we see in nature are very good, but that is not the way to see God. We must learn how to turn the eyes inwards. The eagerness of the eyes to see outwards should be restricted. When you walk in a busy street, it is difficult to hear the man speak with whom you are walking, because of the noise of the passing carriages. He cannot hear you because there is so much noise. The mind is going outwards, and you cannot hear the man who is next to you. In the same way, this world around us is making such a noise that it draws the mind outwards. How can we see the Self? This going outwards must be stopped. That is what is meant by turning the eyes inwards, and then alone the glory of the Lord within will be seen.

What is this Self? We have seen that It is even beyond the intellect. We learn from the same Upanishad that this Self is eternal and omnipresent, that you and I and all of us are omnipresent beings, and that the Self is changeless. Now this omnipresent Being can be only one. There cannot be two beings who are equally omnipresent — how could that be? There cannot be two beings who are infinite, and the result is, there is really only one Self, and you, I, and the whole universe are but one, appearing as many. "As the one fire entering into the world manifests itself in various ways, even so that one Self, the Self of all, manifests Itself in every form." But the question is: If this Self is perfect and pure, and the One Being of the universe, what becomes of It when It goes into the impure body, the wicked body, the good body, and so on? How can It remain perfect? "The one sun is the cause of vision in every eye, yet it is not touched by the defects in the eyes of any." If a man has jaundice he sees everything as yellow; the cause of his vision is the sun, but his seeing everything as yellow does not touch the sun. Even so this One Being, though the Self of every one, is not touched by the purities or impurities outside. "In this world where everything is evanescent, he who knows Him who never changes, in this world of insentience, he who knows the one sentient Being, in this world of many, he who knows this One and sees Him in his own soul, unto him belongs eternal bliss, to none else, to none else. There the sun shines not, nor the stars, nor the lightning flashes, what to speak of fire? He shining, everything shines; through His light everything becomes effulgent. When all the desires that trouble the heart cease, then the mortal becomes immortal, and here one attains Brahman. When all the crookedness of the heart disappears, when all its knots are cut asunder, then alone the mortal becomes immortal. This is the way. May this study bless us; may it maintain us; may it give us strength, may it become energy in us; may we not hate each other; peace unto all!"

This is the line of thought that you will find in the Vedanta philosophy. We see first that here is a thought entirely different from what you see anywhere else in the world. In the oldest parts of the Vedas the search was the same as in other books, the search was outside. In some of the old, old books, the question was raised, "What was in the beginning? When there was neither aught nor naught, when darkness was covering darkness, who created all this?" So the search began. And they began to talk about the angels, the Devas, and all sorts of things, and later on we find that they gave it up as hopeless. In their day the search was outside and they could find nothing; but in later days, as we read in the Vedas, they had to look inside for the self-existent One. This Is the one fundamental idea in the Vedas, that our search in the stars, the nebulae, the Milky Way, in the whole of this external universe leads to nothing, never solves the problem of life and death. The wonderful mechanism inside had to be analysed, and it revealed to them the secret of the universe; nor star or sun could do it. Man had to be anatomised; not the body, but the soul of man. In that soul they found the answer. What was the answer they found? That behind the body, behind even the mind, there is the self-existent One. He dies not, nor is He born. The self-existent One it omnipresent, because He has no form. That which has no form or shape, that which is not limited by space or time, cannot live in a certain place. How can it? It is everywhere, omnipresent, equally present through all of us.

What is the soul of man? There was one party who held that there is a Being, God, and an infinite number of souls besides, who are eternally separate from God in essence, and form, and everything. This is dualism. This is the old, old crude idea. The answer given by another party was that the soul was a part of the infinite Divine Existence. Just as this body is a little world by itself, and behind it is the mind or thought, and behind that is the individual soul, similarly, the whole world is a body, and behind that is the universal mind, and behind that is the universal Soul. Just as this body is a portion of the universal body, so this mind is a portion of the universal mind, and the soul of man a portion of the universal Soul. This is what is called the Vishishtâdvaita, qualified monism. Now, we know that the universal Soul is infinite. How can infinity have parts? How can it be broken up, divided? It may be very poetic to say that I am a spark of the Infinite, but it is absurd to the thinking mind. What is meant by dividing Infinity? Is it something material that you can part or separate it into pieces? Infinite can never be divided. If that were possible, it would be no more Infinite. What is the conclusion then? The answer is, that Soul which is the universal is you; you are not a part but the whole of It. You are the whole of God. Then what are all these varieties? We find so many millions of individual souls. What are they? If the sun reflects upon millions of globules of water, in each globule is the form, the perfect image of the sun; but they are only images, and the real sun is only one. So this apparent soul that is in every one of us is only the image of God, nothing beyond that. The real Being who is behind, is that one God. We are all one there. As Self, there is only one in the universe. It is in me and you, and is only one; and that one Self has been reflected in all these various bodies as various different selves. But we do not know this; we think we are separate from each other and separate from Him. And so long as we think this, misery will be in the world. This is hallucination.

Then the other great source of misery is fear. Why does one man injure another? Because he fears he will not have enough enjoyment. One man fears that, perhaps, he will not have enough money, and that fear causes him to injure others and rob them. How can there be fear if there is only one existence? If a thunderbolt falls on my head, it was I who was the thunderbolt, because I am the only existence. If a plague comes, it is I; if a tiger comes, it is I. If death comes, it is I. I am both death and life. We see that fear comes with the idea that there are two in the universe. We have always heard it preached, "Love one another". What for? That doctrine was preached, but the explanation is here. Why should I love every one? Because they and I are one. Why should I love my brother? Because he and I are one. There is this oneness; this solidarity of the whole universe. From the lowest worm that crawls under our feet to the highest beings that ever lived — all have various bodies, but are the one Soul. Through all mouths, you eat; through all hands, you work; through all eyes, you see. You enjoy health in millions of bodies, you are suffering from disease in millions of bodies. When this idea comes, and we realise it, see it, feel it, then will misery cease, and fear with it. How can I die? There is nothing beyond me. Fear ceases, and then alone comes perfect happiness and perfect love. That universal sympathy, universal love, universal bliss, that never changes, raises man above everything. It has no reactions and no misery can touch it; but this little eating and drinking of the world always brings a reaction. The whole cause of it is this dualism, the idea that I am separate from the universe, separate from God. But as soon as we have realised that "I am He, I am the Self of the universe, I am eternally blessed, eternally free" — then will come real love, fear will vanish, and all misery cease.

YAJNAVALKYA AND MAITREYI

We say, "That day is indeed a bad day on which you do not hear the name of the Lord, but a cloudy day is not a bad day at all." Yâjnavalkya was a great sage. You know, the Shastras in India enjoin that every man should give up the world when he becomes old. So Yajnavalkya said to his wife, "My beloved, here is all my money, and my possessions, and I am going away." She replied, "Sir, if I had this whole earth full of wealth, would that give me immortality?" Yajnavalkya said, "No, it will not. You will be rich, and that will be all, but wealth cannot give us immortality." She replied, "what shall I do to gain that through which I shall become immortal? If you know, tell me." Yajnavalkya replied, "You have been always my beloved; you are more beloved now by this question. Come, take your seat, and I will tell you; and when you have heard, meditate upon it." He said, "It is not for the sake of the husband that the wife loves the husband, but for the sake of the Âtman that she loves the husband, because she loves the Self. None loves the wife for the sake of the wife; but it is because one loves the Self that one loves the wife. None loves the children for the children; but because one loves the Self, therefore one loves the children. None loves wealth on account of the wealth; but because one loves the Self, therefore one loves wealth. None loves the Brâhmin for the sake of the Brahmin; but because one loves the Self, one loves the Brahmin. So, none loves the Kshatriya for the sake of the Kshatriya, but because one loves the Self. Neither does any one love the world on account of the world, but because one loves the Self. None, similarly, loves the gods on account of the gods, but because one loves the Self. None loves a thing for that thing's sake; but it is for the Self that one loves it. This Self, therefore, is to be heard, reasoned about, and meditated upon. O my Maitreyi, when that Self has been heard, when that Self has been seen, when that Self has been realised, then, all this becomes known." What do we get then? Before us we find a curious philosophy. The statement has been made that every love is selfishness in the lowest sense of the word: because I love myself, therefore I love another; it cannot be. There have been philosophers in modern times who have said that self is the only motive power in the world. That is true, and yet it is wrong. But this self is but the shadow of that real Self which is behind. It appears wrong and evil because it is small. That infinite love for the Self, which is the universe, appears to be evil, appears to be small, because it appears through a small part. Even when the wife loves the husband, whether she knows it or not, she loves the husband for that Self. It is selfishness as it is manifested in the world, but that selfishness is really but a small part of that Self-ness. Whenever one loves, one has to love in and through the Self. This Self has to be known. What is the difference? Those that love the Self without knowing what It is, their love is selfishness. Those that love, knowing what that Self is, their love is free; they are sages. "Him the Brahmin gives up who sees the Brahmin anywhere else but in the Self. Him the Kshatriya gives up who sees the Kshatriya anywhere else but in the Self. The world gives him up who sees this world anywhere but in that Atman. The gods give him up who loves the gods knowing them to be anywhere else but in the Atman. Everything goes away from him who knows everything as something else except the Atman. These Brahmins, these Kshatriyas, this world, these gods, whatever exists, everything is that Atman". Thus he explains what he means by love.

Every time we particularise an object, we differentiate it from the Self. I am trying to love a woman; as soon as that woman is particularised, she is separated from the Atman, and my love for her will not be eternal, but will end in grief. But as soon as I see that woman as the Atman, that love becomes perfect, and will never suffer. So with everything; as soon as you are attached to anything in the universe, detaching it from the universe as a whole, from the Atman, there comes a reaction. With everything that we love outside the Self, grief and misery will be the result. If we enjoy everything in the Self, and as the Self, no misery or reaction will come. This is perfect bliss. How to come to this ideal? Yajnavalkya goes on to tell us the process by which to reach that state. The universe is infinite: how can we take every particular thing and look at it as the Atman, without knowing the Atman? "As with a drum when we are at a distance we cannot catch the sound, we cannot conquer the sound; but as soon as we come to the drum and put our hand on it, the sound is conquered. When the conch-shell is being blown, we cannot catch or conquer the sound, until we come near and get hold of the shell, and then it is conquered. When the Vina is being played, when we have come to the Vina, we get to the centre whence the sound is proceeding. As when some one is burning damp fuel, smoke and sparks of various kinds come, even so, from this great One has been breathed out knowledge; everything has come out of Him. He breathed out, as it were, all knowledge. As to all water, the one goal is the ocean; as to all touch, the skin is the one centre; as of all smell, the nose is the one centre; as of all taste, the tongue is the one goal; as of all form, the eyes are the one goal; as of all sounds, the ears are the one goal; as of all thought, the mind is the one goal; as of all knowledge, the heart is the one goal; as of all work, the hands are the one goal; as a morsel of salt put into the sea-water melts away, and we cannot take it back, even so, Maitreyi, is this Universal Being eternally infinite; all knowledge is in Him. The whole universe rises from Him, and again goes down into Him. No more is there any knowledge, dying, or death." We get the idea that we have all come just like sparks from Him, and when you know Him, then you go back and become one with Him again. We are the Universal.

Maitreyi became frightened, just as everywhere people become frightened. Said she, "Sir, here is exactly where you have thrown a delusion over me. You have frightened me by saying there will be no more gods; all individuality will be lost. There will be no one to recognise, no one to love, no one to hate. What will become of us?" "Maitreyi, I do not mean to puzzle you, or rather let it rest here. You may be frightened. Where there are two, one sees another, one hears another, one welcomes another, one thinks of another, one knows another. But when the whole has become that Atman, who is seen by whom, who is to be heard by whom, who is to be welcomed by whom, who is to be known by whom?" That one idea was taken up by Schopenhauer and echoed in his philosophy. Through whom we know this universe, through what to know Him? How to know the knower? By what means can we know the knower? How can that be? Because in and through that we know everything. By what means can we know Him? By no means, for He is that means.

So far the idea is that it is all One Infinite Being. That is the real individuality, when there is no more division, and no more parts; these little ideas are very low, illusive. But yet in and through every spark of the individuality is shining that Infinite. Everything is a manifestation of the Atman. How to reach that? First you make the statement, just as Yajnavalkya himself tells us: "This Atman is first to be heard of." So he stated the case; then he argued it out, and the last demonstration was how to know

That, through which all knowledge is possible. Then, last, it is to be meditated upon. He takes the contrast, the microcosm and the macrocosm, and shows how they are rolling on in particular lines, and how it is all beautiful. "This earth is so blissful, so helpful to every being; and all beings are so helpful to this earth: all these are manifestations of that Self-effulgent One, the Atman." All that is bliss, even in the lowest sense, is but the reflection of Him. All that is good is His reflection, and when that reflection is a shadow it is called evil. There are no two Gods. When He is less manifested, it is called darkness, evil; and when He is more manifested, it is called light. That is all. Good and evil are only a question of degree: more manifested or less manifested. Just take the example of our own lives. How many things we see in our childhood which we think to be good, but which really are evil, and how many things seem to be evil which are good! How the ideas change! How an idea goes up and up! What we thought very good at one time we do not think so good now. So good and evil are but superstitions, and do not exist. The difference is only in degree. It is all a manifestation of that Atman; He is being manifested in everything; only, when the manifestation is very thick we call it evil; and when it is very thin, we call it good. It is the best, when all covering goes away. So everything that is in the universe is to be meditated upon in that sense alone, that we can see it as all good, because it is the best. There is evil and there is good; and the apex, the centre, is the Reality. He is neither evil nor good; He is the best. The best can be only one, the good can be many and the evil many. There will be degrees of variation between the good and the evil, but the best is only one, and that best, when seen through thin coverings, we call different sorts of good, and when through thick covers, we call evil. Good and evil are different forms of superstition. They have gone through all sorts of dualistic delusion and all sorts of ideas, and the words have sunk into the hearts of human beings, terrorising men and women and living there as terrible tyrants. They make us become tigers. All the hatred with which we hate others is caused by these foolish ideas which we have imbibed since our childhood — good and evil. Our judgment of humanity becomes entirely false; we make this beautiful earth a hell; but as soon as we can give up good and evil, it becomes a heaven.

"This earth is blissful ('sweet' is the literal translation) to all beings and all beings are sweet to this earth; they all help each other. And all the sweetness is the Atman, that effulgent, immortal One who is inside this earth." Whose is this sweetness? How can there be any sweetness but He? That one sweetness is manifesting itself in various ways. Wherever there is any love, any sweetness in any human being, either in a saint or a sinner, either in an angel or a murderer, either in the body, mind, or the senses, it is He. Physical enjoyments are but He, mental enjoyments are but He, spiritual enjoyments are but He. How can there be anything but He? How can there be twenty thousand gods and devils fighting with each other? Childish dreams! Whatever is the lowest physical enjoyment is He, and the highest spiritual enjoyment is He. There is no sweetness but He. Thus says Yajnavalkya. When you come to that state and look upon all things with the same eye, when you see even in the drunkard's pleasure in drink only that sweetness, then you have got the truth, and then alone you will know what happiness means, what peace means, what love means; and so long as toll make these vain distinctions, silly, childish, foolish superstitions, all sorts of misery will come. But that immortal One, the effulgent One, He is inside the earth, it is all His sweetness, and the same sweetness is in the body. This body is the earth, as it were, and inside all the powers of the body, all the enjoyments of the body, is He; the eyes see, the skin touches; what are all these enjoyments? That Self-effulgent One who is in the body, He is the Atman. This world, so sweet to all beings, and every being so sweet to it, is but the Self-effulgent; the Immortal is the bliss in that world. In us also, He is that bliss. He is the Brahman. "This air is so sweet to all beings, and all beings are so sweet to it. But He who is that Self-effulgent Immortal Being in the air — is also in this body. He is expressing Himself as the life of all beings. This sun is so sweet to all beings. All beings are so sweet to this sun. He who is the Self-effulgent Being in the sun, we reflect Him as the smaller light. What can be there but His reflection? He is in the body, and it is His reflection which makes us see the light. This moon is so sweet to all, and every one is so sweet to the moon, but that Self-effulgent and Immortal One who is the soul of that moon, He is in us expressing Himself as mind. This lightning is so beautiful, every one is so sweet to the lightning, but the Self-effulgent and Immortal One is the soul of this lightning, and is also in us, because all is that Brahman. The Atman, the Self, is the king of all beings." These ideas are very helpful to men; they are for meditation. For instance, meditate on the earth; think of the earth and at the same time know that we have That which is in the earth, that both are the same. Identify the body with the earth, and identify the soul with the Soul behind. Identify the air with the soul that is in the air and that is in me. They are all one, manifested in different forms. To realise this unity is the end and aim of all meditation, and this is what Yajnavalkya was trying to explain to Maitreyi.

SOUL, NATURE, AND GOD

According to the Vedanta philosophy, man consists of three substances, so to say. The outermost is the body, the gross form of man, in which are the instruments of sensation, such as the eyes, nose, ears, and so forth. This eye is not the organ of vision; it is only the instrument. Behind that is the organ. So, the ears are not the organs of hearing; they are the instruments, and behind them is the organ, or what, in modern physiology, is called the centre. The organs are called Indriyas in Sanskrit. If the centre which governs the eyes be destroyed, the eyes will not see; so with all our senses. The organs, again, cannot sense anything by themselves, until there be something else attached to them. That something is the mind. Many times you have observed that you were deeply engaged in a certain thought, and the clock struck and you did not hear it. Why? The ear was there; vibrations entered it and were carried into the brain, yet you did not hear, because the mind was not joined to the organ. The impressions of external objects are carried to the organs, and when the mind is attached to them, it takes the impressions and gives them, as it were, a colouring, which is called egoism, "I". Take the case of a mosquito biting me on the finger when I am engaged in some work. I do not feel it, because my mind is joined to something else. Later, when my mind is joined to the impression conveyed to the Indriyas, a reaction comes. With this reaction I become conscious of the mosquito. So even the mind joining itself to the organs is not sufficient; there must come the reaction in the form of will. This faculty from which the reaction comes, the faculty of knowledge or intellect, is called "Buddhi" First, there must be the external instrument, next the organ, next the mind must join itself to the organ, then must come the reaction of intellect, and when all these things are complete, there immediately flashes the idea, "I and the external object", and there is a perception, a concept, knowledge. The external organ, which is only the instrument, is in the body, and behind that is the internal organ which is finer; then there is the mind, then the intellectual faculty, then egoism, which says, "I" — I see, I hear, and so forth. The whole process is carried on by certain forces; you may call them vital forces; in Sanskrit they are called Prâna. This gross part of man, this body, in which are the external instruments, is called in Sanskrit, Sthula Sharira, the gross body; behind it comes the series, beginning with the organs, the mind, the intellect, the egoism. These and the vital forces form a compound which is called the fine body, the Sukshma Sharira. These forces are composed of very fine elements, so fine that no amount of injury to this body can destroy them; they survive all the shocks given to this body. The gross body we see is composed of gross material, and as such it is always being renewed and changing continuously. But the internal organs, the mind, the intellect, and the egoism are composed of the finest material, so fine that they will endure for aeons and aeons. They are so fine that they cannot be resisted by anything; they can get through any obstruction. The gross body is non-intelligent, so is the fine, being composed of fine matter. Although one part is called mind, another the intellect, and the third egoism, yet we see at a glance that no one of them can be the "Knower". None of them can be the perceiver, the witness, the one for whom action is made, and who is the seer of the action. All these movements in the mind, or the faculty of intellection, or egoism, must be for some one else. These being composed of fine matter cannot be self-effulgent. Their luminosity cannot be in themselves. This manifestation of the table, for instance, cannot be due to any material thing. Therefore there must be some one behind them all, who is the real manifester, the real seer, the real enjoyer and He in Sanskrit is called the Atman, the Soul of man, the real Self of man. He it is who really sees things. The external instruments and the organs catch the impressions and convey them to the mind, and the mind to the intellect, and the intellect reflects them as on a mirror, and back of it is the Soul that looks on them and gives His orders and His directions. He is the ruler of all these instruments, the master in the house, the enthroned king in the body. The faculty of egoism, the faculty of intellection, the faculty of cogitation, the organs, the instruments, the body, all of them obey His commands. It is He who is manifesting all of these. This is the Atman of man. Similarly, we can see that what is in a small part of the universe must also be in the whole universe. If conformity is the law of the universe, every part of the universe must have been built on the same plan as the whole. So we naturally think that behind the gross material form which we call this universe of ours, there must be a universe of finer matter, which we call thought, and behind that there must be a Soul, which makes all this thought possible, which commands, which is the enthroned king of this universe. That soul which is behind each mind and each body is called Pratyagâtman, the individual Atman, and that Soul which is behind the universe as its guide, ruler, and governor, is God.

The next thing to consider is whence all these things come. The answer is: What is meant by coming? If it means that something can be produced out of nothing, it is impossible. All this creation, manifestation, cannot be produced out of zero. Nothing can be produced without a cause, and the effect is but the cause reproduced. Here is a glass. Suppose we break it to pieces, and pulverise it, and by means of chemicals almost annihilate it. Will it go back to zero? Certainly not. The form will break, but the particles of which it is made will be there; they will go beyond our senses, but they remain, and it is quite possible that out of these materials another glass may be made. If this is true in one case, it will be so in every case. Something cannot be made out of nothing. Nor can something be made to go back to nothing. It may become finer and finer, and then again grosser and grosser. The raindrop is drawn from the ocean in the form of vapour, and drifts away through the air to the mountains; there it changes again into water and flows back through hundreds of miles down to the mother ocean. The seed produces the tree. The tree dies, leaving only the seed. Again it comes up as another tree, which again ends in the seed, and so on. Look at a bird, how from; the egg it springs, becomes a beautiful bird, lives its life and then dies, leaving only other eggs, containing germs of future birds. So with the animals; so with men. Everything begins, as it were, from certain seeds, certain rudiments, certain fine forms, and becomes grosser and grosser as it develops; and then again it goes back to that fine form and subsides. The whole universe is going on in this way. There comes a time when this whole universe melts down and becomes finer and at last disappears entirely, as it were, but remains as superfine matter. We know through modern science and astronomy that this earth is cooling down, and in course of time it will become very cold, and then it will break to pieces and become finer and finer until it becomes ether once more. Yet the particles will all remain to form the material out of which another earth will be projected. Again that will disappear, and another will come out. So this universe will go back to its causes, and again its materials will come together and take form, like the wave that goes down, rises again, and takes shape. The acts of going back to causes and coming out again, taking form, are called in Sanskrit Sankocha and Vikâsha, which mean shrinking and expanding. The whole universe, as it were, shrinks, and then it expands again. To use the more accepted words of modern science, they are involved and evolved. You hear about evolution, how all forms grow from lower ones, slowly growing up and up. This is very true, but each evolution presupposes an involution. We know that the sum total of energy that is displayed in the universe is the same at all times, and that matter is indestructible. By no means can you take away one particle of matter. You cannot take away a foot-pound of energy or add one. The sum total is the same always. Only the manifestation varies, being involved and evolved. So this cycle is the evolution out of the involution of the previous cycle, and this cycle will again be involved, getting finer and finer, and out of that will come the next cycle. The whole universe is going on in this fashion. Thus we find that there is no creation in the sense that something is created out of nothing. To use a better word, there is manifestation, and God is the manifester of the universe. The universe, as it were, is being breathed out of Him, and again it shrinks into Him, and again He throws it out. A most beautiful simile is given in the Vedas — "That eternal One breathes out this universe and breathes it in." Just as we can breathe out a little particle of dust and breathe it in again. That is all very good, but the question may be asked: How we, it at the first cycle? The answer is: What is the meaning of a first cycle? There was none. If you can give a beginning to time, the whole concept of time will be destroyed. Try to think of a limit where time began, you have to think of time beyond that limit. Try to think where space begins, you will have to think of space beyond that. Time and space are infinite, and therefore have neither beginning nor end. This is a better idea than that God created the universe in five minutes and then went to sleep, and since then has been sleeping. On the other hand, this idea will give us God as the Eternal Creator. Here is a series of waves rising and falling, and God is directing this eternal process. As the universe is without beginning and without end, so is God. We see that it must necessarily be so, because if we say there was a time when there was no creation, either in a gross or a fine form, then there was no God, because God is known to us as Sâkshi, the Witness of the universe. When the universe did not exist, neither did He. One concept follows the other. The idea of the cause we get from the idea of the effect, and if there is no effect, there will be no cause. It naturally follows that as the universe is eternal, God is eternal.

The soul must also be eternal. Why? In the first place we see that the soul is not matter. It is neither a gross body, nor a fine body, which we call mind or thought. It is neither a physical body, nor what in Christianity is called a spiritual body. It is the gross body and the spiritual body that are liable to change. The gross body is liable to change almost every minute and dies, but the spiritual body endures through long periods, until one becomes free, when it also falls away. When a man becomes free, the spiritual body disperses. The gross body disintegrates every time a man dies. The soul not being made of any particles must be indestructible. What do we mean by destruction? Destruction is disintegration of the materials out of which anything is composed. If this glass is broken into pieces, the materials will disintegrate, and that will be the destruction of the glass. Disintegration of particles is what we mean by destruction. It naturally follows that nothing that is not composed of particles can be destroyed, can ever be disintegrated. The soul is not composed of any materials. It is unity indivisible. Therefore it must be indestructible. For the same reasons it must also be without any beginning. So the soul is without any beginning and end.

We have three entities. Here is nature which is infinite, but changeful. The whole of nature is without beginning and end, but within it are multifarious changes. It is like a river that runs down to the sea for thousands of years. It is the same river always, but it is changing every minute, the particles of water are changing their position constantly. Then there is God, unchangeable, the ruler; and there is the soul unchangeable as God, eternal but under the ruler. One is the master, the other the servant, and the third one is nature.

God being the cause of the projection, the continuance, and the dissolution of the universe, the cause must be present to produce the effect. Not only so, the cause becomes the effect. Glass is produced out of certain materials and certain forces used by the manufacturer. In the glass there are those forces plus the materials. The forces used have become the force of adhesion, and if that force goes the glass will fall to pieces; the materials also are undoubtedly in the glass. Only their form is changed. The cause has become the effect. Wherever you see an effect you can always analyze it into a cause, the cause manifests itself as the effect. It follows, if God is the cause of the universe, and the universe is the effect, that God has become the universe. If souls are the effect, and God the cause, God has become the souls. Each soul, therefore, is a part of God. "As from a mass of fire an infinite number of sparks fly, even so from the Eternal One all this universe of souls has come out."

We have seen that there is the eternal God, and there is eternal nature. And there is also an infinite number of eternal souls. This is the first stage in religion, it is called dualism, the stage when man sees himself and God eternally separate, when God is a separate entity by Him, self and man is a separate entity by himself and nature is a separate entity by itself. This is dualism, which holds that the subject and the object are opposed to each other in everything. When man looks at nature, he is the subject and nature the object. He sees the dualism between subject and object. When he looks at God, he sees God as object and himself as the subject. They are entirely separate. This is the dualism between man and God. This is generally the first view of religion.

Then comes another view which I have just shown to you. Man begins to find out that if God is the cause of the universe and the universe the effect, God Himself must have become the universe and the souls, and he is but a particle of which God is the whole. We are but little beings, sparks of that mass of fire, and the whole universe is a manifestation of God Himself. This is the next step. In Sanskrit, it is called Vishishtâdvaita. Just as I have this body and this body covers the soul, and the soul is in and through this body, so this whole universe of infinite souls and nature forms, as it were, the body of God. When the period of involution comes, the universe becomes finer and finer, yet remains the body of God. When the gross manifestation comes, then also the universe remains the body of God. Just as the human soul is the soul of the human body and minds so God is the Soul of our souls. All of you have heard this expression in every religion, "Soul of our souls". That is what is meant by it. He, as it were, resides in them, guides them, is the ruler of them all. In the first view, that of dualism, each one of us is an individual, eternally separate from God and nature. In the second view, we are individuals, but not separate from God. We are like little particles floating in one mass, and that mass is God. We are individuals but one in God. We are all in Him. We are all parts of Him, and therefore we are One. And yet between man and man, man and God there is a strict individuality, separate and yet not separate.

Then comes a still finer question. The question is: Can infinity have parts? What is meant by parts of infinity? If you reason it out, you will find that it is impossible. Infinity cannot be divided, it always remains infinite. If it could be divided, each part would be infinite. And there cannot be two infinites. Suppose there were, one would limit the other, and both would be finite. Infinity can only be one, undivided. Thus the conclusion will be reached that the infinite is one and not many, and that one Infinite Soul is reflecting itself through thousands and thousands of mirrors, appearing as so many different souls. It is the same Infinite Soul, which is the background of the universe, that we call God. The same Infinite Soul also is the background of the human mind which we call the human soul.

COSMOLOGY

There are two worlds, the microcosm, and the macrocosm, the internal and the external. We get truth from both of these by means of experience. The truth gathered from internal experience is psychology, metaphysics, and religion; from external experience, the physical sciences. Now a perfect truth should be in harmony with experiences in both these worlds. The microcosm must bear testimony to the macrocosm, and the macrocosm to the microcosm; physical truth must have its counterpart in the internal world, and the internal world must have its verification outside. Yet, as a rule, we find that many of these truths are in conflict. At one period of the world's history, the internals become supreme, and they begin to fight the externals. At the present time the externals, the physicists, have become supreme, and they have put down many claims of psychologists and metaphysicians. So far as my knowledge goes, I find that the real, essential parts of psychology are in perfect accord with the essential parts of modern physical knowledge. It is not given to one individual to be great in every respect; it is not given to one race or nation to be equally strong in the research of all fields of knowledge. The modern European nations are very strong in their research of external physical knowledge, but they are not so strong in their study of the inner nature of man. On the other hand, the Orientals have not been very strong in their researches of the external physical world, but very strong in their researches of the internal. Therefore we find that Oriental physics and other sciences are not in accordance with Occidental Sciences; nor is Occidental psychology in harmony with Oriental psychology. The Oriental physicists have been routed by Occidental scientists. At the same time, each claims to rest on truth; and as we stated before, real truth in any field of knowledge will not contradict itself; the truths internal are in harmony with the truths external.

We all know the theories of the cosmos according to the modern astronomers and physicists; and at the same time we all know how woefully they undermine the theology of Europe, how these scientific discoveries that are made act as a bomb thrown at its stronghold; and we know how theologians have in all times attempted to put down these researches.

I want here to go over the psychological ideas of the Orientals about cosmology and all that pertains to it, and you will find how wonderfully they are in accordance with the latest discoveries of modern science; and where there is disharmony, you will find that it is modern science which lacks and not they. We all use the word nature. The old Sânkhya philosophers called it by two different names, Prakriti, which is very much the same as the word nature, and the more scientific name, Avyakta, undifferentiated, from which everything proceeds, such as atoms, molecules, and forces, mind, thought, and intelligence. It is startling to find that the philosophers and metaphysicians of India stated ages ago that mind is material. What are our present materialists trying to do, but to show that mind is as much a product of nature as the body? And so is thought, and, we shall find by and by, intelligence also: all issue from that nature which is called Avyakta, the undifferentiated. The Sankhyas define it as the equilibrium of three forces, one of which is called Sattva, another Rajas, and the third Tamas. Tamas, the lowest force, is that of attraction; a little higher is Rajas, that of repulsion; and the highest is the balance of these two, Sattva; so that when these two forces, attraction and repulsion, are held in perfect control by the Sattva there is no creation, no movement in the world. As soon as this equilibrium is lost, the balance is disturbed, and one of these forces gets stronger than the other, motion sets in, and creation begins. This state of things goes on cyclically, periodically. That is to say, there is a period of disturbance of the balance, when forces begin to combine and recombine, and things project outwards. At the same time, everything has a tendency to go back to the primal state of equilibrium, and the time comes when that total annihilation of all manifestation is reached. Again, after a period, the whole thing is disturbed, projected outwards, and again it slowly goes down — like waves. All motion, everything in this universe, can be likened to waves undergoing successive rise and fall. Some of these philosophers hold that the whole universe quiets down for a period. Others hold that this quieting down applies only to systems; that is to say, that while our system here, this solar system, will quiet down and go back into the undifferentiated state, millions of other systems will go the other way, and will project outwards. I should rather favour the second opinion, that this quieting down is not simultaneous over the whole of the universe, and that in different parts different things go on. But the principle remains the same, that all we see — that is, nature herself — is progressing in successive rises and falls. The one stage, falling down, going back to balance, the perfect equilibrium, is called Pralaya, the end of a cycle. The projection and the Pralaya of the universe have been compared by theistical writers in India to the outbreathing and inbreathing of God; God, as it were, breathes out the universe, and it comes into Him again. When it quiets down, what becomes of the universe? It exists, only in finer forms, in the form of cause, as it is called in the Sankhya philosophy. It does not get rid of causation, time, and space; they are there, only it comes to very fine and minute forms. Supposing that this whole universe begins to shrink, till every one of us becomes just a little molecule, we should not feel the change at all, because everything relating to us would be shrinking at the same time. The whole thing goes down, and again projects out, the cause brings out the effect, and so it goes on.

What we call matter in modern times was called by; the ancient psychologists Bhutas, the external elements. There is one element which, according to them, is eternal ; every other element is produced out of this one. It is called Âkâsha. It is somewhat similar to the idea of ether of the moderns, though not exactly similar. Along with this element, there is the primal energy called Prâna. Prana and Akasha combine and recombine and form the elements out of them. Then at the end of the Kalpa; everything subsides, and goes back to Akasha and Prana. There is in the Rig-Veda, the oldest human writing in existence, a beautiful passage describing creation, and it is most poetical — "When there was neither aught nor naught, when darkness was rolling over darkness, what existed?" and the answer is given, "It then existed without vibration". This Prana existed then, but there was no motion in it; Ânidavâtam means "existed without vibration". Vibration had stopped. Then when the Kalpa begins, after an immense interval, the Anidavatam (unvibrating atom) commences to vibrate, and blow after blow is given by Prana to Akasha. The atoms become condensed, and as they are condensed different elements are formed. We generally find these things very curiously translated; people do not go to the philosophers or the commentators for their translation, and have not the brains to understand them themselves. A silly man reads three letters of Sanskrit and translates a whole book. They translate the, elements as air, fire, and so on; if they would go to the commentators, they would find they do not mean air or anything of the sort.

The Akasha, acted upon by the repeated blows of Prana, produces Vâyu or vibrations. This Vayu vibrates, and the vibrations growing more and more rapid result in friction giving rise to heat, Tejas. Then this heat ends in liquefaction, Âpah. Then that liquid becomes solid. We had ether, and motion, then came heat, then it became liquefied, and then it condensed into gross matter; and it goes back in exactly the reverse way. The solid will be liquefied and will then be converted into a mass of heat, and that will slowly get back into motion; that motion will stop, and this Kalpa will be destroyed. Then, again it will come back and again dissolve into ether. Prana cannot work alone without the help of Akasha. All that we know in the form of motion, vibration, or thought is a modification of the Prana, and everything that we know in the shape of matter, either as form or as resistance, is a modification of the Akasha. The Prana cannot live alone, or act without a medium; when it is pure Prana, it has the Akasha itself to live in, and when it changes into forces of nature, say gravitation, or centrifugal force, it must have matter. You have never seen force without matter or matter without force; what we call force and matter are simply the gross manifestations of these same things, which, when superfine, are called Prana and Akasha. Prana you can call in English life, the vital force; but you must not restrict it to the life of man; at the same time you must not identify it with Spirit, Atman. So this goes on. Creation cannot have either a beginning or an end; it is an eternal on-going.

We shall state another position of these old psychologists, which is that all gross things are the results of fine ones. Everything that is gross is composed of fine things, which they call the Tanmâtras, the fine particles. I smell a flower. To smell, something must come in contact with my nose; the flower is there, but I do not see it move towards me. That which comes from the flower and in contact with my nose is called the Tanmatra, fine molecules of that flower. So with heat, light and everything. These Tanmatras can again be subdivided into atoms. Different philosophers have different theories, and we know these are only theories. It is sufficient for our purpose to know that everything gross is composed of things that are very, very fine. We first get the gross elements which we feel externally, and then come the fine elements with which the nose, eyes, and ears come in contact. Ether waves touch my eyes; I cannot see them, yet I know they must come in contact with my eyes before I can see light.

Here are the eyes, but the eyes do not see. Take away the brain centre; the eyes will still be there, as also the picture of the outside world complete on the retinae; yet the eyes will not see. So the eyes are only a secondary instrument, not the organ of vision. The organ of vision is the nerve-centre in the brain. Likewise the nose is an instrument, and there is an organ behind it. The senses are simply the external instruments. It may be said that these different organs, Indriyas, as they are called in Sanskrit, are the real seats of perception.

It is necessary for the mind to be joined to an organ to perceive. It is a common experience that we do not hear the clock strike when we happen to be buried in study. Why? The ear was there, the sound was carried through it to the brain; yet it was not heard, because the mind did not attach itself to the organ of hearing.

There is a different organ for each different instrument. For, if one served for all, we should find that when the mind joined itself to it, all the senses would be equally active. But it is not so, as we have seen from the instance of the clock. If there was only one organ for all the instruments, the mind would see and hear at the same time, would see and hear and smell at the same time, and it would be impossible for it not to do all these at one and the same time. Therefore it is necessary that there should be a separate organ for each sense. This has been borne out by modern physiology. It is certainly possible for us to hear and see at the same time, but that is because the mind attaches itself partially to the two centres.

What are the organs made of? We see that the instruments — eyes, nose, and ears — are made of gross materials. The organs are also made of matter. Just as the body is composed of gross materials, and manufactures Prana into different gross forces, so the organs are composed of the fine elements, Akasha, Vayu, Tejas, etc., and manufacture Prana into the finer forces of perception. The organs, the Prana functions, the mind and the Buddhi combined, are called the finer body of man — the Linga or Sukshma Sharira. The Linga Sharira has a real form because everything material must have a form.

The mind is called the Manas, the Chitta in Vritti or vibrating, the unsettled state. If you throw a stone in a lake, first there will be vibration, and then resistance. For a moment the water will vibrate and then it will react on the stone. So when any impression comes on the Chitta, it first vibrates a little. That is called the Manas. The mind carries the impression farther in, and presents it to the determinative faculty, Buddhi, which reacts. Behind Buddhi is Ahamkâra, egoism, the self-consciousness which says, "I am". Behind Ahamkara is Mahat, intelligence, the highest form of nature's existence. Each one is the effect of the succeeding one. In the case of the lake, every blow that comes to it is from the external world, while in the case of the mind, the blow may come either from the external or the internal world. Behind the intelligence is the Self of man, the Purusha, the Atman, the pure, the perfect, who alone is the seer, and for whom is all this change.

Man looks on all these changes; he himself is never impure; but through what the Vedantists call Adhyâsa, by reflection, by implication, he seems to be impure. It is like the appearance of a crystal when a red or a blue flower is brought before it: the colour is reflected on it, but the crystal itself is pure. We shall take it for granted that there are many selves, and each self is pure and perfect; various kinds of gross and fine matter superimpose themselves on the self and make it multicoloured. Why does nature do all this? Nature is undergoing all these changes for the development of the soul; all this creation is for the benefit of the soul, so that it may be free. This immense book which we call the universe is stretched out before man so that he may read; and he discovers eventually that he is an omniscient and omnipotent being. I must here tell you that some of our best psychologists do not believe in God in the sense in which you believe in Him. The father of our psychology, Kapila, denies the existence of God. His idea is that a Personal God is quite unnecessary; nature itself is sufficient to work out the whole of creation. What is called the Design Theory, he knocked on the head, and said that a more childish theory was never advanced. But he admits a peculiar kind of God. He says we are all struggling to get free; and when we become free, we can, as it were, melt away into nature, only to come out at the beginning of the next cycle and be its ruler. We come out omniscient and omnipotent beings. In that sense we can be called Gods; you and I and the humblest beings can be Gods in different cycles. He says such a God will be temporal; but an eternal God, eternally omnipotent and ruler of the universe cannot be. If there was such a God, there would be this difficulty: He must be either a bound spirit or a free one. A God who is perfectly free would not create: there is no necessity for it. If He were bound, He would not create, because He could not: He would be powerless. In either case, there cannot be any omniscient or omnipotent eternal ruler. In our scriptures, wherever the word God is mentioned, he says, it means those human beings who have become free.

Kapila does not believe in the unity of all souls. His analysis, so far as it goes, is simply marvellous. He is the father of Indian thinkers; Buddhism and other systems are the outcome of his thought.

According to his psychology, all souls can regain their freedom and their natural rights, which are omnipotence and omniscience. But the question arises: Where is this bondage? Kapila says it is without beginning. But if it is without beginning, it must be without end, and we shall never be free. He says that though bondage is without beginning, it is not of that constant uniform character as the soul is. In other words, nature (the cause of bondage) is without beginning and end, but not in the same sense as soul, because nature has no individuality; it is like a river which gets a fresh body of water every moment; the sum total of these bodies of water is the river, but the river is not a constant quantity. Everything in nature is constantly changing, but the soul never changes; so, as nature is always changing, it is possible for the soul to come out of its bondage.

The whole of the universe is built upon the same plan as a part of it. So, just as I have a mind, there is a cosmic mind. As in the individual, so in the universal. There is the universal gross body; behind that, a universal fine body; behind that, a universal mind; behind that, a universal egoism, or consciousness; and behind that, a universal intelligence. And all this is in nature, the manifestation of nature, not outside of it.

We have the gross bodies from our parents, as also our consciousness. Strict heredity says my body is a part of my parents' bodies, the material of my consciousness and egoism is a part of my parents'. We can add to the little portion inherited from our parents by drawing upon the universal consciousness. There is an infinite storehouse of intelligence out of which we draw what we require; there is an infinite storehouse of mental force in the universe out of which we are drawing eternally; but the seed must come from the parents. Our theory is heredity coupled with reincarnation. By the law of heredity, the reincarnating soul receives from parents the material out of which to manufacture a man.

A STUDY OF THE SANKHYA PHILOSOPHY

Some of the European philosophers have asserted that this world exists because I exist; and if I do not exist, the world will not exist. Sometimes it is stated thus: If all the people in the world were to die, and there were no more human beings, and no animals with powers of perception and intelligence, all these manifestations would disappear. But these European philosophers do not know the psychology of it, although they know the principle; modern philosophy has got only a glimpse of it. This becomes easy of understanding when looked at from the Sankhya point of view. According to Sankhya, it is impossible for anything to be, which has not as its material, some portion of my mind. I do not know this table as it is. An impression from it comes to the eyes, then to, the Indriya, and then to the mind; and the mind reacts, and that reaction is what I call the table. It is just the same as throwing a stone in a lake; the lake throws a wave towards the stone; this wave is what we know. What is external nobody knows; when I try to know it, it has to become that material which I furnish. I, with my own mind, have furnished the material for my eyes. There is something which is outside, which is only, the occasion, the suggestion, and upon that suggestion I project my mind; and it takes the form that I see. How do we all see the same things? Because we all have; similar parts of the cosmic mind. Those who have like minds will see like things, and those who have not will not see alike.

Prakriti is called by the Sânkhya philosophers indiscrete, and defined as the perfect balance of the materials in it; and it naturally follows that in perfect balance there cannot be any motion. In the primal state before any manifestation, when there was no motion but perfect balance, this Prakriti was indestructible, because decomposition or death comes from instability or change. Again, according to the Sankhya, atoms are not the primal state. This universe does not come out of atoms: they may be the secondary or the tertiary state. The primordial material may form into atoms and become grosser and bigger things; and as far as modern investigations go, they rather point towards the same conclusion. For instance, in the modern theory of ether, if you say ether is atomic, it will not solve anything. To make it clearer, say that air is composed of atoms, and we know that ether is everywhere, interpenetrating, omnipresent, and that these air atoms are floating, as it were, in ether. If ether again be composed of atoms, there will still be spaces between every two atoms of ether. What fills up these? If you suppose that there is another ether still finer which does this, there will again be other spaces between the atoms of that finer ether which require filling up, and so it will be regressus ad infinitum, what the Sankhya philosophers call the "cause leading to nothing" So the atomic theory cannot be final. According to Sankhya, nature is omnipresent, one omnipresent mass of nature, in which are the causes of everything that exists. What is meant by cause? Cause is the fine state of the manifested state; the unmanifested state of that which becomes manifested. What do you mean by destruction? It is reverting to the cause If you have a piece of pottery and give it a blow, it is destroyed. What is meant by this is that the effects go back to their own nature, they materials out of which the pottery was created go back into their original state. Beyond this idea of destruction, any idea such as annihilation is on the face of it absurd. According to modern physical science, it can be demonstrated that all destruction means that which Kapila said ages ago — simply reverting to the cause. Going back to the finer form is all that is meant by destruction. You know how it can be demonstrated in a laboratory that matter is indestructible. At this present stage of our knowledge, if any man stands up and says that matter or this soul becomes annihilated, he is only making himself, ridiculous; it is only uneducated, silly people who would advance such a proposition; and it is curious that modern knowledge coincides with what those old philosophers taught. It must be so, and that is the proof of truth. They proceeded in their inquiry, taking up mind as the basis; they analysed the mental part of this universe and came to certain conclusions, which we, analysing the physical part, must come to, for they both must lead to the same centre.

You must remember that the first manifestation of this Prakriti in the cosmos is what the Sankhya calls "Mahat". We may call it intelligence — the great principle, its literal meaning. The first change in Prakriti is this intelligence; I would not translate it by self-consciousness, because that would be wrong. Consciousness is only a part of this intelligence. Mahat is universal. It covers all the grounds of sub-consciousness, consciousness, and super-consciousness; so any one state of consciousness, as applied to this Mahat, would not be sufficient. In nature, for instance, you note certain changes going on before your eyes which you see and understand, but there are other changes, so much finer, that no human perception can catch them. The are from the same cause, the same Mahat is making these changes. Out of Mahat comes universal egoism. These are all substance. There is no difference between matter and mind, except in degree. The substance is the same in finer or grosser form; one changes into the other, and this exactly coincides with the conclusions of modern physiological research. By believing in the teaching that the mind is not separate from the brain, you will be saved from much fighting and struggling. Egoism again changes into two varieties. In one variety it changes into the organs. Organs are of two kinds, organs of sensation and organs of reaction. They are not the eyes or the ears, but back of those are what you call brain-centres, and nerve-centres, and so on. This egoism, this matter or substance, becomes changed, and out of this material are manufactured these centres. Of the same substance is manufactured the other variety, the Tanmatras, fine particles of matter, which strike our organs of perception and bring about sensations. You cannot perceive them but only know they are there. Out of the Tanmatras is manufactured the gross matter — earth, water, and all the things that we see and feel. I want to impress this on your mind. It is very, hard to grasp it, because in Western countries the ideas are so queer about mind and matter. It is hard to get those impressions out of our brains. I myself had a tremendous difficulty, being educated in Western philosophy in my boyhood. These are all cosmic things. Think of this universal extension of matter, unbroken, one substance, un-differentiated, which is the first state of everything, and which begins to change in the same way as milk becomes curd. This first change is called Mahat. The substance Mahat changes into the grosser matter called egoism. The third change is manifested as universal sense-organs, and universal fine particles, and these last again combine and become this gross universe which with eyes, nose, and ears, we see, smell, and hear. This is the cosmic plan according to the Sankhya, and what is in the cosmos must also be microcosmic. Take an individual man. He has first a part of undifferentiated nature in him, and that material nature in him becomes changed into this Mahat, a small particle of this universal intelligence, and this particle of universal intelligence in him becomes changed into egoism, and then into the sense-organs and the fine particles of matter which combine and manufacture his body. I want this to be clear, because it is the stepping-stone to Sankhya, and it is absolutely necessary for you to understand it, because this is the basis of the philosophy of the whole world. There is no philosophy in the world that is not indebted to Kapila. Pythagoras came to India and studied this philosophy, and that was the beginning of the philosophy of the Greeks. Later, it formed the Alexandrian school, and still later, the

Gnostic. It became divided into two; one part went to Europe and Alexandria, and the other remained in India; and out of this, the system of Vyasa was developed. The Sankhya philosophy of Kapila was the first rational system that the world ever saw. Every metaphysician in the world must pay homage to him. I want to impress on your mind that we are bound to listen to him as the great father of philosophy. This wonderful man, the most ancient of philosophers, is mentioned even in the Shruti: "O Lord, Thou who produced the sage Kapila in the Beginning." How wonderful his perceptions were, and if there is ant proof required of the extraordinary power of the perception of Yogis, such men are the proof. They had no microscopes or telescopes. Yet how fine their perception was, how perfect and wonderful their analysis of things!

I will here point out the difference between Schopenhauer and the Indian philosophy. Schopenhauer says that desire, or will, is the cause of everything. It is the will to exist that make us manifest, but we deny this. The will is identical with the motor nerves. When I see an object there is no will; when its sensations are carried to the brain, there comes the reaction, which says "Do this", or "Do not do this", and this state of the ego-substance is what is called will. There cannot be a single particle of will which is not a reaction. So many things precede will. It is only a manufactured something out of the ego, and the ego is a manufacture of something still higher — the intelligence — and that again is a modification of the indiscrete nature. That was the Buddhistic idea, that whatever we see is the will. It is psychologically entirely wrong, because will can only be identified with the motor nerves. If you take out the motor nerves, a man has no will whatever. This fact, as is perhaps well known to you, has been found out after a long series of experiments made with the lower animals.

We will take up this question. It is very important to understand this question of Mahat in man, the great principle, the intelligence. This intelligence itself is modified into what we call egoism, and this intelligence is the cause of all the powers in the body. It covers the whole ground, sub-consciousness, consciousness, and super-consciousness. What are these three states? The sub-conscious state we find in animals, which we call instinct. This is almost infallible, but very limited. Instinct rarely fails. An animal almost instinctively knows a poisonous herb from an edible one, but its instinct is very limited. As soon as something new comes, it is blind. It works like a machine. Then comes a higher state of knowledge which is fallible and makes mistakes often, but has a larger scope, although it is slow, and this you call reason. It is much larger than instinct, but instinct is surer than reason. There are more chances of mistakes in reasoning than in instinct. There is a still higher state of the mind, the super-conscious, which belongs only to Yogis, to men who have cultivated it. This is infallible and much more unlimited in its scope than reason. This is the highest state. So we must remember, this Mahat is the real cause of all that is here, that which manifests itself in various ways, covers the whole ground of sub-conscious, conscious, and super-conscious, the three states in which knowledge exists.

Now comes a delicate question which is being always asked. If a perfect God created the universe, why is there imperfection in it? What we call the universe is what we see, and that is only this little plane of consciousness and reason; beyond that we do not see at all. Now the very question is an impossible one. If I take only a small portion out of a mass of something and look at it, it seems to be inharmonious. Naturally. The universe is inharmonious because we make it so. How? What is reason? What is knowledge? Knowledge is finding the association about things. You go into the street and see a man and say, I know this is a man; because you remember the impressions on your mind, the marks on the Chitta. You have seen many men, and each one has made an impression on your mind; and as you see this man, you refer this to your store and see many similar pictures there; and when you see them, you are satisfied, and you put this new one with the rest. When a new impression comes and it has associations in your mind, you are satisfied; and this state of association is called knowledge. Knowledge is, therefore, pigeon-holing one experience with the already existing fund of experience, and this is one of the great proofs of the fact that you cannot have any knowledge until you have already a fund in existence. If you are without experience, as some European philosophers think, and that your mind is a tabula rasa to begin with, you cannot get any knowledge, because the very fact of knowledge is the recognition of the new by means of associations already existing in the mind. There must be a store at hand to which to refer a new impression. Suppose a child is born into this world without such a fund, it would be impossible for him ever to get any knowledge. Therefore, the child must have been previously in a state in which he had a fund, and so knowledge is eternally increasing. Slow me a way of getting round this argument. It is a mathematical fact. Some Western schools of philosophy also hold that there cannot be any knowledge without a fund of past knowledge. They have framed the idea that the child is born with knowledge. These Western philosophers say that the impressions with which the child comes into the world are not due to the child's past, but to the experiences of his forefathers: it is only hereditary transmission. Soon they will find out that this idea is all wrong; some German philosophers are now giving hard blows to these heredity ideas. Heredity is very good, but incomplete, it only explains the physical side. How do you explain the environments influencing us? Many causes produce one effect. Environment is one of the modifying effects. We make our own environment: as our past is, so we find the present environment. A drunken man naturally gravitates to the lowest slums of the city.

You understand what is meant by knowledge. Knowledge is pigeon-holing a new impression with old ones, recognising a new impression. What is meant by recognition? Finding associations with similar impressions that one already has. Nothing further is meant by knowledge. If that is the case, if knowledge means finding the associations, then it must be that to know anything we have to set the whole series of its similars. Is it not so? Suppose you take a pebble; to find the association, you have to see the whole series of pebbles similes to it. But with our perception of the universe as a whole we cannot do that, because in the pigeon-hole of our mind there is only one single record of the perception, we have no other perception of the same nature or class, we cannot compare it with any other. We cannot refer it to its associations. This bit of the universe, cut off by our consciousness, is a startling new thing, because we have not been able to find its associations. Therefore, we are struggling with it, and thinking it horrible, wicked, and bad; we may sometimes think it is good, but we always think it is imperfect. It is only when we find its associations that the universe can be known. We shall recognise it when we go beyond the universe and consciousness, and then the universe will stand explained. Until we can do that, all the knocking of our heads against a wall will never explain the universe, because knowledge is the finding of similars, and this conscious plane only gives us one single perception of it. So with our idea of God. All that we see of God is only a part just as we see only one portion of the universe, and all the rest is beyond human cognition. "I, the universal; so great am I that even this universe is but a part of Me." That is why we see God as imperfect, and do not understand Him. The only way to understand Him and the universe is to go beyond reason, beyond consciousness. "When thou goest beyond the heard and the hearing, the thought and the thinking, then alone wilt thou come to Truth." "Go thou beyond the scriptures, because they teach only up to nature, up to the three qualities." When we go beyond them, we find the harmony, and not before.

The microcosm and the macrocosm are built on exactly the same plan, and in the microcosm we know only one part, the middle part. We know neither the sub-conscious, nor the super-conscious. We know the conscious only. If a man stands up and says, "I am a sinner", he makes an untrue statement because he does not know himself. He is the most ignorant of men; of himself he knows only one part, because his knowledge covers only a part of the ground he is on. So with this universe, it is possible to know only a part of it with the reason, not the whole of it; for the sub-conscious, the conscious and the super-conscious, the individual Mahat and the universal Mahat, and all the subsequent modifications, constitute the universe.

What makes nature (Prakriti) change? We see so far that everything, all Prakriti, is Jada, insentient. It is all compound and insentient. Wherever there is law, it is proof that the region of its play is insentient. Mind, intelligence, will, and everything else is insentient. But they are all reflecting the sentiency, the "Chit" of some being who is beyond all this, whom the Sankhya philosophers call "Purusha". The Purusha is the unwitting cause of all the changes in the universe. That is to say, this Purusha, taking Him in the universal sense, is the God of the universe. It is said that the will of the Lord created the universe. It is very good as a common expression, but we see it cannot be true. How could it be will? Will is the third or fourth manifestation in nature. Many things exist before it, and what created them? Will is a compound, and everything that is a compound is a product of nature. Will, therefore, could not create nature. So, to say that the will of the Lord created the universe is meaningless. Our will only covers a little portion of self-consciousness and moves our brain. It is not will that is working your body or that is working the universe. This body is being moved by a power of which will is only a manifestation in one part. Likewise in the universe there is will, but that is only one part of the universe. The whole of the universe is not guided by will; that is why we cannot explain it by the will theory. Suppose I take it for granted that it is will moving the body, then, when I find I cannot work it at will, I begin to fret and fume. It is my fault, because I had no right to take the will theory for granted. In the same way, if I take the universe and think it is will that moves it and find things which do not coincide, it is my fault. So the Purusha is not will, neither can it be intelligence, because intelligence itself is a compound. There cannot be any intelligence without some sort of matter corresponding to the brain. Wherever there is intelligence, there must be something akin to that matter which we call brain which becomes lumped together into a particular form and serves the purpose of the brain. Wherever there is intelligence, there must be that matter in some form or other. But intelligence itself is a compound. What then is this Purusha? It is neither intelligence nor will, but it is the cause of all these. It is its presence that sets them all going and combining. It does not mix with nature; it is not intelligence, or Mahat; but the Self, the pure, is Purusha. "I am the witness, and through my witnessing, nature is producing; all that is sentient and all that is insentient."

What is this sentiency in nature? We find intelligence is this sentiency which is called Chit. The basis of sentiency is in the Purusha, it is the nature of Purusha. It is that which cannot be explained but which is the cause of all that we call knowledge. Purusha is not consciousness, because consciousness is a compound; buts whatever is light and good in consciousness belongs to Purusha. Purusha is not conscious, but whatever is light in intelligence belongs to Purusha. Sentiency is in the Purusha, but the Purusha is not intelligent, not knowing. The Chit in the Purusha plus Prakriti is what we see around us. Whatever is pleasure and happiness and light in the universe belongs to Purusha; but it is a compound, because it is Purusha plus Prakriti. "Wherever there is any happiness, wherever there is any bliss, there is a spark of that immortality which is God." "Purusha is the; great attraction of the universe; though untouched by and unconnected with the universe, yet it attracts the whole; universe." You see a man going after gold, because behind it is a spark of the Purusha though mixed up with a good deal of dirt. When a man loves his children or a woman her husband, what is the attracting power? A spark of Purusha behind them. It is there, only mixed up with "dirt". Nothing else can attract. "In this world of insentiency the Purusha alone is sentient." This is the Purusha of the Sankhya. As such, it necessarily follows that the Purusha must be omnipresent. That which is not omnipresent must be limited. All limitations are caused; that which is caused must have a beginning and end. If the Purusha is limited, it will die, will not be free, will not be final, but must have some cause. Therefore it is omnipresent. According to Kapila, there are many Purushas; not one, but an infinite number of them. You and I have each of us one, and so has everyone else; an infinite number of circles, each one infinite, running through this universe. The Purusha is neither mind nor matter, the reflex from it is all that we know. We are sure if it is omnipresent it has neither death nor birth. Nature is casting her shadow upon it, the shadow of birth and death, but it is by its nature pure. So far we have found the philosophy of the Sankhya wonderful.

Next we shall take up the proofs against it. So far the analysis is perfect, the psychology incontrovertible. We find by the division of the senses into organs and instruments that they are not simple, but compound; by dividing egoism into sense and matter, we find that this is also material and that Mahat is also a state of matter, and finally we find the Purusha. So far there is no objection. But if we ask the Sankhya the question, "Who created nature?" — the Sankhya says that the Purusha and the Prakriti are uncreate and omnipresent, and that of this Purusha there is an infinite number. We shall have to controvert these propositions, and find a better solution, and by so doing we shall come to Advaitism. Our first objection is, how can there be these two infinites? Then our argument will be that the Sankhya is not a perfect generalization, and that we have not found in it a perfect solution. And then we shall see how the Vedantists grope out of all these difficulties and reach a perfect solution, and yet all the glory really belongs to the Sankhya. It is very easy to give a finishing touch to a building when it is constructed.

SANKHYA AND VEDANTA

I shall give you a résumé of the Sânkhya philosophy, through which we have been going. We, in this lecture, want to find where its defects are, and where Vedanta comes in and supplements it. You must remember that according to Sankhya philosophy, nature is the cause of all these manifestations which we call thought, intellect, reason, love, hatred, touch, taste, and matter. Everything is from nature. This nature consists of three sorts of elements, called Sattva, Rajas, and Tamas. These are not qualities, but elements, the materials out of which the whole universe is evolved. In the beginning of a cycle these remain in equilibrium; and when creation comes, they begin to combine and recombine and manifest as the universe. The first manifestation is what the Sankhya calls the Mahat or Intelligence, and out of that comes consciousness. According to Sankhya, this is an element (Tattva). And out of consciousness are evolved Manas or mind, the organs of the senses, and the Tanmâtras (particles of sound, touch, etc.). All the fine particles are evolved from consciousness, and out of these fine particles come the gross elements which we call matter. The Tanmatras cannot be perceived; but when they become gross particles, we can feel and sense them.

The Chitta, in its threefold function of intelligence, consciousness, and mind, works and manufactures the forces called Prâna. You must at once get rid of the idea that Prana is breath. Breath is one effect of Prana. By Prana are meant the nervous forces governing and moving the whole body, which also manifest themselves as thought. The foremost and most obvious manifestation of Prana is the breathing motion. Prana acts upon air, and not air upon it. Controlling the breathing motion is prânâyâma. Pranayama is practised to get mastery over this motion; the end is not merely to control the breath or to make the lungs strong. That is Delsarte, not Pranayama. These Pranas are the vital forces which manipulate the whole body, while they in their turn are manipulated by other organs in the body, which are called mind or internal organs. So far so good. The psychology is very clear and most precise; and yet it is the oldest rational thought in the world! Wherever there is any philosophy or rational thought, it owes something or other to Kapila. Pythagoras learnt it in India, and taught it in Greece. Later on Plato got an inkling of it; and still later the Gnostics carried the thought to Alexandria, and from there it came to Europe. So wherever there is any attempt at psychology or philosophy, the great father of it is this man, Kapila. So far we see that his psychology is wonderful; but we shall have to differ with him on some points, as we go on. We find that the basic principle on which Kapila works, is evolution. He makes one thing evolve out of another, because his very definition of causation is "the cause reproduced in another form," and because the whole universe, so far as we see it, is progressive and evolving. We see clay; in another form, we call it a pitcher. Clay was the cause and the pitcher the effect. Beyond this we cannot have any idea of causation. Thus this whole universe is evolved out of a material, out of Prakriti or nature. Therefore, the universe cannot be essentially different from its cause. According to Kapila, from undifferentiated nature to thought or intellect, not one of them is what he calls the "Enjoyer" or "Enlightener". Just as is a lump of clay, so is a lump of mind. By itself the mind has no light; but ate see it reasons. Therefore there must be some one behind it, whose light is percolating through Mahat and consciousness, and subsequent modifications, and this is what Kapila calls the Purusha, the Self of the Vedantin. According to Kapila, the Purusha is a simple entity, not a compound; he is immaterial, the only one who is immaterial, and all these various manifestations are material. I see a black-board. First, the external instruments will bring that sensation to the nerve-centre, to the Indriya according to Kapila; from the centre it will go to the mind and make an impression; the mind will present it to the Buddhi, but Buddhi cannot act; the action comes, as it were, from the Purusha behind. These, so to speak, are all his servants, bringing the sensations to him, and he, as it were, gives the orders, reacts, is the enjoyer, the perceiver, the real One, the King on his throne, the Self of man, who is immaterial. Because he is immaterial, it necessarily follows that he must be infinite, he cannot have any limitation whatever. Each one of the Purushas is omnipresent; each one of us is omnipresent, but we can act only through the Linga Sharira, the fine body. The mind, the self-consciousness, the organs, and the vital forces compose the fine body or sheath, what in Christian philosophy is called the spiritual body of man. It is this body that gets salvation, or punishment, or heaven, that incarnates and reincarnates, because we see from the very beginning that the going and the coming of the Purusha or soul are impossible. Motion means going or coming, and what goes or comes from one place to another cannot be omnipresent. Thus far we see from Kapila's psychology that the soul is infinite, and that the soul is the only thing which is not composed of nature. He is the only one that is outside of nature, but he has got bound by nature, apparently. Nature is around him, and he has identified himself with it. He thinks, "I am the Linga Sharira", "I am the gross matter, the gross body", and as such he enjoys pleasure and pain, but they do not really belong to him, they belong to this Linga Sharira or the fine body.

The meditative state is called always the highest state by the Yogi, when it is neither a passive nor an active state; in it you approach nearest to the Purusha. The soul has neither pleasure nor pain; it is the witness of everything, the eternal witness of all work, but it takes no fruits from any work. As the sun is the cause of sight of every eye, but is not itself affected by any defects in the eye or as when a crystal has red or blue flowers placed before it, the crystal looks red or blue, and yet it is neither; so, the soul is neither passive nor active, it is beyond both. The nearest way of expressing this state of the soul is that it is meditation. This is Sankhya philosophy.

Next, Sankhya says, that the manifestation of nature is for the soul; all combinations are for some third person. The combinations which you call nature, these constant changes are going on for the enjoyment of the soul, for its liberation, that it may gain all this experience from the lowest to the highest. When it has gained it, the soul finds it was never in nature, that it was entirely separate, that it is indestructible, that it cannot go and come; that going to heaven and being born again were in nature, and not in the soul. Thus the soul becomes free. All nature is working for the enjoyment and experience of the soul. It is getting this experience in order to reach the goal, and that goal is freedom. But the souls are many according to the Sankhya philosophy. There is an infinite number of souls. The other conclusion of Kapila is that there is no God as the Creator of the universe. Nature is quite sufficient by itself to account for everything. God is not necessary, says the Sankhya.

The Vedanta says that the Soul is in its nature Existence absolute, Knowledge absolute, Bliss absolute. But these are not qualities of the Soul: they are one, not three, the essence of the Soul; and it agrees with the Sankhya in thinking that intelligence belongs to nature, inasmuch as it comes through nature. The Vedanta also shows that what is called intelligence is a compound. For instance, let us examine our perceptions. I see a black-board. How does the knowledge come? What the German philosophers call "the thing-in-itself" of the blackboard is unknown, I can never know it. Let us call it x. The black-board x acts on my mind, and the mind reacts. The mind is like a lake. Throw a stone in a lake and a reactionary wave comes towards the stone; this wave is not like the stone at all, it is a wave. The black-board x is like a stone which strikes the mind and the mind throws up a wave towards it, and this wave is what we call the black-board. I see you. You as reality are unknown and unknowable. You are x and you act upon my mind, and the mind throws a wave in the direction from which the impact comes, and that wave is what I call Mr. or Mrs. So-and-so. There are two elements in the perception, one coming from outside and the other from inside, and the combination of these two, x+ mind, is our external universe. All knowledge is by reaction. In the case of a whale it has been determined by calculation how long after its tail is struck, its mind reacts and the whale feels the pain. Similar is the case with internal perception. The real self within me is also unknown and unknowable. Let us call it y. When I know myself as so-and-so, it is y+ the mind. That y strikes a blow on the mind. So our whole world is x+ mind (external), and y + mind (internal), x and y standing for the thing-in-itself behind the external and the internal worlds respectively.

According to Vedanta, the three fundamental factors of consciousness are, I exist, I know, and I am blessed The idea that I have no want, that I am restful, peaceful, that nothing can disturb me, which comes from time to time, is the central fact of our being, the basic principle of our life; and when it becomes limited, and becomes a compound, it manifests itself as existence phenomenal, knowledge phenomenal, and love. Every man exists, and every man must know, and every man is mad for love. He cannot help loving. Through all existence, from the lowest to the highest, all must love. The y, the internal thing-in-itself, which, combining with mind, manufactures existence, knowledge, and love, is called by the Vedantists. Existence absolute, Knowledge absolute, Bliss absolute. That real existence is limitless, unmixed, uncombined, knows no change, is the free soul; when it gets mixed up, muddled up, as it were, with the mind, it becomes what we call individual existence. It is plant life, animal life, human life, just as universal space is cut off in a room, in a jar, and so on. And that real knowledge is not what we know, not intuition, nor reason, nor instinct. When that degenerates and is confused, we call it intuition; when it degenerates more, we call it reason; and when it degenerates still more, we call it instinct. That knowledge itself is Vijnâna, neither intuition, nor reason nor instinct. The nearest expression for it is all-knowingness. There is no limit to it, no combination in it. That bliss, when it gets clouded over, we call love, attraction for gross bodies or fine bodies, or for ideas. This is only a distorted manifestation of that blessedness. Absolute Existence, absolute Knowledge, and absolute Blessedness are not qualities of the soul, but the essence; there is no difference between them and the soul. And the three are one; we see the one thing in three different aspects. They are beyond all relative knowledge. That eternal knowledge of the Self percolating through the brain of man becomes his intuition, reason, and so on. Its manifestation varies according to the medium through which it shines. As soul, there is no difference between man and the lowest animal, only the latter's brain is less developed and the manifestation through it which we call instinct is very dull. In a man the brain is much finer, so the manifestation is much clearer, and in the highest man it becomes entirely clear. So with existence; the existence which we know, the limited sphere of existence, is simply a reflection of that real existence which is the nature of the soul. So with bliss; that which we call love or attraction is but the rejection of the eternal blessedness of the Self. With manifestation comes limitation, but the unmanifested, the essential nature of the soul, is unlimited; to that blessedness there is no limit. But in love there is limitation. I love you one day, I hate you the next. My love increases one day and decreases the next, because it is only a manifestation.

The first point we will contend with Kapila is his idea of God. Just as the series of modifications of Prakriti, beginning with the individual intellect and ending with the individual body, require a Purusha behind, as the ruler and governor, so, in the Cosmos, the universal intellect, the universal egoism, the universal mind, all universal fine and gross materials, must have a ruler and governor. How will the cosmic series become complete without the universal Purusha behind them all as the ruler and governor? If you deny a universal Purusha behind the cosmic series, we deny your Purusha behind the individual series. If it be true that behind the series of graded, evolved individual manifestations, there stands One that is beyond them all, the Purusha who is not composed of matter, the very same logic will apply to the case of universal manifestations. This Universal Self which is beyond the universal modifications of Prakriti is what is called Ishwara, the Supreme Ruler, God.

Now comes the more important point of difference. Can there be more than one Purusha? The Purusha, we have seen, is omnipresent and infinite. The omnipresent, the infinite, cannot be two. If there are two infinites A and B, the infinite A would limit the infinite B, because the infinite B is not the infinite A, and the infinite A is not the infinite B. Difference in identity means exclusion, and exclusion means limitation. Therefore, A and B, limiting each other, cease to be infinites. Hence, there can be but one infinite, that is, one Purusha.

Now we will take up our x and y and show they are one. We have shown how what we call the external world is x + mind, and the internal world y + mind; x and y are both quantities unknown and unknowable. All difference is due to time, space, and causation. These are the constituent elements of the mind. No mentality is possible without them. You can never think without time, you can never imagine anything without space, and you can never have anything without causation. These are the forms of the mind. Take them away, and the mind itself does not exist. All difference is, therefore, due to the mind. According to Vedanta, it is the mind, its forms, that have limited x and y apparently and made them appear as external and internal worlds. But x and y, being both beyond the mind, are without difference and hence one. We cannot attribute any quality to them, because qualities are born of the mind. That which is qualityless must be one; x is without qualities, it only takes qualities of the mind; so does y; therefore these x and y are one. The whole universe is one. There is only one Self in the universe, only One Existence, and that One Existence, when it passes through the forms of time, space, and causation, is called by different names, Buddhi, fine matter, gross matter, all mental and physical forms. Everything in the universe is that One, appearing in various forms. When a little part of it comes, as it were, into this network of time, space, and causation, it takes forms; take off the network, and it is all one. Therefore in the Advaita philosophy, the whole universe is all one in the Self which is called Brahman. That Self when it appears behind the universe is called God. The same Self when it appears behind this little universe, the body, is the soul. This very soul, therefore, is the Self in man. There is only one Purusha, the Brahman of the Vedanta; God and man, analysed, are one in It. The universe is you yourself, the unbroken you; you are throughout the universe. "In all hands you work, through all mouths you eat, through all nostrils you breathe through all minds you think." The whole universe is you; the universe is your body; you are the universe both formed and unformed. You are the soul of the universe and its body also. You are God, you are the angels, you are man, you are animals, you are the plants, you are the minerals, you are everything; the manifestation of everything is you. Whatever exists is you. You are the Infinite. The Infinite cannot be divided. It can have no parts, for each part would be infinite, and then the part would be identical with the whole, which is absurd. Therefore the idea that you are Mr. So-and-so can never be true; it is a day-dream. Know this and be free. This is the Advaita conclusion. "I am neither the body, nor the organs, nor am I the mind; I am Existence, Knowledge, and Bliss absolute; I am He." This is true knowledge; all reason and intellect, and everything else is ignorance. Where is knowledge for me, for I am knowledge itself! Where is life for me, for I am life itself! I am sure I live, for I am life, the One Being, and nothing exists except through me, and in me, and as me. I am manifested through the elements, but I am the free One. Who seeks freedom? Nobody. If you think that you are bound, you remain bound; you make your own bondage. If you know that you are free, you are free this moment. This is knowledge, knowledge of freedom. Freedom is the goal of all nature.

THE GOAL

Delivered in San Francisco, March 27, 1900

We find that man, as it were, is always surrounded by something greater than himself, and he is trying to grasp the meaning of this. Man will ever [seek] the highest ideal. He knows that it exists and that religion is the search after the highest ideal. At first all his searches were in the external plane — placed in heaven, in different places — just according to [his grasp] of the total nature of man.

[Later,] man began to look at himself a little closer and began to find out that the real "me" was not the "me" that he stands for ordinarily. As he appears to the senses is not the same as he really is. He began to [search] inside of himself, and found out that ... the same ideal he [had placed] outside of himself is all the time within; what he was worshipping outside was his own real inner nature. The difference between dualism and monism is that when the ideal is put outside [of oneself], it is dualism. When God is [sought] within, it is monism.

First, the old question of why and wherefore ... How is it that man became limited? How did the Infinite become finite, the pure become impure? In the first place, you must never forget that this question can never be answered [by] any dualistic hypothesis.

Why did God create the impure universe? Why is man so miserable, made by a perfect, infinite, merciful Father? Why this heaven and earth, looking at which we get our conception of law? Nobody can imagine anything that he has not seen.

All the tortures we feel in this life, we put in another place and that is our hell....

Why did the infinite God make this world? [The dualist says:] Just as the potter makes pots. God the potter; we the pots.... In more philosophical language the question is: How is it taken for granted that the real nature of man is pure, perfect, and infinite? This is the one difficulty found in any system of monism. Everything else is clean and clear. This question cannot be answered. The monists say the question itself is a contradiction.

Take the system of dualism — the question is asked why God created the world. This is contradictory. Why? Because — what is the idea of God? He is a being who cannot be acted upon by anything outside.

You and I are not free. I am thirsty. There is something called thirst, over which I have no control, [which] forces me to drink water. Every action of my body and even every thought of my mind is forced out of me. I have got to do it. That is why I am bound . . . . I am forced to do this, to have this, and so on . . . . And what is meant by why and wherefore? [Being subject to external forces.] Why do you drink water? Because thirst forces you. You are a slave. You never do anything of your own will because you are forced to do everything. Your only motive for action is some force. . . .

The earth, by itself, would never move unless something forced it. Why does the light burn? It does not burn unless somebody comes and strikes a match. Throughout nature, everything is bound. Slavery, slavery! To be in harmony with nature is [slavery]. What is there in being the slave of nature and living in a golden cage? The greatest law and order is in the [knowledge that man is essentially free and divine] Now we see that the question why and wherefore can only be asked [in ignorance]. I can only be forced to do something through something else.

[You say] God is free. Again you ask the question why God creates the world. You contradict yourself. The meaning of God is entirely free will. The question put in logical language is this: What forced Him, who can never be forced by anybody, to create the world? You say in the same question, What forced Him? The question is nonsense. He is infinite by His very nature; He is free. We shall answer questions when you can ask them in logical language. Reason will tell you that there is only one Reality, nothing else. Wherever dualism has risen, monism came to a head and drove it out.

There is only one difficulty in understanding this. Religion is a common-sense, everyday thing. The man in the street knows it if you put it in his language and not [if it is put] in a philosopher's language. It is a common thing in human nature to [project itself]. Think of your feeling with the child. [You identify yourself with it. Then] you have two bodies. [Similarly] you can feel through your husband's mind Where can you stop? You can feel in infinite bodies.

Nature is conquered by man every day. As a race, man is manifesting his power. Try in imagination to put a limit to this power in man. You admit that man as a race has infinite power, has [an] infinite body. The only question is what you are. Are you the race or one [individual]? The moment you isolate yourself, everything hurts you. The moment you expand and feel for others, you gain help. The selfish man is the most miserable in the world. The happiest is the man who is not at all selfish. He has become the whole creation, the whole race and God [is] within him. . . . So in dualism — Christian, Hindu, and all religions — the code of ethics . . . . is: Do not be selfish . . . . things for others! Expand! . . . .

The ignorant can be made to understand [this] very easily, and the learned can be made to understand still more easily. But the man who has just got a speck of learning, him God himself cannot make understand. [The truth is,] you are not separate [from this universe]; Just as your Spirit] is [not] separate from the rest of you. If [not] so, you could not see anything, could not feel anything. Our bodies are simply little whirlpools in the ocean of matter. Life is taking a turn and passing on, in another form . . . . The sun, the moon, the stars, you and I are mere whirlpools. Why did I select [a particular mind as mine? It is] simply a mental whirlpool in the ocean of mind.

How else is it possible that my vibration reaches you just now? If you throw a stone in the lake, it raises a vibration and [that stirs] the water into vibration. I throw my mind into the state of bliss and the tendency is to raise the same bliss in your mind. How often in your mind or heart [you have thought something] and without [verbal] communication, [others have got your thought]? Everywhere we are one.... That is what we never understand. The whole [universe] is composed of time, space, and causation. And God [appears as this universe].... When did nature begin? When you [forgot your true nature and] became [bound by time, space, and causation].

This is the [rotating] circle of your bodies and yet that is your infinite nature.... That is certainly nature — time, space, and causation. That is all that is meant by nature. Time began when you began to think. Space began when you got the body; otherwise there cannot be any space. Causation began when you became limited. We have to have some sort of answer. There is the answer. [Our limitation] is play. Just for the fun of it. Nothing binds you; nothing forces [you. You were] never bound. We are all acting our parts in this [play] of our own invention.

But let us bring another question about individuality. Some people are so afraid of losing their individuality. Wouldn't it be better for the pig to lose his pig-individuality if he can become God? Yes. But the poor pig does not think so at the time. Which state is my individuality? When I was a baby sprawling on the floor trying to swallow my thumb? Was that the individuality I should be sorry to lose? Fifty years hence I shall look upon this present state and laugh, just as I [now] look upon the baby state. Which of these individualities shall I keep ?...

We are to understand what is meant by this individuality.... [There are two opposite tendencies:] one is the protection of the individuality, the other is the intense desire to sacrifice the individuality.... The mother sacrifices all her own will for the needy baby.... When she carries the baby in her arms, the call of individuality, of self-preservation is no more heard. She will eat the worst food, but her children will have the best. So for all the people we love we are ready to die.

[On the one hand] we are struggling hard to keep up this individuality; on the other hand, trying to kill it. With what result? Tom Brown may struggle hard. He is [fighting] for his individuality. Tom dies and there is not a ripple anywhere upon the surface of the earth. There was a Jew born nineteen hundred years ago, and he never moved a finger to keep his individuality.... Think of that! That Jew never struggled to protect his individuality. That is why he became the greatest in the world. This is what the world does not know.

In time we are to be individuals. But in what sense? What is the individuality of man? Not Tom Brown, but God in man. That is the [true] individuality. The more man has approached that, the more he has given up his false individuality. The more he tries to collect and gain everything [for himself], the less he is an individual. The less he has thought of [himself], the more he has sacrificed all individuality during his lifetime,... the more he is an individual. This is one secret the world does not understand.

We must first understand what is meant by individuality. It is attaining the ideal. You are man now, [or] you are woman. You will change all the time. Can you stop? Do you want to keep your minds as they are now — the angels, hatreds, jealousies, quarrels, all the thousand and one things in the mind? Do you mean to say that you will keep them? ... You cannot stop anywhere ... until perfect conquest has been achieved, until you are pure and you are perfect.

You have no more anger when you are all love, bliss, infinite existence.... Which of your bodies will you keep? You cannot stop anywhere until you come to life that never ends. Infinite life! You stop there. You have a little knowledge now and are always trying to get more. Where will you stop? Nowhere, until you become one with life itself....

Many want pleasure [as] the goal. For that pleasure they seek only the senses. On the higher planes much pleasure is to be sought. Then on spiritual planes. Then in himself — God within him. The man whose pleasure is outside of [himself] becomes unhappy when that outside thing goes. You cannot depend for this pleasure upon anything in this universe. If all my pleasures are in myself, I must have pleasure there all the time because I can never lose my Self.... Mother, father, child, wife, body, wealth — everything I can lose except my self . . . bliss in the Self All desire is contained in the Self. . . . This is individuality which never changes, and this is perfect.

. . . And how to get it? They find what the great souls of this world — all great men and women — found [through sustained discrimination]. . . . What of these dualistic theories of twenty gods, thirty gods? It does not matter. They all had the one truth, that this false individuality must go. . . . So this ego — the less there is of it, the nearer I am to that which I really am: the universal body. The less I think of my own individual mind, the nearer I am to that universal mind. The less I think of my own soul, the nearer I am to the universal soul.

We live in one body. We have some pain, some pleasure. Just for this little pleasure we have by living in this body, we are ready to kill everything in the universe to preserve ourselves. If we had two bodies, would not that be much better? So on and on to bliss. I am in everybody. Through all hands I work; through all feet I walk. I speak through every mouth; I live in every body. Infinite my bodies, infinite my minds. I lived in Jesus of Nazareth, in Buddha, in Mohammed — in all the great and good of the past, of the present. I am going to live in all that [may] come afterwards. Is that theory [No, it is the truth.]

If you can realise this, how infinitely more pleasurable that will be. What an ecstasy of joy! Which one body is so great that we need here anything [of] the body. . . After living in all the bodies of others, all the bodies there are in this world, what becomes of us? [We become one with the Infinite. And] that is the goal. That is the only way. One [man] says, "If I know the truth, I shall be melted away like butter." I wish people would be, but they are too tough to be melted so quickly!

What are we to do to be free? Free you are already. . . . How could the free ever be bound? It is a lie. [You were] never bound. How could the unlimited ever be limited by anything? Infinite divided by infinite, added to infinite, multiplied by infinite [remains] infinite. You are infinite; God is infinite. You are all infinite. There cannot be two existences, only one. The Infinite can never be made finite. You are never bound. That is all. . . . You are free already. You have reached the goal — all there is to reach. Never allow the mind to think that you have not reached the goal. . . .

Whatever we [think] that we become. If you think you are poor sinners you hypnotise yourselves: "I am a miserable, crawling worm." Those who believe in hell are in hell when they die; those who say that they will go to heaven [go to heaven].

It is all play. . . . [You may say,] "We have to do something; let us do good." [But] who cares for good and evil? Play! God Almighty plays. That is all. . . .You are the almighty God playing. If you want to play on the side and take the part of a beggar, you are not [to blame someone else for making that choice]. You enjoy being the beggar. You know your real nature [to be divine]. You are the king and play you are a beggar. . . . It is all fun. Know it and play. That is all there is to it. Then practice it. The whole universe is a vast play. All is good because all is fun. This star comes and crashes with our earth, and we are all dead. [That too is fun.] You only think fun the little things that delight your senses! . . .

[We are told that there is] one good god here, and one bad god there always on the watch to grab me the moment I make a mistake. . . . When I was a child I was told by someone that God watches everything. I went to bed and looked up and expected the ceiling of the room to open. [Nothing happened.] Nobody is watching us except ourselves. No Lord except our [own Self]; no nature but what we feel. Habit is second nature; it is first nature also. It is all there is of nature. I repeat [something] two or three times; it becomes my nature. Do not be miserable! Do not repent! What is done is done. If you burn yourself, [take the consequences].

. . . Be sensible. We make mistakes; what of that? That is all in fun. They go so crazy over their past sins, moaning and weeping and all that. Do not repent! After having done work, do not think of it. Go on! Stop not! Don't look back! What will you gain by looking back? You lose nothing, gain nothing.

You are not going to be melted like butter. Heavens and hells and incarnations — all nonsense!

Who is born and who dies? You are having fun, playing with worlds and all that. You keep this body as long as you like. If you do not like it, do not have it. The Infinite is the real; the finite is the play. You are the infinite body and the finite body in one. Know it! But knowledge will not make any difference; the play will go on.... Two words — soul and body — have been joined. [Partial] knowledge is the cause. Know that you are always free. The fire of knowledge burns down all the [impurities and limitations]. I am that Infinite....

You are as free as you were in the beginning, are now, and always will be. He who knows that he is free is free; he who knows that he is bound is bound.

What becomes of God and worship and all that? They have their place. I have divided myself into God and me; I become the worshipped and I worship myself. Why not? God is I. Why not worship my Self? The universal God — He is also my Self. It is all fun. There is no other purpose.

What is the end and aim of life? None, because I [know that I am the Infinite]. If you are beggars, you can have aims. I have no aims, no want, no purpose. I come to your country, and lecture — just for fun. No other meaning. What meaning can be there? Only slaves do actions for somebody else. You do actions for nobody else. When it suits you, you worship. You can join the Christians, the Mohammedans, the Chinese, the Japanese. You can worship all the gods that ever were and are ever going to be....

I am in the sun, the moon, and the stars. I am with God and I am in all the gods. I worship my Self.

There is another side to it. I have kept it in reserve. I am the man that is going to be hanged. I am all the wicked. I am getting punished in hells. That [also] is fun. This is the goal of philosophy [to know that I am the Infinite]. Aims, motives, purposes, and duties live in the background....

This truth is first to be listened to then to be thought about. Reason, argue it out by all manner of means. The enlightened know no more than that. Know it for certain that you are in everything.

That is why you should not hurt anybody, because in hurting them you hurt yourself.... [Lastly,] this is to be meditated upon. Think upon it. Can you realise there will come a time when everything will crumble in the dust and you will stand alone? That moment of ecstatic joy will never leave you. You will actually find that you are without bodies. You never had bodies.

I am One, alone, through all eternity. Whom shall I fear? It is all my Self. This is continuously to be meditated upon. Through that comes realisation. It is through realisation that you become a [blessing] to others....

"Thy face shines like [that of] one who has known God."[3] That is the goal. This is not to be preached as I am doing. "Under a tree I saw a teacher, a boy of sixteen; the disciple was an old man of eighty. The teacher was teaching in silence, and the doubts of the disciple vanished."[4] And who speaks? Who lights a candle to see the sun? When the truth [dawns], no witness is necessary. You know it.... That is what you are going to do:... realise it. [first think of it. Reason it out. Satisfy your curiosity. Then [think] of nothing else. I wish we never read anything. Lord help us all! Just see what [a learned] man becomes.

"This is said, and that is said...."

"What do *you* say, my friend?"

"I say nothing." [He quotes] everybody else's thought; but he thinks nothing. If this is education, what is lunacy? Look at all the men who wrote!... These modern writers, not two sentences their own! All quotations....

There is not much value in books, and in [secondhand] religion there is no value whatsoever. It is like eating. Your religion would not satisfy me Jesus saw God and Buddha saw God. If you have not seen God, you are no better than the atheist. Only he is quiet, and you talk much and disturb the world with your talk. Books and bibles and scriptures are of no use. I met an old man when I was a boy; [he did not study any scripture, but he transmitted the truth of God by a touch].

---

3. Chhândogya. IV. ix. 2.

4. Dakshinâmurtistotram, 12.

Silence ye teachers of the world. Silence ye books. Lord, Thou alone speak and Thy servant listeneth. . . . If truth is not there, what is the use of this life? We all think we will catch it, but we do not. Most of us catch only dust. God is not there. If no God, what is the use of life? Is there any resting-place in the universe? [It is up to us to find it]; only we do not [search for it intensely. We are] like a little piece of maw carried on in the current.

If there is this truth, if there is God, it must be within us. . . . [I must be able to say,] "I have seen Him with my eyes," Otherwise I have no religion. Beliefs, doctrines, sermons do not make religion. It is realisation, perception of God [which alone is religion]. What is the glory of all these men whom the world worships? God was no more a doctrine [for them. Did they believe] because their grandfather believed it? No. It was the realisation of the Infinite, higher than their own bodies, minds, and everything. This world is real inasmuch as it contains a little bit [of] the reflection of that God. We love the good man because in his face shines the reflection a little more. We must catch it ourselves. There is no other way.

That is the goal. Struggle for it! Have your own Bible. Have your own Christ. Otherwise you are not religious. Do not talk religion. Men talk and talk. "Some of them, steeped in darkness, in the pride of their hearts think that they have the light. And not only [that], they offer to take others upon their shoulders and both fall into the pit."[5] . . .

No church ever saved by itself. It is good to be born in a temple, but woe unto the person who dies in a temple or church. Out of it! . . . It was a good beginning, but leave it! It was the childhood place . . . but let it be! . . . Go to God directly. No theories, no doctrines. Then alone will all doubts vanish. Then alone will all crookedness be made straight. . . .

In the midst of the manifold, he who sees that One; in the midst of this infinite death, he who sees that one life; in the midst of the manifold, he who sees that which never changes in his own soul — unto him belongs eternal peace.

---

5. Katha, I. ii. 5.

REPORTS IN AMERICAN NEWSPAPERS

NOTE: These reports from American newspapers have been given exactly as they were in the original. The wrong spellings of proper names, faulty punctuation and grammar have been left uncorrected. — *Publisher.*

DIVINITY OF MAN

Ada Record, February 28, 1894

The lecture on the Divinity of Man by Swami Vive Kananda,[6] the Hindu monk, drew a packed house at the Opera last Friday evening [February 22].

He stated that the fundamental basis of all religions was belief in the soul which is the real man, and something beyond both mind and matter, and proceeded to demonstrate the proposition. The existence of things material are dependent on something else. The mind is mortal because changeable. Death is simply a change.

The soul uses the mind as an instrument and through it affects the body. The soul should be made conscious of its powers. The nature of man is pure and holy but it becomes clouded. In our religion every soul is trying to regain its own nature. The mass of our people believe in the individuality of the soul. We are forbidden to preach that ours is the only true religion. Continuing the speaker said: "I am a spirit and not matter. The religion of the West hopes to again live with their body. Ours teaches there can not be such a state. We say freedom of the soul instead of salvation." The lecture proper lasted but 30 minutes but the president of the lecture committee had announced that at the close of the lecture the speaker would answer any questions propounded him. He gave that opportunity and liberal use was made of the privilege. They came from preachers and professors, physicians and philosophers, from citizens and students, from saints and sinners, some were written but dozens arose in their seats and propounded their questions directly. The speaker responded to all — mark the word, please — in an affable manner and in several instances turned the laugh on the inquirer. They kept up the fusilade for nearly an hour; when the speaker begged to be excused from further labor there yet remained a large pile of unanswered questions. He was an artful dodger on many of the questions. From his answers we glean the following additional statements in regard to the Hindu belief and teachings: They believe in the incarnation of man. One of their teachings is to the effect that their God Krishna was born of a virgin about 5000 years ago in the North of India. The story is very similar to the Biblical history of Christ, only their God was accidently killed. They believe in evolution and the transmigration of souls: i.e. our souls once inhabited some other living thing, a bird, fish or animal, and on our death will go into some other organism. In reply to the inquiry where these souls were before they came into this world he said they were in other worlds. The soul is the permanent basis of all existence. There was no time when there was no God, therefore no time when there was no creation. Buddhists [sic] do not believe in a personal god; I am no Buddhist. Mohammed is not worshipped in the same sense as Christ. Mohammed believes in Christ but denies he is God. The earth was peopled by evolution and not special selection [creation]. God is the creator and nature the created. We do not have prayer save for the children and then only to improve the mind. Punishment for sin is comparatively immediate. Our actions are not of the soul and can therefore be impure. It is our spirit that becomes perfect and holy. There is no resting place for the soul. It has no material qualities. Man assumes the perfect state when he realizes he is a spirit. Religion is the manifestation of the soul nature. The deeper they see is what makes one holier than another. Worship is feeling the holiness of God. Our religion does not believe in missions and teaches that man should love God for love's sake and his neighbor in spite of himself. The people of the West struggle too hard; repose is a factor of civilization. We do not lay our infirmities to God. There is a tendency toward a union of religions.

---

6. In the earlier days Swami Vivekananda's name was thus misspelt by the American Press. — Publisher.

SWAMI VIVEKANANDA ON INDIA

Bay City Daily Tribune, March 21, 1894

Bay City had a distinguished visitor yesterday in the person of Swami Vive Kananda, the much talked of Hindoo monk. He arrived at noon from Detroit where he has been the guest of Senator Palmer and proceeded immediately to the Fraser house. There he was seen by a reporter for The Tribune.

Kananda spoke entertainingly of his country and his impressions of this country. He came to America via the Pacific and will return via the Atlantic. "This is a great land," he said, "but I wouldn't like to live here. Americans think too much of money. They give it preference over everything else. Your people have much to learn. When your nation is as old as ours you will be wiser. I like Chicago very much and Detroit is a nice place."

Asked how long he intended remaining in America, he replied: "I do not know. I am trying to see most of your country. I go east next and will spend some time at Boston and New York. I have visited Boston but not to stay. When I have seen America I shall go to Europe. I am very anxious to visit Europe. I have never been there."

Concerning himself the easterner said he was 30 years old. He was born at Calcutta and educated at a college in that city. His profession calls him to all parts of the country, and he is at all times the guest of the nation. India has a population of 285,000,000," he said. "Of these about 65,000,000 are Mohammedans and most of the others Hindoos. There are only about 600,000 Christians in the country, and of these at least 250,000 are Catholics. Our people do not, as a rule, embrace Christianity; they are satisfied with their own religion. Some go into Christianity for mercenary motives. They are free to do as they wish. We say let everybody have his own faith. We are a cunning nation. We do not believe in bloodshed. There are wicked men in our country and they are in the majority, same as in your country. It is unreasonable to expect people to be angels."

Vive Kananda will lecture in Saginaw to-night.

Lecture Last Night

The lower floor of the opera house was comfortably filled when the lecture began last evening. Promptly at 8:15 o'clock Swami Vive Kananda made his appearance on the stage, dressed in his beautiful oriental costume. He was introduced in a few words by Dr. C. T. Newkirk.

The first part of the discourse consisted of an explanation of the different religions of India and of the theory of transmigration of souls. In connection with the latter, the speaker said it was on the same basis as the theory of conservation was to the scientist. This latter theory, he said, was first produced by a philosopher of his country. They did not believe in a creation. A creation implied making something out of nothing. That was impossible. There was no beginning of creation, just as there was no beginning of time. God and creation are as two lines — without end, without beginning, without [?] parallel. Their theory of creation is, "It is, was, and is to be." They think all punishment is but re-action. If we put our hand in the fire it is burned. That is the re-action of the action. The future condition of life is determined by the present condition. They do not believe God punishes. "You, in this land," said the speaker, "praise the man who does not get angry and denounce the man who does become angry. And yet thousands of people throughout this country are every day accusing God of being angry. Everybody denounces Nero, who sat and played on his instrument while Rome was burning, and yet thousands of your people are accusing God of doing the same thing today."

The Hindoos have no theory of redemption in their religion. Christ is only to show the way. Every man and woman is a divine being, but covered as though by a screen, which their religion is trying to remove. The removal of that Christians call salvation, they, freedom. God is the creator, preserver, and destroyer of the universe.

The speaker then sought to vindicate the religions of his country. He said it had been proven that the entire system of the Roman Catholic Church had been taken from the books of Buddhism. The people of the west should learn one thing from India — toleration.

Among other subjects which he held up and overhauled were: The Christian missionaries, the zeal of the Presbyterian church and its non-toleration, the dollar-worshipping in this country, and the priests. The latter he said were in the business for the dollars there were in it, and wanted to know how long they would stay in the church if they had to depend on getting their pay from God. After speaking briefly on the Caste system in India, our civilization in the south, our general knowledge of the mind, and various other topics the speaker concluded his remarks.

RELIGIOUS HARMONY

Saginaw Evening News, March 22, 1894

Swami Vive Kananda, the much talked of Hindoo monk, spoke to a small but deeply interested audience last evening at the academy of music on "The Harmony of Religions". He was dressed in oriental costume and received an extremely cordial reception. Hon. Rowland Connor gracefully introduced the speaker, who devoted the first portion of his lecture to an explanation of the different religions of India and of the theory of transmigration of souls. The first invaders of India, the Aryans, did not try to exterminate the population of India as the Christians have done when they went into a new land, but the endeavour was made to elevate persons of brutish habits. The Hindoo is disgusted with those people of his own country who do not bathe and who eat dead animals. The Northern people of India have not tried to force their customs on the southerns, but the latter gradually adopted many ways of the former class. In southernmost portions of India there are a few persons who are Christians and who have been so for thousands [?] of years. The Spaniards came to Ceylon with Christianity. The Spaniards thought that their God commanded them to kill and murder and to tear down heathen temples.

If there were not different religions no one religion would survive. The Christian needs his selfish religion. The Hindoo needs his own creed. Those which were founded on a book still stand. Why could not the Christian convert the Jew? Why could they not make the Persians Christians? Why not so with the Mohammedans? Why cannot any impression be made upon China or Japan? The Buddhists, the first missionary religion, have double the number of converts of any other religion and they did not use the sword. The Mohammedans used the most force, and they number the least of the three great missionary, religions. The Mohammedans have had their day. Every day you read of Christian nations acquiring land by bloodshed. What missionaries preach against this? Why should the most bloodthirsty nations exalt an alleged religion which is not the religion of Christ? The Jews and the Arabs were the fathers of Christianity, and how have they been persecuted by the Christians! The Christians have been weighed in the balance in India and found wanting.

The speaker did not wish to be unkind, but he wanted to show Christians how they looked in other eyes. The Missionaries who preach the burning pit are regarded with horror. The Mohammedans rolled wave after wave over India, waving the sword, and today where are they? The farthest that all religions can see is the existence of a spiritual entity. So no religion can teach beyond this point. In every religion there is the essential truth and nonessential casket in which this jewel lies. The believing in the Jewish book or the Hindoo book is non-essential. Circumstances change, the receptacle is different; but the central truth remains. The essentials being the same, the educated people of every community retain the essentials. The shell of the oyster is not attractive, but the pearls are within. Before a small fraction of the world is converted Christianity will be divided into many creeds. That is the law of nature. Why take a single instrument from the great religious orchestras of the earth? Let the grand symphony go on. Be pure, urged the speaker, give up superstition and see the wonderful harmony of nature. Superstition gets the better of religion. All the religions are good since the essentials are the same. Each man should have the perfect exercise of his individuality but these individualities form a perfect whole. This marvellous condition is already in existence. Each creed has had something to add to the wonderful structure.

The speaker sought throughout to vindicate the religions of his country and said that it had been proven that the entire system of the Roman Catholic Church had been taken from the books of Buddhism. He dilated at some length on the high code of morality and purity of life that the ethics of Buddha taught but allowed that as far as the belief in the personality of God was concerned, agnosticism prevailed, the main thing being to follow out Buddha's precepts which were, "Be good, be moral, be perfect."

FROM FAR OFF INDIA

Saginaw Courier-Herald, March 22, 1894

Seated in the lobby of the Hotel Vincent yesterday evening was a strong and regular featured man of fine presence, whose swarthy skin made more pronounced the pearly whiteness of his even teeth. Under a broad and high forehead his eyes betoken intelligence. This gentleman was Swami Vive Kananda, the Hindoo preacher. Mr. Kananda's conversation is in pure and grammatically constructed English sentences, to which his slightly foreign accent lends piquancy. Readers of the Detroit papers are aware that Mr. Kananda has lectured in that city a number of times and aroused the animosity of some on account of his strictures upon Christians. The *Courier-Herald* representative had a few moments' conversation with the learned Buddhist [?] just before he left for the Academy, where he was to lecture. Mr. Kananda said in conversation that he was surprised at the lapses from the paths of rectitude which were so common among Christians, but that there was good and bad to be found among members of all religious bodies. One statement he made was decidedly un-American. Upon being asked if he had been investigating our institutions, he replied: "No, I am a preacher only." This displayed both a want of curiosity and narrowness, which seemed foreign to one who appeared to be so well versed upon religious topics as did the Buddhist [?] preacher.

From the hotel to the Academy was but a step and at 8 o'clock Rowland Connor introduced to a small audience the lecturer, who was dressed in a long orange colored robe, fastened by a red sash, and who wore a turban of windings of what appeared to be a narrow shawl.

The lecturer stated at the opening that he had not come as a missionary, and that it was not the part of a Buddhist to convert others from their faiths and beliefs. He said that the subject of his address would be, "The Harmony of Religions". Mr. Kananda said that many ancient religions had been founded, and were dead and gone.

He said that the Buddhists [Hindus] comprise two-thirds of the race, and that the other third comprised those of all other believers. He said that the Buddhists have no place of future torment for men. In that they differ from the Christians, who will forgive a man for five minutes in this world and condemn him to everlasting punishment in the next. Buddha was the first to teach the universal brotherhood of man. It is a cardinal principle of the Buddhist faith today. The Christian preaches it, but does not practice its own teachings.

He instanced the condition of the Negro in the South, who is not allowed in hotels nor to ride in the same cars with white men, and is a being to whom no decent man will speak. He said that he had been in the South, and spoke from his knowledge and observation.

AN EVENING WITH OUR HINDU COUSINS

Northampton Daily Herald, April 16, 1894

For Swami Vive Kananda proved conclusively that all our neighbors across the water, even the remotest, are our close cousins differing only a trifle in color, language, customs and religion, the silver-tongued Hindu monk prefacing his address in city hall Saturday evening [April 14] by an historic sketch of the origin of his own and all other leading nations of the earth which demonstrated the truth that race-kinship is more of a simple fact than many know or always care to admit.

The informal address that followed regarding some of the customs of the Hindu people was more of the nature of a pleasant parlor talk, expressed with the easy freedom of the conversational adept, and to those of his hearers possessing a natural and cultivated interest in the subject both the man and his thought were intensely interesting for more reasons than can be given here. But to others the speaker was disappointing in not covering a larger scope in his word-pictures, the address, although extremely lengthy for the American lecture-platform, referring to very few of the "customs and manners" of the peculiar people considered, and of whose personal, civil, home, social and religious life much more would have been gladly heard from this one of the finest representatives of this oldest of races, which the average student of human nature should find preeminently interesting but really knows the least about.

The allusions to the life of the Hindu began with a picture of the birth of the Hindu boy, his introduction to educational training, his marriage, slight reference to the home life but not what was expected, the speaker diverging frequently to make comparative comments on the customs and ideas of his own and English-speaking races, socially, morally and religiously, the inference in all cases being clearly in favor of his own, although most courteously, kindly and gracefully expressed. Some of his auditors who are tolerably well posted as to social and family conditions among the Hindoos of all classes would have liked to have asked the speaker a challenging question or two on a good many of the points he touched upon. For instance, when he so eloquently and beautifully portrayed the Hindu idea of womanhood as the divine motherhood ideal, to be forever reverenced, even worshipped with a devotion of loyalty such as the most woman-respecting unselfish and truest of American sons, husbands and fathers cannot even conceive of, one would have liked to know what the reply would have been to the query as to how far this beautiful theory is exemplified in practice in the majority of Hindu homes, which hold wives, mothers, daughters and sisters.

The rebuke to the greed for gain, the national vice of luxury-seeking, self-seeking the "dollar-caste" sentiment which taints the dominant white European and American races to their mortal danger, morally and civilly, was only too just and superbly well-put, the slow, soft, quiets unimpassioned musical voice embodying its thought with all the power and fire of the most vehement physical utterance, and went straight to the mark like the "Thou art the man" of the prophet. But when this learned Hindu nobleman by birth, nature and culture attempts to prove — as he repeatedly did in his frequent and apparently half-unconscious digressions from the special point under consideration — that the distinctively self-centred, self-cultivating, preeminently self-soulsaving, negative and passive, not to say selfishly indolent religion of his race has proven itself superior in its usefulness to the world to the vitally aggressive, self-forgetful, do-good unto-others-first-last-and-always, go-ye-into-all-the-world and work religion which we call Christianity, in whose name nine tenths of all the really practical moral, spiritual and philanthropic work of the world has been and is being done, whatever sad and gross mistakes have been made by its unwise zealots, he attempts a large contract.

But to see and hear Swami Vive Kananda is an opportunity which no intelligent fair-minded

American ought to miss if one cares to see a shining light of the very finest product of the mental, moral and spiritual culture of a race which reckons its age by thousands where we count ours by hundreds and is richly worth the study of every mind.

Sunday afternoon [April 15] the distinguished Hindu spoke to the students of Smith college at the vesper service, the Fatherhood of God and the Brotherhood of man being, virtually, his theme, and that the address made a deep impression is evinced by the report of every auditor, the broadest liberality of true religious sentiment and precept characterizing the whole trend of thought.

THE MANNERS AND CUSTOMS OF INDIA

Boston Herald, May 15, 1894

Association Hall was crowded with ladies yesterday, to hear Swami Vivekananda, the Brahmin[7] Monk talk about "The Religion of India" [actually "The Manners and Customs of India"], for the benefit of the ward 16 day nursery [actually, Tyler-street Day Nursery]. The Brahmin monk has become a fad in Boston, as he was in Chicago last year, and his earnest, honest, cultured manner has won many friends for him.

The Hindoo nation is not given to marriage, he said, not because we are women haters, but because our religion teaches us to worship women. The Hindoo is taught to see in every woman his mother, and no man wants to marry his mother. God is mother to us. We don't care anything about God in heaven; it is mother to us. We consider marriage a low vulgar state, and if a man does marry, it is because he needs a helpmate for religion.

You say we ill-treat our women. What nation in the world has not ill-treated its women? In Europe or America a man can marry a woman for money, and, after capturing her dollars, can kick her out. In India, on the contrary, when a woman marries for money, her children are considered slaves, according to our teaching, and when a rich man marries, his money passes into the hands of his wife, so that he would be scarcely likely to turn the keeper of his money out of doors.

You say we are heathens, we are uneducated, uncultivated, but we laugh in our sleeves at your want of refinement in telling us such things. With us, quality and birth make caste, not money. No amount of money can do anything for you in India. In caste the poorest is as good as the richest, and that is one of the most beautiful things about it.

Money has made warfare in the world, and caused Christians to trample on each other's necks. Jealousy, hatred and avariciousness are born of money-getters. Here it is all work, hustle and bustle. Caste saves a man from all this. It makes it possible for a man to live with less money, and it brings work to all. The man of caste has time to think of his soul; and that is what we want in the society of India.

The Brahmin is born to worship God, and the higher his caste, the greater his social restrictions are. Caste has kept us alive as a nation, and while it has many defects, it has many more advantages.

Mr. Vivekananda described the universities and colleges of India, both ancient and modern, notably the one at Benares, that has 20,000 students and professors.

When you judge my religion, he continued, you take it that yours is perfect and mine wrong; and when you criticise the society of India you suppose it to be uncultured just so far as it does not conform to your standard. That is nonsense.

In reference to the matter of education, the speaker said that the educated men of India become professors, while the less educated become priests.

---

7. Meaning Hindu. — *Publisher*.

THE RELIGIONS OF INDIA

Boston Herald, May 17, 1894

The Brahmin monk, Swami Vivekananda, lectured yesterday afternoon in Association Hall on "The Religions of India", in aid of the Ward 16 Day Nursery. There was a large attendance.

The speaker first gave an account of the Mahommedans, who formed, he said, one-fifth of the population. They believed in both Old and New Testaments, but Jesus Christ they regarded only as a prophet. They had no church organization, though there was reading of the Koran.

The Parsees, another race, called their sacred book the Zend-Avesta, and believed in two warring deities, Armuzd the good and Ahriman the evil. They believed that finally the good would triumph over the evil. Their moral code was summed up in the words: "Good thought, good words, good deeds."

The Hindus proper looked up to the Vedas as their religious scripture. They held each individual to the customs of caste, but gave him full liberty to think for himself in religious matters. A part of their method was to seek out some holy man or prophet in order to take advantage of the spiritual current that flowed through him.

The Hindus had three different schools of religion — the dualistic, the qualified monistic and the monistic — and these three were regarded as stages through which each individual naturally passed in the course of his religious development.

All three believed in God, but the dualistic school believed that God and man were separate entities, while the monistic declared that there was only one existence in the universe, this unitary existence teeing neither God nor soul, but something beyond.

The lecturer quoted from the Vedas to show the character of the Hindu religion, and declared that, to find God, one must search one's own heart.

Religion did not consist of pamphlets or books; it consisted of looking into the human heart, and finding there the truths of God and immortality.

"Whomsoever I like," said the Vedas, "him I create a prophet," and to be a prophet was all there was of religion.

The speaker brought his lecture to a close by giving an account of the Jains, who show remarkable kindness to dumb animals, and whose moral law is summed up in the words: "Not to injure others is the highest good."

SECTS AND DOCTRINES IN INDIA

Harvard Crimson, May 17, 1894

Swami Vivekananda, the Hindoo monk, gave an address last evening in Sever Hall under the auspices of the Harvard Religious Union. The address was very interesting, the clear and eloquent voice of the speaker, and his low, earnest delivery making his words singularly impressive.

There are various sects and doctrines in India, said Vivekananda, some of which accept the theory of a personal God, and others which believe that God and the universe are one; but whatever sect the Hindoo belongs to he does not say that his is the only right belief, and that all others must be wrong. He believes that there are many ways of coming to God; that a man who is truly religious rises above the petty quarrels of sects or creed. In India if a man believes that he is a spirit, a soul, and not a body, then he is said to have religion and not till then.

To become a monk in India it is necessary to lose all thought of the body; to look upon other human beings as souls. So monks can never marry. Two vows are taken when a man becomes a monk, poverty and chastity. He is not allowed to receive or possess any money whatever. The first ceremony to be performed on joining the order is to be burnt in effigy, which supposed to destroy once for all the old body, name and caste. The man then receives a new name, and is allowed to go forth and preach or travel, but must take no money for what he does.

LESS DOCTRINE AND MORE BREAD

Baltimore American, October 15, 1894

The Lyceum Theater was crowded last night at the first of a series of meetings by the Vrooman Brothers. The subject discussed was "Dynamic Religion".

Swami Vivekananda, the high priest [?] from India, was the last speaker. He spoke briefly, and was listened to with marked attention. His English and his mode of delivery were excellent. There is a foreign accent to his syllables, but not enough to prevent him from being plainly understood. He was dressed in the costume of his native country, which was decidedly picturesque. He said he could speak but briefly after the oratory that had preceded him, but he could add his endorsement to all that had been said. He had traveled a great deal, and preached to all kinds of people. He had found that the particular kind of doctrine preached made little difference. What is wanted is practical sort of work. If such ideas could not be carried out, he would lose his faith in humanity. The cry all over the world is "less doctrine and more bread". He thought the sending of missionaries to India all right; he had no objections to offer, but he thought it would be better to send fewer men and more money. So far as India was concerned, she had religious doctrine to spare. Living up to the doctrines was needed more than more doctrines. The people of India, as well as the people all over the world, had been taught to pray, but prayer with the lips was not enough; people should pray with their hearts. "A few people in the world," he said, "really try to do good. Others look on and applaud, and think that they themselves have done great good. Life is love, and when a man ceases to do good to others, he is dead spiritually."

On Sunday evening next Swami Vivekananda will make the address of the evening at the Lyceum.

Sun, October 15, 1894

Vivekananda sat on the stage last night with imperturbable stolidity until it came his turn to speak. Then his manner changed and he spoke with force and feeling. He followed the Vrooman brothers and said there was little to add to what had been said save his testimony as a "man from the Antipodes".

"We have doctrines enough," he continued. "What we want now is practical work as presented in these speeches. When asked about the missionaries sent to India I reply all right. But we want money more and men less. India has bushels full of doctrines and to spare. What is wanted is the means to carry them out.

"Prayer may be done in different ways. Prayer with the hands is yet higher than prayer with the lips and is more saving.

"All religions teach us to do good for our brothers. Doing good is nothing extraordinary — it is the only way to live. Everything in nature tends to expansion for life and contraction for death. It is the same in religion. Do good by helping others without ulterior motives. The moment this ceases contraction and death follow."

THE RELIGION OF BUDDHA

Morning Herald, October 22, 1894

An audience which filled the Lyceum Theatre [Baltimore] from pit to dome assembled last night at the second of the series of meetings held by the Vrooman Brothers in the interest of "Dynamic Religion". Fully 3,000 persons were present. Addresses were made by the Rev. Hiram Vrooman, Rev. Walter Vrooman and Rev. Swami Vivekananda, the Brahmin High Priest now visiting this city. The speakers of the evening were seated on the stage, the Rev. Vivekananda being an object of particular interest to all. He wore a yellow turban and a red robe tied in at the waste [sic] with a sash of the same color, which added to the Oriental cast of his features and invested him with a peculiar interest. His personality seemed to be the feature of the evening. His address was delivered in an easy, unembarrassed manner, his diction being perfect and his accent similar to that of a cultured member of the Latin race familiar with the English language. He said in part:

The High Priest Speaks

"Buddha began to found the religion of India 600 years before the birth of Christ He found the religion of India at that time mainly engaged in eternal discussions upon the nature of the human soul. There was no remedy according to the ideas then prevailing for the cure of religious ills but sacrifices of animals, sacrificial altars and similar methods.

"In the midst of this system a priest [?] was born who was a member of one of the leading families who was the founder of Buddhism. His was, in the first place, not the founding of a new religion, but a movement of reformation. He believed in the good of all. His religion, as formulated by him, consisted of the discovery of three things: First, 'There is an evil'; second, 'What is the cause of this evil?' This he ascribed to the desires of men to be superior to others, an evil that could be cured by unselfishness. Third, 'This evil is curable by becoming unselfish'. Force, he concluded, could not cure it; dirt cannot wash dirt; hate cannot cure hate.

"This was the basis of his religion. So long as society tries to cure human selfishness by laws and institutions whose aim is to force others to do good to their neighbors, nothing can be done. The remedy is not to place trick against trick and force against force. The only remedy is in making unselfish men and women. You may enact laws to cure present evils, but they will be of no avail.

"Buddha found in India too much talking about God and His essence and too little work. He always insisted upon this fundamental truth, that we are to be pure and holy, and that we are to help others to be holy also. He believed that man must go to work and help others; find his soul in others; find his life in others. He believed that in the conjunction of doing good to others is the only good we do ourselves. [sic] He believed that there was always in the world too much theory and too little practice. A dozen Buddhas in India at the present time would do good, and one Buddha in this country would also be beneficial.

"When there is too much doctrine, too much belief in my father's religion, too much rational superstition, a change is needed. Such doctrine produces evil, and a reformation is necessary."

At the conclusion of Mr. Vivekananda's address there was a hearty burst of applause.

Baltimore American, October 22, 1894

The Lyceum Theater was crowded to the doors last night at the second meeting of the series conducted by the Vrooman brothers on "Dynamic Religion". Swami Vivekananda, of India, made the principal address. He spoke on the Buddhist religion, and told of the evils which existed among the people of India, at the time of the birth of Buddha. The social inequalities in India, he said, were at that period a thousand times greater than anywhere else in the world. "Six hundred years before Christ," he continued, "the priesthood of India exercised great influence over the minds of the people, and between the upper and nether millstone of intellectuality and learning the people were ground. Buddhism, which is the religion of more than two-third of the human family, was not founded as an entirely new religion, but rather as a reformation which carried off the corruption of the times. Buddha seems to have been the only prophet who did everything for others and absolutely nothing for himself. He gave up his home and all the enjoyments of life to spend his days in search of the medicine for the terrible disease of human misery. In an age when men and priests were discussing the essence of the deity, he discovered what people had overlooked, that misery existed. The cause of evil is our desire to be superior to others and our selfishness. The moment that the world becomes unselfish all evil will vanish. So long as society tries to cure evil by laws and institutions, evil will not be cured. The world has tried this method ineffectually for thousands of years. Force against force never cures, and the only cure for evil is unselfishness. We need to teach people to obey the laws rather than to make more laws. Buddhism was the first missionary religion of the world but it was one of the teachings of Buddhism not to antagonize any other religion. Sects weaken their power for good by making war on each other."

ALL RELIGIONS ARE GOOD

Washington Post, October 29, 1894

Mr. Kananda spoke yesterday at the People's Church on the invitation of Dr. Kent, pastor of the church. His talk in the morning was a regular sermon, dealing entirely with the spiritual side of religion, and presenting the, to orthodox sects, rather original proposition that there is good in the foundation of every religion, that all religions, like languages, are descended from a common stock, and that each is good in its corporal and spiritual aspects so long as it is kept free from dogma and fossilism. The address in the afternoon was more in the form of a lecture on the Aryan race, and traced the descent of the various allied nationalities by their language, religion and customs from the common Sanskrit stock.

After the meeting, to a Post reporter Mr. Kananda said: "I claim no affiliation with any religious sect, but occupy the position of an observer, and so far as I may, of a teacher to mankind. All religion to me is good. About the higher mysteries of life and existence I can do no more than speculate, as others do. Reincarnation seems to me to be the nearest to a logical explanation for many things with which we are confronted in the realm of religion. But I do not advance it as a doctrine. It is no more than a theory at best, and is not susceptible of proof except by personal experience, and that proof is good only for the man who has it. Your experience is nothing to me, nor mine to you. I am not a believer in miracles — they are repugnant to me in matters of religion. You might bring the world tumbling down about my ears, but that would be no proof to me that there was a God, or that you worked by his agency, if there was one.

He Believes It Blindly

"I must, however, believe in a past and a hereafter as necessary to the existence of the present. And if we go on from here, we must go in other forms, and so comes any belief in reincarnation. But I can prove nothing, and any one is welcome to deprive me of the theory of reincarnation provided they will show me something better to replace it. Only up to the present I have found nothing that offers so satisfactory an explanation to me."

Mr. Kananda is a native of Calcutta, and a graduate of the government university there. He speaks English like a native, having received his university training in that tongue. He has had good opportunity to observe the contact between the native and the English, and it would disappoint a foreign missionary worker to hear him speak in very unconcerned style of the attempts to convert the natives. In this connection he was asked what effect the Western teaching was having on the thought of the Orient.

"Of course," he said, "no thought of any sort can come into a country without having its effect, but the effect of Christian teaching on Oriental thought is, if it exists, so small as to be imperceptible. The Western doctrines have made about as much impression there as have the Eastern doctrines here, perhaps not so much. That is, among the higher thinkers of the country. The effect of the missionary work among the masses is imperceptible. When converts are made they of course drop at once out of the native sects, but the mass of the population is so great that the converts of the missionaries have very little effect that can be seen."

The Yogis Are Jugglers

When asked whether he knew anything of the

alleged miraculous performances of the yogis and adepts Mr. Kananda replied that he was not interested in miracles, and that while there were of course a great many clever jugglers in the country, their performances were tricks. Mr. Kananda said that he had seen the mango trick but once, and then by a fakir on a small scale. He held the same view about the alleged attainments of the lamas. "There is a great lack of trained, scientific, and unprejudiced observers in all accounts of these phenomena," said he, "so that it is hard to select the false from the true."

THE HINDU VIEW OF LIFE

Brooklyn Times, December 31, 1894

The Brooklyn Ethical Association, at the Pouch Gallery last night, tendered a reception to Swami Vivekananda.... Previous to the reception the distinguished visitor delivered a remarkably interesting lecture on "The Religions of India". Among other things he said:

"The Hindoo's view of life is that we are here to learn; the whole happiness of life is to learn; the human soul is here to love learning and get experience. I am able to read my Bible better by your Bible, and you will learn to read your Bible the better by my Bible. If there is but one religion to be true, all the rest must be true. The same truth has manifested itself in different forms, and the forms are according to the different circumstances of the physical or mental nature of the different nations.

"If matter and its transformation answer for all that we have, there is no necessity for supposing the existence of a soul. But it can [not] be proven that thought has been evolved out of matter. We can not deny that bodies inherit certain tendencies, but those tendencies only mean the physical configuration through which a peculiar mind alone can act in a peculiar way. These peculiar tendencies in that soul have been caused by past actions. A soul with a certain tendency will take birth in a body which is the fittest instrument for the display of that tendency, by the laws of affinity. And this is in perfect accord with science, for science wants to explain everything by habit, and habit is got through repetitions. So these repetitions are also necessary to explain the natural habits of a new-born soul. They were not got in this present life; therefore, they must have come down from past lives.

"All religions are so many stages. Each one of them represents the stage through which the human soul passes to realize God. Therefore, not one of them should be neglected. None of the stages are dangerous or bad. They are good. Just as a child becomes a young man, and a young man becomes an old man, so they are travelling from truth to truth; they become dangerous only when they become rigid, and will not move further — when he ceases to grow. If the child refuses to become an old man, then he is diseased, but if they steadily grow, each step will lead them onward until they reach the whole truth. Therefore, we believe in both a personal and impersonal God, and at the same time we believe in all the religions that were, all the religions that are, and all the religions that will be in the world. We also believe we ought not only tolerate these religions, but to accept them.

"In the material physical world, expansion is life, and contraction is death. Whatever ceases to expand ceases to live. Translating this in the moral world we have: If one would expand, he must love, and when he ceases to love he dies. It is your nature; you must, because that is the only law of life. Therefore, we must love God for love's sake, so we must do our duty for duty's sake; we must work for work's sake without looking for any reward — know that you are purer and more perfect, know that this is the real temple of God."

Brooklyn Daily Eagle, December 31, 1894

After referring to the views of the Mohammedans, the Buddhists and other religious schools of India, the speaker said that the Hindoos received their religion through the revelations of the Vedas, who teach that creation is without beginning or end. They teach that man is a spirit living in a body. The body will die, but the man will not. The spirit will go on living. The soul was not created from nothing for creation means a combination and that means a certain future dissolution. If then the soul was created it must die. Therefore, it was not created. He might be asked how it is that we do not remember anything of our past lives. This could be easily explained. Consciousness is the name only of the surface of the mental ocean, and within its depths are stored up all our experiences. The desire was to find out something that was stable. The mind, the body, all nature, in fact, is changing. This question of finding something that was infinite had long been discussed. One school of which the modern Buddhists are the representatives, teach that everything that could not be solved by the five senses was nonexistent. That every object is dependent upon all others, that it is a delusion that man is an independent entity. The idealists, on the other hand, claim that each individual is an independent body. The true solution of this problem is that nature is a mixture of dependence and independence, of reality and idealism. There is a dependence which is proved by the fact that the movements of our bodies are controlled by our minds, and our minds are controlled by the spirit within us, which Christians call the soul. Death is but a change. Those who have passed beyond and are occupying high positions there are but the same as those who remain here, and those who are occupying lower positions there are the same as others here. Every human being is a perfect being. If we sit down in the dark and lament that it is so dark it will profit us nothing, but if we procure matches and strike a light, the darkness goes out immediately. So, if we sit down and lament that our bodies are imperfect, that our souls are imperfect, we are not profited. When we call in the light of reason, then this darkness of doubt will disappear. The object of life is to learn. Christians can learn from the Hindus, and the Hindus from Christians. He could read his Bible better after reading ours. "Tell your children," he said, "that religion is a positive something, and not a negative something. It is not the teachings of men, but a growth, a development of something higher within our nature that seeks outlet. Every child born into the world is born with a certain accumulated experience. The idea of independence which possesses us shows there is something in us besides mind and body. The body and mind are dependent. The soul that animates us is an independent factor that creates this wish for freedom. If we are not free how can we hope to make the world good or perfect? We hold that we are makers of ourselves, that what we have we make ourselves. We have made it and we can unmake it. We believe in God, the Father of us all, the Creator and Preserver of His children, omnipresent and omnipotent. We believe in a personal God, as you do, but we go further. We believe that we are He. We believe in all the religions that have gone before, in all that now exist and in all that are to come. The Hindu bows down to the all religion [sic] for in this world the idea is addition, not subtraction. We would make up a bouquet of all beautiful colors for God, the Creator, who is a personal God. We must love Cod for love's sake, we must do our duty to Him for duty's sake, and must work for Him for work's sake and must worship Him for worship's sake.

"Books are good but they are only maps. Reading a book by direction of a man I read that so many inches of rain fell during the year. Then he told me to take the book and squeeze it between my hands. I did so and not a drop of water came from it. It was the idea only that the book conveyed. So we can get good from books, from the temple, from the church, from anything, so long as it leads us onward and upward. Sacrifices, genuflections, rumblings and mutterings are not religion. They are all good if they help us to come to a perception of the perfection which we shall realize when we come face to face with Christ. These are words or instructions to us by which we may profit. Columbus, when he discovered this continent, went back and told his countrymen that he had found the new world. They would not believe him, or some would not, and he told them to go and search for themselves. So with us, we read these truths and come in and find the truths for ourselves and then we have a belief which no one can take from us."

After the lecture an opportunity was given those present to question the speaker on any point on which they wished to have his views. Many of them availed themselves of this offer.[8]

IDEALS OF WOMANHOOD

Brooklyn Standard Union, January 21, 1895

Swami Vivekananda, after being presented to the audience by Dr. Janes, president of the Ethical Association, said in part:

"The product of the slums of any nation cannot be the criterion of our judgment of that nation. One may collect the rotten, worm-eaten apples under every apple tree in the world, and write a book about each of them, and still know nothing of the beauty and possibilities of the apple tree. Only in the highest and best can we judge a nation — the fallen are a race by themselves. Thus it is not only proper, but just and right, to judge a custom by its best, by its ideal.

"The ideal of womanhood centres in the Arian race of India, the most ancient in the worlds history. In that race, men and women were priests, 'sabatimini [saha-dharmini],' or co-religionists, as the Vedas call them. There every family had its hearth or altar, on which, at the time of the wedding, the marriage fire was kindled, which was kept alive, until either spouse died, when the funeral pile was lighted from its spark. There man and wife together offered their sacrifices, and this idea was carried so far that a man could not even pray alone, because it was held that he was only half a being, for that reason no unmarried man could become a priest. The same held true in ancient Rome and Greece.

"But with the advent of a distinct and separate priest-class, the co-priesthood of the woman in all these nations steps back. First it was the Assyrian race, coming of semitic blood, which proclaimed the doctrine that girls have no voice, and no right, even when married. The Persians drank deep of this Babylonian idea, and by them it was carried to Rome and to Greece, and everywhere woman degenerated.

"Another cause was instrumental in bringing this about — the change in the system of marriage. The earliest system was a matriarchal one; that is, one in which the mother was the centre, and in which the girls acceded to her station. This led to the curious system of the Polianders [polyandrous], where five and six brothers often married one wife. Even the Vedas contain a trace of it in the provision, that when a man died without leaving any children, his widow was permitted to live with another man, until she became a mother; but the children she bore did not belong to their father, but to her dead husband. In later years the widow was allowed to marry again, which the modern idea forbids her to do.

"But side by side with these excrescences a very intense idea of personal purity sprang up in the nation. On every page the Vedas preach personal purity. The laws in this respect were extremely strict. Every boy and girl was sent to the university, where they studied until their twentieth or thirtieth year; there the least impurity was punished almost cruelly. This idea of personal purity has imprinted itself deeply into the very heart of the race, amounting almost to a mania. The most conspicuous example of it is to be found in the capture of Chito [Chitor] by the Mohammedans. The men defended the town against tremendous odds; and when the women saw that defeat was inevitable they lit a monstrous fire on the market place, and when the enemy broke down the gates 74,500 women jumped on the huge funeral pile and perished in the flames. This noble example has been handed down in India to the present time, when every letter bears the words '74,500,' which means that any one who unlawfully reads the letter, thereby becomes guilty of a crime similar to the one which drove those noble women of Chito to their death.

"The next period is that of the monks; it came

---

8. See *Complete Works*, Vol. V. in the Section, "Questions and Answers".

with the advent of Buddhism, which taught that only the monks could reach the 'nirvana', something similar to the Christian heaven. The result was that all India became one huge monastery; there was but one object, one battle — to remain pure. All the blame was cast onto women, and even the proverbs warned against them. 'What is the gate to hell?' was one of them, to which the answer was: 'Woman'. Another read: 'What is the chain which binds us all to dust? Woman'. Another one: 'Who is the blindest of the blind? He who is deceived by woman.'

"The same idea is to be found in the cloisters of the West. The development of all monasticism always meant the degeneration of women.

"But eventually another idea of womanhood arose. In the West it found its ideal in the wife, in India in the mother. But do not think that the priests were altogeher responsible for this change. I know they always lay claim to everything in the world and I say this, although I am myself a priest. I'll bend my knees to every prophet in every religion and clime, but candor compels me to say, that here in the West the development of women was brought about by men like John Stuart Mill and the revolutionary French philosophers. Religion has done something, no doubt, but not all. Why, in Asia Minor, Christian bishops to this day keep a harem!

"The Christian ideal is that which is found in the Anglo-Saxon race. The Mohammedan woman differs vastly from her western sisters in so far as her social and intellectual development is not so pronounced. But do not, on that account, think that the Mohammedan woman is unhappy, because it is not so. In India woman has enjoyed property rights since thousands of years. Here a man may disinherit his wife, in India the whole estate of the deceased husband must go to the wife, personal property absolutely, real property for life.

"In India the mother is the centre of the family and our highest ideal, She is to us the representative of God, as God is the mother of the Universe. It was a female sage who first found the unity of God, and laid down this doctrine in one of the first hymns of the Vedas. Our God is both personal and absolute, the absolute is male, the personal, female. And thus it comes that we now say: 'The first manifestation of God is the hand that rocks the cradle.' He is of the 'arian' race, who is born through prayer, and he is a nonarian, who is born through sensuality.

"This doctrine of prenatal influence is now slowly being recognized, and science as well as religion calls out: 'Keep yourself holy, and pure.' So deeply has this been recognized in India, that there we even speak of adultery in marriage, except when marriage is consummated in prayer. And I and every good Hindoo believe, that my mother was pure and holy, and hence I owe her everything that I am. That is the secret of the race — chastity."

TRUE BUDDHISM

Brooklyn Standard Union, February 4, 1895

Swami Vivekananda, being presented by Dr. Janes, the president of the Ethical Association, under whose auspices these lectures are given, said in part: "The Hindoo occupies a unique position towards Buddhism. Like Christ, who antagonized the Jews, Buddha antagonized the prevailing religion of India; but while Christ was rejected by his countrymen, Buddha was accepted as God Incarnate. He denounced the priestcraft at the very doors of their temples, yet to-day he is worshipped by them.

"Not, however, the creed which bears his name. What Buddha taught, the Hindoo believes, but what the Buddhists teach, we do not accept. For the teachings of the Great Master, spread out broadcast over the land, came back in tradition, colored by the channels through which they passed.

"In order to understand Buddhism fully we must go-back to the mother religion from which it came. The books of Veda have two parts; the first, Cura makanda [Karma Kanda], contains the sacrificial portion, while the second part, the Vedanta, denounces sacrifices, teaching charity and love, but not death. Each sect took up what portion it liked.

The charvaka, or materialist, basing his doctrine on the first part, believed that all was matter and that there is neither a heaven nor a hell, neither a soul nor a God. The second sect, the Gains [Jains], were very moral atheists, who, while rejecting the idea of a God, believed that there is a soul, striving for more perfect development. These two sects were called the heretics. A third sect was called orthodox, because it accepted the Vedas, although it denied the existence of a personal God, believing that everything sprang from the atom or nature.

"Thus the intellectual world was divided before Buddha came. But for a correct understanding of his religion, it is also necessary to speak of the caste then existing. The Vedas teach that he who knows God is a Brahma [Brâhmin]; he who protects his fellows is a Chocta [Kshatriya], while he who gains his livelihood in trade is a Visha [Vaishya]. These different social diversions [divisions] developed or degenerated into iron-bound casts [castes], and an organized and crystallized priestcraft stood upon the neck of the nation. At this time Buddha was born, and his religion is therefore the culmination of an attempt at a religious and a social reformation.

"The air was full of the din of discussion; 20,000 blind priests were trying to lead 20,000,000 [?] blind men, fighting amongst themselves. What was more needed at that time than for a Buddha to preach? 'Stop quarreling, throw your books aside, be perfect!' Buddha never fought true castes, for they are nothing but the congregation of those of a particular natural tendency, and they are always valuable. But Buddha fought the degenerated castes with their hereditary privileges, and spoke to the Brahmins: 'True Brahmins are not greedy, nor criminal nor angry — are you such? If not, do not mimic the genuine, real men. Caste is a state, not an iron-bound class, and every one who knows and loves God is a true Brahmin.' And with regard to the sacrifices, he said: 'Where do the Vedas say that sacrifices make us pure? They may please, perhaps, the angels, but they make us no better. Hence, let off these mummeries — love God and strive to be perfect.'

"In later years these doctrines of Buddha were forgotten. Going to lands yet unprepared for the reception of these noble truths, they came back tainted with the foibles of these nations. Thus the Nihilists arose — a sect whose doctrine it was that the whole universe, God and soul, had no basis, but that everything is continually changing. They believed in nothing but the enjoyment of the moment, which eventually resulted in the most revolting orgies. That, however, is not the doctrine of Buddha, but a horrible degeneration of it, and honor to the Hindoo nation, who stood up and drove it out.

"Every one of Buddha's teachings is founded in the Vedantas. He was one of those monks who wanted to bring out the truths, hidden in those books and in the forest monasteries. I do not believe that the world is ready for them even now; it still wants those lower religions, which teach of a personal God. Because of this, the original Buddhism could not hold the popular mind, until it took up the modifications, which were reflected back from Thibet and the Tartars. Original Buddhism was not at all nihilistic. It was but an attempt to combat cast and priestcraft; it was the first in the world to stand as champion of the dumb animals, the first to break down the caste, standing between man and man."

Swami Vivekananda concluded his lecture with the presentation of a few pictures from the life of Buddha, the 'great one, who never thought a thought and never performed a deed except for the good of others; who had the greatest intellect and heart, taking in all mankind and all the animals, all embracing, ready to give up his life for the highest angels as well as for the lowest worm." He first showed how Buddha, for the purpose of saving a herd of sheep, intended for a king's sacrifice, had thrown himself upon the altar, and thus accomplished his purpose. He next pictured how the great prophet had parted from his wife and baby at the cry of suffering mankind, and how, lastly, after his teachings had been universally accepted in India, he accepted the invitation of a despised Pariah, who dined him on swine's flesh, from the effects of which he died.

INDIA'S GIFT TO THE WORLD

Brooklyn Standard Union, February 27, 1895

Swami Vivekananda, the Hindoo monk, delivered a lecture Monday night under the auspices of the Brooklyn Ethical Association before a fairly large audience at the hall of the Long Island Historical Society, corner Pierrepont and Clinton streets. His subject was "India's Gift to the World".

He spoke of the wondrous beauties of his native land, "where stood the earliest cradle of ethics, arts, sciences, and literature, and the integrity of whose sons and the virtue of whose daughters have been sung by all travelers." Then the lecturer showed in rapid details, what India has given to the world.

"In religion," he said, "she has exerted a great influence on Christianity, as the very teachings of Christ would [could] be traced back to those of Buddha." He showed by quotations from the works of European and American scientists the many points of similarity between Buddha and Christ. The latter's birth, his seclusion from the world, the number of his apostles, and the very ethics of his teachings are the same as those of Buddha, living many hundred years before him.

"Is it mere chance," the lecturer asked, "or was Buddha's religion but the foreshadowing of that of Christ? The majority of your thinkers seem to be satisfied in the latter explanation, but there are some bold enough to say that Christianity is the direct offspring of Buddhism just as the earliest heresy in the Christian religion — the Monecian [Manichaean] heresy — is now universally regarded as the teaching of a sect of Buddhists. But there is more evidence that Christianity is founded in Buddhism. We find it in recently discovered inscriptions from the reign of Emperor Oshoka [Asoka] of India, about 300 B.C., who made treaties with all the Grecian kings, and whose missionaries discriminated [disseminated ?] in those very parts, where, centuries after, Christianity flourished, the principles of the Buddhistic religion. Thus it is explained, why you have our doctrine of trinity, of incarnation of God, and of our ethics, and why the service in our temples is so much alike to that in your present Catholic churches, from the mass to the chant and benediction. Buddhism had all these long before you. Now use your own judgment on these premise — we Hindoos stand ready to be convinced that yours is the earlier religion, although we had ours some three hundred years before yours was even thought of.

"The same holds good with respect to sciences. India has given to antiquity the earliest scientific physicians, and, according to Sir William Hunter, she has even contributed to modern medical science by the discovery of various chemicals and by teaching you how to reform misshapen ears and noses. Even more it has done in mathematics, for algebra, geometry, astronomy, and the triumph of modern science — mixed mathematics — were all invented in India, just so much as the ten numerals, the very cornerstone of all present civilization, were discovered in India, and are in reality, Sanskrit words.

"In philosophy we are even now head and shoulders above any other nation, as Schopenhauer, the great German philosopher, has confessed. In music India gave to the world her system of notation, with the seven cardinal notes and the diatonic scale, all of which we enjoyed as early as 350 B.C., while it came to Europe only in the eleventh century. In philology, our Sanskrit language is now universally acknowledged to be the foundation of all European languages, which, in fact, are nothing but jargonized Sanskrit.

"In literature, our epics and poems and dramas rank as high as those of any language; our 'Shaguntala' [Shakuntala] was summarized by Germany's greatest poet, as 'heaven and earth united'. India has given to the world the fables of Aesop, which were copied by Aesop from an old Sanskrit book; it has given the Arabian Nights, yes, even the story of Cinderella and the Bean Stalks. In manufacture, India was the first to make cotton and purple [dye], it was proficient in all works of jewelry, and the very word 'sugar', as well as the article itself, is the product of India. Lastly she has invented the game of chess and the cards and the dice. So great, in fact, was the superiority of India in every respect, that it drew to her borders the hungry cohorts of Europe, and thereby indirectly brought about the discovery of America.

"And now, what has the world given to India in return for all that? Nothing but nullification [vilification] and curse and contempt. The world waded in her children's life-blood, it reduced India to poverty and her sons and daughters to slavery, and now it adds insult to injury by preaching to her a religion which can only thrive on the destruction of every other religion. But India is not afraid. It does not beg for mercy at the hands of any nation. Our only fault is that we cannot: fight to conquer; but we trust in the eternity of truth. India's message to the world is first of all, her blessing; she is returning good for the evil which is done her, and thus she puts into execution this noble idea, which had its origin in India. Lastly, India's message is, that calm goodness, patience and gentleness will ultimately triumph. For where are the Greeks, the onetime masters of the earth? They are gone. Where are the Romans, at the tramp of whose cohorts the world trembled? Passed away. Where are the Arabs, who in fifty years had carried their banners from the Atlantic to the Pacific? and where are the Spaniards, the cruel murderers of millions of men? Both races are nearly extinct; but thanks to the morality of her children, the kinder race will never perish, and she will yet see the hour of her triumph."

At the close of the lecture, which was warmly applauded, Swami Vivekananda answered a number of questions in regard to the customs of India. He denied positively the truth of the statement published in yesterday's [February 25] Standard Union, to the effect that widows are ill-treated in India. The law guarantees her not only her own property, before marriage, but also all she received from her husband, at whose death, if there be no direct heirs, the property goes to her. Widows seldom marry in India, because of the scarcity of men. He also stated that the self-sacrifices of wives at the death of their husbands as well as the fanatical self-destruction under the wheels of the Juggernaut, have wholly stopped, and referred his hearers for proof to Sir William Hunter's "History of the Indian Empire".

CHILD WIDOWS OF INDIA

Daily Eagle, February 27, 1895

Swami Vivekananda, the Hindu monk, lectured in Historical hall Monday night under the auspices of the Brooklyn Ethical association, on "India's Gift to the World". There were about two hundred and fifty people in the hall when the Swami stepped on the platform. Much interest was manifested on account of the denial by Mrs. James McKeen, president of the Brooklyn Ramabai circle, which is interested in Christian work in India, of the statement attributed to the lecture that the child widows of India were not protected [ill-treated]. In no part of his lecture was reference made to this denial, but after he had concluded, one of the audience asked the lecturer what explanation he had to make to the statement. Swami Vivekananda said that it was untrue that child widows were abused or ill treated in any way. He added:

"It is a fact that some Hindus marry very young. Others marry when they have attained a fair age and some do not marry at all. My grandfather was married when quite a child. My father when he was 14 years old and I am 30 years old and am not yet married. When a husband dies all his possessions go to his widow. If a widow is poor she is the same as poor widows in any other country. Old men sometimes marry children, but if the husband was wealthy it was all the better for the widow the sooner he died. I have traveled all over India, but failed to see a case of the ill treatment mentioned. At one time there were religious fanatics, widows, who threw themselves into a fire and were consumed by the flames at the death of their husbands. The Hindus did not believe in this, but did not prevent it, and it was not until the British obtained control of India that it was finally prohibited. These women were considered saints and in many instances monuments were erected to their memory."

SOME CUSTOMS OF THE HINDUS

Brooklyn Standard Union, April 8, 1895

A special meeting of the Brooklyn Ethical Association with an address by Swami Vivekananda, the Hindu monk as the main feature, was held at the Pouch Gallery, of Clinton avenue, last night. "Some customs of the Hindus what they mean, and how they are misinterpreted," was the subject treated. A large throng of people filled the spacious gallery.

Dressed in his Oriental costume, his eyes bright, and a flush mantling his face, Swami Vivekananda started to tell of his people, of his country, and its customs. He desired only that justice be shown to him and to his. In the beginning of his discourse he said he would give a general idea of India. He said it was not a country but a continent; that erroneous ideas had been promulgated by travellers who had never seen the country. He said that there were nine separate languages spoken and over 100 different dialects. He spoke severely of those who wrote about his country, and said their brains were addled by superstition, and that they had an idea that everyone outside of the pale of their own religion was a horrible blackguard. One of the customs that had often been misinterpreted was the brushing of the teeth by the Hindus. They never put hair or skin in their mouths, but use a plant. "Hence a man wrote," said the speaker, "that the Hindus get up early in the morning and swallow a plant." He said the [custom of widows throwing themselves under the] car of juggernaut did not exist, never had, and that no one knew how such a story started.

Swami Vivekananda's talk on caste was most comprehensive and interesting. He said it was not a granted [graded] system of classes, but that each caste thought itself to be superior to all the others. He said it was a trade guild and not a religious institution. He said that it had been in existence from time immemorial, and explained how at first only certain rights were hereditary, but how afterward the ties were bound closer, and intermarriage and eating and drinking were restricted to each caste.

The speaker told of the effect that the mere presence of a Christian or Mohammedan would have on a Hindu household. He said that it was veritable pollution for a white man to step into a Hindu's presence, and that after receiving one outside of his religion, the Hindu always took a bath.

The Hindu monk abused [?] the order of the Pariahs roundly, saying they did all the menial work, ate carrion and were the scavengers. He also said that the people who wrote books on India came only into contact with these people, and not with genuine Hindus. He described the trial of one who broke the rules of caste, and said that the only punishment inflicted was the refusal of the particular caste to intermarry or drink or eat with him or his children. All other ideas were erroneous.

In explaining the defects of caste, the speaker said that in preventing competition it produced stagnation, and completely blocked the progress of the people. He said that in taking away brutality it stopped social improvements. In checking competition it increased population. In its favor, he said, were the facts that it was the only ideal of equality and fraternity. That money had nothing to do with social standing in the caste. All were equal. He said that the fault of all the great reformers was that they thought caste was due only to religious representation, instead of ascribing it to the right source, namely, the curious social conditions. He spoke very bitterly of the attempts of the English and Mohammedans to civilize the country by the bayonet and fire and sword. He said that to abolish caste one must change the social conditions completely ant destroy the entire economic system of the country. Better, he said, that the waves of the [Bay of] Bengal flow and drown all rather than this. English civilization was composed of the three "B's" — Bible, bayonet, and brandy. "That is civilization, and it has been carried to such an extent that the average income of a Hindu is 50 cents a month. Russia is outside, saying. 'Let's civilize a little,' and England goes on and on."

The monk grew excited as he walked up and down, talking rapidly about the way the Hindus had been treated. He scored the foreign educated Hindus, and described their return to their native land, "full of champagne and new ideas". He said that child-marriage was bad, because the West said so, and that the mother-in-law could torture her daughter-in-law with impunity, as the son could not interfere. He said that the foreigners took every opportunity to abuse the heathen, because they had so many evils of their own that they wanted to cover them up. He said that each nation must work out its own salvation, and that no one else could solve its problems.

In speaking of India's benefactors he asked whether America had ever heard of David Herr [Hare], who established the first college for women, and who had devoted so much of his life to education.

The speaker gave a number of Indian proverbs that were not at all complimentary to the English. In closing he made an earnest appeal for his land. He said:

"It matters not as long as India is true to herself and to her religion. But a blow has been struck at her heart by this awful godless West when she sends hypocrisy and atheism into her midst. Instead of sending bushels of abuses, carloads of vituperation and shiploads of condemnations, let an endless stream of love go forth. Let us all be men"

Discovery Publisher is a multimedia publisher whose mission is to inspire and support personal transformation, spiritual growth and awakening. We strive with every title to preserve the essential wisdom of the author, spiritual teacher, thinker, healer, and visionary artist.

www.ingramcontent.com/pod-product-compliance
Lightning Source LLC
Chambersburg PA
CBHW080242170426
43192CB00014BA/2532